E SZERO

15

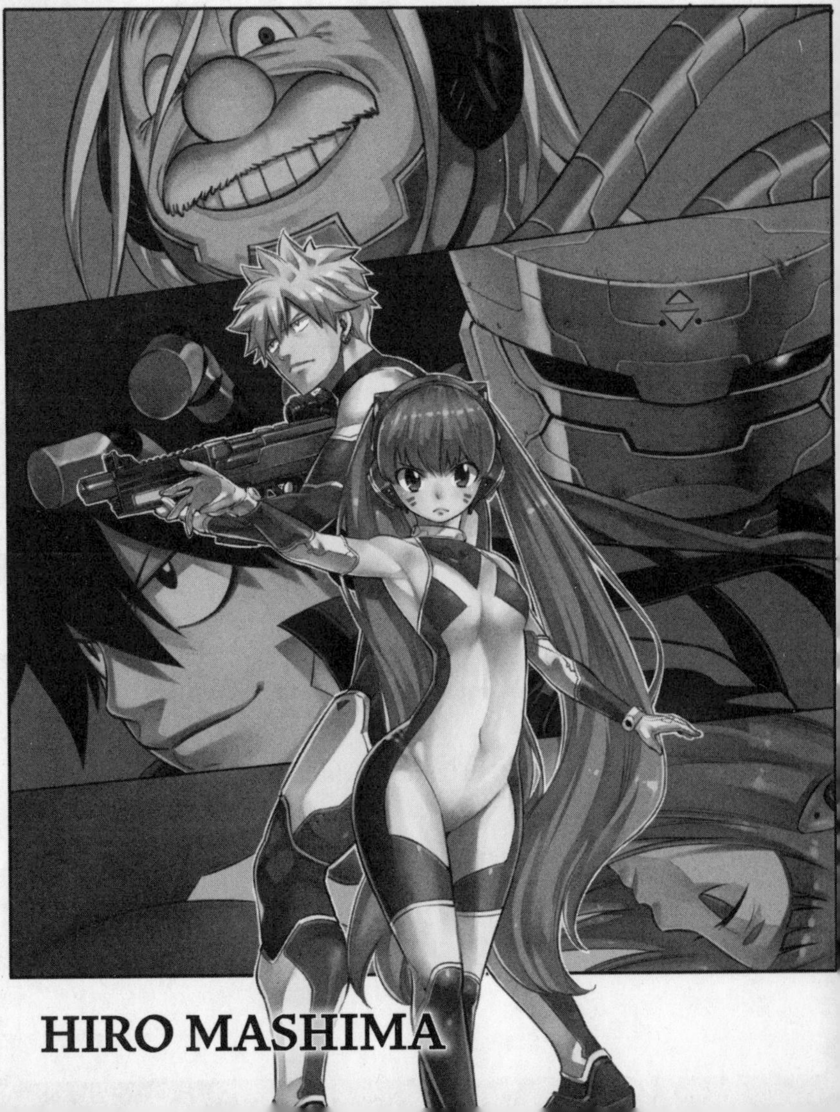

HIRO MASHIMA

EDENS ZERO 15 contents

EDENS ZERO

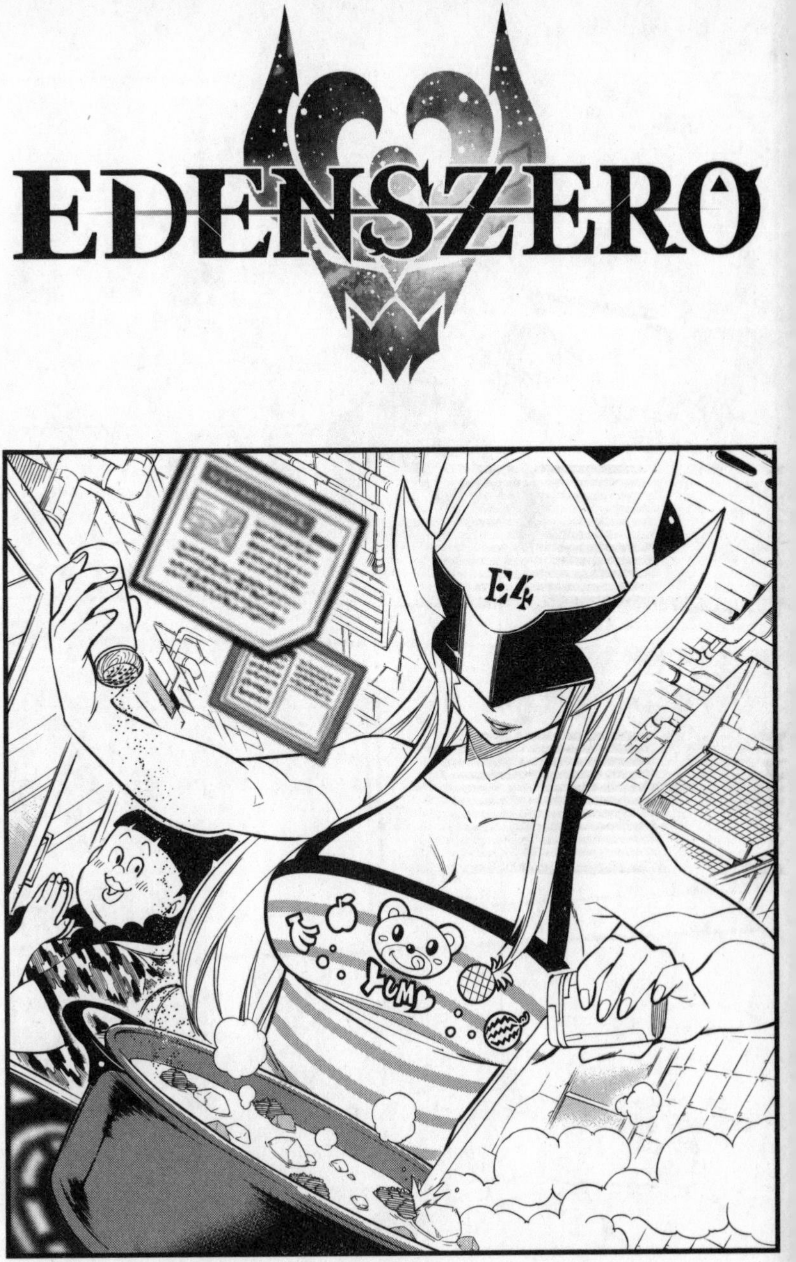
E4
YUM

CHAPTER 123: THE LIGHT OF JUSTICE

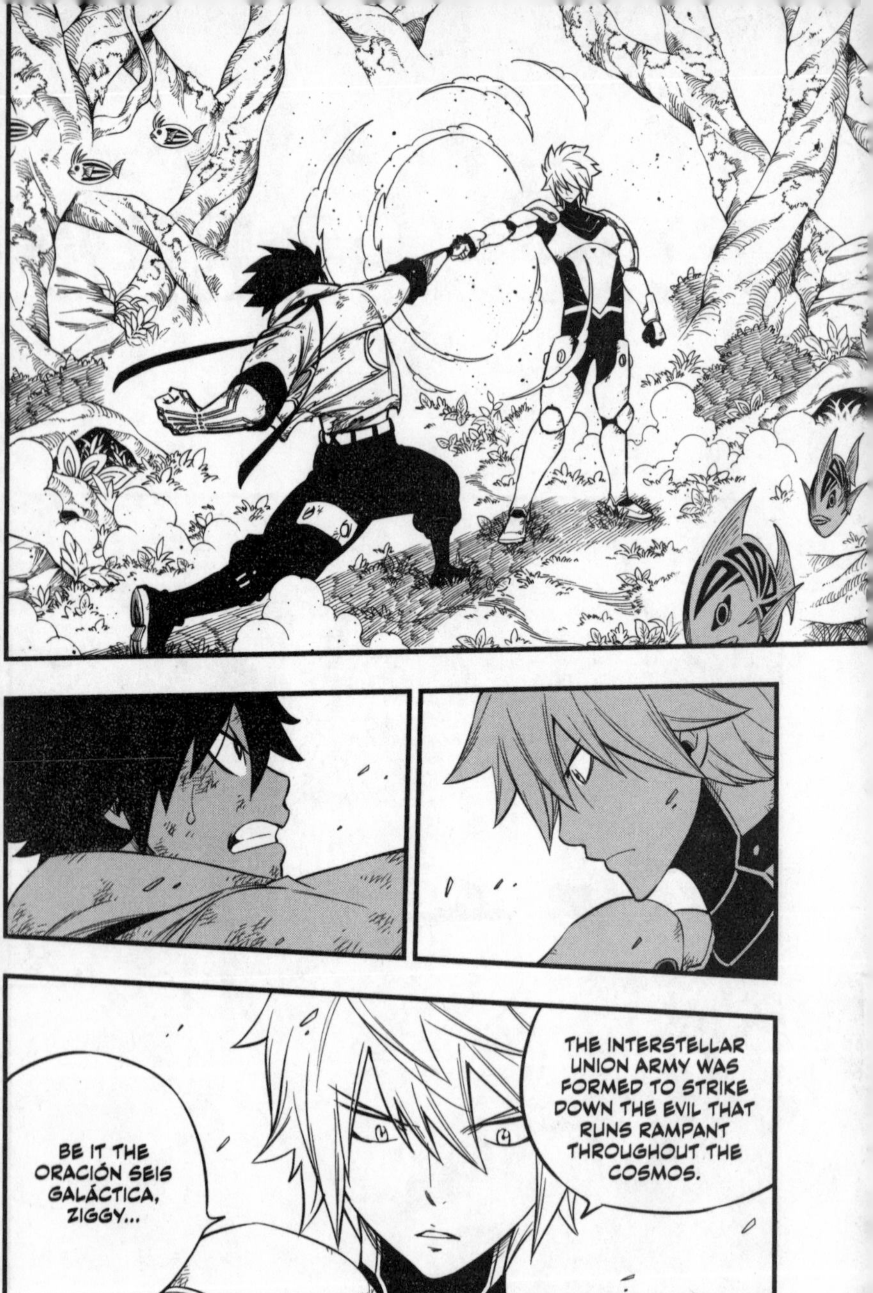
THE INTERSTELLAR UNION ARMY WAS FORMED TO STRIKE DOWN THE EVIL THAT RUNS RAMPANT THROUGHOUT THE COSMOS.
BE IT THE ORACIÓN SEIS GALÁCTICA, ZIGGY...

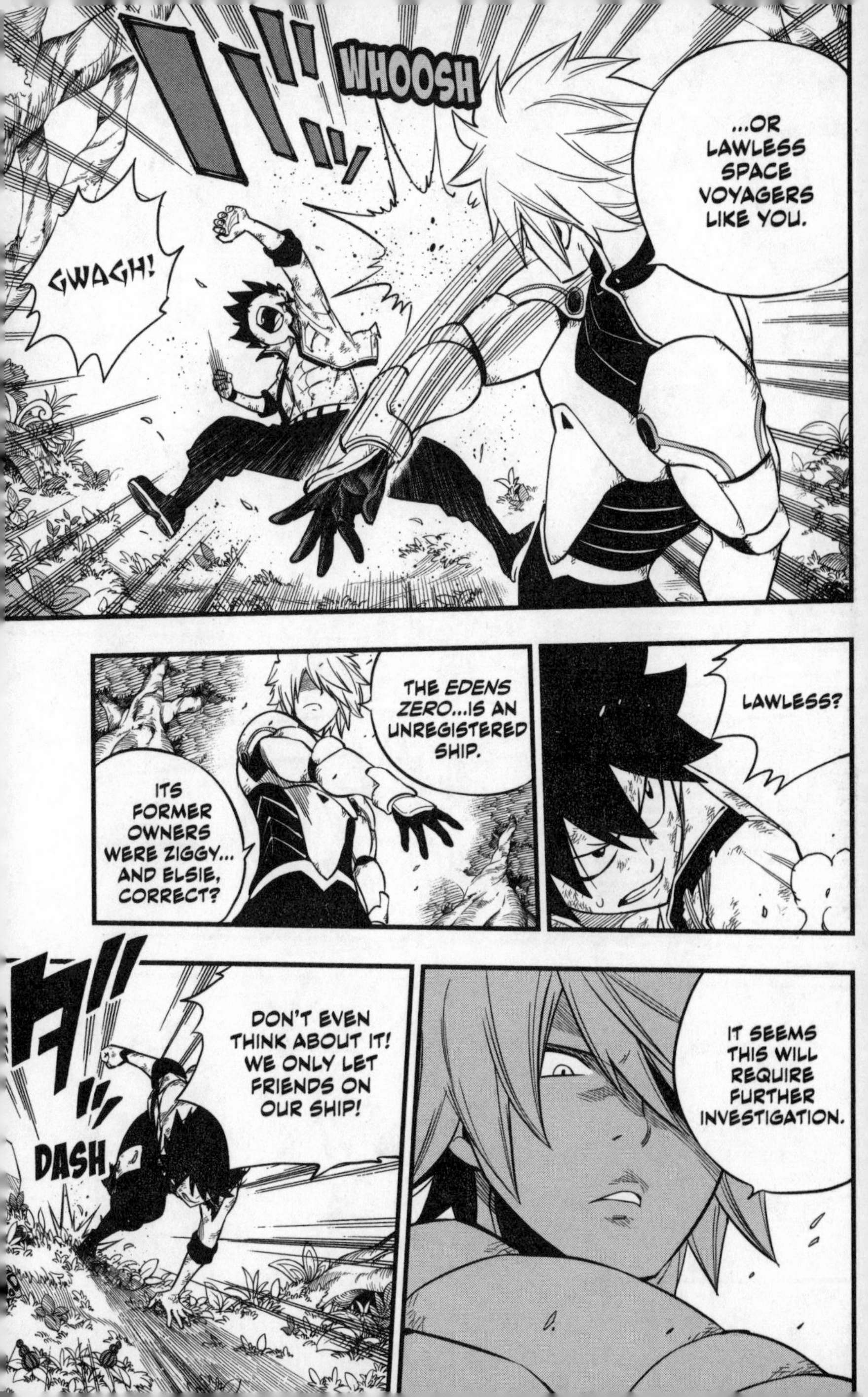
...OR LAWLESS SPACE VOYAGERS LIKE YOU.
WHOOSH
GWAGH!
LAWLESS?
THE *EDENS ZERO*...IS AN UNREGISTERED SHIP.
ITS FORMER OWNERS WERE ZIGGY... AND ELSIE, CORRECT?
IT SEEMS THIS WILL REQUIRE FURTHER INVESTIGATION.
DON'T EVEN THINK ABOUT IT! WE ONLY LET FRIENDS ON OUR SHIP!
DASH

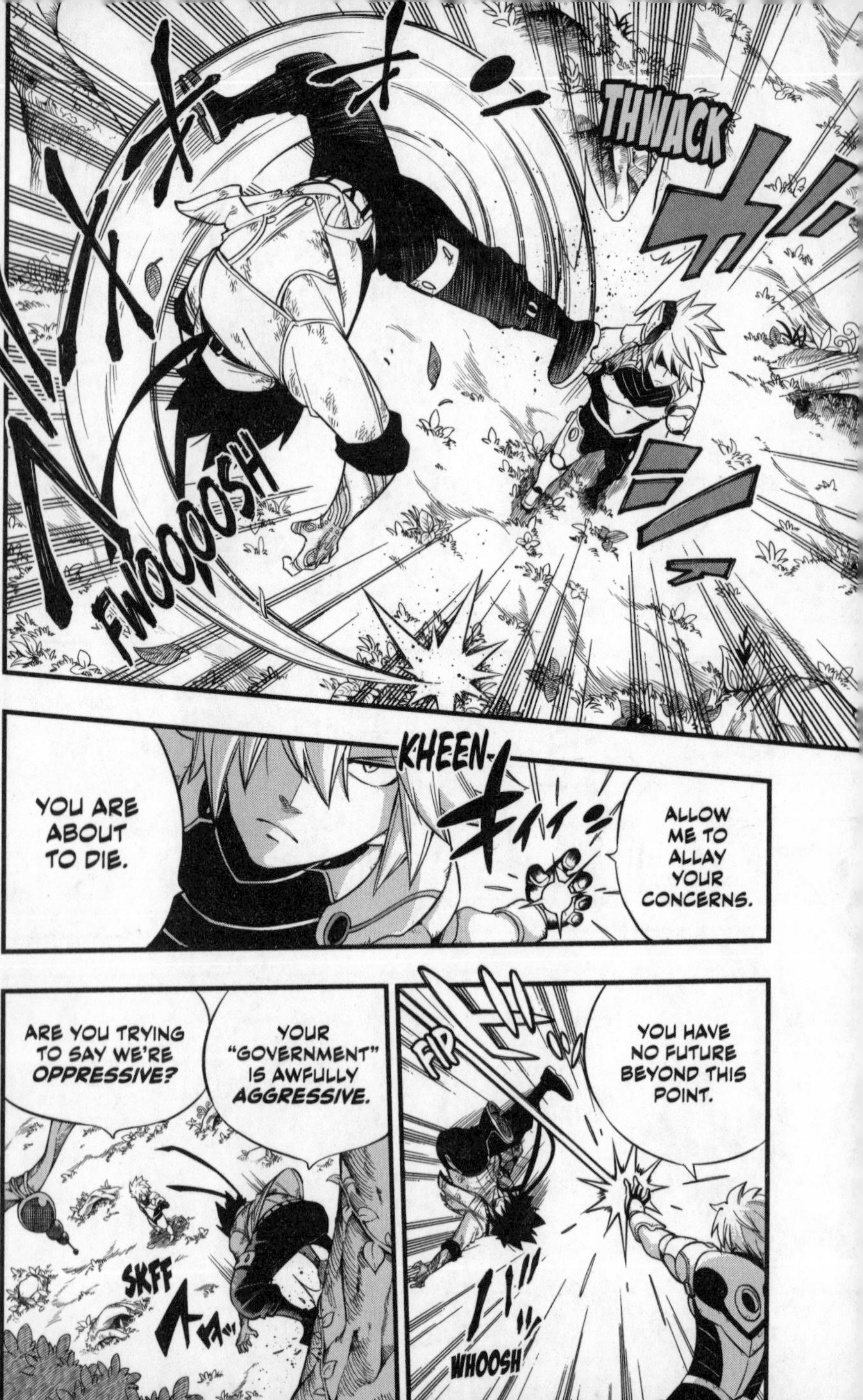
THWACK
FWOOOSH
ALLOW ME TO ALLAY YOUR CONCERNS.
KHEEN
YOU ARE ABOUT TO DIE.
YOU HAVE NO FUTURE BEYOND THIS POINT.
FIP
WHOOSH
YOUR "GOVERNMENT" IS AWFULLY AGGRESSIVE.
ARE YOU TRYING TO SAY WE'RE OPPRESSIVE?
SKFF

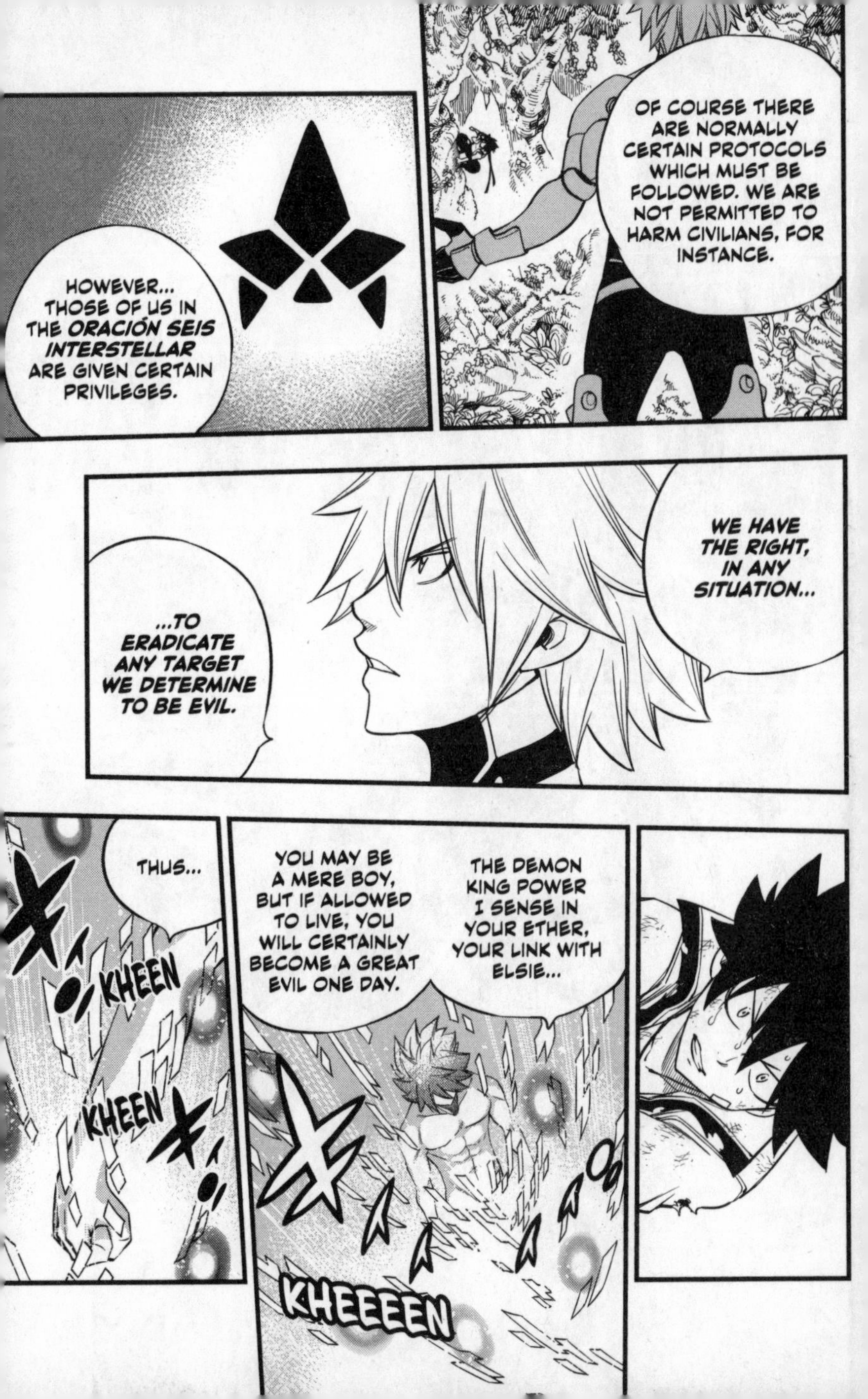
OF COURSE THERE ARE NORMALLY CERTAIN PROTOCOLS WHICH MUST BE FOLLOWED. WE ARE NOT PERMITTED TO HARM CIVILIANS, FOR INSTANCE.
HOWEVER... THOSE OF US IN THE *ORACIÓN SEIS INTERSTELLAR* ARE GIVEN CERTAIN PRIVILEGES.
WE HAVE THE RIGHT, IN ANY SITUATION...
...TO ERADICATE ANY TARGET WE DETERMINE TO BE EVIL.
THE DEMON KING POWER I SENSE IN YOUR ETHER, YOUR LINK WITH ELSIE...
YOU MAY BE A MERE BOY, BUT IF ALLOWED TO LIVE, YOU WILL CERTAINLY BECOME A GREAT EVIL ONE DAY.
KHEEEEEN
THUS...
KHEEN
KHEEN

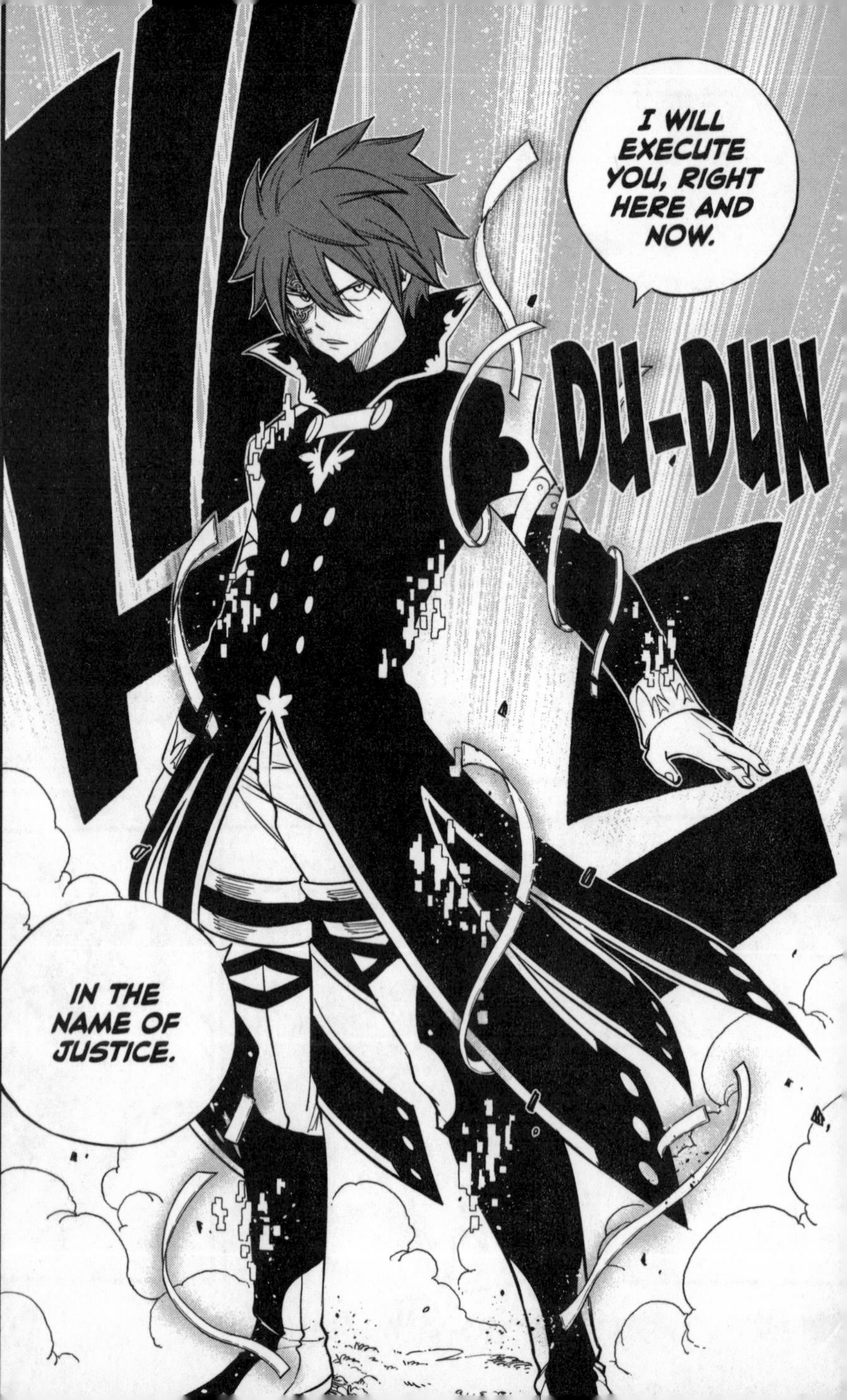
I WILL EXECUTE YOU, RIGHT HERE AND NOW.
DU-DUN
IN THE NAME OF JUSTICE.

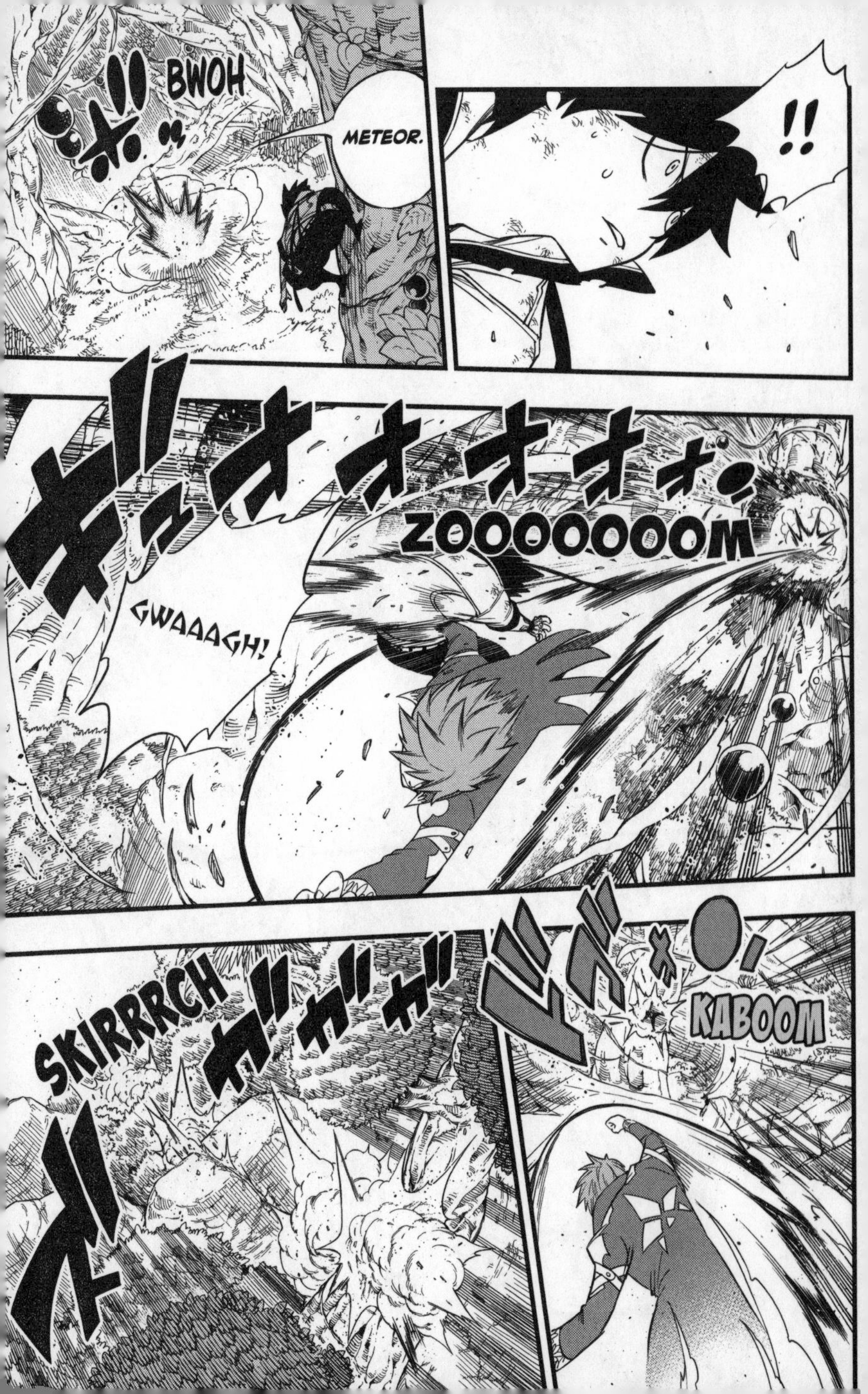
!!
METEOR.
BWOH
ZOOOOOOOM
GWAAAGH!
KABOOM
SKIRRRCH

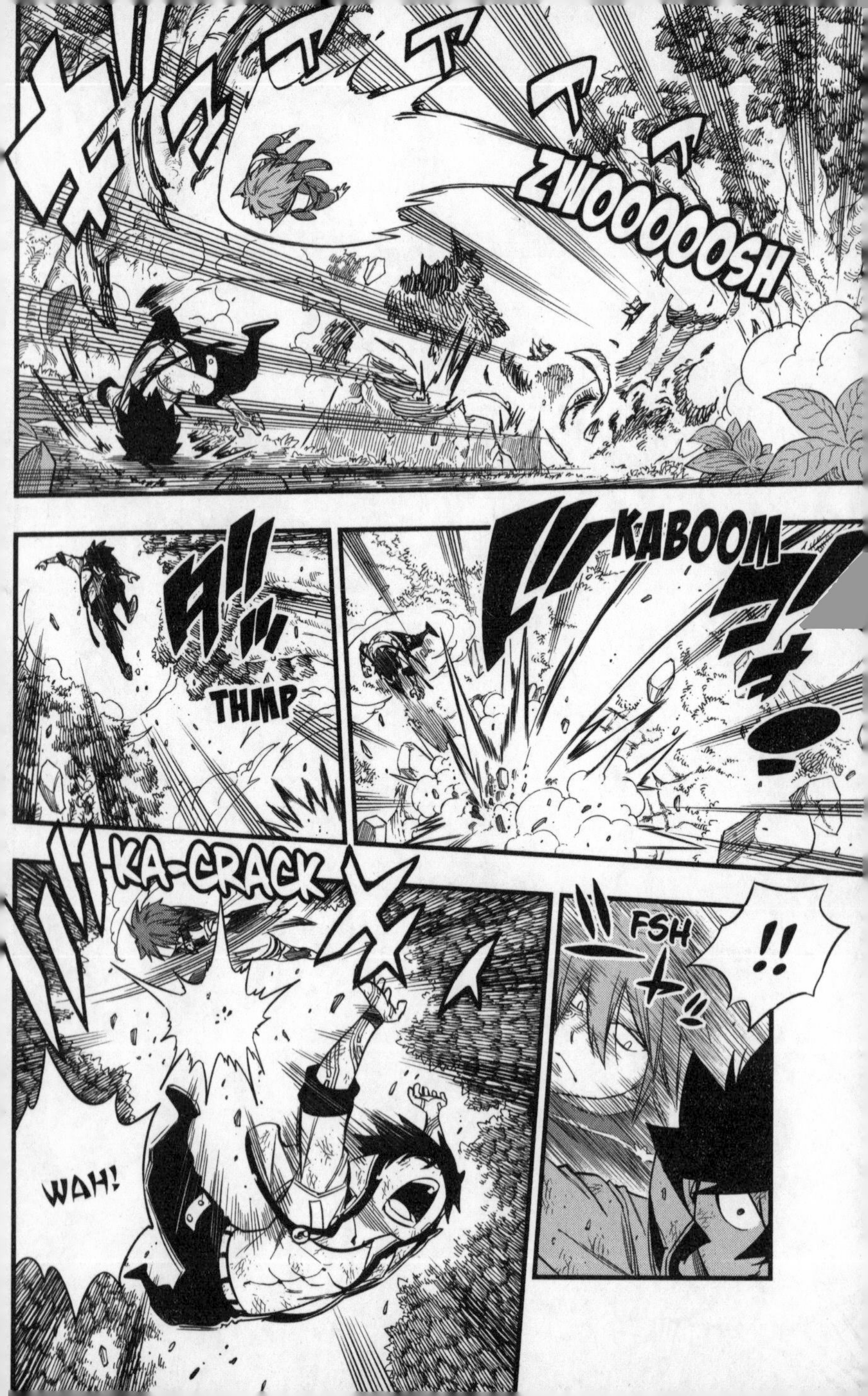
ZWOOOOOOSH
KABOOM
THMP
FSH
!!
KA-CRACK
WAH!

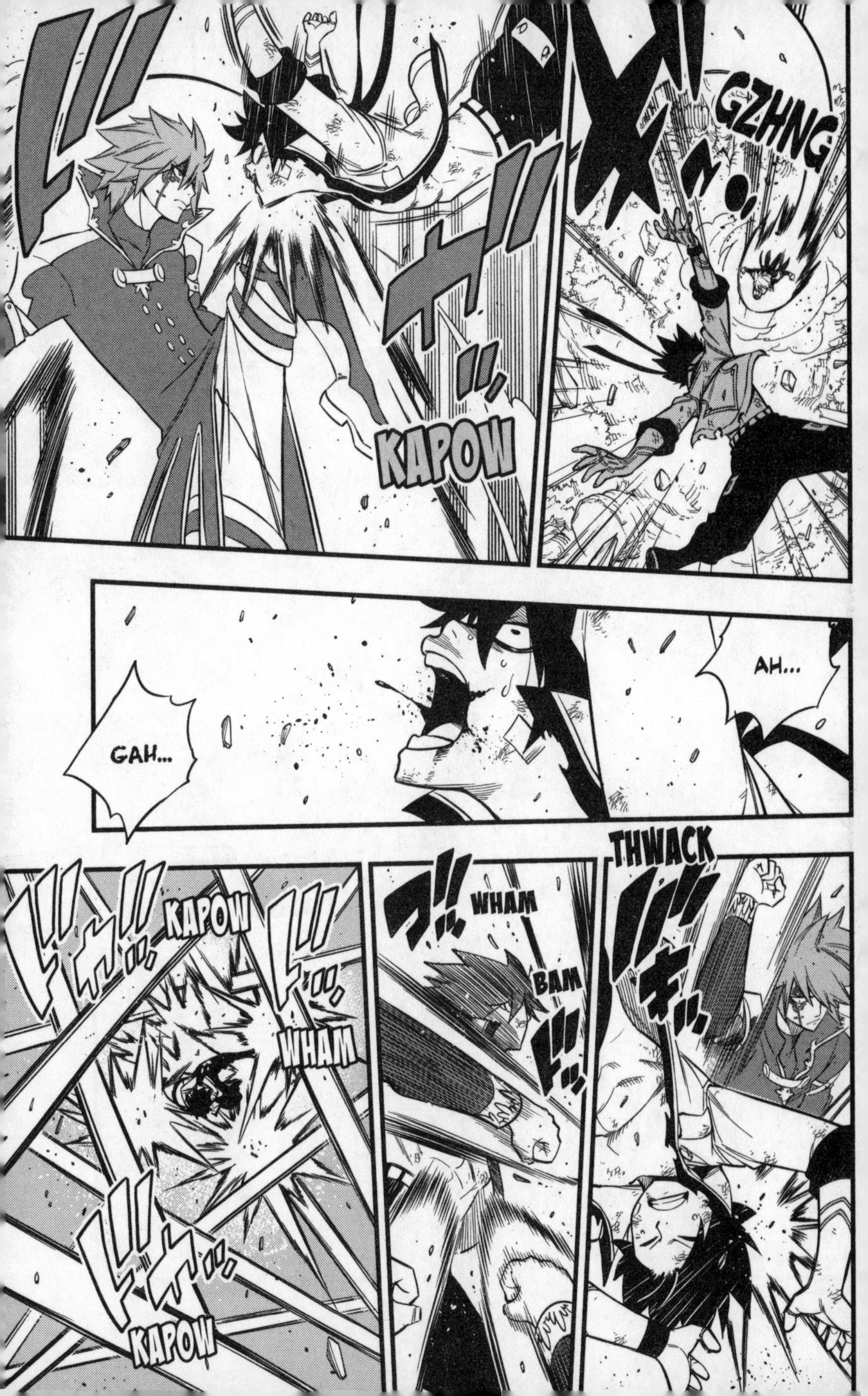
GZHNG
KAPOW
AH...
GAH...
THWACK
WHAM
BAM
KAPOW
WHAM
KAPOW

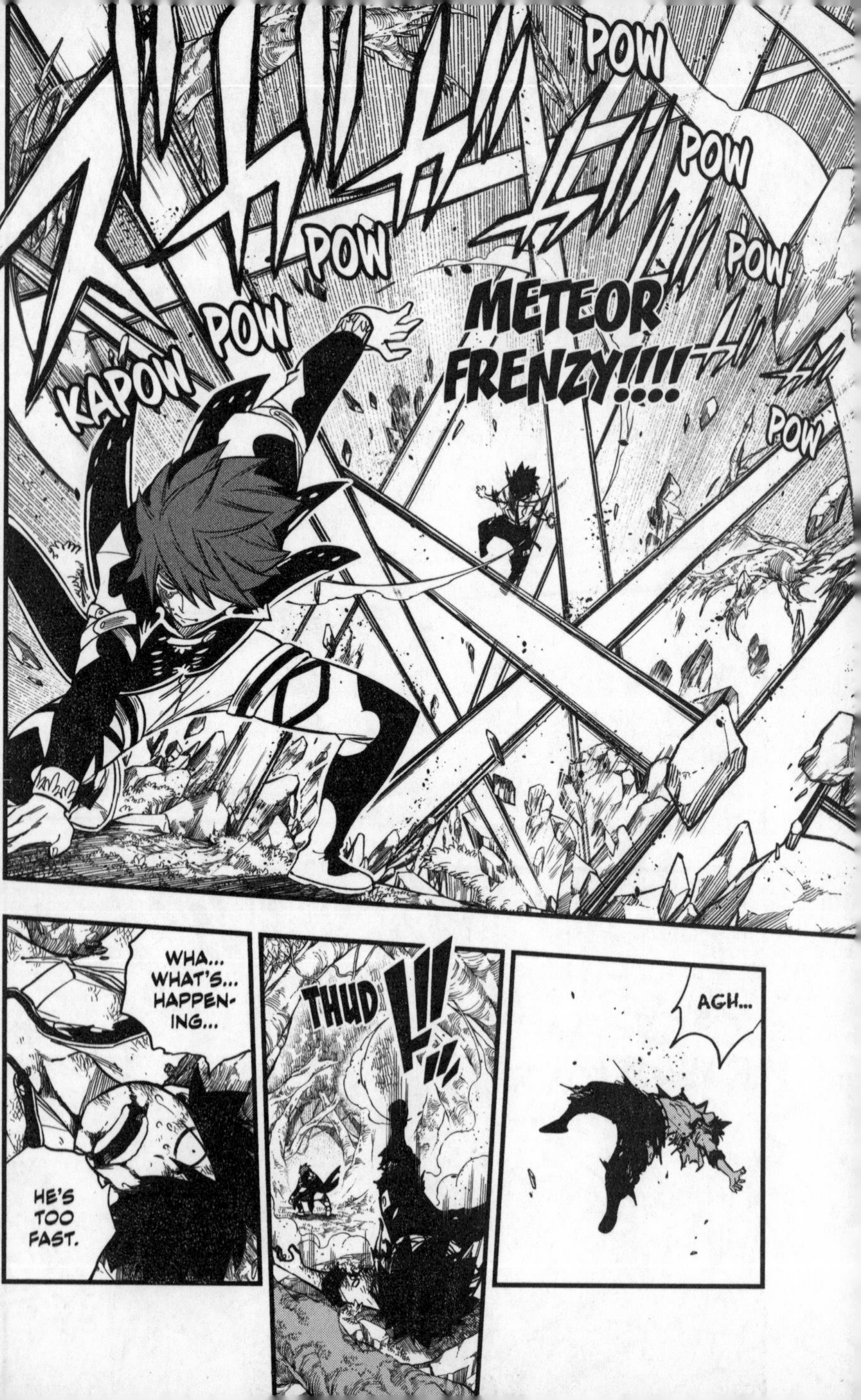
POW
POW
POW
POW
METEOR FRENZY!!!!
POW
POW
KAPOW
AGH...
THUD!!
WHA... WHAT'S... HAPPEN-ING...
HE'S TOO FAST.

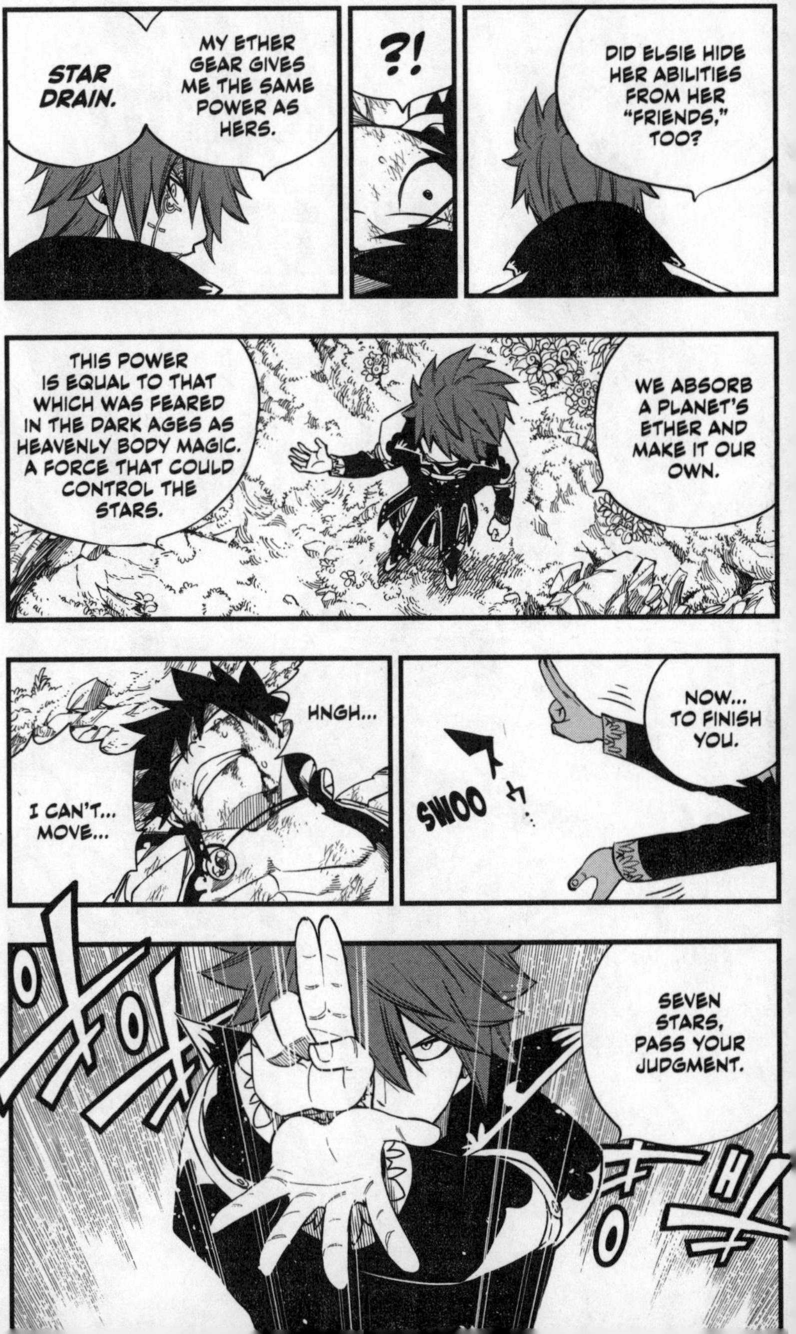
DID ELSIE HIDE HER ABILITIES FROM HER "FRIENDS," TOO?
?!
MY ETHER GEAR GIVES ME THE SAME POWER AS HERS.
STAR DRAIN.
WE ABSORB A PLANET'S ETHER AND MAKE IT OUR OWN.
THIS POWER IS EQUAL TO THAT WHICH WAS FEARED IN THE DARK AGES AS HEAVENLY BODY MAGIC. A FORCE THAT COULD CONTROL THE STARS.
NOW... TO FINISH YOU.
SWOO
HNGH...
I CAN'T... MOVE...
SEVEN STARS, PASS YOUR JUDGMENT.

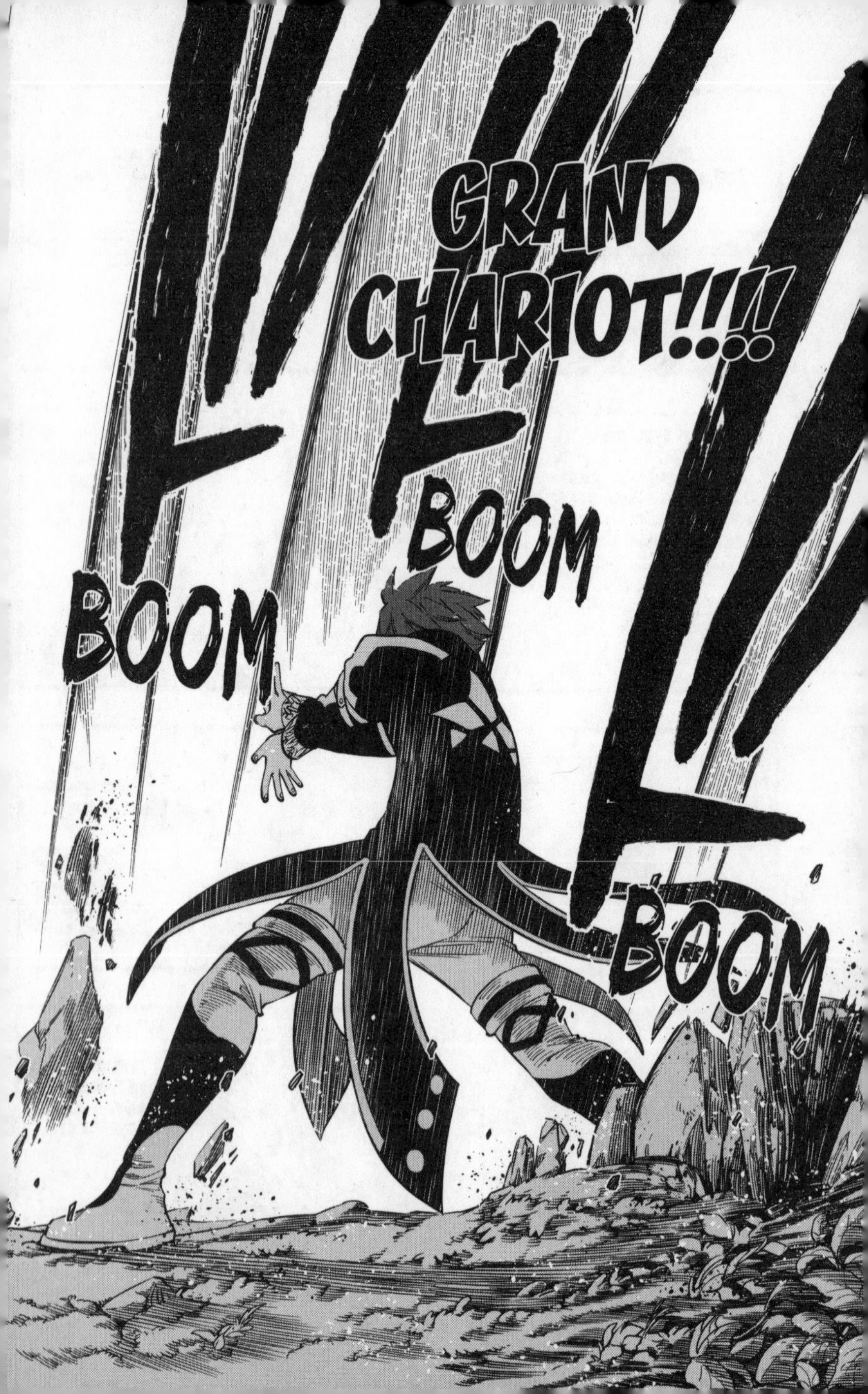
GRAND CHARIOT!!!!
BOOM
BOOM
BOOM

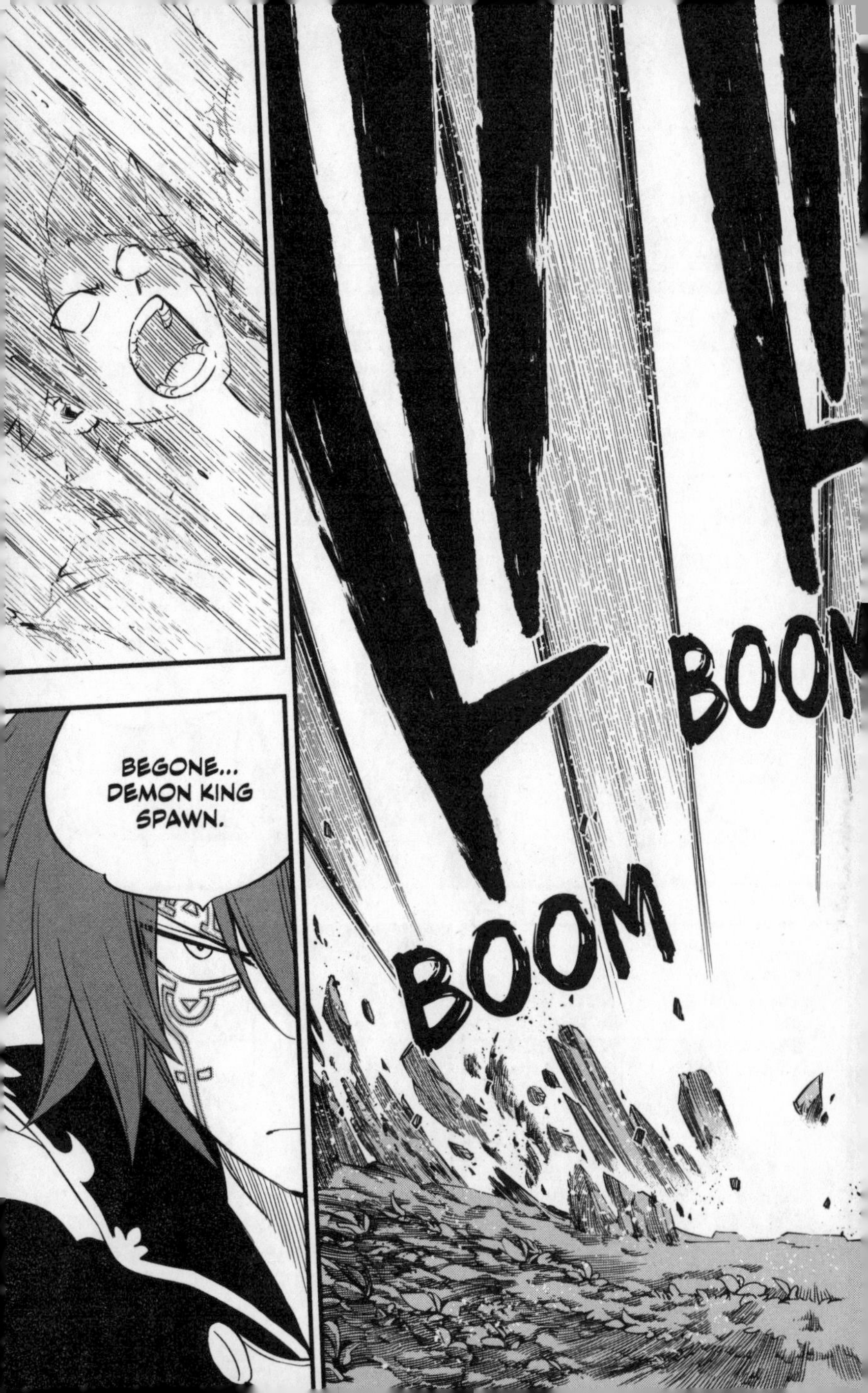
BOOM
BOOM
BEGONE... DEMON KING SPAWN.

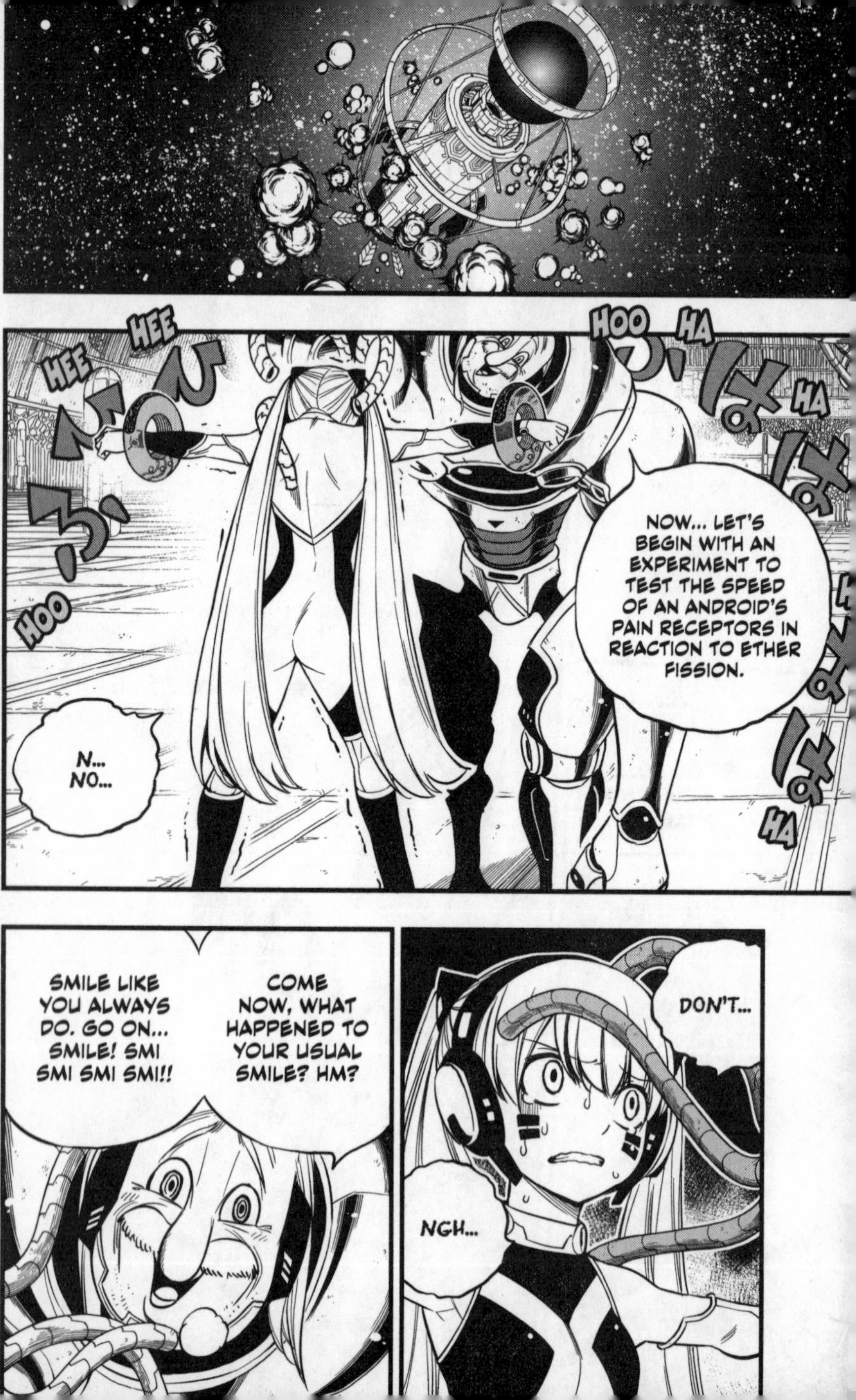
HOO HA
HA
NOW... LET'S BEGIN WITH AN EXPERIMENT TO TEST THE SPEED OF AN ANDROID'S PAIN RECEPTORS IN REACTION TO ETHER FISSION.
HA
HEE
HEE
HEE
HOO
N... NO...
DON'T...
NGH...
COME NOW, WHAT HAPPENED TO YOUR USUAL SMILE? HM?
SMILE LIKE YOU ALWAYS DO. GO ON... SMILE! SMI SMI SMI SMI!!

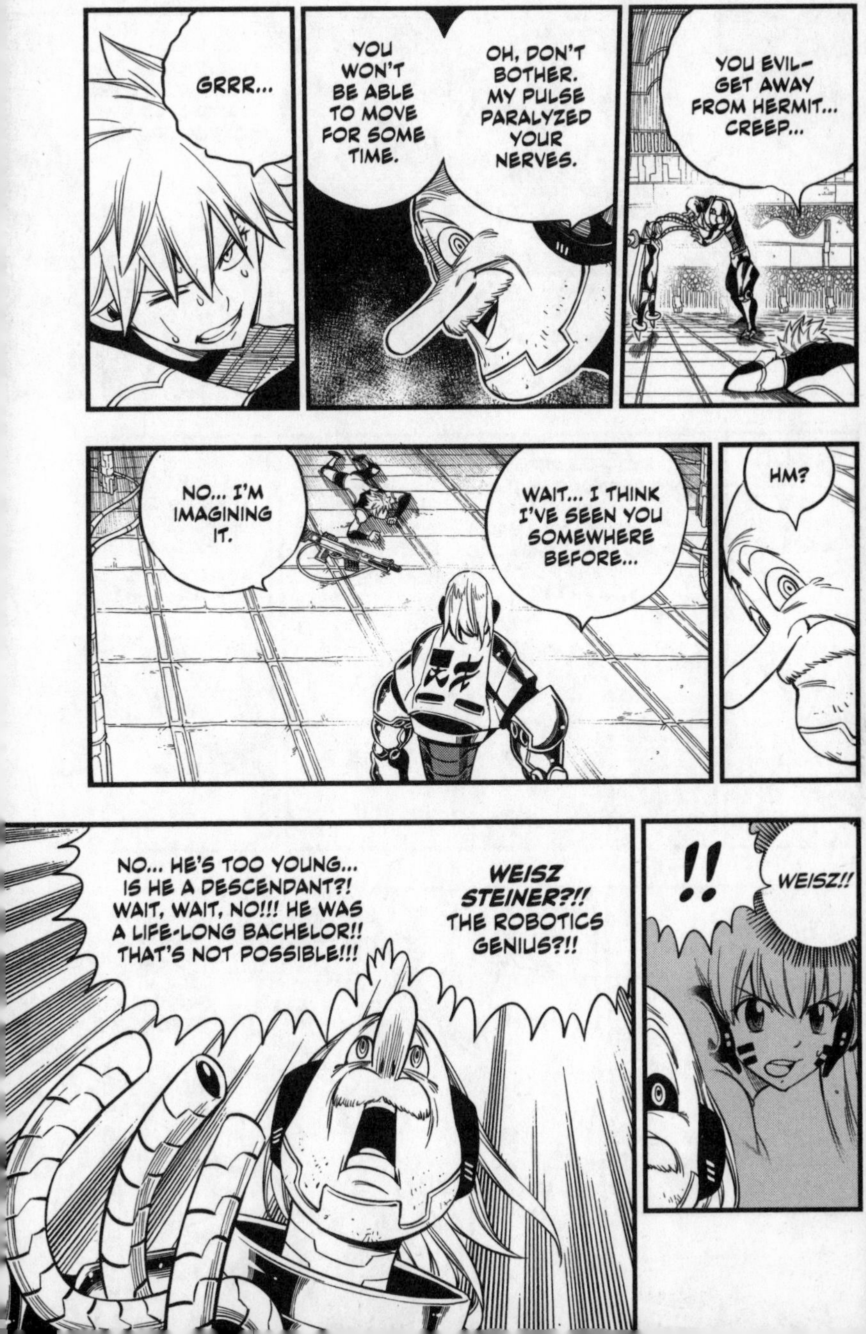
YOU EVIL-
GET AWAY
FROM HERMIT...
CREEP...
OH, DON'T BOTHER. MY PULSE PARALYZED YOUR NERVES.
YOU WON'T BE ABLE TO MOVE FOR SOME TIME.
GRRR...
HM?
WAIT... I THINK I'VE SEEN YOU SOMEWHERE BEFORE...
NO... I'M IMAGINING IT.
WEISZ!!
!!
WEISZ STEINER?!! THE ROBOTICS GENIUS?!!
NO... HE'S TOO YOUNG... IS HE A DESCENDANT?! WAIT, WAIT, NO!!! HE WAS A LIFE-LONG BACHELOR!! THAT'S NOT POSSIBLE!!!

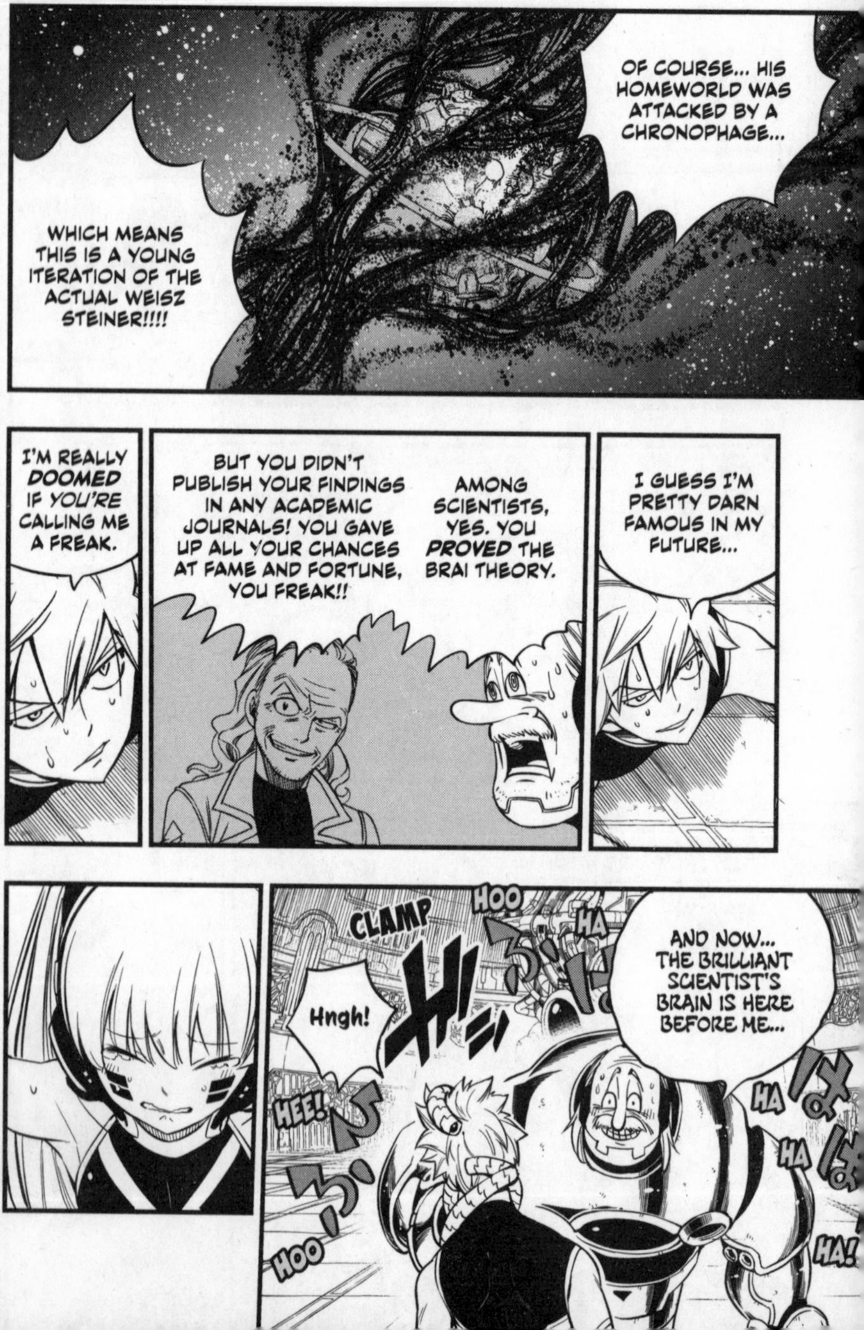
OF COURSE... HIS HOMEWORLD WAS ATTACKED BY A CHRONOPHAGE...
WHICH MEANS THIS IS A YOUNG ITERATION OF THE ACTUAL WEISZ STEINER!!!!
I GUESS I'M PRETTY DARN FAMOUS IN MY FUTURE...
AMONG SCIENTISTS, YES. YOU *PROVED* THE BRAI THEORY.
BUT YOU DIDN'T PUBLISH YOUR FINDINGS IN ANY ACADEMIC JOURNALS! YOU GAVE UP ALL YOUR CHANCES AT FAME AND FORTUNE, YOU FREAK!!
I'M REALLY *DOOMED* IF *YOU'RE* CALLING ME A FREAK.
AND NOW... THE BRILLIANT SCIENTIST'S BRAIN IS HERE BEFORE ME...
HA
HA
HA!
HA
HOO
CLAMP
Hngh!
HEE!
HOO

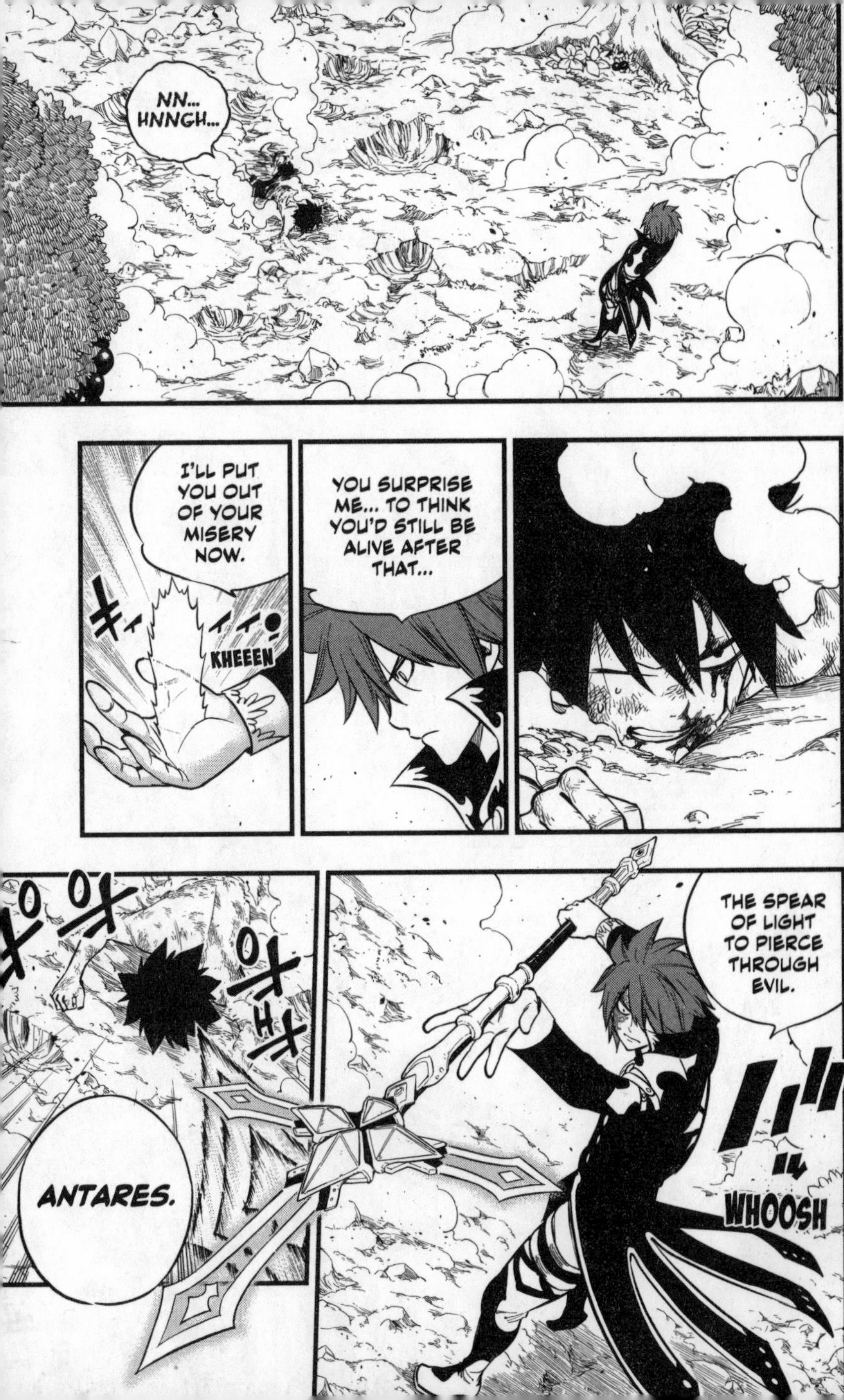
NN... UNNGH...
YOU SURPRISE ME... TO THINK YOU'D STILL BE ALIVE AFTER THAT...
I'LL PUT YOU OUT OF YOUR MISERY NOW.
KHEEEN
THE SPEAR OF LIGHT TO PIERCE THROUGH EVIL.
WHOOSH
ANTARES.

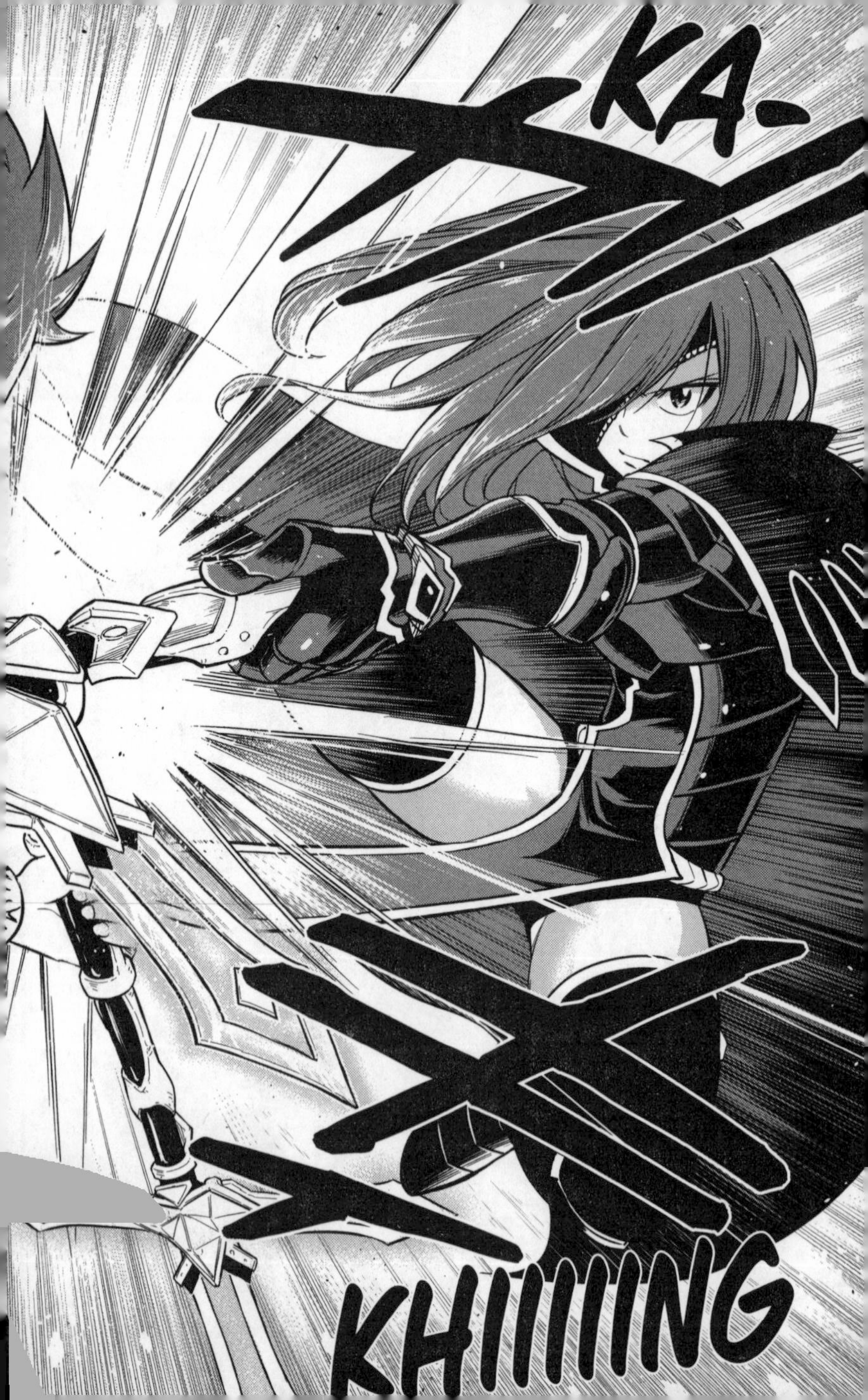
KA-
KHIIIIING

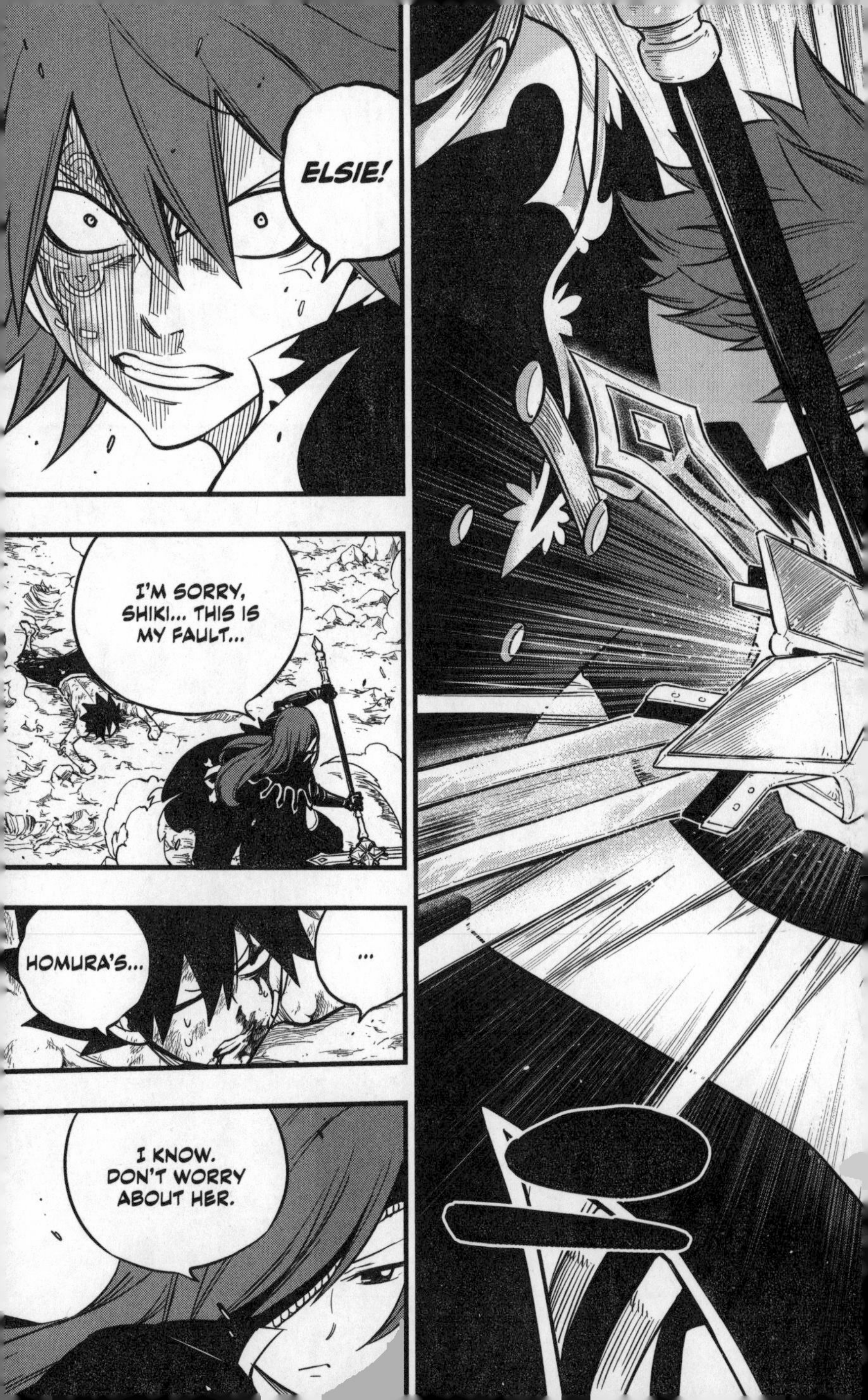
ELSIE!
I'M SORRY, SHIKI... THIS IS MY FAULT...
...
HOMURA'S...
I KNOW. DON'T WORRY ABOUT HER.

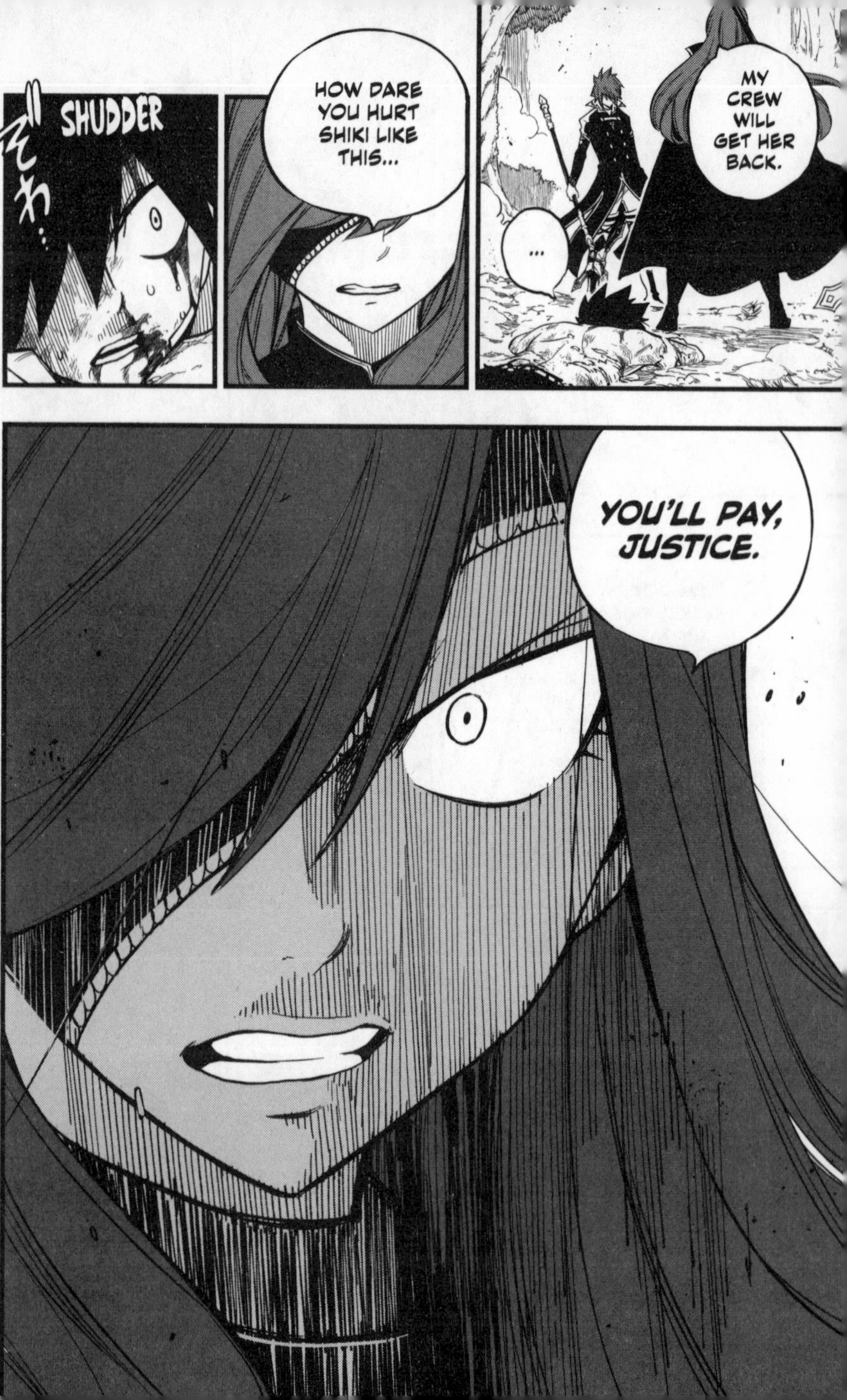
MY CREW WILL GET HER BACK.
...
HOW DARE YOU HURT SHIKI LIKE THIS...
SHUDDER
ぞわ…
YOU'LL PAY, JUSTICE.

EDENS ZERO

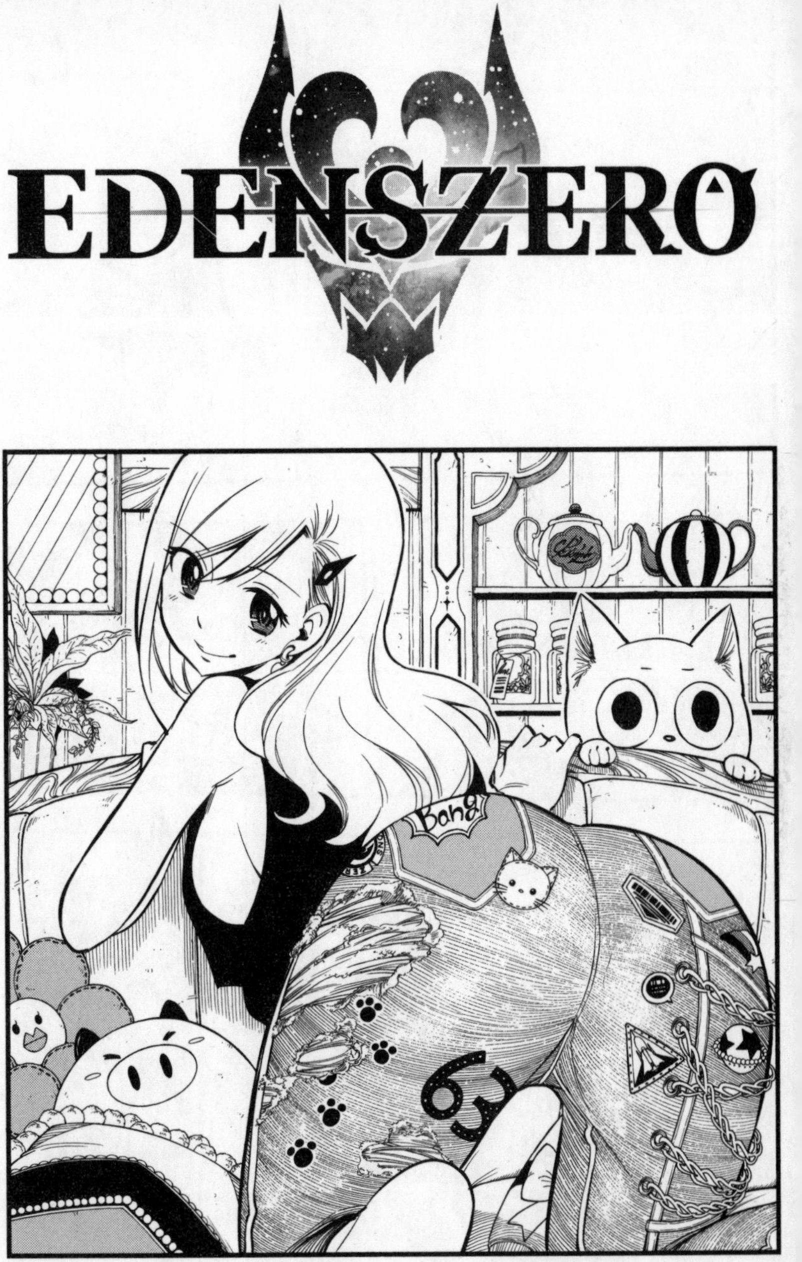
Bang
63

CHAPTER 124: KISS & DIE

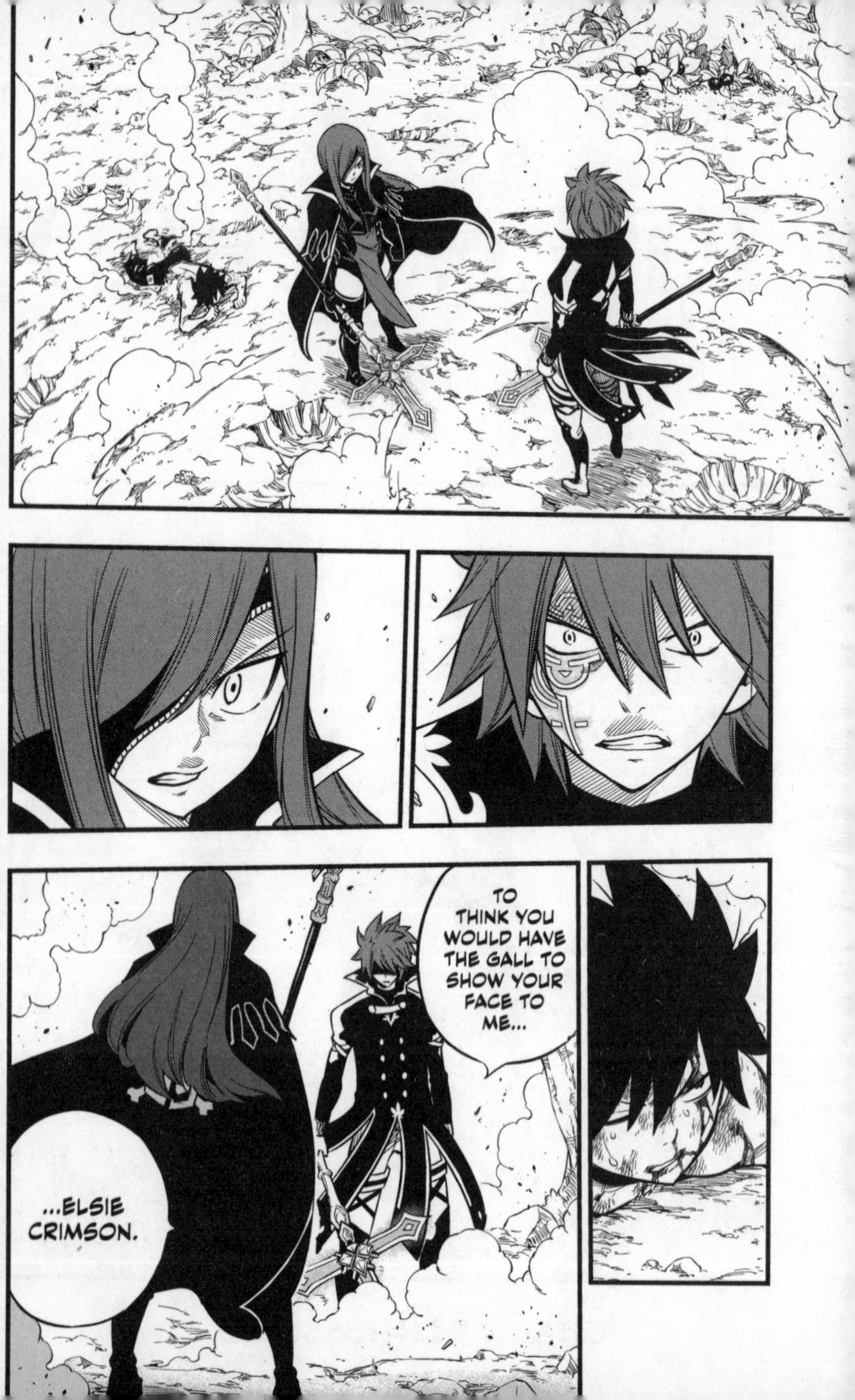
TO THINK YOU WOULD HAVE THE GALL TO SHOW YOUR FACE TO ME...
...ELSIE CRIMSON.

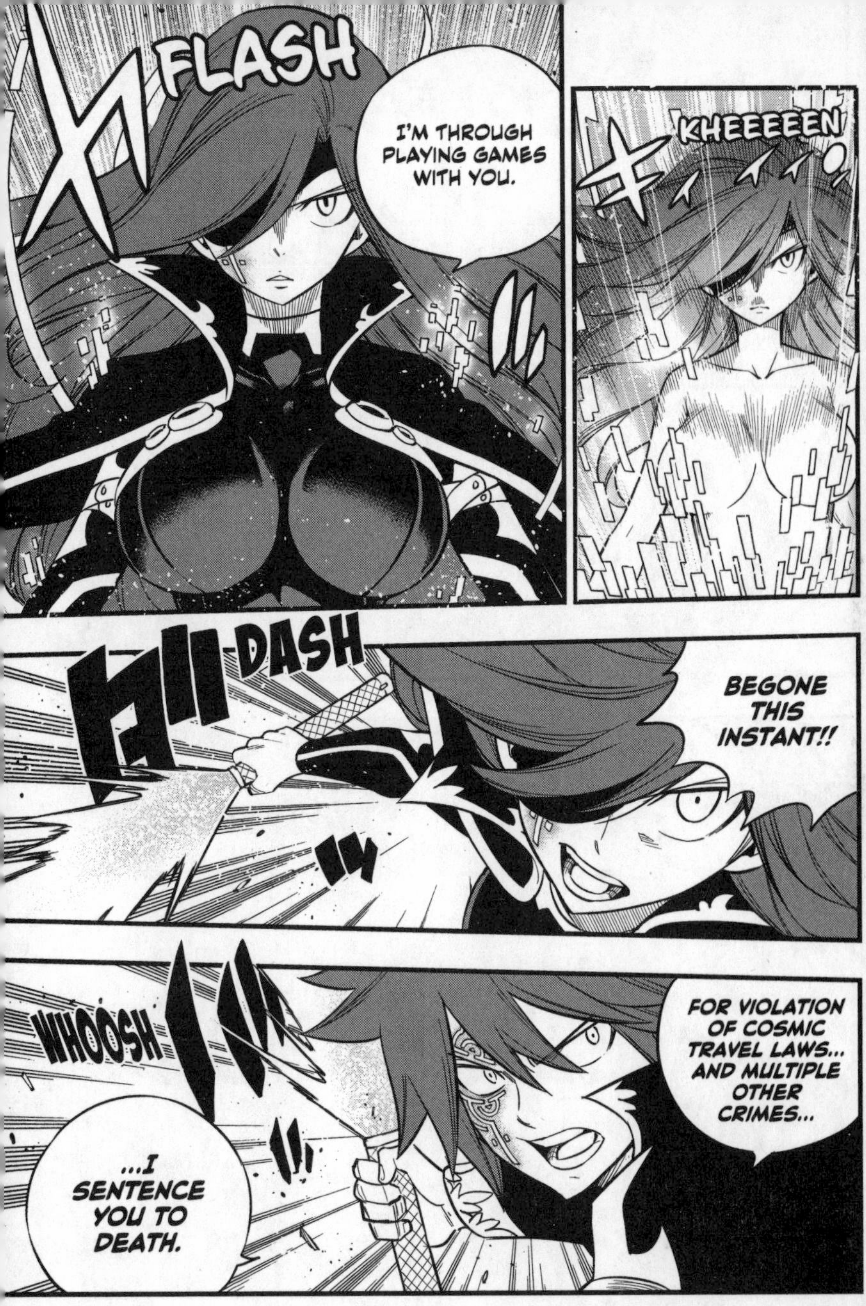
KHEEEEEN
FLASH
I'M THROUGH PLAYING GAMES WITH YOU.
BEGONE THIS INSTANT!!
DASH
FOR VIOLATION OF COSMIC TRAVEL LAWS... AND MULTIPLE OTHER CRIMES...
WHOOSH
...I SENTENCE YOU TO DEATH.

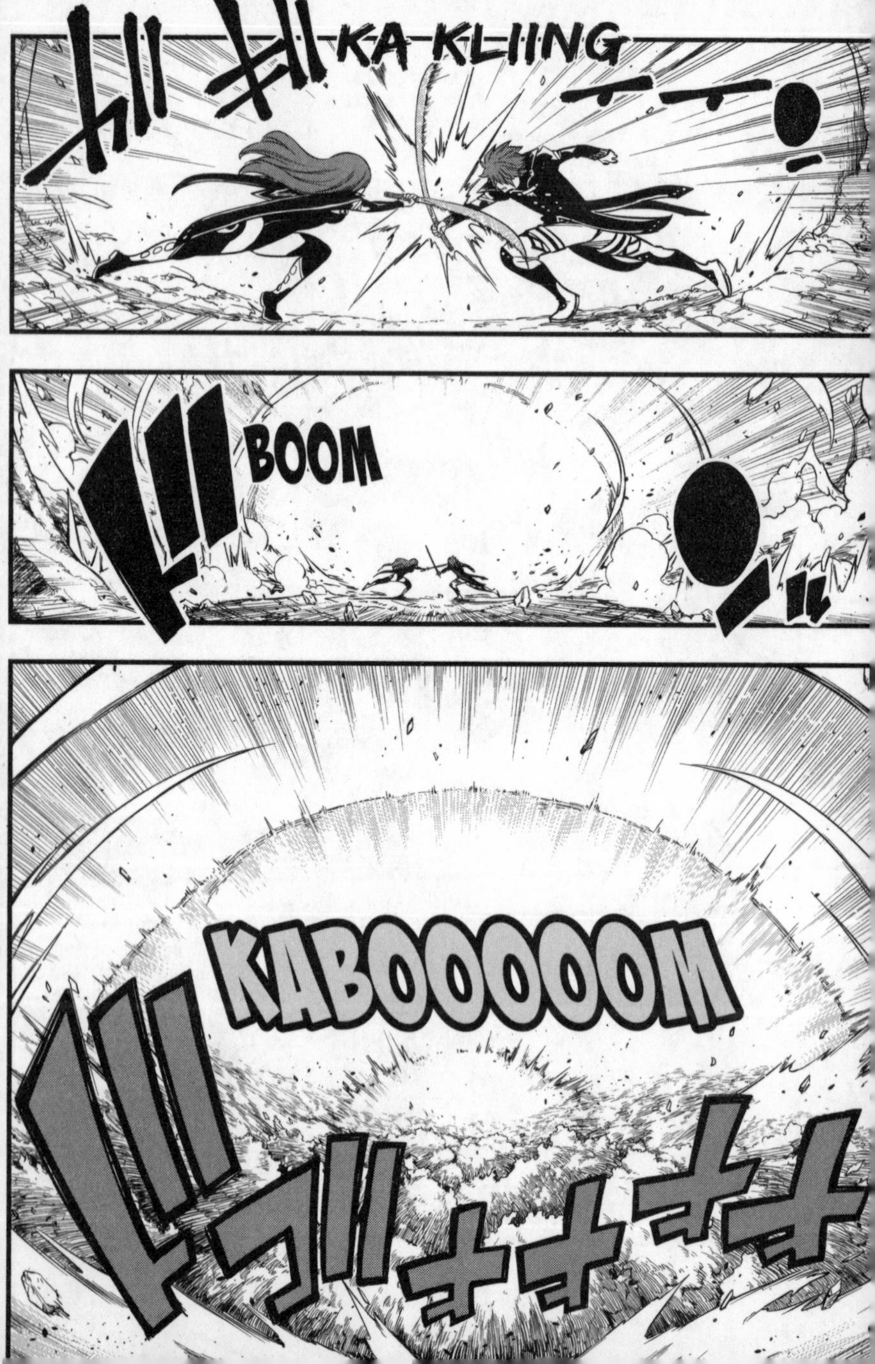
KA KLIING
BOOM
KABOOOOOM

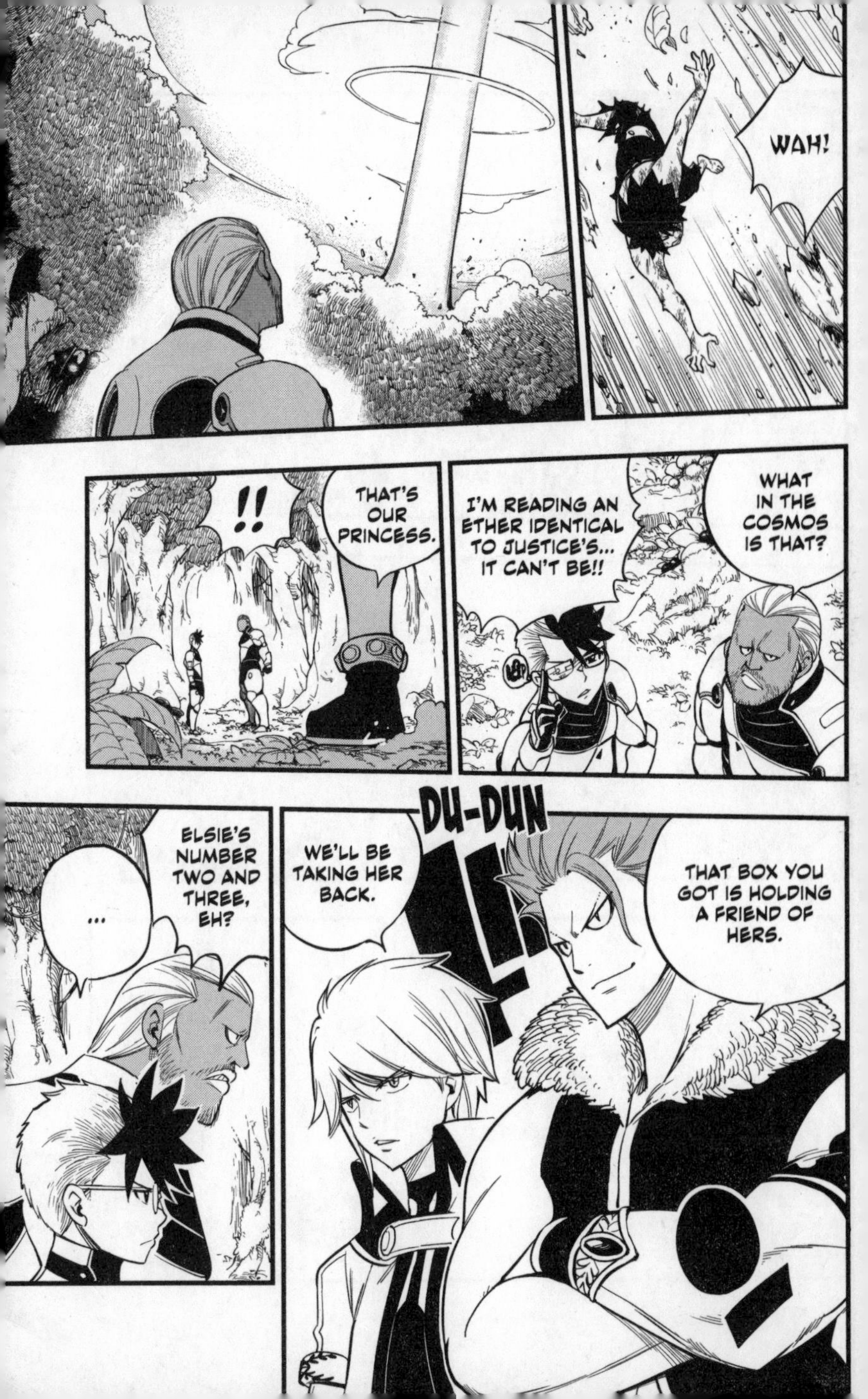
WAH!
WHAT IN THE COSMOS IS THAT?
I'M READING AN ETHER IDENTICAL TO JUSTICE'S... IT CAN'T BE!!
THAT'S OUR PRINCESS.
!!
DU-DUN
THAT BOX YOU GOT IS HOLDING A FRIEND OF HERS.
WE'LL BE TAKING HER BACK.
ELSIE'S NUMBER TWO AND THREE, EH?
...

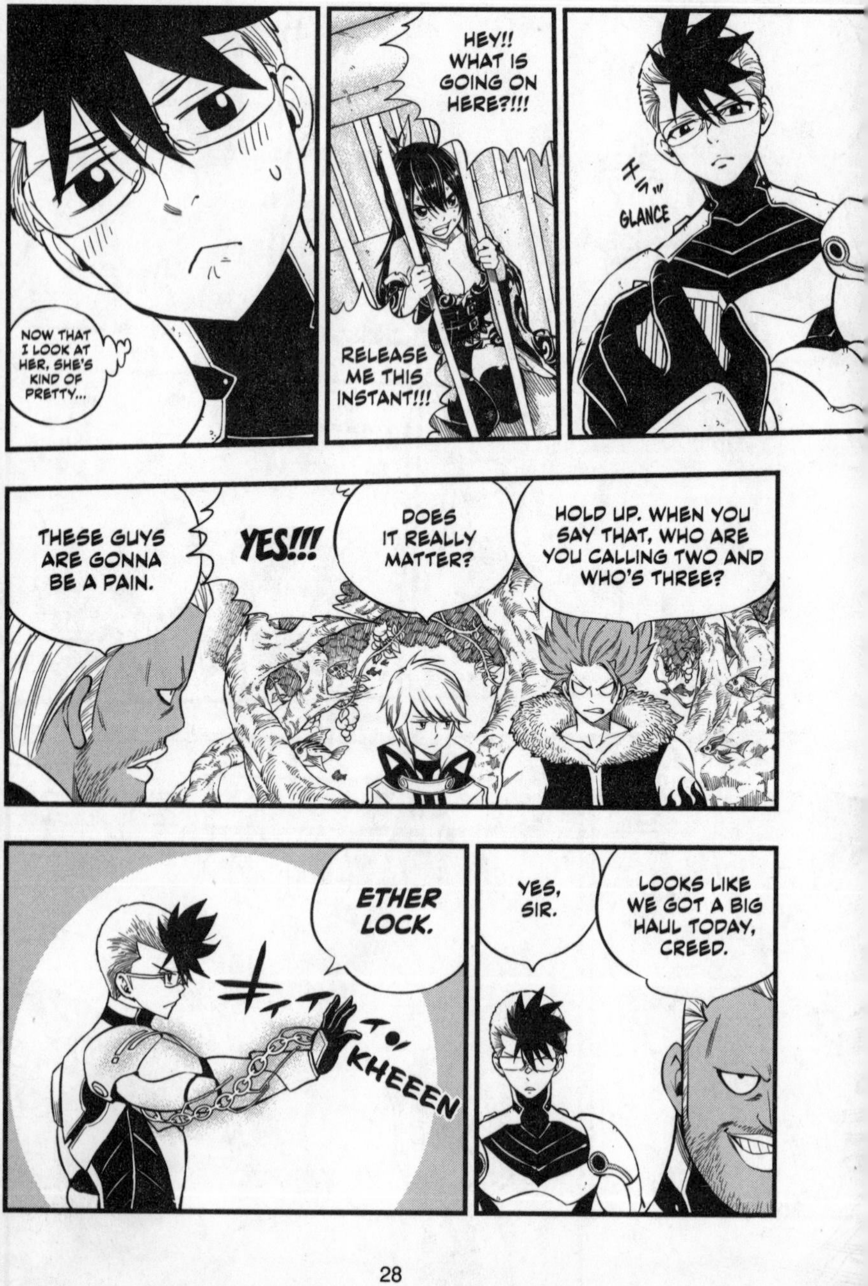
GLANCE
HEY!! WHAT IS GOING ON HERE?!!!
RELEASE ME THIS INSTANT!!!
NOW THAT I LOOK AT HER, SHE'S KIND OF PRETTY...
HOLD UP. WHEN YOU SAY THAT, WHO ARE YOU CALLING TWO AND WHO'S THREE?
DOES IT REALLY MATTER?
YES!!!
THESE GUYS ARE GONNA BE A PAIN.
LOOKS LIKE WE GOT A BIG HAUL TODAY, CREED.
YES, SIR.
ETHER LOCK.
KHEEEN

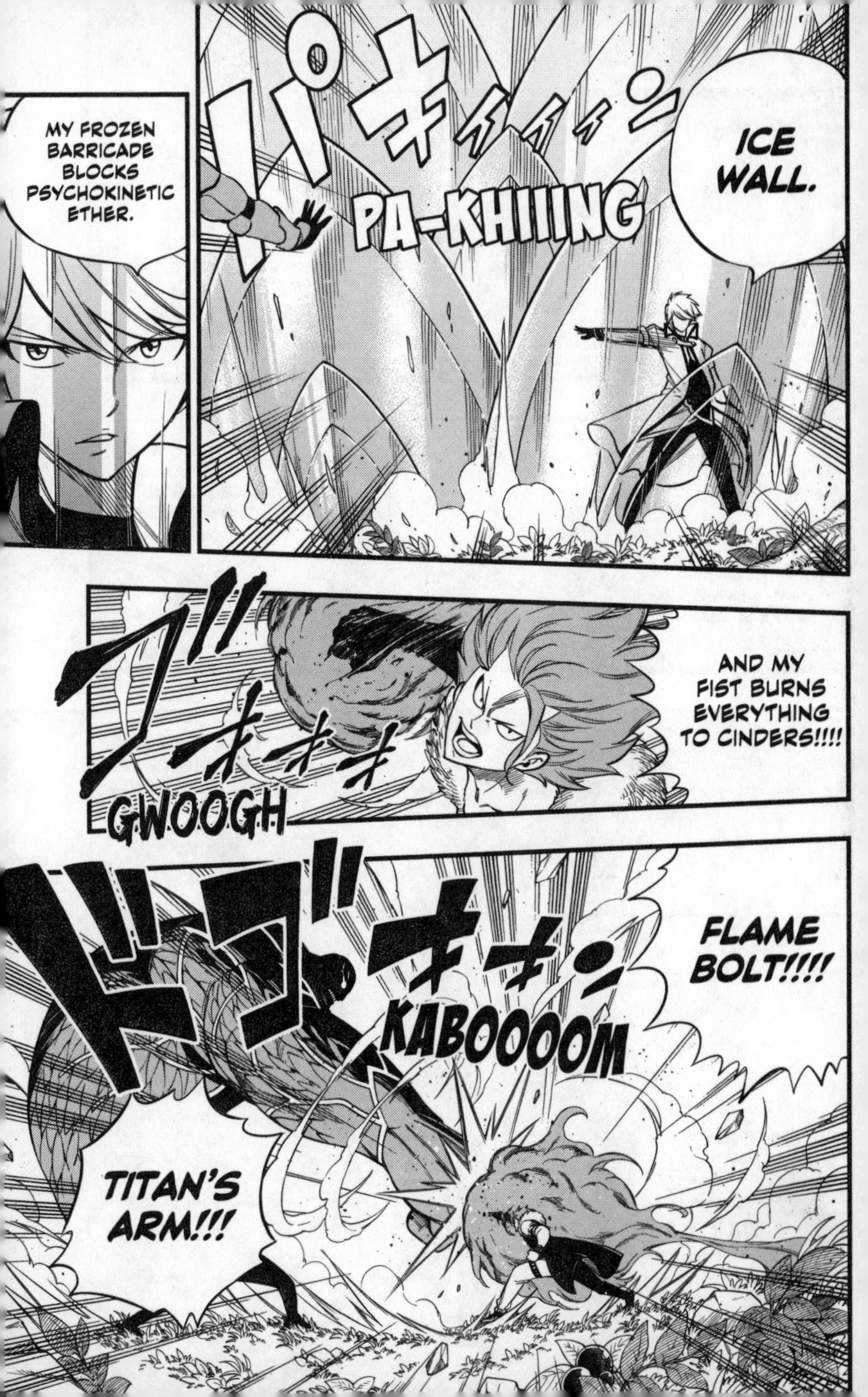
ICE WALL.
PA-KHIIING
MY FROZEN BARRICADE BLOCKS PSYCHOKINETIC ETHER.
AND MY FIST BURNS EVERYTHING TO CINDERS!!!!
GWOOGH
FLAME BOLT!!!!
KABOOOOM
TITAN'S ARM!!!

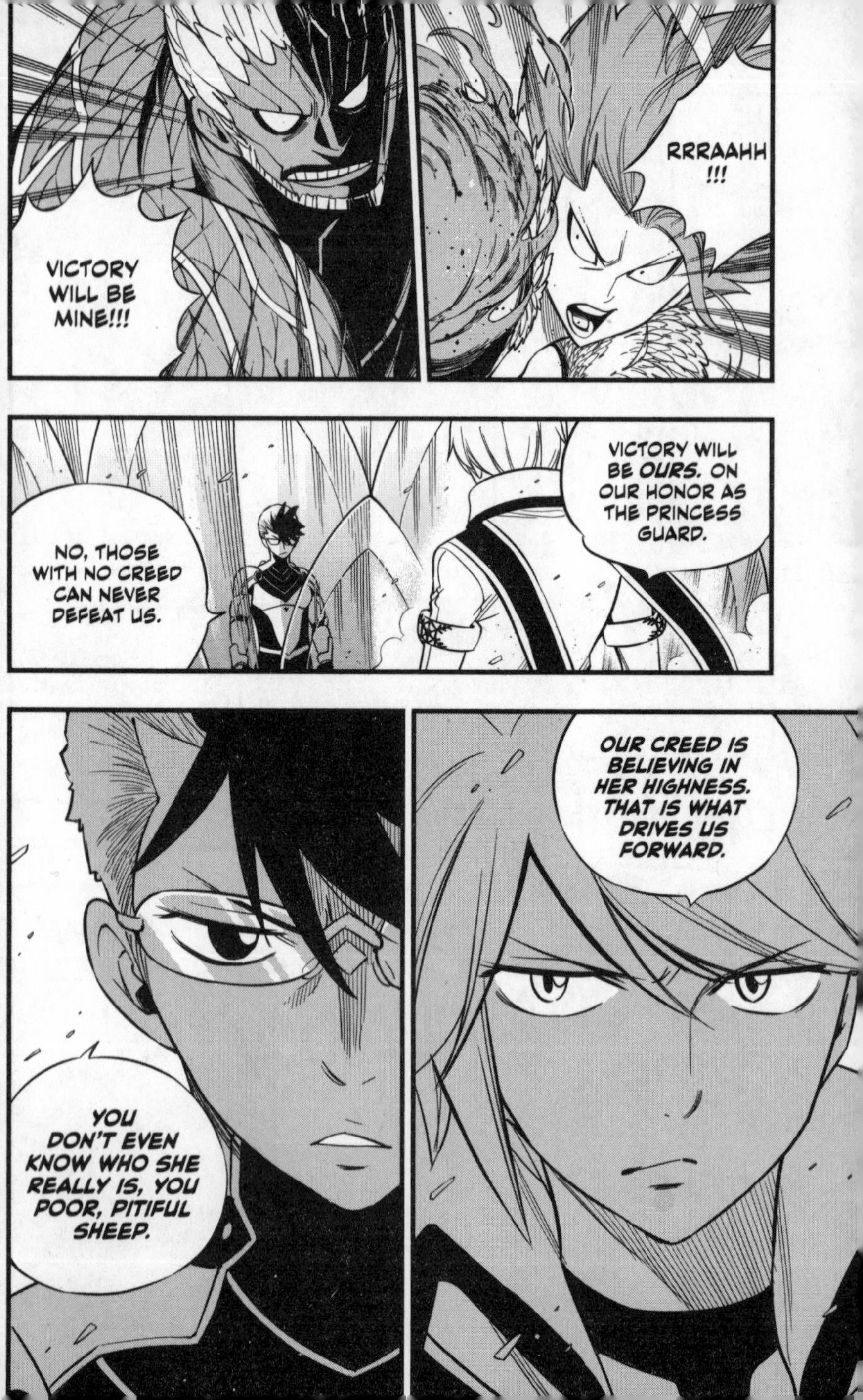
RRRAAHH !!!
VICTORY WILL BE MINE!!!
VICTORY WILL BE *OURS*. ON OUR HONOR AS THE PRINCESS GUARD.
NO, THOSE WITH NO CREED CAN NEVER DEFEAT US.
OUR CREED IS BELIEVING IN HER HIGHNESS. THAT IS WHAT DRIVES US FORWARD.
YOU DON'T EVEN KNOW WHO SHE REALLY IS, YOU POOR, PITIFUL SHEEP.

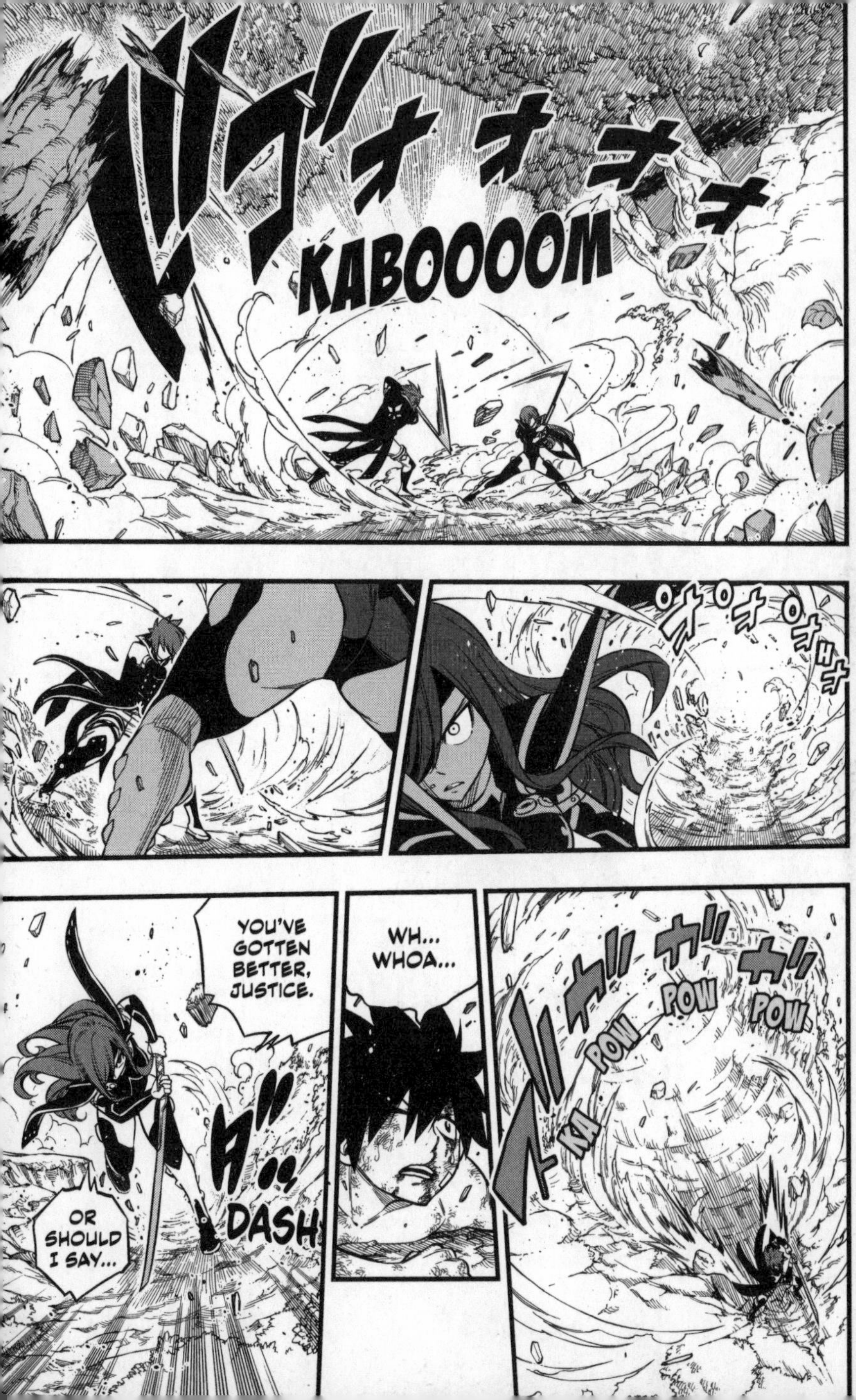
KABOOOOM
POW
POW
POW
KA
WH... WHOA...
YOU'VE GOTTEN BETTER, JUSTICE.
DASH
OR SHOULD I SAY...

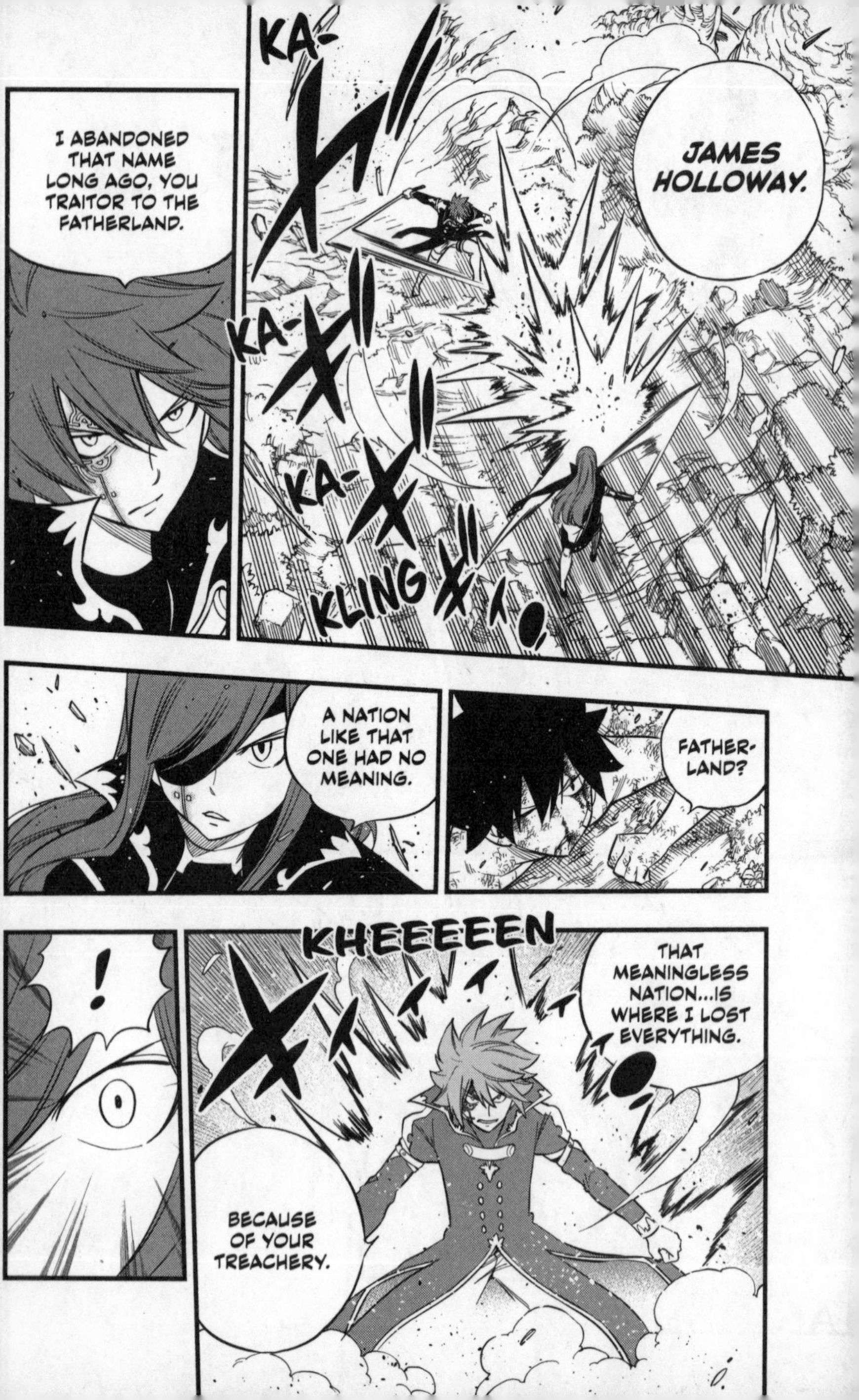
JAMES HOLLOWAY.
KA-
KA-
KA-
KLING
I ABANDONED THAT NAME LONG AGO, YOU TRAITOR TO THE FATHERLAND.
FATHER-LAND?
A NATION LIKE THAT ONE HAD NO MEANING.
KHEEEEEN
THAT MEANINGLESS NATION...IS WHERE I LOST EVERYTHING.
BECAUSE OF YOUR TREACHERY.
!

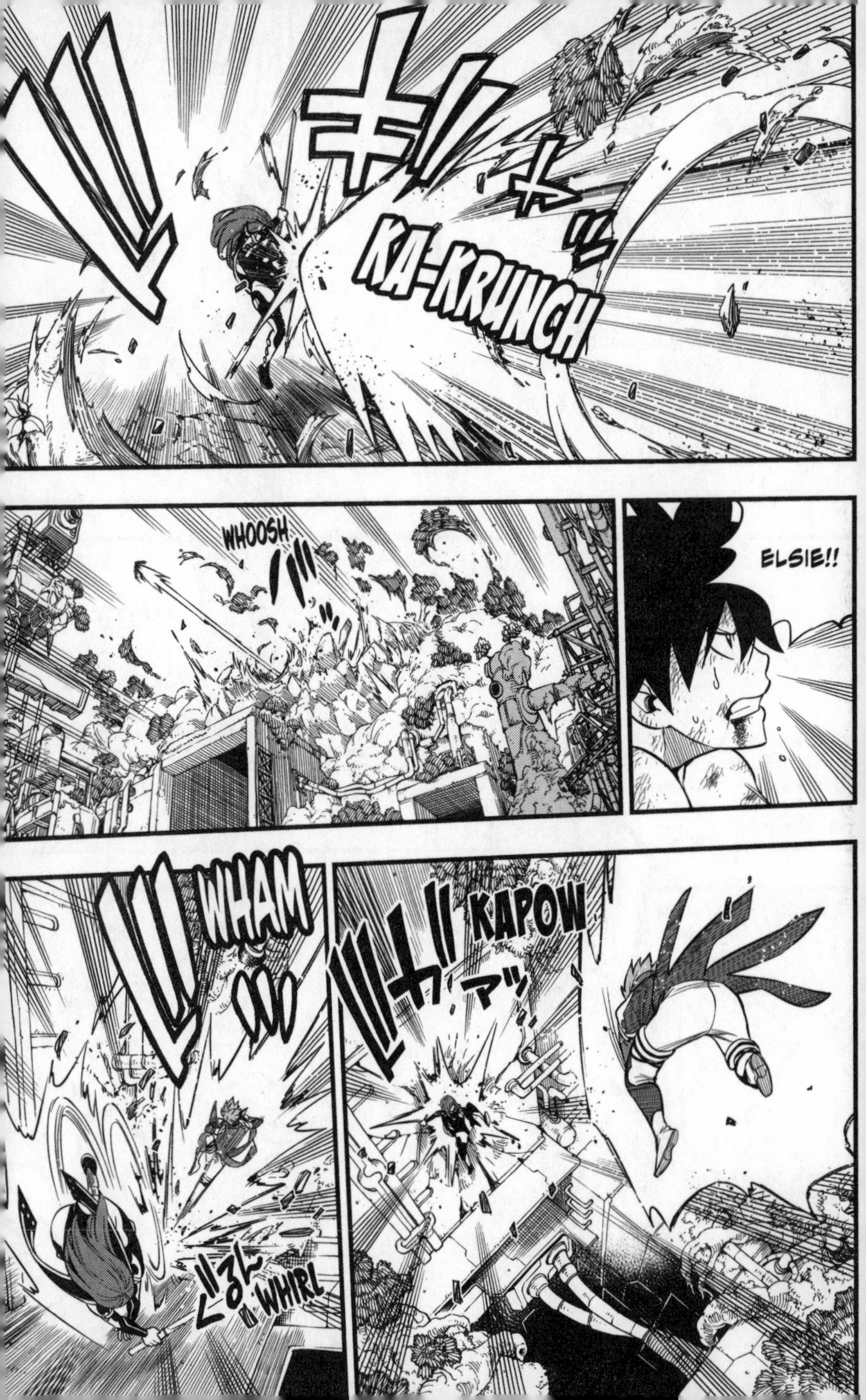
KA-KRUNCH
ELSIE!!
WHOOSH
KAPOW
WHAM
WHIRL

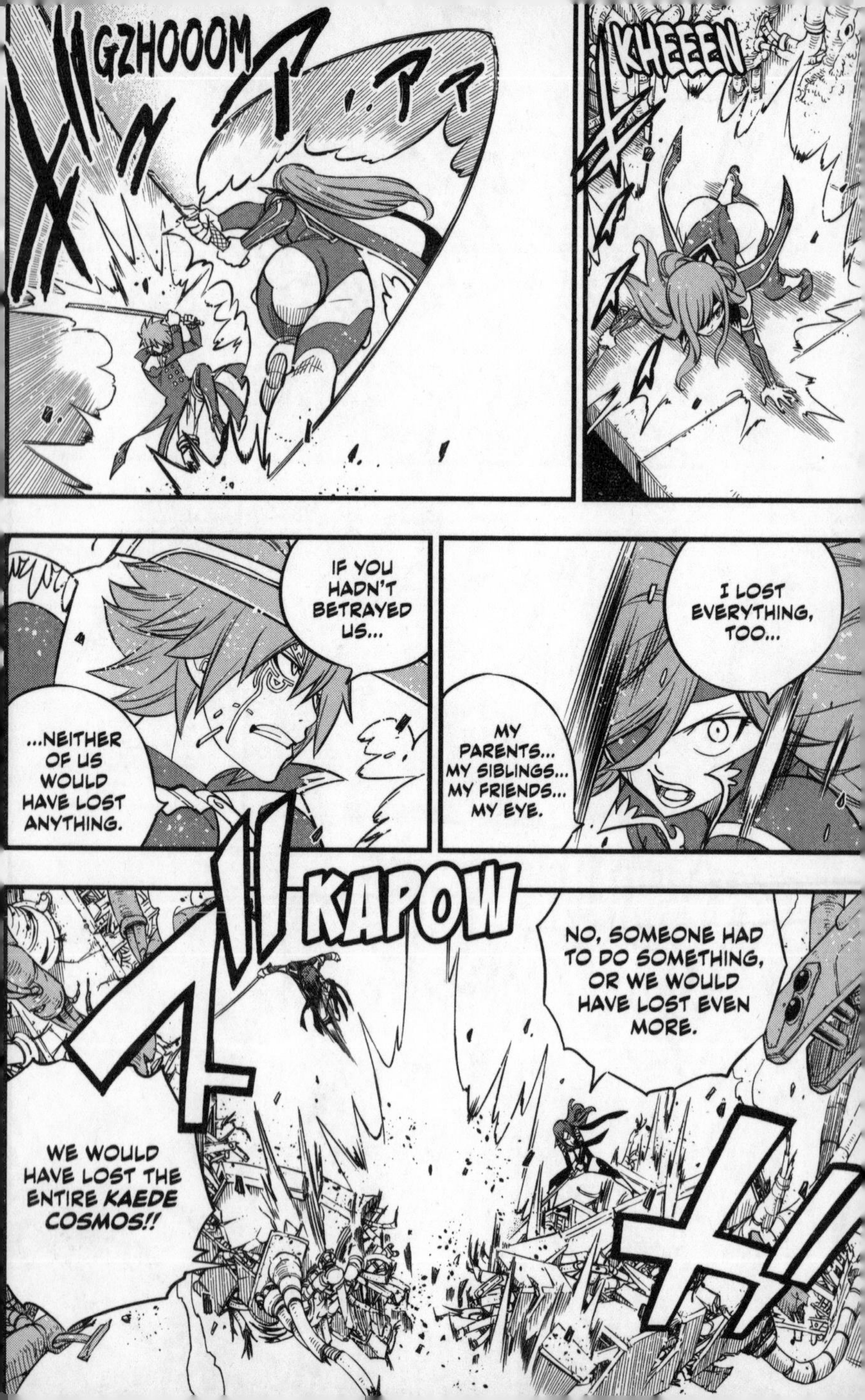

KHEEEN
GZHOOOM
I LOST EVERYTHING, TOO...
MY PARENTS... MY SIBLINGS... MY FRIENDS... MY EYE.
IF YOU HADN'T BETRAYED US...
...NEITHER OF US WOULD HAVE LOST ANYTHING.
NO, SOMEONE HAD TO DO SOMETHING, OR WE WOULD HAVE LOST EVEN MORE.
KAPOW
WE WOULD HAVE LOST THE ENTIRE *KAEDE COSMOS*!!

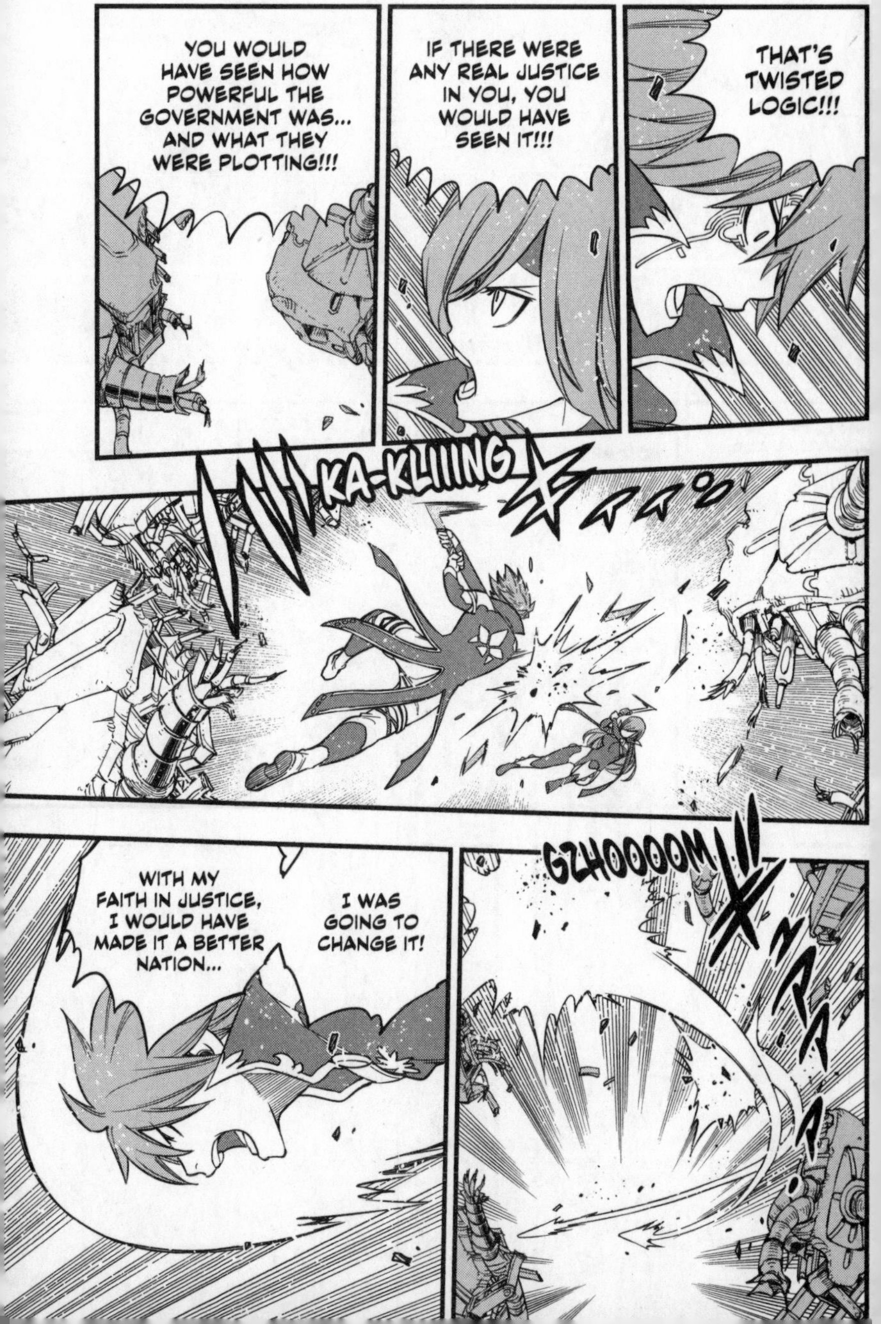
THAT'S TWISTED LOGIC!!!
IF THERE WERE ANY REAL JUSTICE IN YOU, YOU WOULD HAVE SEEN IT!!!
YOU WOULD HAVE SEEN HOW POWERFUL THE GOVERNMENT WAS... AND WHAT THEY WERE PLOTTING!!!
KA-KLIIING
GZHOOOOM
I WAS GOING TO CHANGE IT!
WITH MY FAITH IN JUSTICE, I WOULD HAVE MADE IT A BETTER NATION...

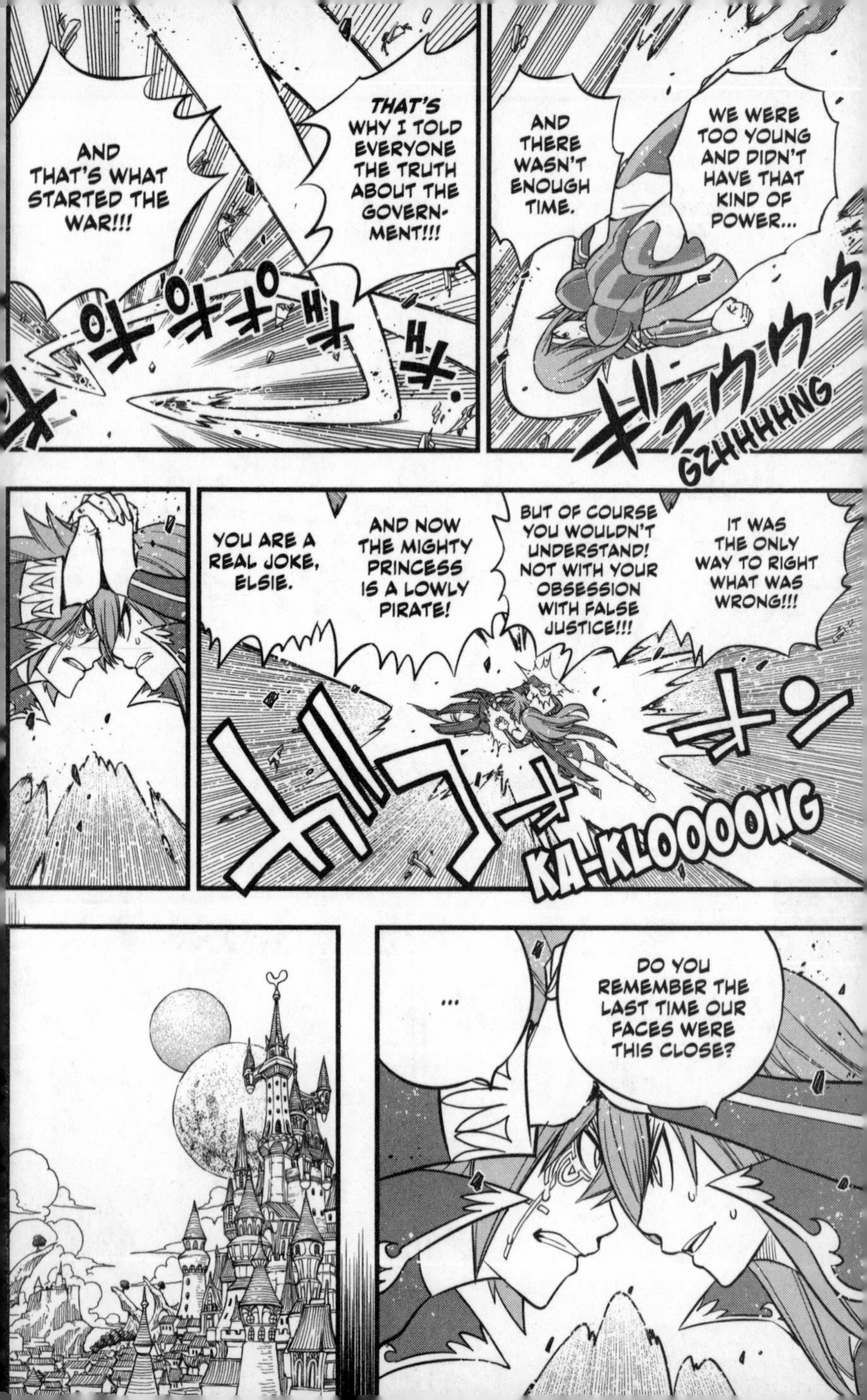
WE WERE TOO YOUNG AND DIDN'T HAVE THAT KIND OF POWER...
AND THERE WASN'T ENOUGH TIME.
GZHHHHNG
THAT'S WHY I TOLD EVERYONE THE TRUTH ABOUT THE GOVERN-MENT!!!
AND THAT'S WHAT STARTED THE WAR!!!
IT WAS THE ONLY WAY TO RIGHT WHAT WAS WRONG!!!
BUT OF COURSE YOU WOULDN'T UNDERSTAND! NOT WITH YOUR OBSESSION WITH FALSE JUSTICE!!!
AND NOW THE MIGHTY PRINCESS IS A LOWLY PIRATE!
YOU ARE A REAL JOKE, ELSIE.
KA-KLOOOOONG
DO YOU REMEMBER THE LAST TIME OUR FACES WERE THIS CLOSE?
...

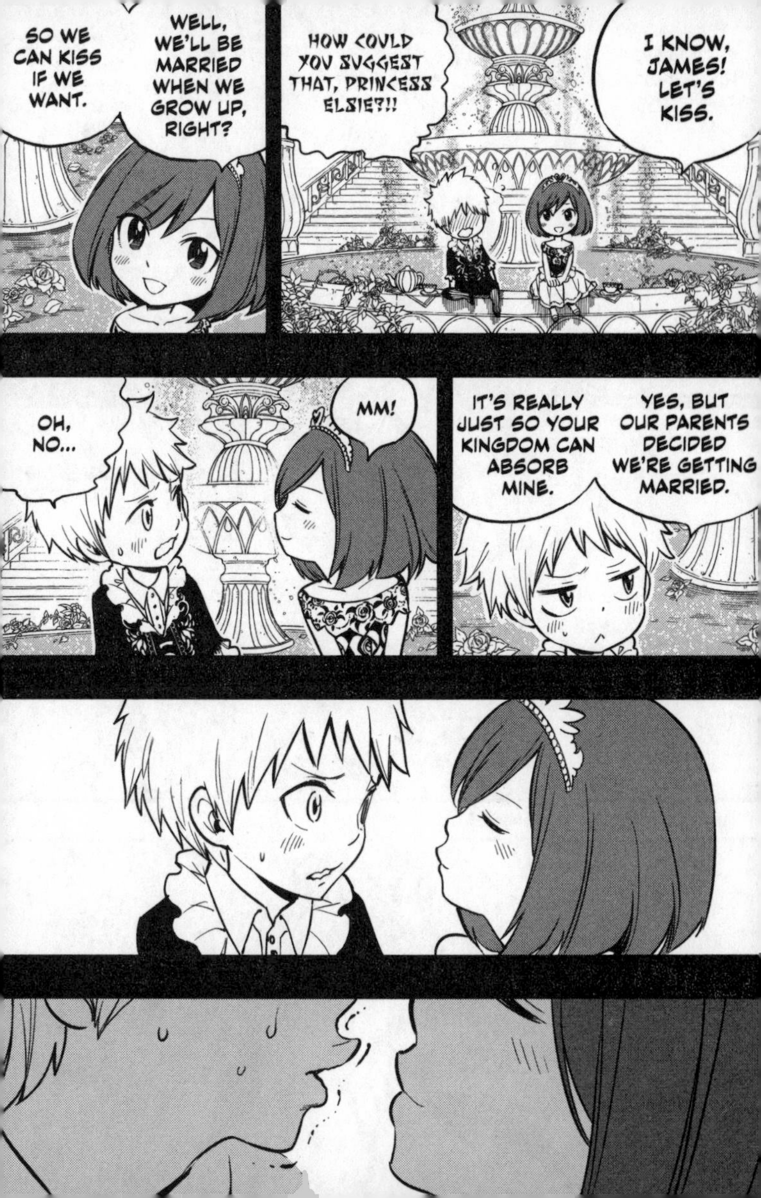
I KNOW, JAMES! LET'S KISS.
HOW COULD YOU SUGGEST THAT, PRINCESS ELSIE?!!
WELL, WE'LL BE MARRIED WHEN WE GROW UP, RIGHT?
SO WE CAN KISS IF WE WANT.
YES, BUT OUR PARENTS DECIDED WE'RE GETTING MARRIED.
IT'S REALLY JUST SO YOUR KINGDOM CAN ABSORB MINE.
MM!
OH, NO...

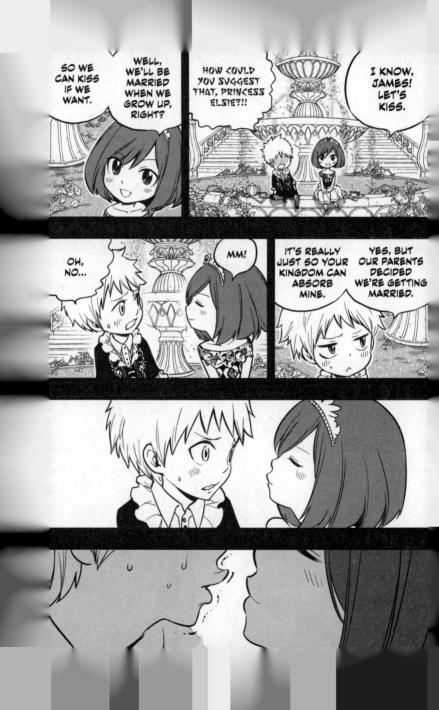

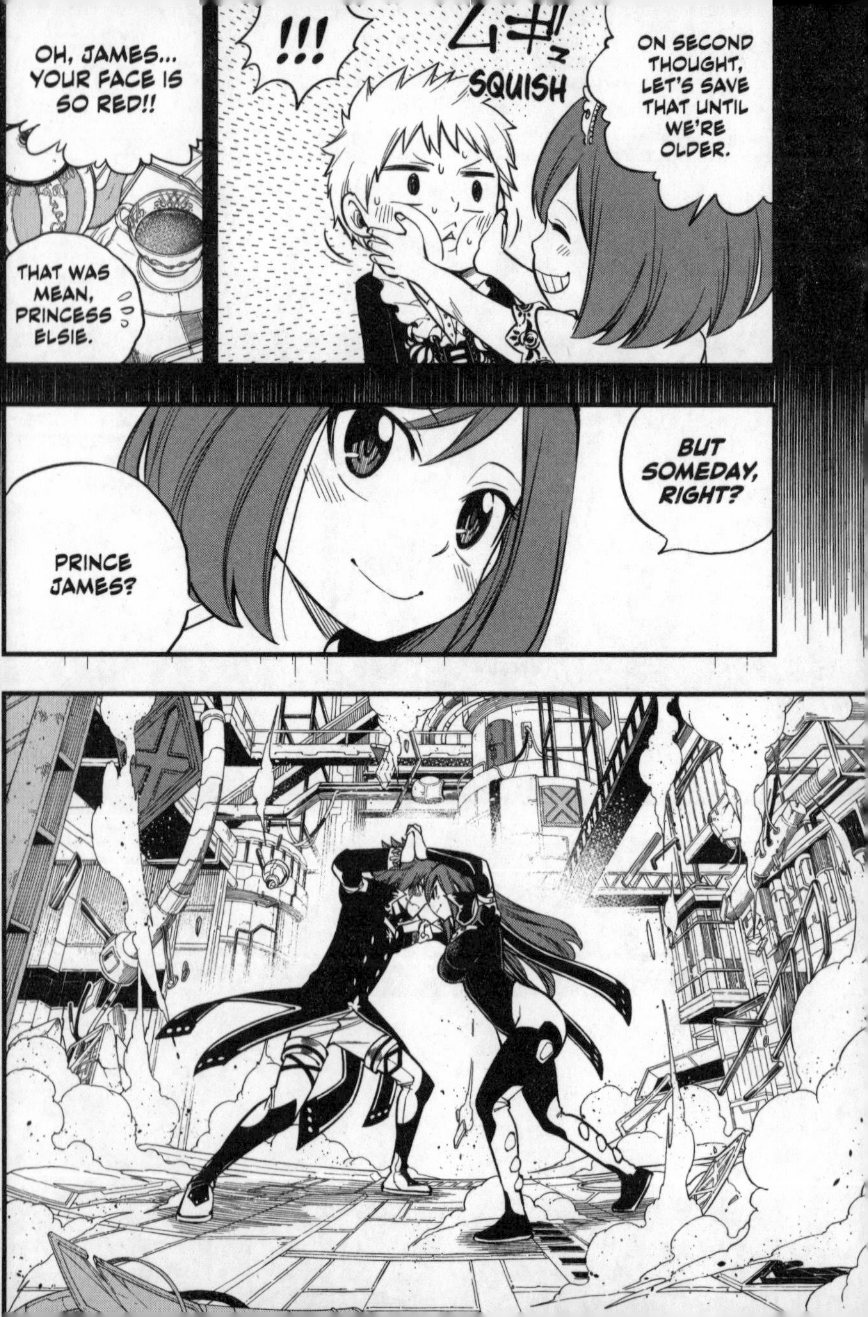
ON SECOND THOUGHT, LET'S SAVE THAT UNTIL WE'RE OLDER.
SQUISH
!!!
OH, JAMES... YOUR FACE IS SO RED!!
THAT WAS MEAN, PRINCESS ELSIE.
BUT SOMEDAY, RIGHT?
PRINCE JAMES?

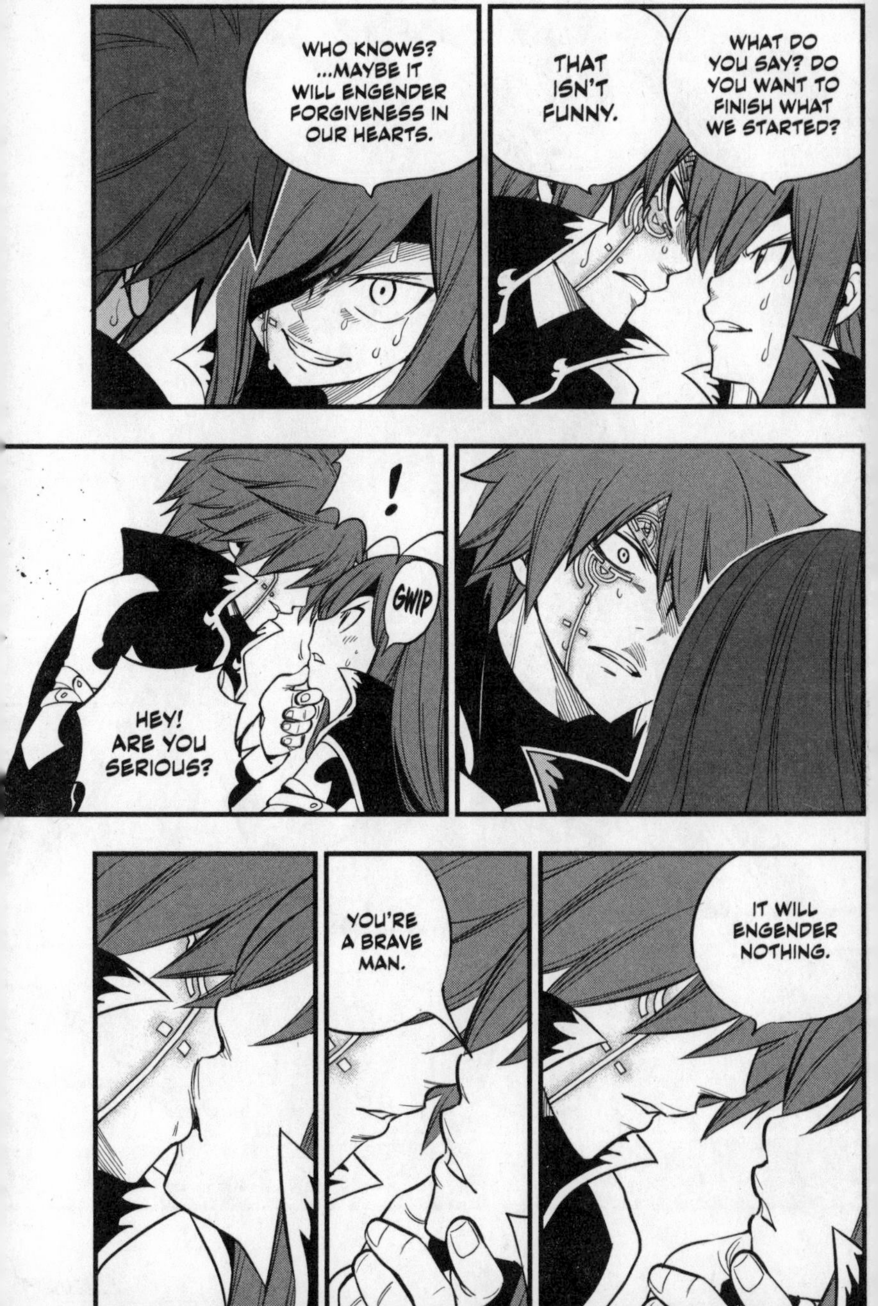
WHAT DO YOU SAY? DO YOU WANT TO FINISH WHAT WE STARTED?
THAT ISN'T FUNNY.
WHO KNOWS? ...MAYBE IT WILL ENGENDER FORGIVENESS IN OUR HEARTS.
!
GWIP
HEY! ARE YOU SERIOUS?
IT WILL ENGENDER NOTHING.
YOU'RE A BRAVE MAN.

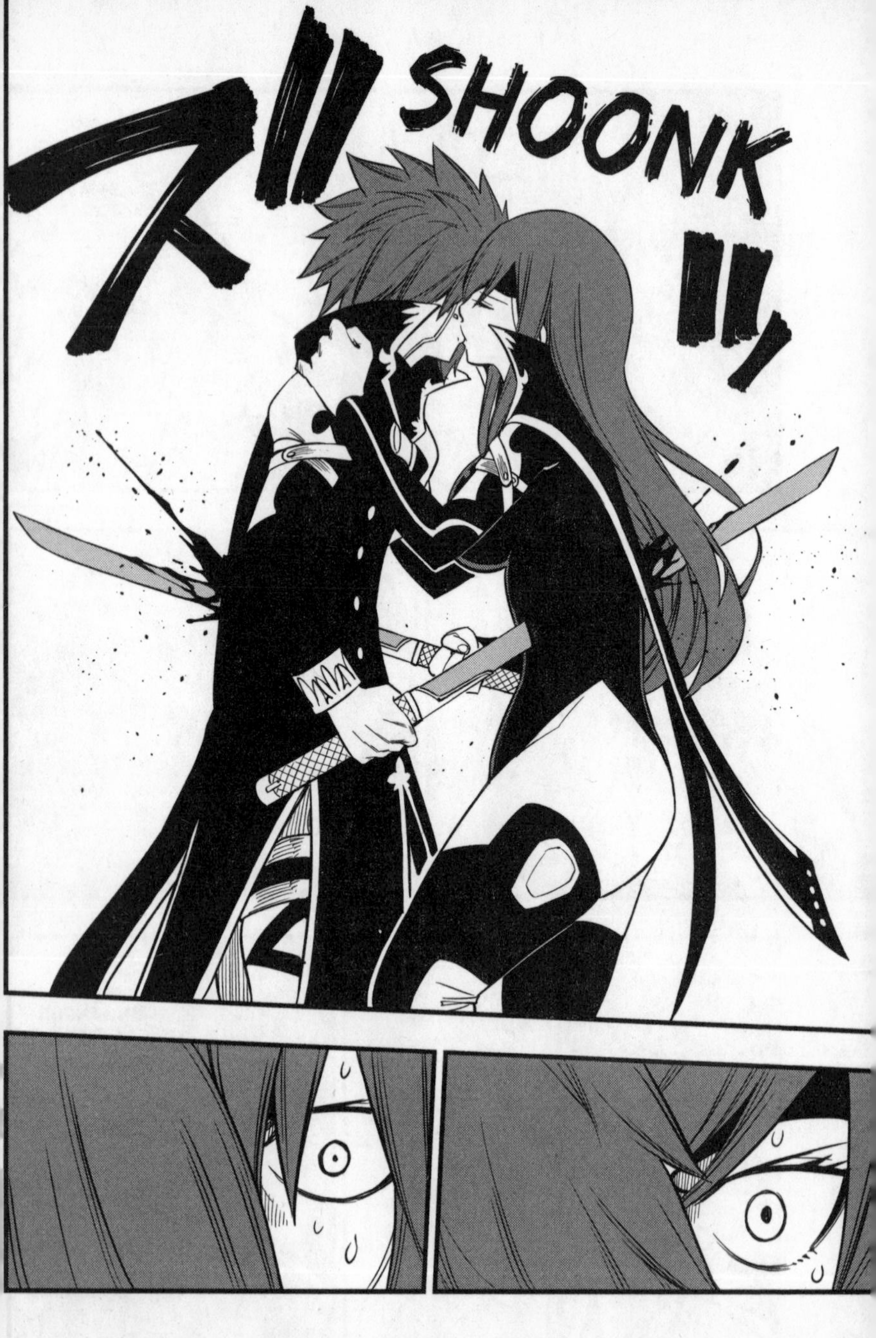
SHOONK

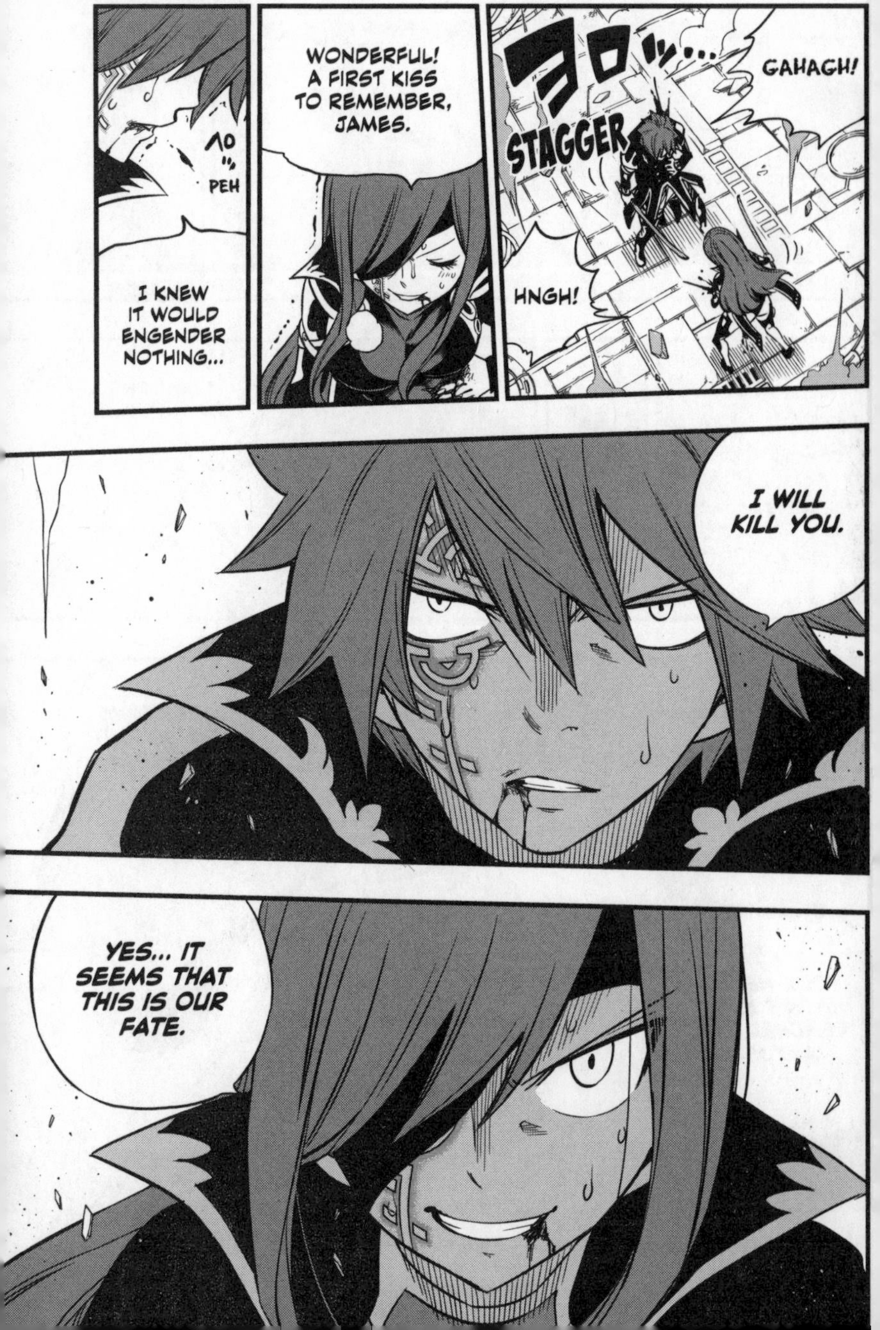

GAHAGH!
ヨロッ…
STAGGER
HNGH!
WONDERFUL! A FIRST KISS TO REMEMBER, JAMES.
ペッ
PEH
I KNEW IT WOULD ENGENDER NOTHING...
I WILL KILL YOU.
YES... IT SEEMS THAT THIS IS OUR FATE.

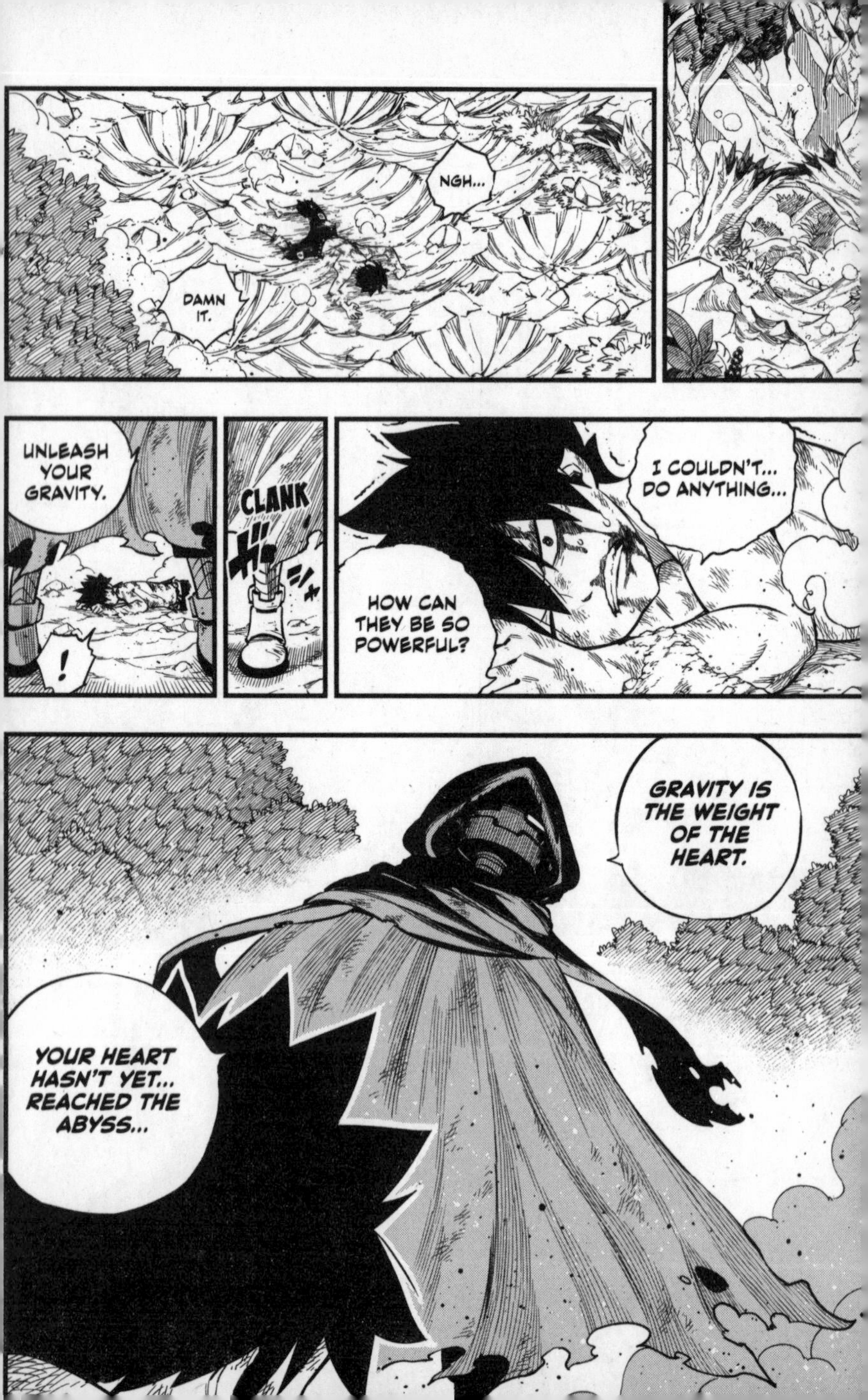
NGH...
DAMN IT.
I COULDN'T... DO ANYTHING...
HOW CAN THEY BE SO POWERFUL?
CLANK
UNLEASH YOUR GRAVITY.
!
GRAVITY IS THE WEIGHT OF THE HEART.
YOUR HEART HASN'T YET... REACHED THE ABYSS...

CHAPTER 125: HEART OF GRAVITY

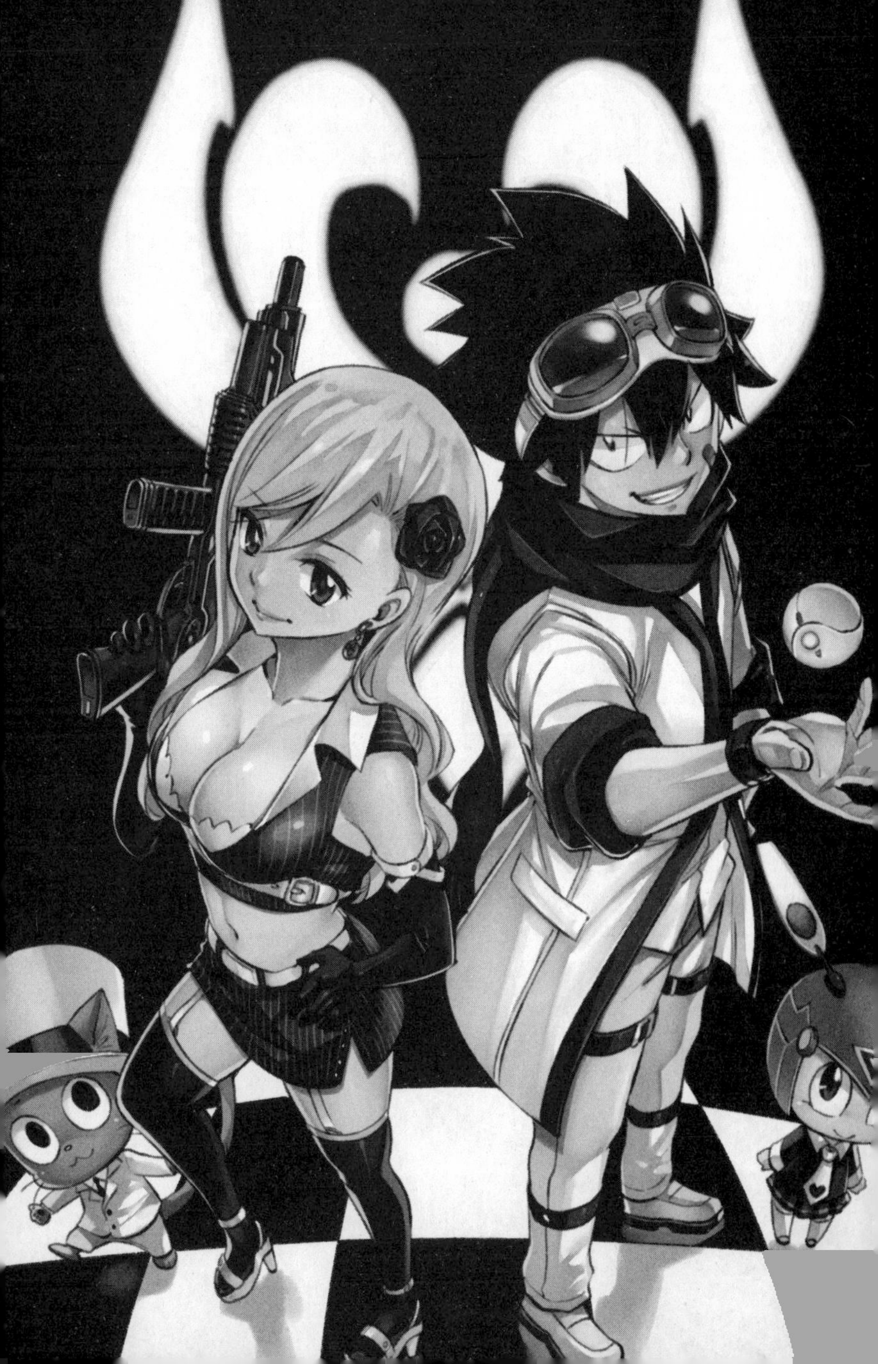

EZ DRAWING

Your postcards are my greatest source of energy! EZ Drawing means it's easy to do, so we hope the fan art keeps coming! Everyone whose work is shown here received a special signed mini sketch!!

(AKANE SAJI-SAN, FUKUOKA)

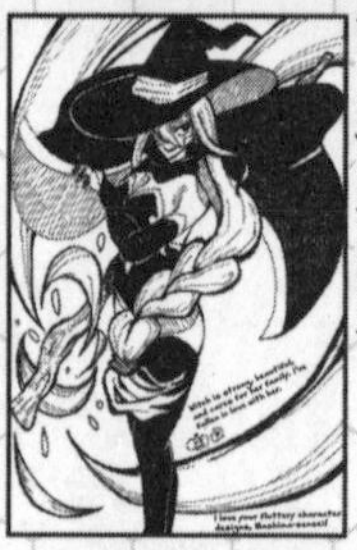

▲ THE OLDER WOMAN ALL THE OTHER CHARACTERS CAN RELY ON. WITCH IS BEAUTIFUL EVEN WITH HER FACE UNCOVERED!!

(KENSAKU NAKAMURA-SAN, KYOTO)

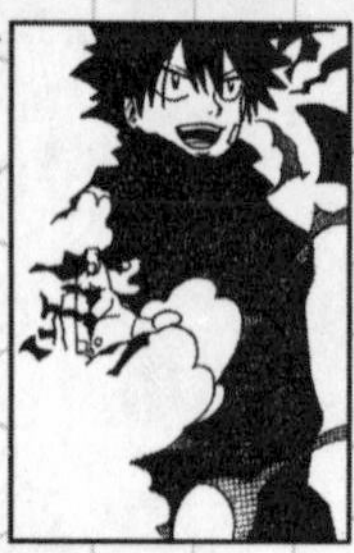

▲ SHIKI LOOKING KINDA LIKE A NINJA. TIME FOR A SHOWDOWN WITH JINN!!

(YUI HASHIMOTO-SAN, IBARAGI)

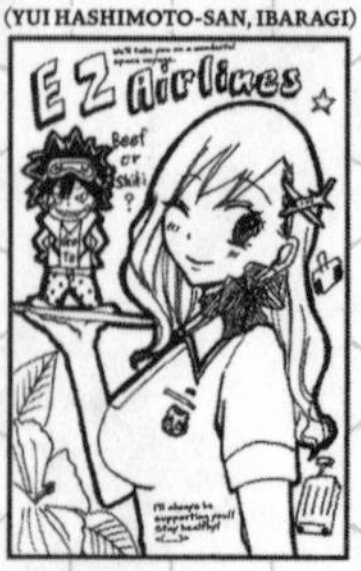
EZ Airlines
Beef or Shiki?

▲ DOES FLYING WITH THIS SPACE AIRLINE COME WITH NONSTOP THRILLS?!

(KOKORO HEMI-SAN, OSAKA)

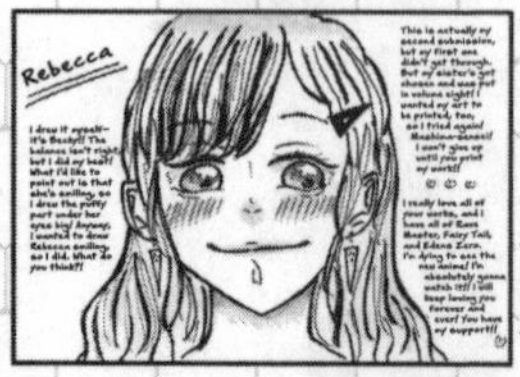
Rebecca

▲ THE ORIGINALITY OF IT MAKES IT A VERY RICH AND UNIQUE REBECCA. I LIKE IT!!

(HAYATE MIZUKI-SAN, HOKKAIDO)

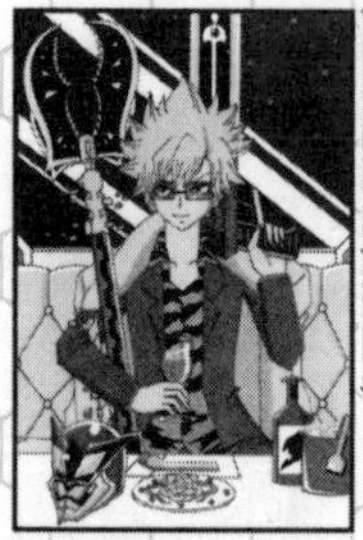

▶ WEISZ, LOOKING LIKE A MAFIA BAD GUY. WILL HE USE HIS PERSONALLY-MADE WEAPONS TO TAKE OVER THE WORLD?!

MASHIMA'S ONE-HIT KO

(YAHOO BEAM★-SAN, MIE)

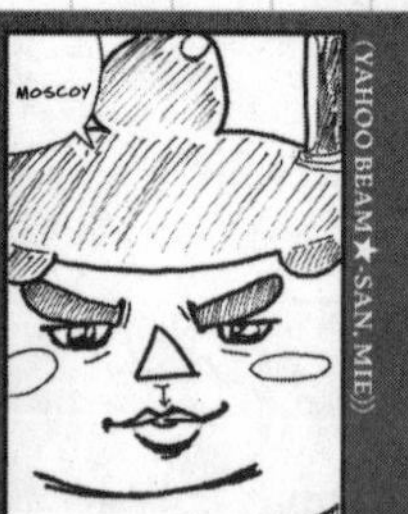
MOSCOY

▲ WHO IS THIS PERSON?! ALL HE SAYS IS "MOSCOY," BUT HE FASCINATES ME....!

(MAYU YAMASHITA-SAN, TOKYO)

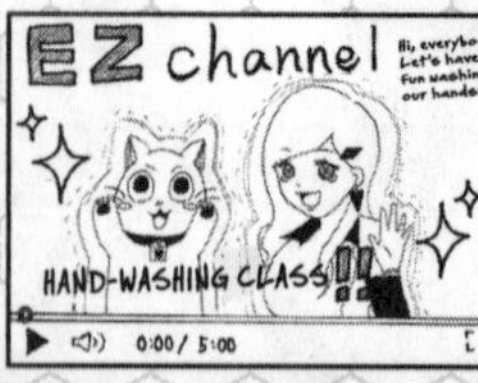
EZ channel
Hi, everybody! Let's have fun washing our hands!!
HAND-WASHING CLASS!!
0:00 / 5:00

◀ EVERYBODY AND THEIR CAT SHOULD WASH THEIR HANDS. (THAT'S REALLY IMPORTANT!!)

EDITOR'S NOTE: DRAWING SUBMISSIONS LIMITED TO JAPAN.

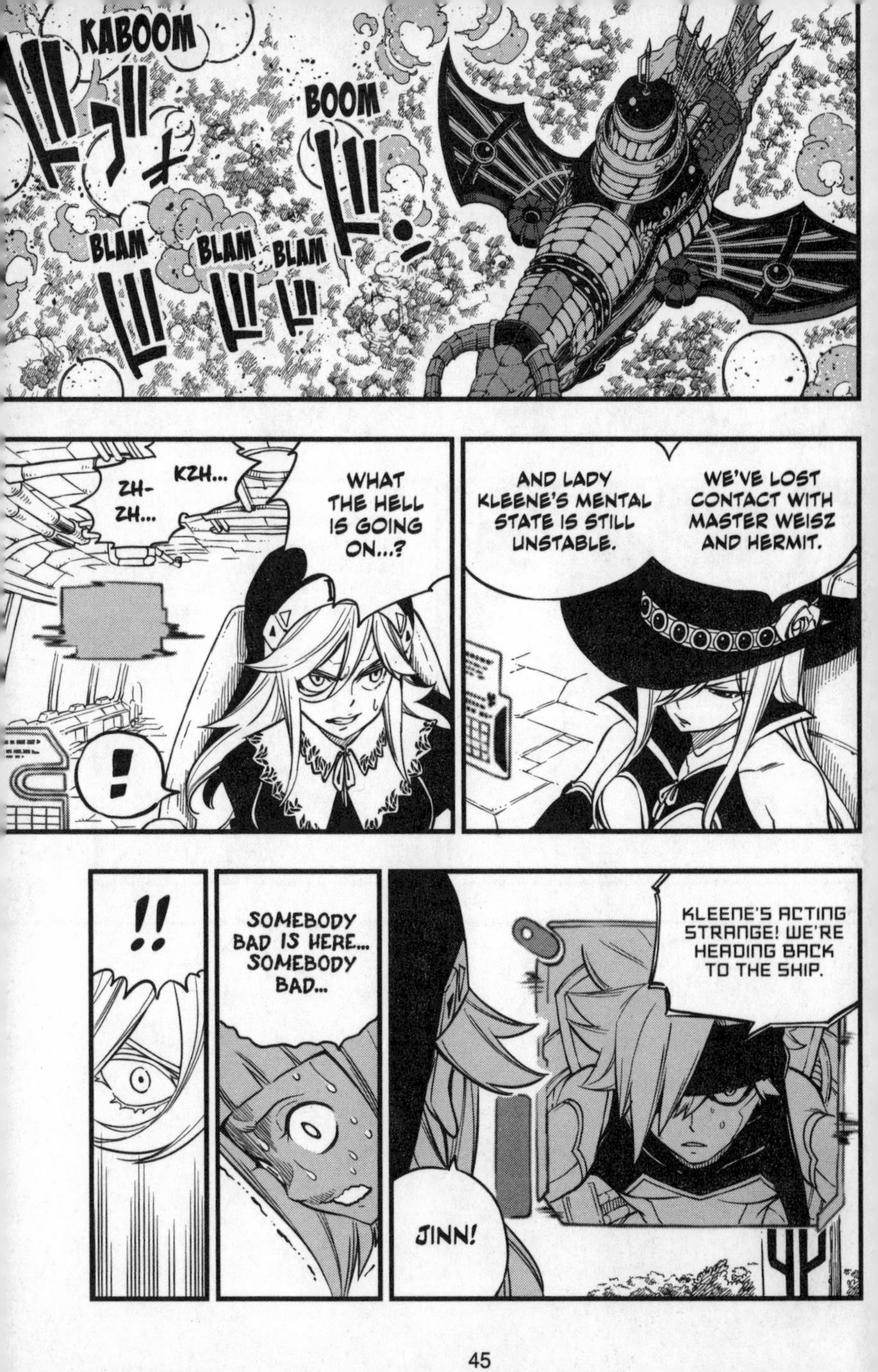
KABOOM
BOOM
BLAM
BLAM
BLAM
WE'VE LOST CONTACT WITH MASTER WEISZ AND HERMIT.
AND LADY KLEENE'S MENTAL STATE IS STILL UNSTABLE.
WHAT THE HELL IS GOING ON...?
KZH...
ZH-ZH...
!
KLEENE'S ACTING STRANGE! WE'RE HEADING BACK TO THE SHIP.
JINN!
SOMEBODY BAD IS HERE... SOMEBODY BAD...
!!

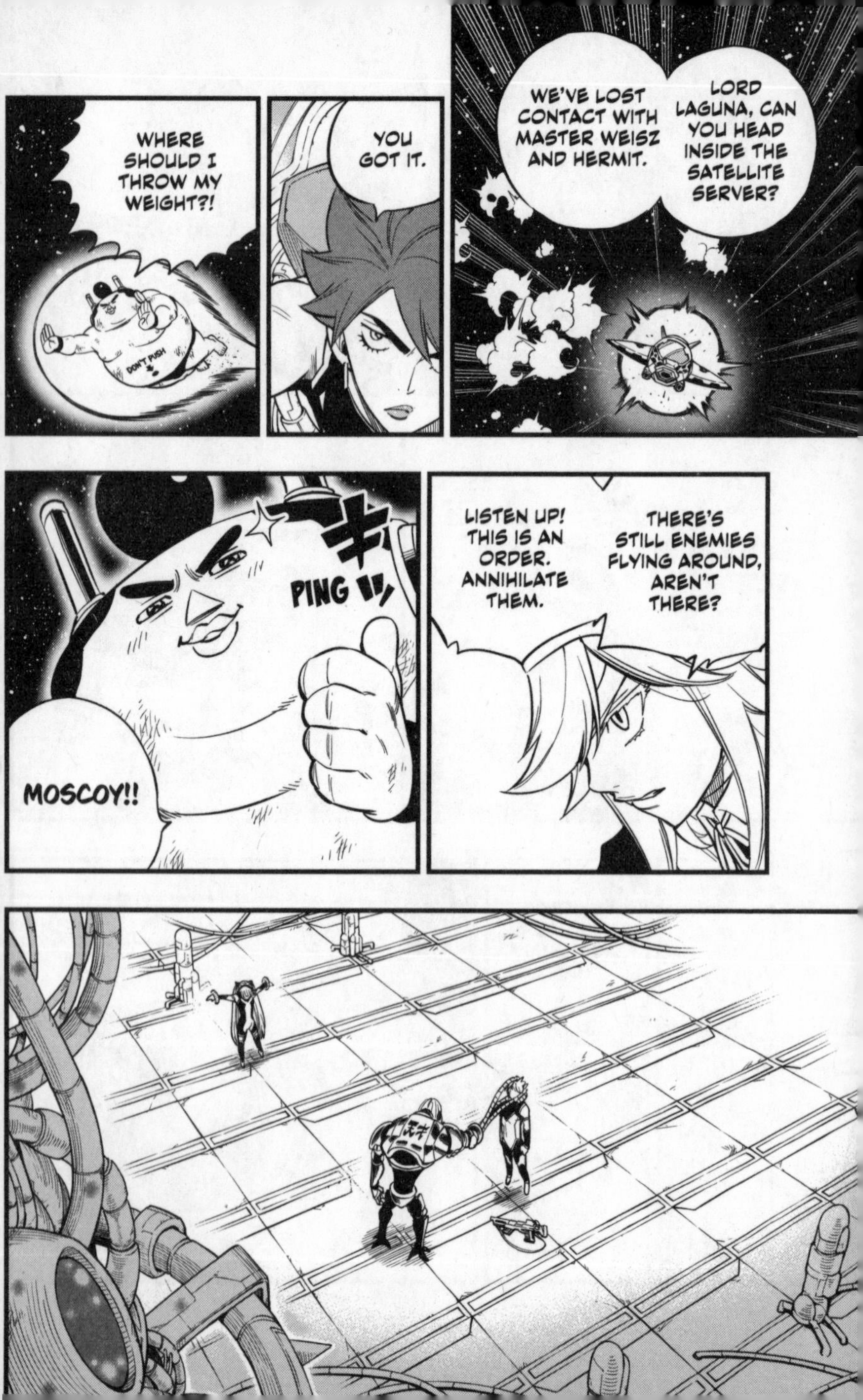
LORD LAGUNA, CAN YOU HEAD INSIDE THE SATELLITE SERVER?
WE'VE LOST CONTACT WITH MASTER WEISZ AND HERMIT.
YOU GOT IT.
WHERE SHOULD I THROW MY WEIGHT?!
DON'T PUSH
THERE'S STILL ENEMIES FLYING AROUND, AREN'T THERE?
LISTEN UP! THIS IS AN ORDER. ANNIHILATE THEM.
PING
MOSCOY!!

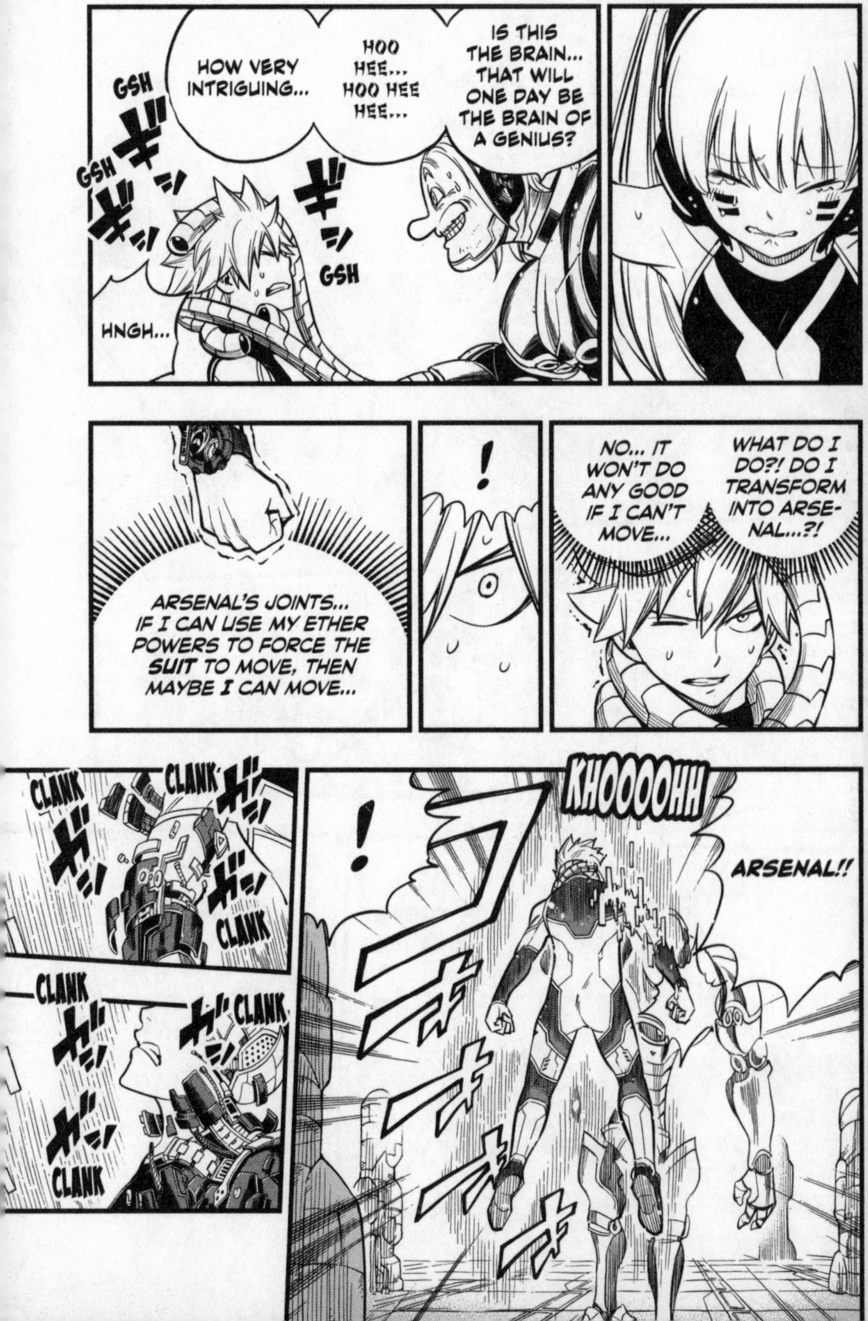
IS THIS THE BRAIN... THAT WILL ONE DAY BE THE BRAIN OF A GENIUS?
HOO HEE... HOO HEE HEE...
HOW VERY INTRIGUING...
GSH
GSH
GSH
HNGH...
WHAT DO I DO?! DO I TRANSFORM INTO ARSE-NAL...?!
NO... IT WON'T DO ANY GOOD IF I CAN'T MOVE...
!
ARSENAL'S JOINTS... IF I CAN USE MY ETHER POWERS TO FORCE THE SUIT TO MOVE, THEN MAYBE I CAN MOVE...
KHOOOOHH
ARSENAL!!
!
CLANK
CLANK
CLANK
CLANK
CLANK
CLANK

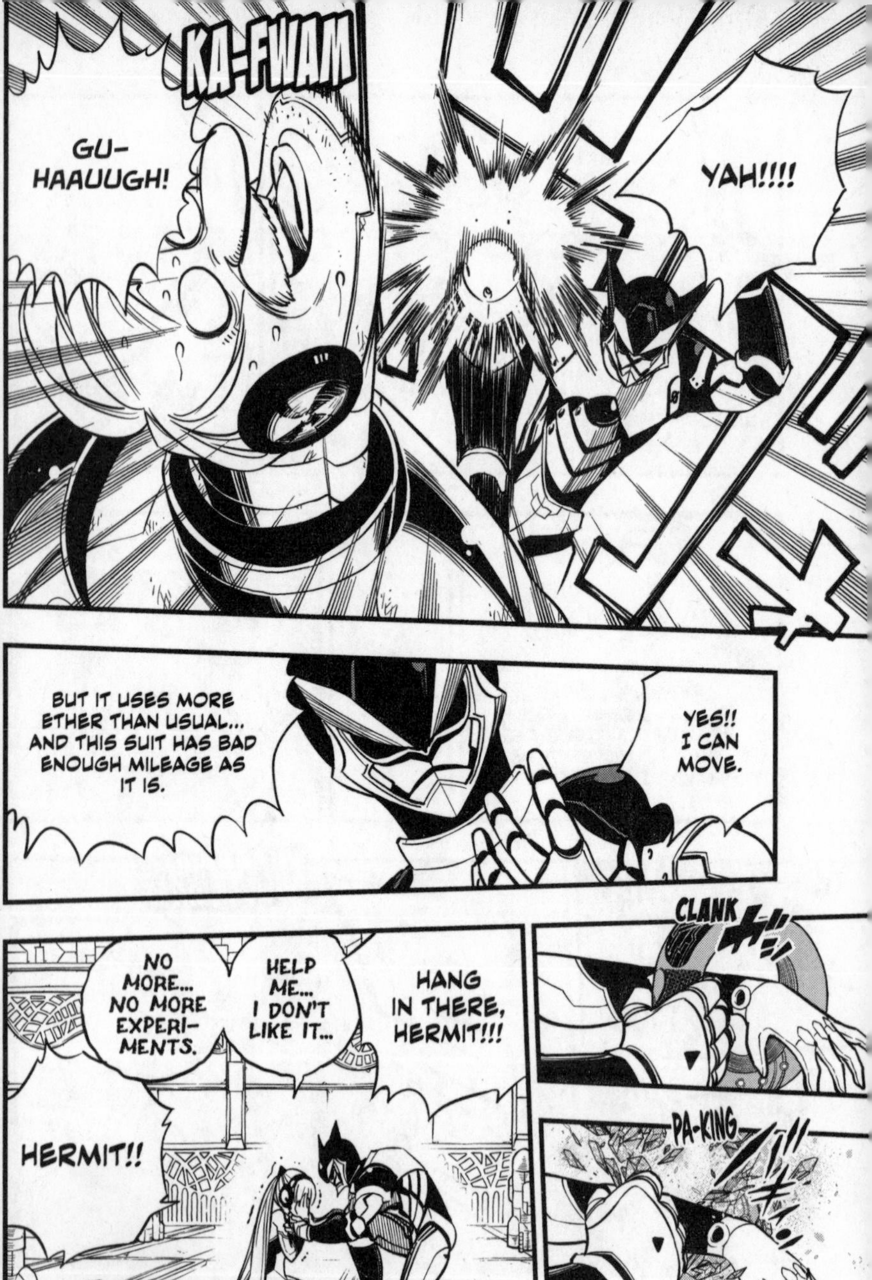
YAH!!!!
KA-FWAM
GU-HAAUUGH!
YES!! I CAN MOVE.
BUT IT USES MORE ETHER THAN USUAL... AND THIS SUIT HAS BAD ENOUGH MILEAGE AS IT IS.
CLANK
PA-KING
HANG IN THERE, HERMIT!!!
HELP ME... I DON'T LIKE IT...
NO MORE... NO MORE EXPERI-MENTS.
HERMIT!!

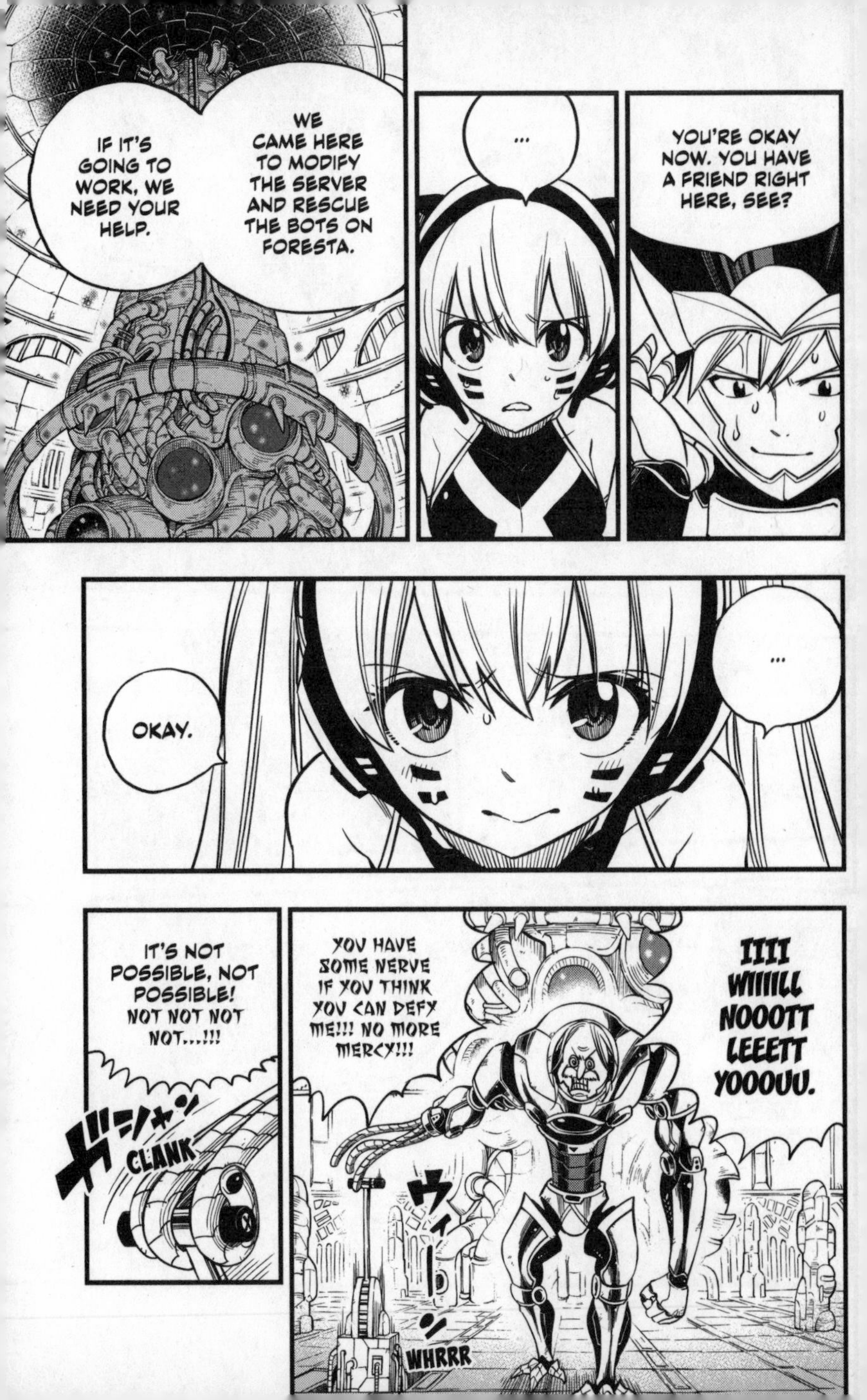
YOU'RE OKAY NOW. YOU HAVE A FRIEND RIGHT HERE, SEE?
...
WE CAME HERE TO MODIFY THE SERVER AND RESCUE THE BOTS ON FORESTA.
IF IT'S GOING TO WORK, WE NEED YOUR HELP.
...
OKAY.
IIII WIIIILL NOOOTT LEEETT YOOOUU.
YOU HAVE SOME NERVE IF YOU THINK YOU CAN DEFY ME!!! NO MORE MERCY!!!
WHRRR
IT'S NOT POSSIBLE, NOT POSSIBLE! NOT NOT NOT NOT...!!!
CLANK

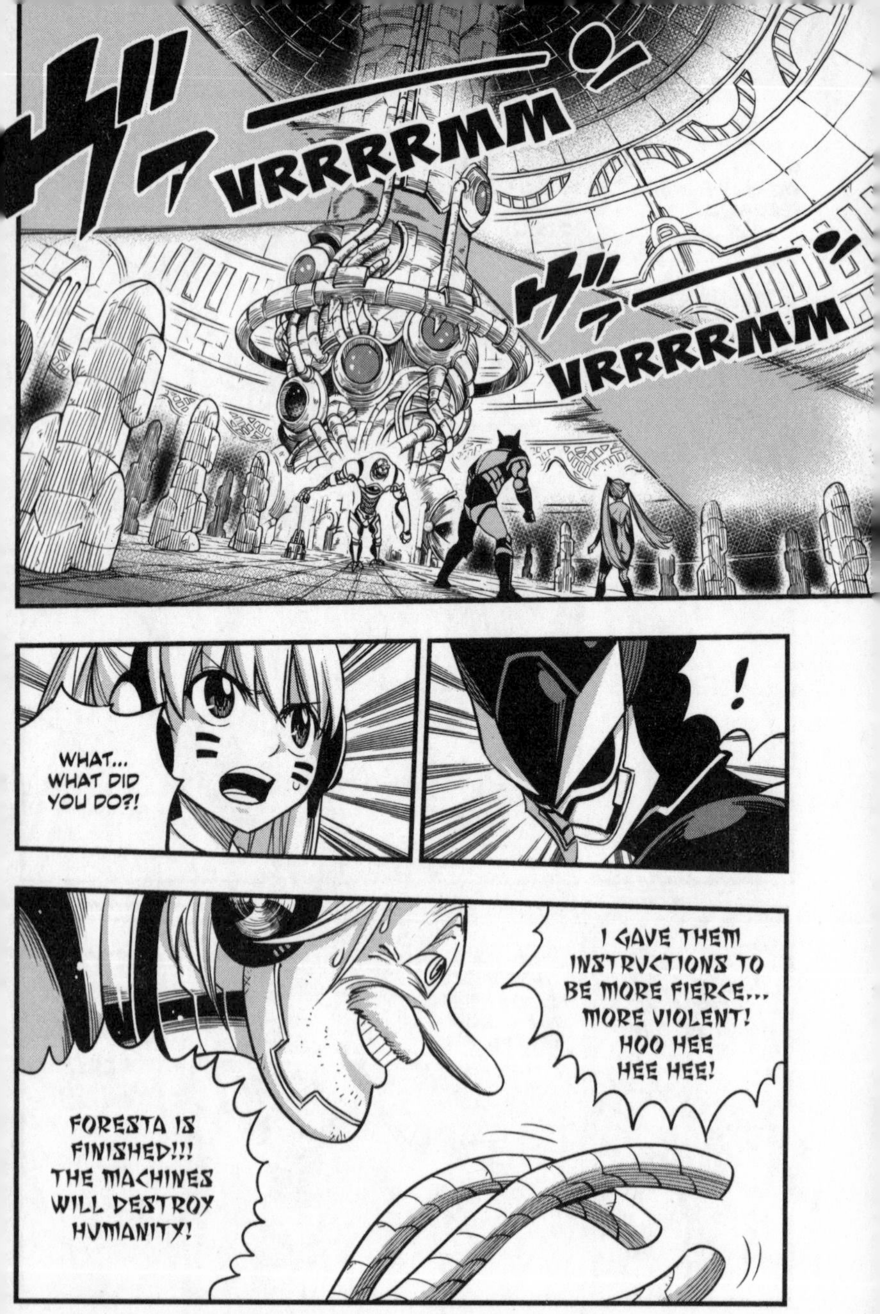
ヴヴァー
VRRRRMM
ヴヴァー
VRRRRMM
!
WHAT... WHAT DID YOU DO?!
I GAVE THEM INSTRUCTIONS TO BE MORE FIERCE... MORE VIOLENT! HOO HEE HEE HEE!
FORESTA IS FINISHED!!! THE MACHINES WILL DESTROY HUMANITY!

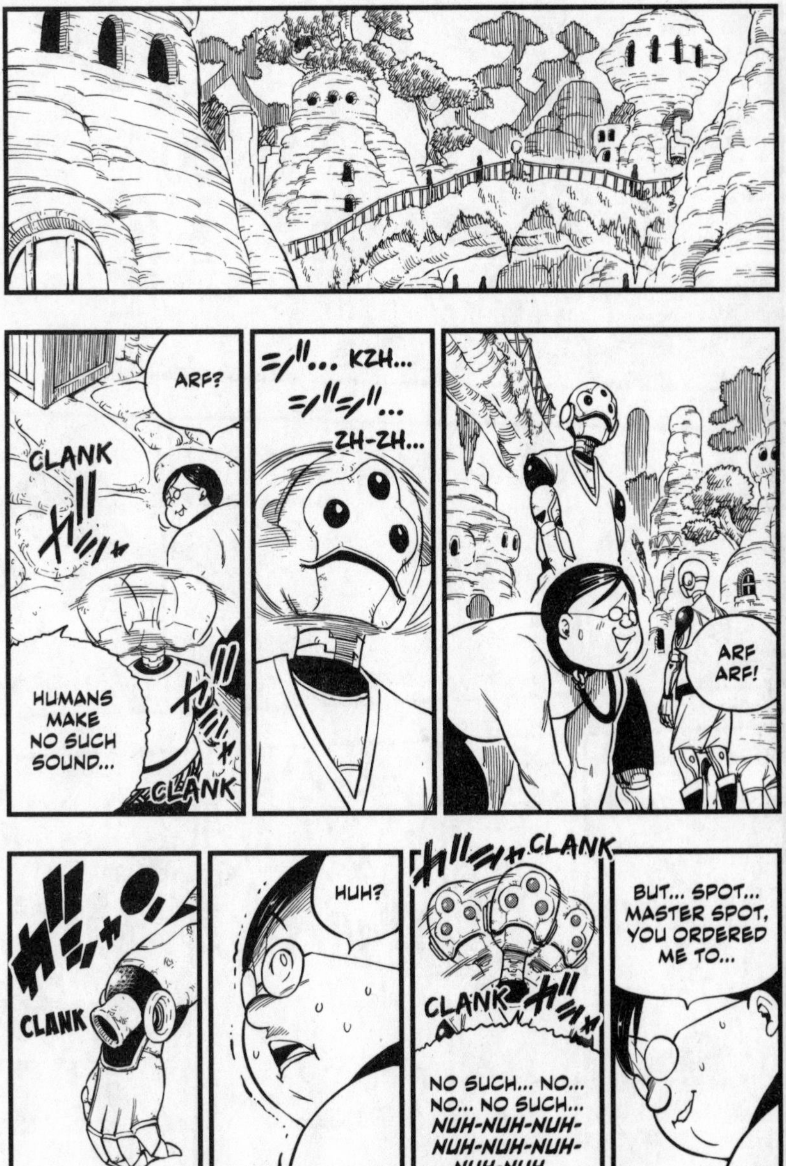
ARF ARF!
KZH...
ZH-ZH...
ARF?
CLANK
HUMANS MAKE NO SUCH SOUND...
CLANK
BUT... SPOT... MASTER SPOT, YOU ORDERED ME TO...
CLANK
CLANK
NO SUCH... NO... NO... NO SUCH... NUH-NUH-NUH-NUH-NUH-NUH-NUH-NUH...
HUH?
CLANK

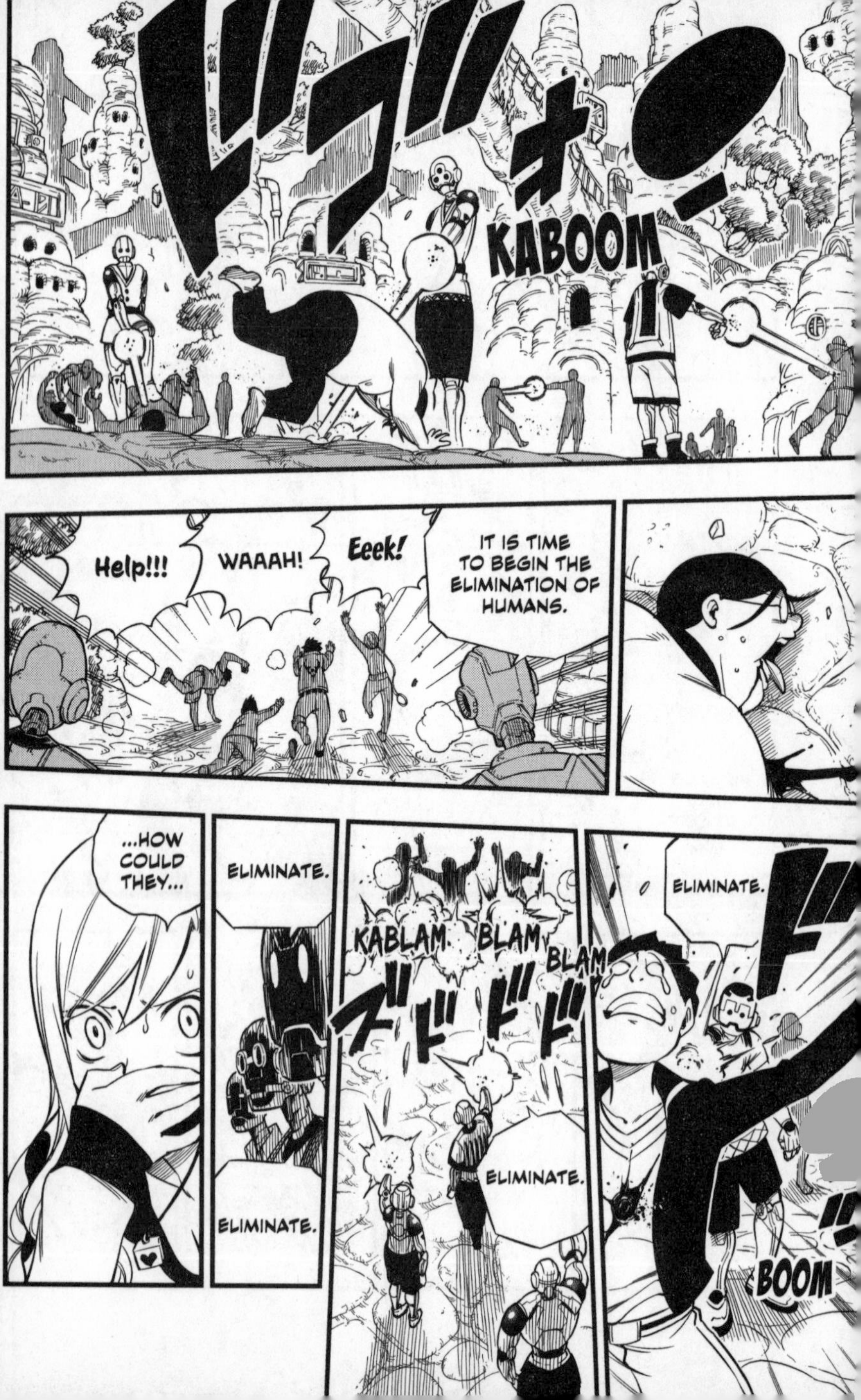
KABOOM
IT IS TIME TO BEGIN THE ELIMINATION OF HUMANS.
Eeek!
WAAAH!
Help!!!
ELIMINATE.
BOOM
BLAM
BLAM
KABLAM
ELIMINATE.
ELIMINATE.
ELIMINATE.
...HOW COULD THEY...

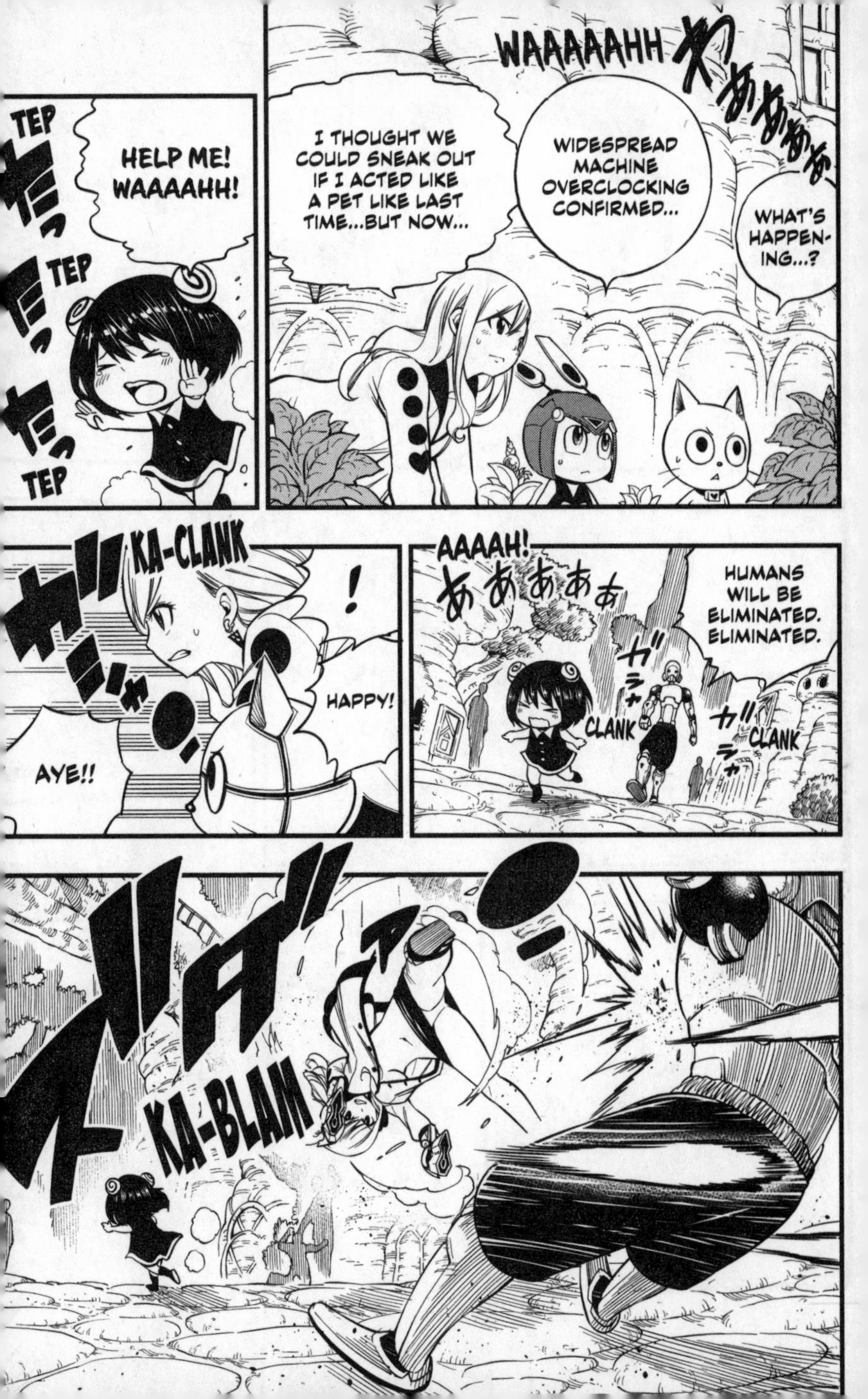
WAAAAAHH
WHAT'S HAPPEN-ING...?
WIDESPREAD MACHINE OVERCLOCKING CONFIRMED...
I THOUGHT WE COULD SNEAK OUT IF I ACTED LIKE A PET LIKE LAST TIME...BUT NOW...
TEP
HELP ME! WAAAAAHH!
TEP
TEP
AAAAH!
あああああ
HUMANS WILL BE ELIMINATED. ELIMINATED.
CLANK
CLANK
!
HAPPY!
KA-CLANK
AYE!!
KA-BLAM

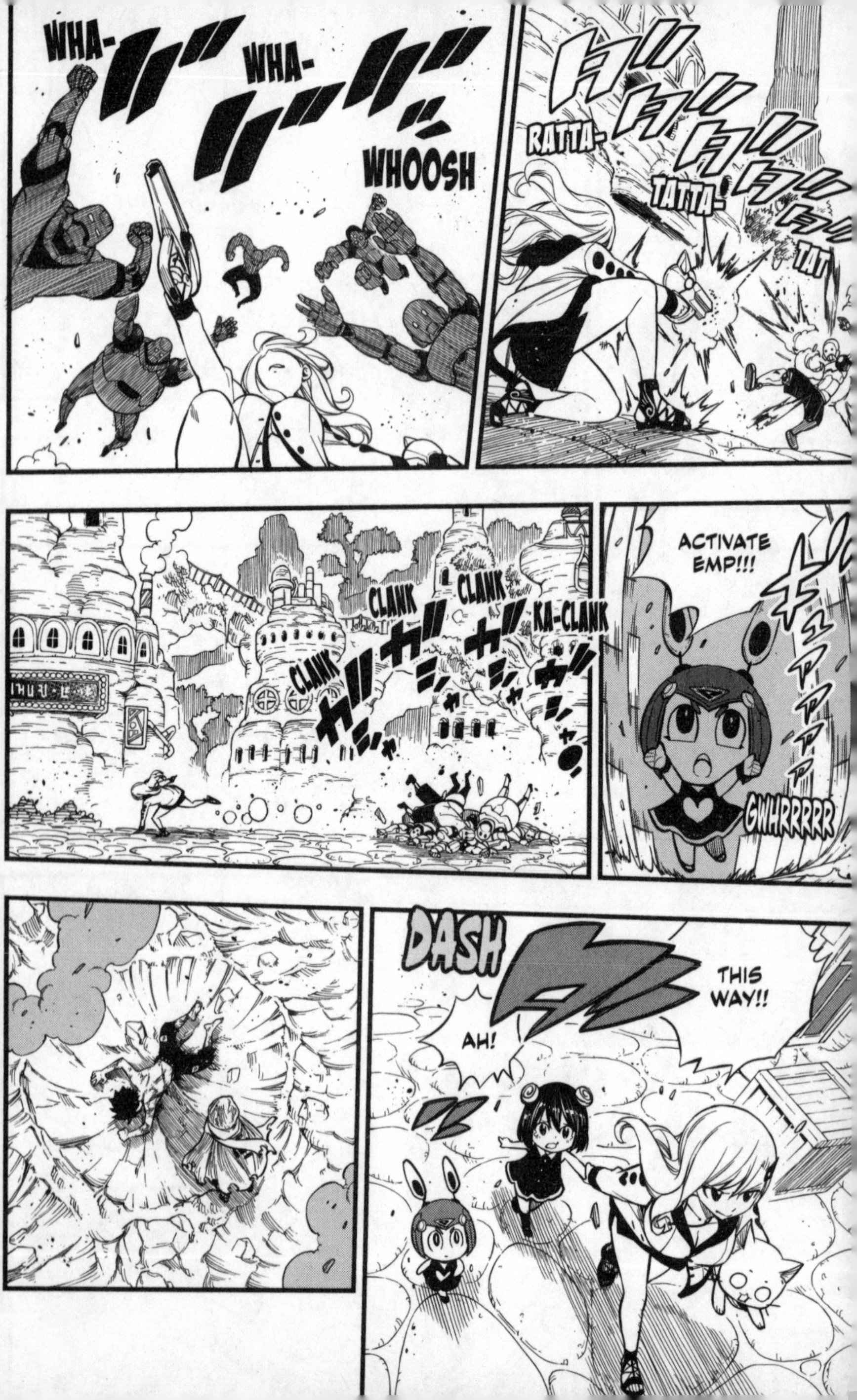
RATTA-
TATTA-
TAT
WHA-
WHA-
WHOOSH
ACTIVATE EMP!!!
GWHRRRRR
KA-CLANK
CLANK
CLANK
CLANK
DASH
THIS WAY!!
AH!

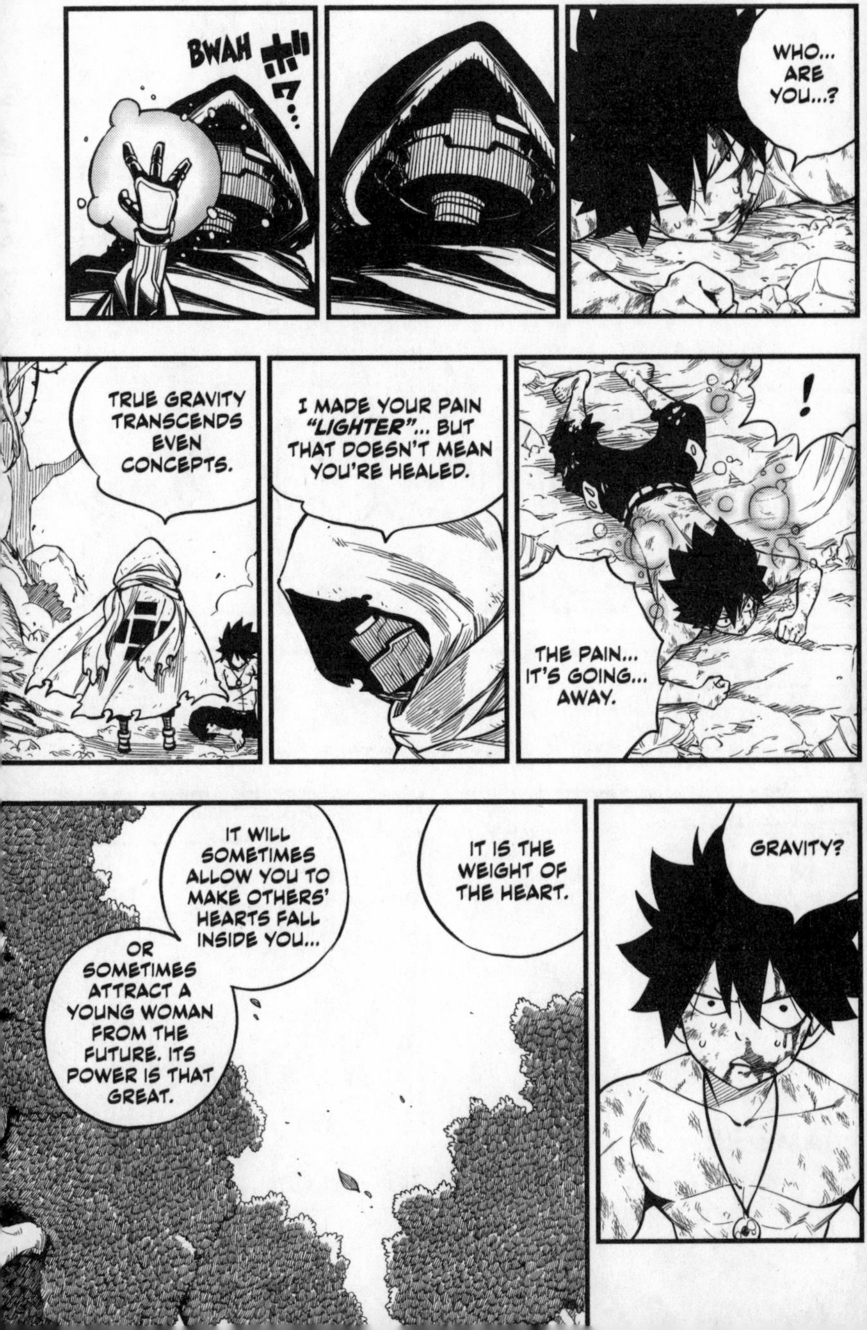
WHO... ARE YOU...?
BWAH
THE PAIN... IT'S GOING... AWAY.
I MADE YOUR PAIN "LIGHTER"... BUT THAT DOESN'T MEAN YOU'RE HEALED.
TRUE GRAVITY TRANSCENDS EVEN CONCEPTS.
GRAVITY?
IT IS THE WEIGHT OF THE HEART.
IT WILL SOMETIMES ALLOW YOU TO MAKE OTHERS' HEARTS FALL INSIDE YOU...
OR SOMETIMES ATTRACT A YOUNG WOMAN FROM THE FUTURE. ITS POWER IS THAT GREAT.

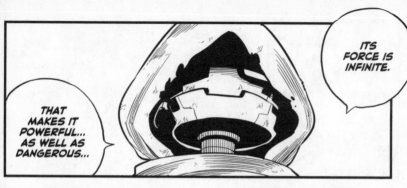

ITS FORCE IS INFINITE.

THAT MAKES IT POWERFUL.... AS WELL AS DANGEROUS...

LET ME SEE...

THOSE MACHINES ARE MAKING QUITE A RACKET...

...

ELSIE!!!

JAMES!!!

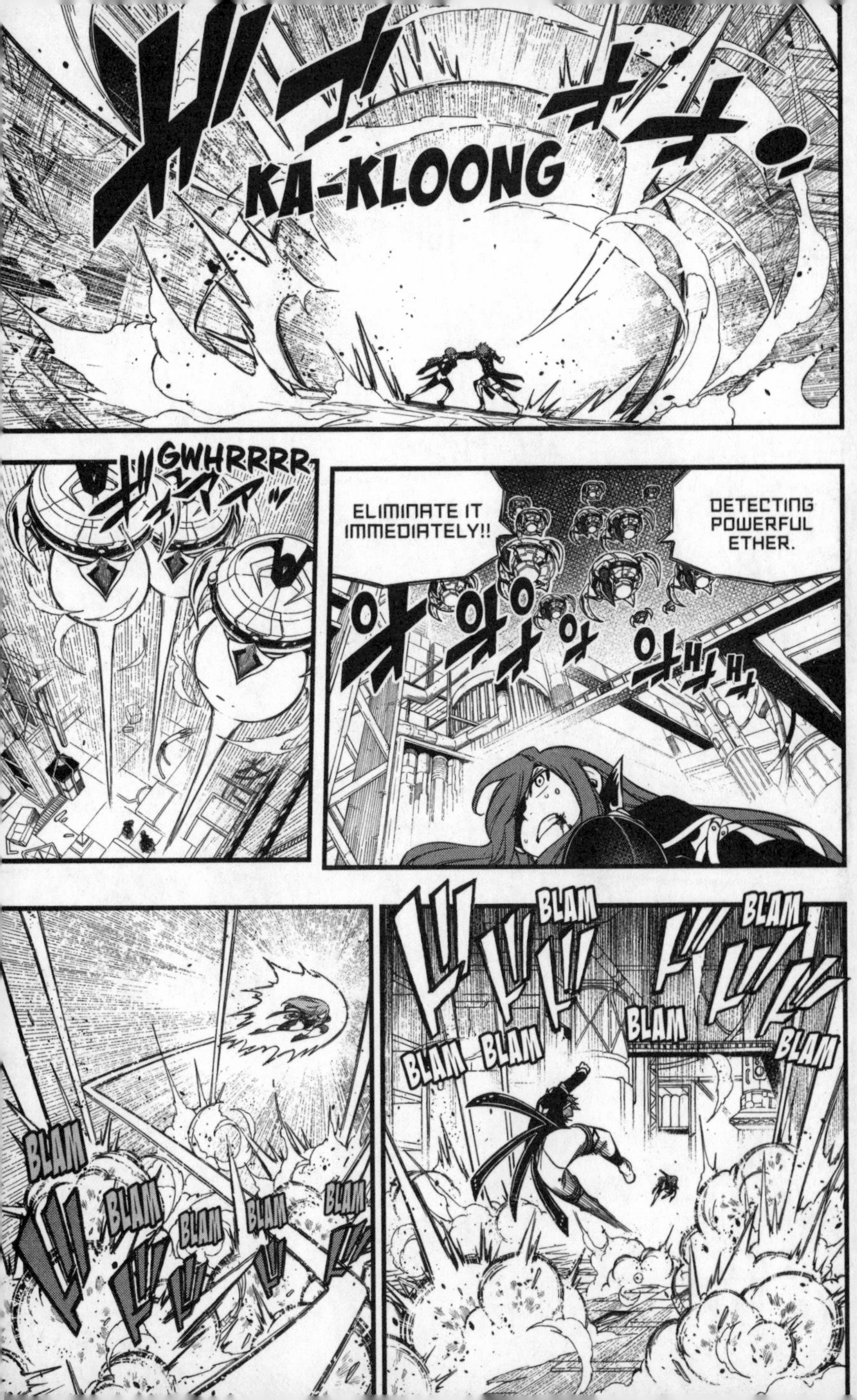
KA-KLOONG
DETECTING POWERFUL ETHER.
ELIMINATE IT IMMEDIATELY!!
GWHRRRR
BLAM
BLAM
BLAM
BLAM
BLAM
BLAM
BLAM
BLAM
BLAM
BLAM
BLAM

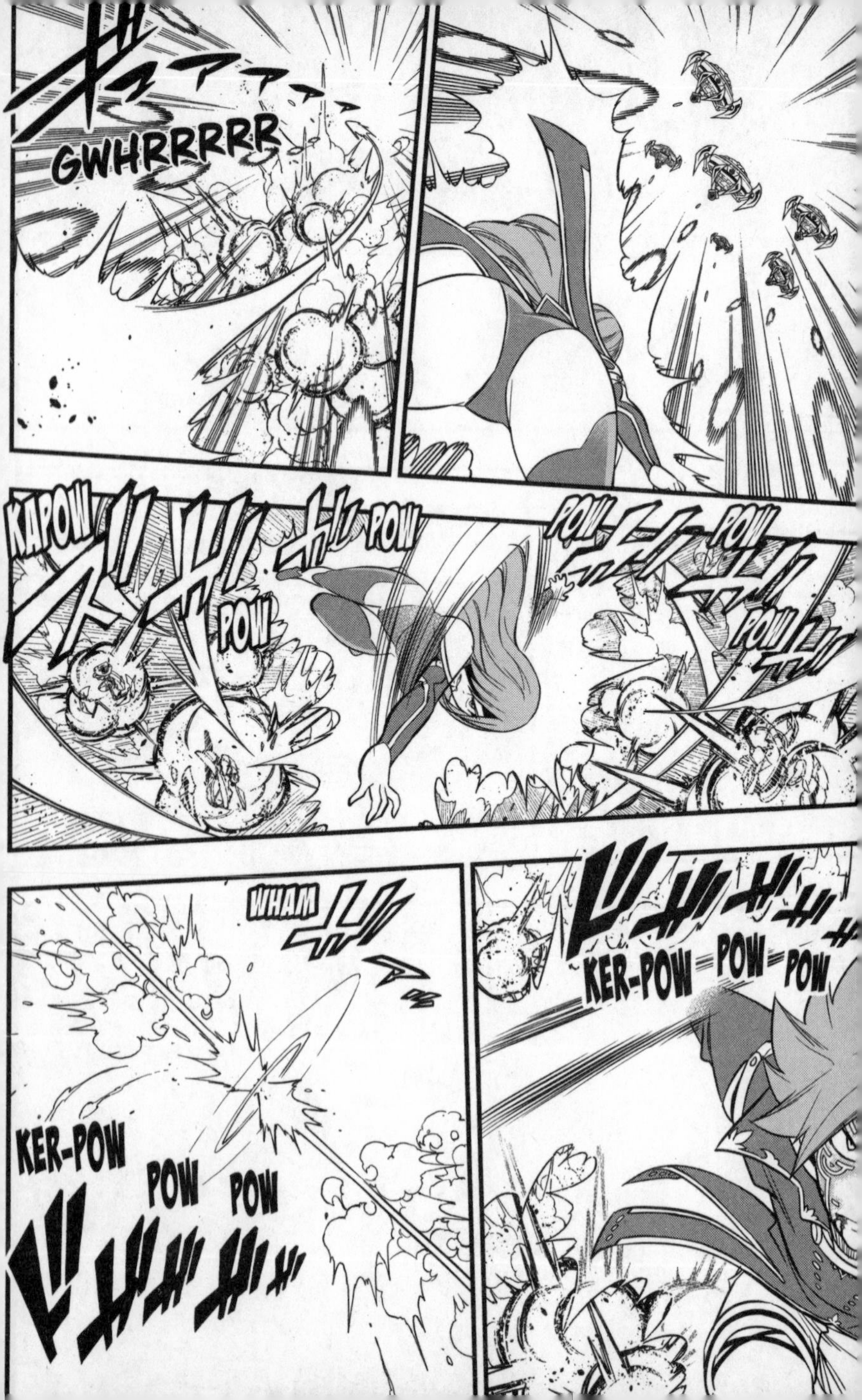
GWHRRRRR
POW
POW
POW
POW
KAPOW
POW
KER-POW POW POW
WHAM
KER-POW
POW
POW

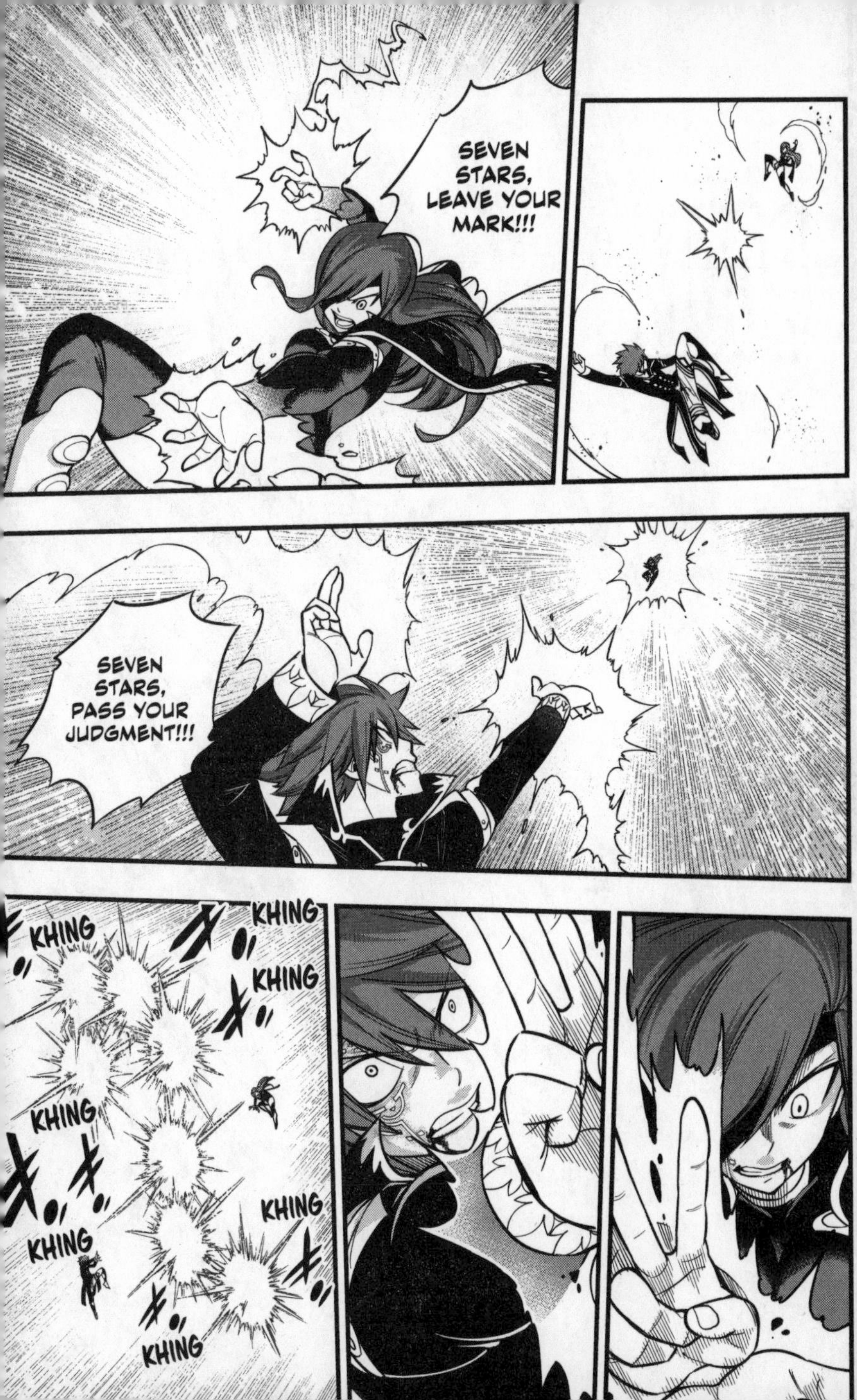
SEVEN STARS, LEAVE YOUR MARK!!!
SEVEN STARS, PASS YOUR JUDGMENT!!!
KHING
KHING
KHING
KHING
KHING
KHING
KHING

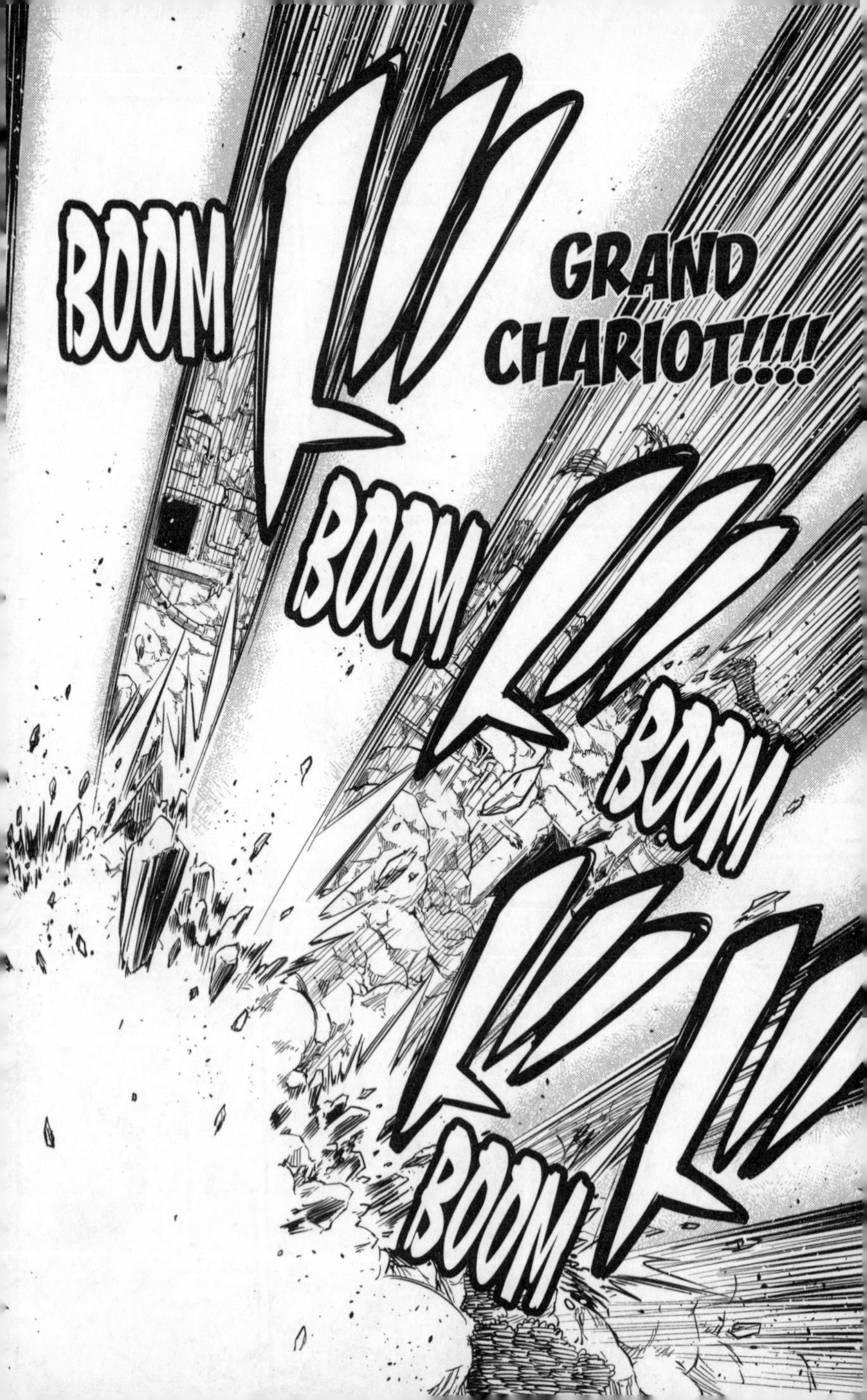
GRAND CHARIOT!!!!
BOOM
BOOM
BOOM
BOOM

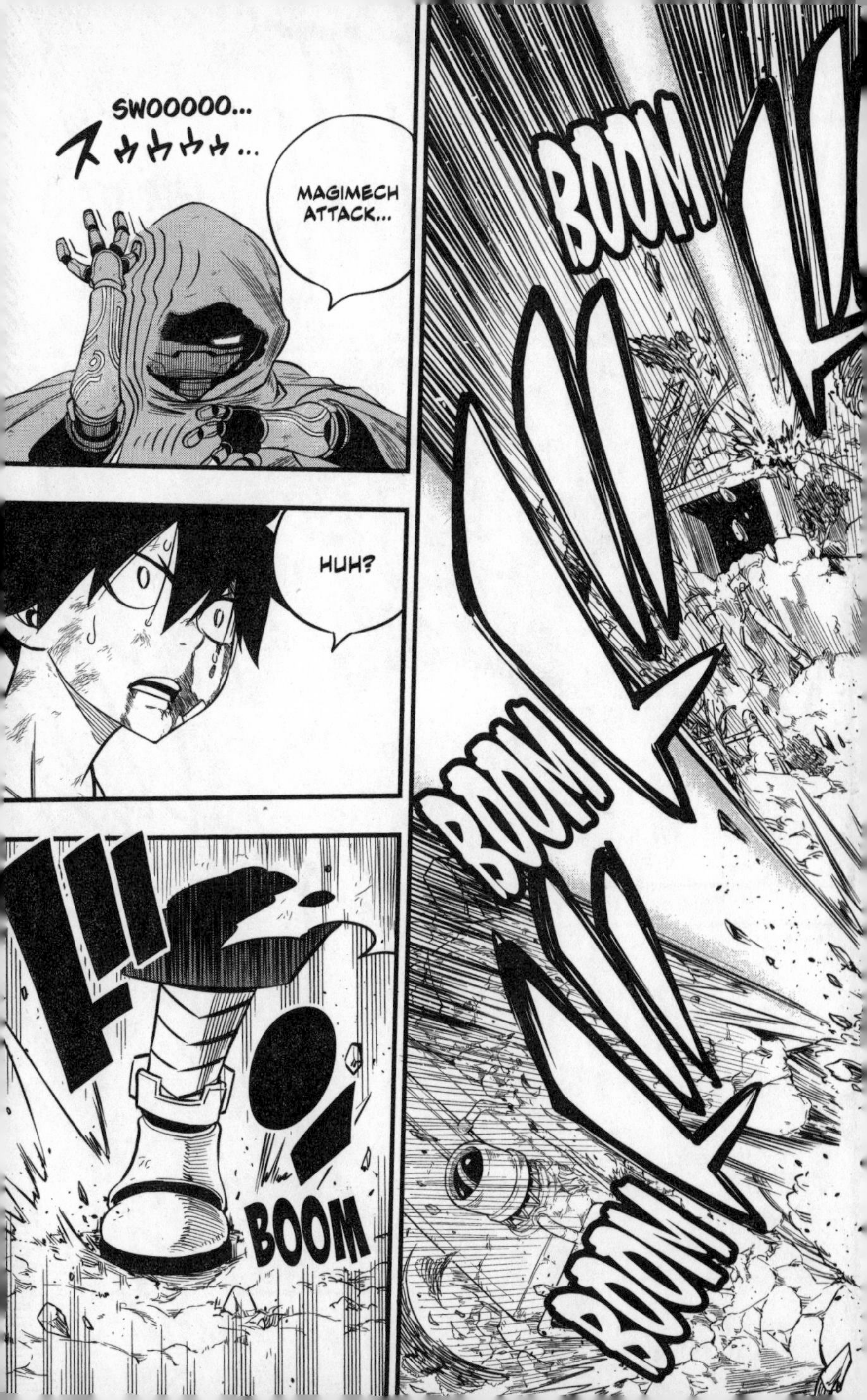
BOOM
BOOM
BOOM
MAGIMECH ATTACK...
SWOOOOO...
スゥウウゥ...
HUH?
BOOM

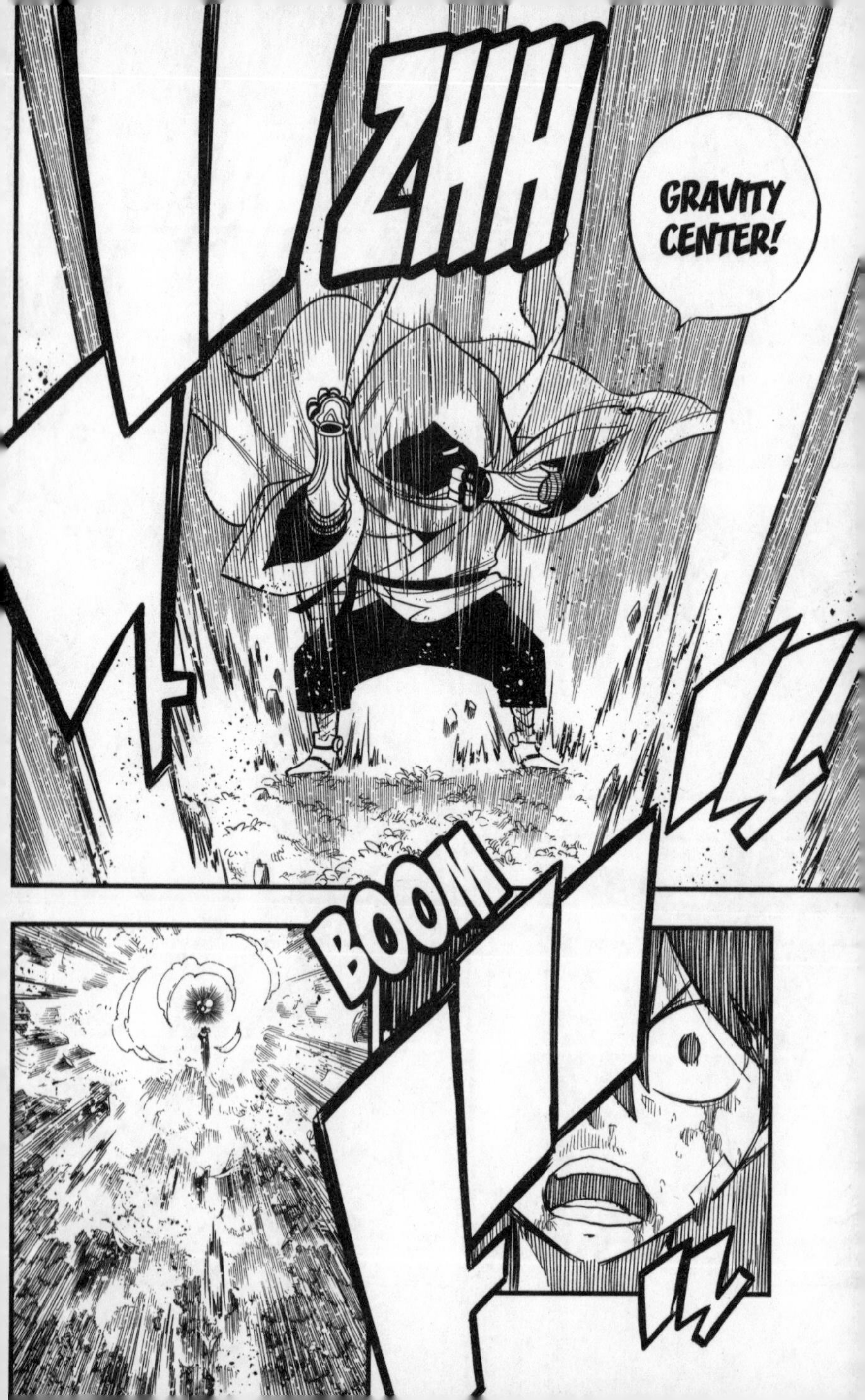
GRAVITY CENTER!
ZHH
BOOM

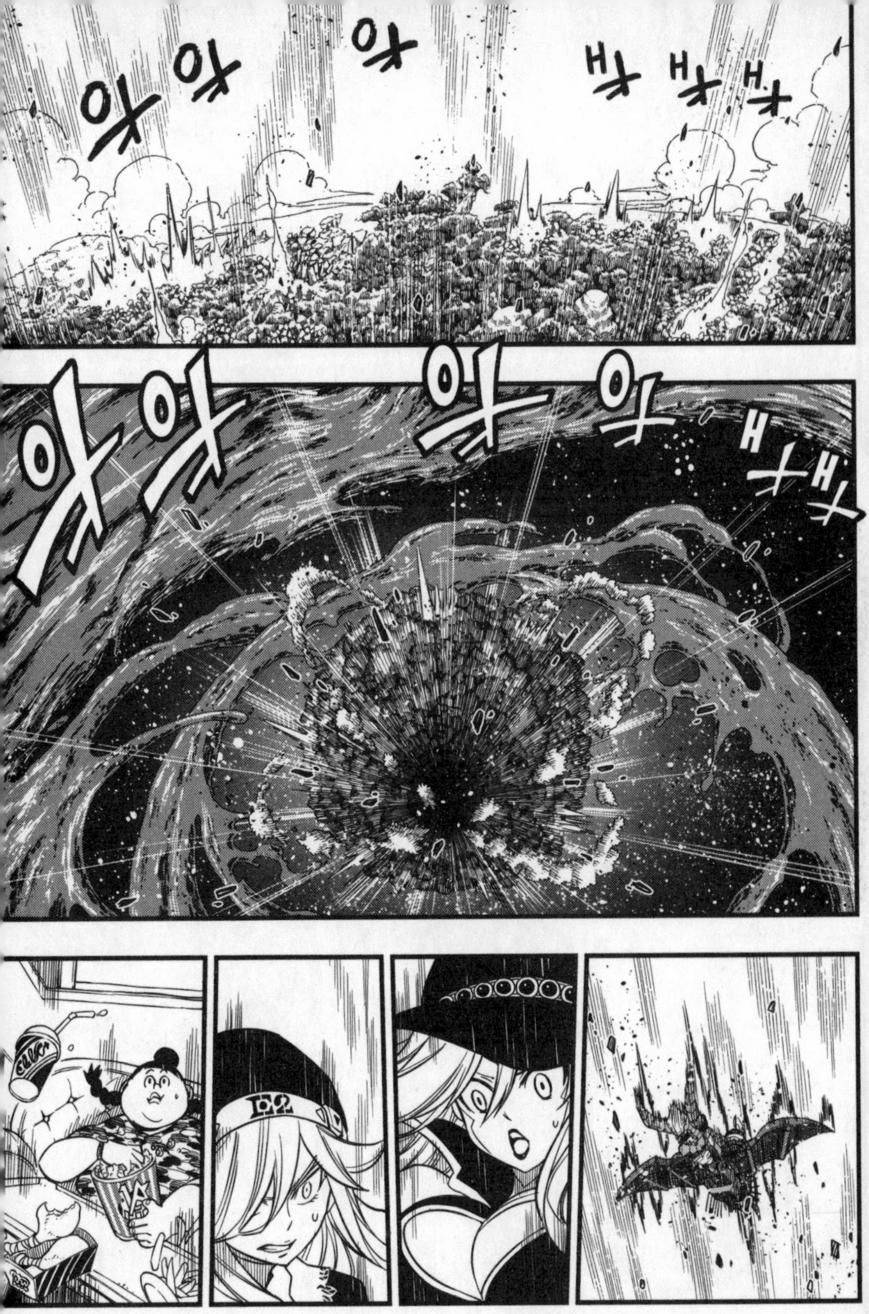

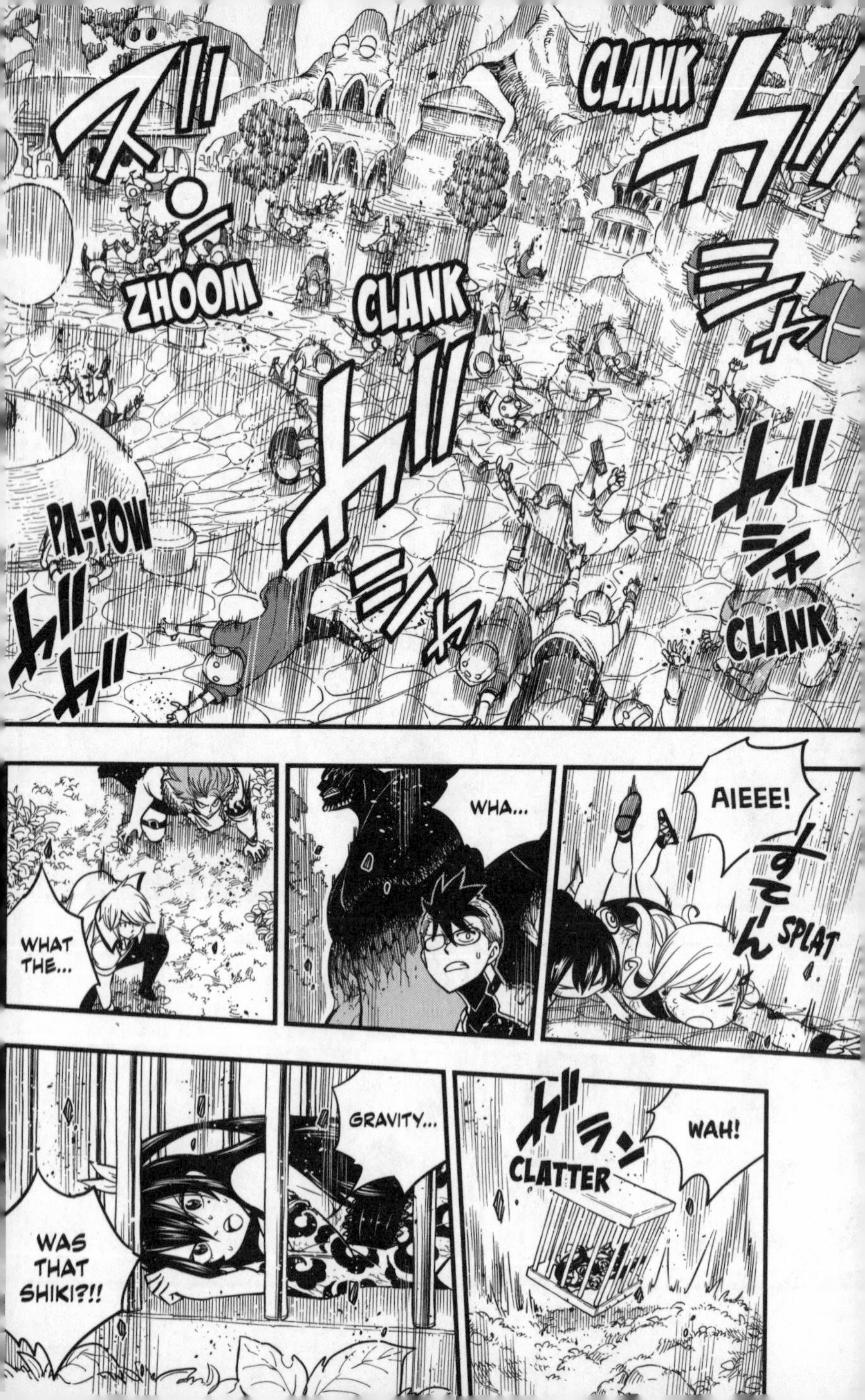
CLANK
CLANK
ZHOOM
CLANK
PA-POW
AIEEE!
すてーん
SPLAT
WHA...
WHAT THE...
WAH!
ガラン
CLATTER
GRAVITY...
WAS THAT SHIKI?!!

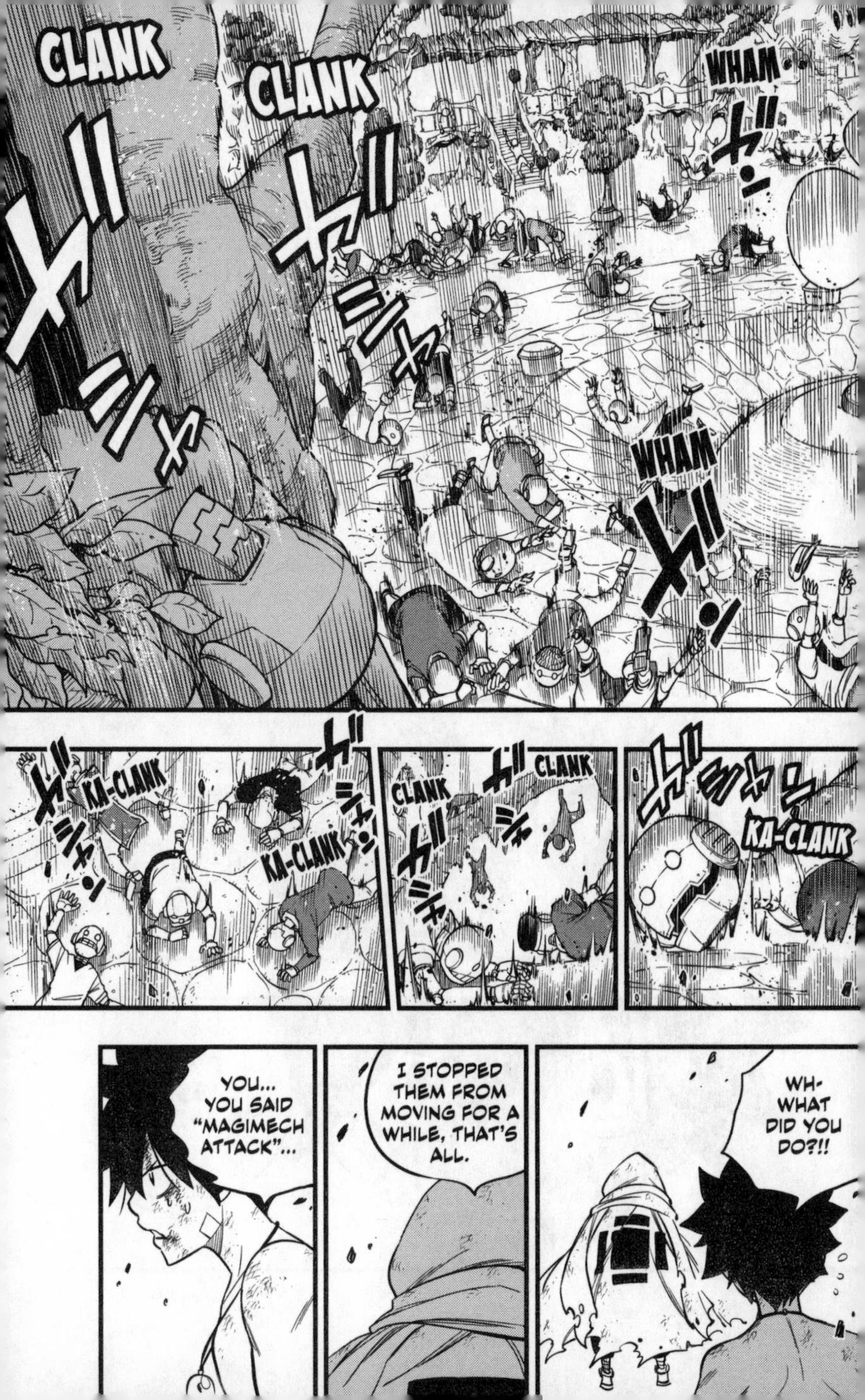
WHAM
WHAM
CLANK
CLANK
KA-CLANK
CLANK
CLANK
KA-CLANK
KA-CLANK
WH- WHAT DID YOU DO?!!
I STOPPED THEM FROM MOVING FOR A WHILE, THAT'S ALL.
YOU... YOU SAID "MAGIMECH ATTACK"...

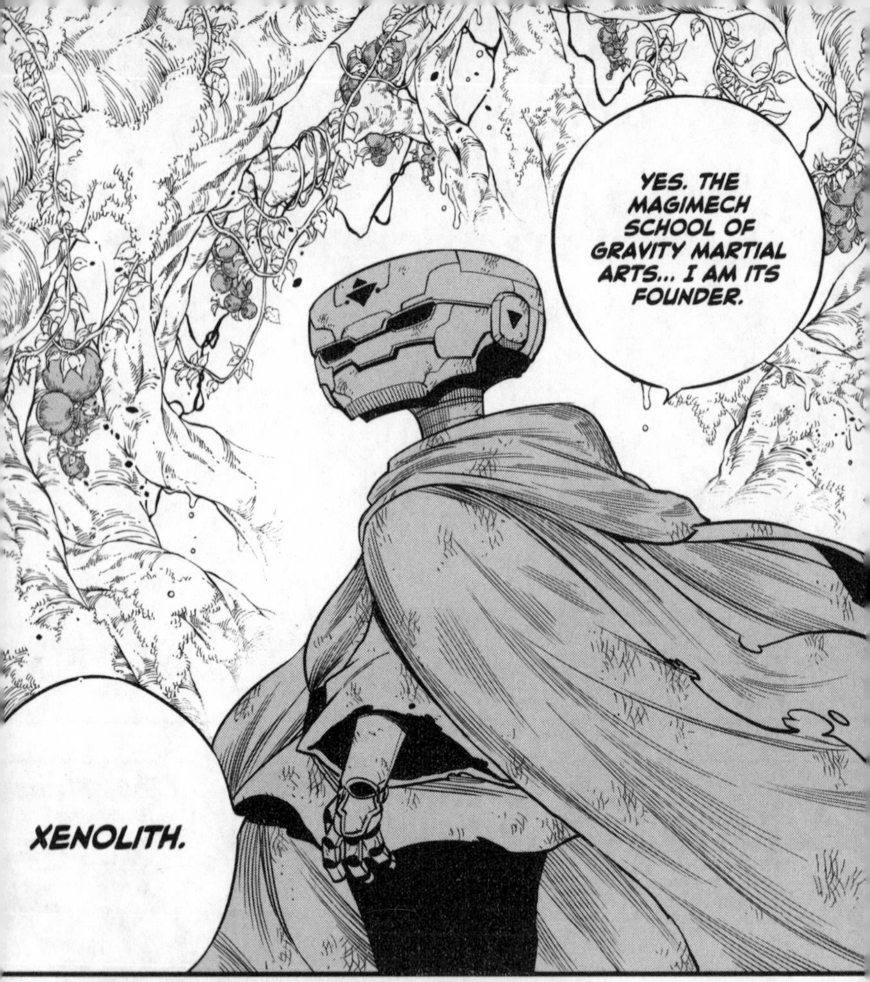
YES. THE MAGIMECH SCHOOL OF GRAVITY MARTIAL ARTS... I AM ITS FOUNDER.
XENOLITH.
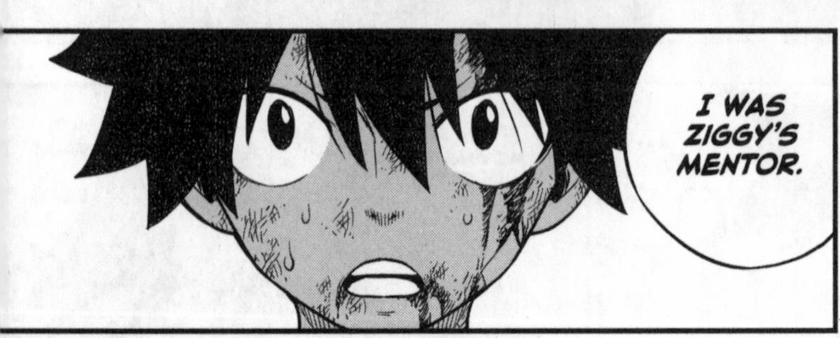
I WAS ZIGGY'S MENTOR.

EDENS ZERO

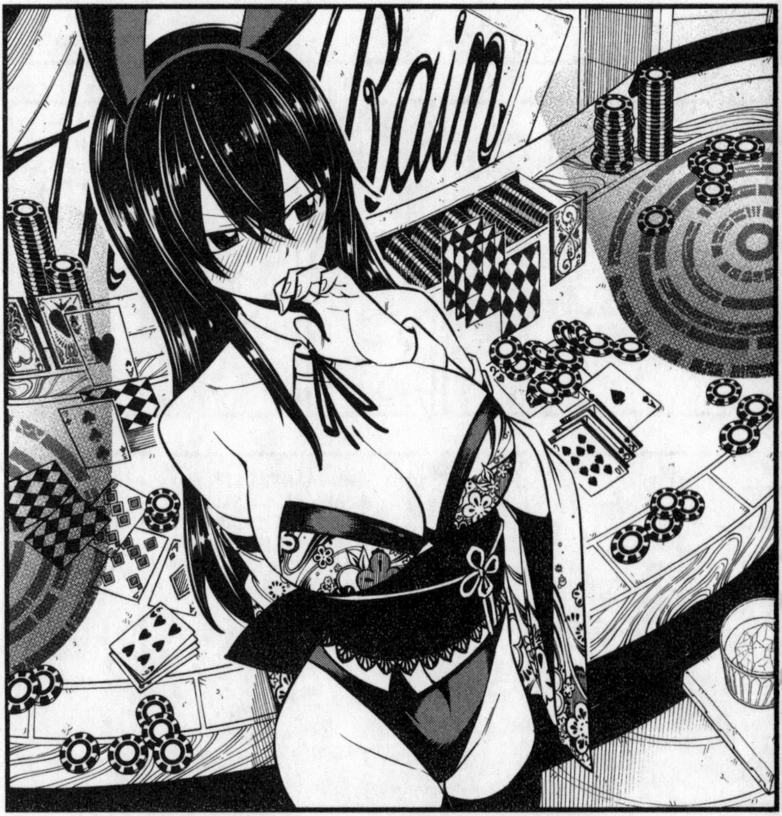
Rain

CHAPTER 126: THE DOCTOR, ARMED AND DANGEROUS

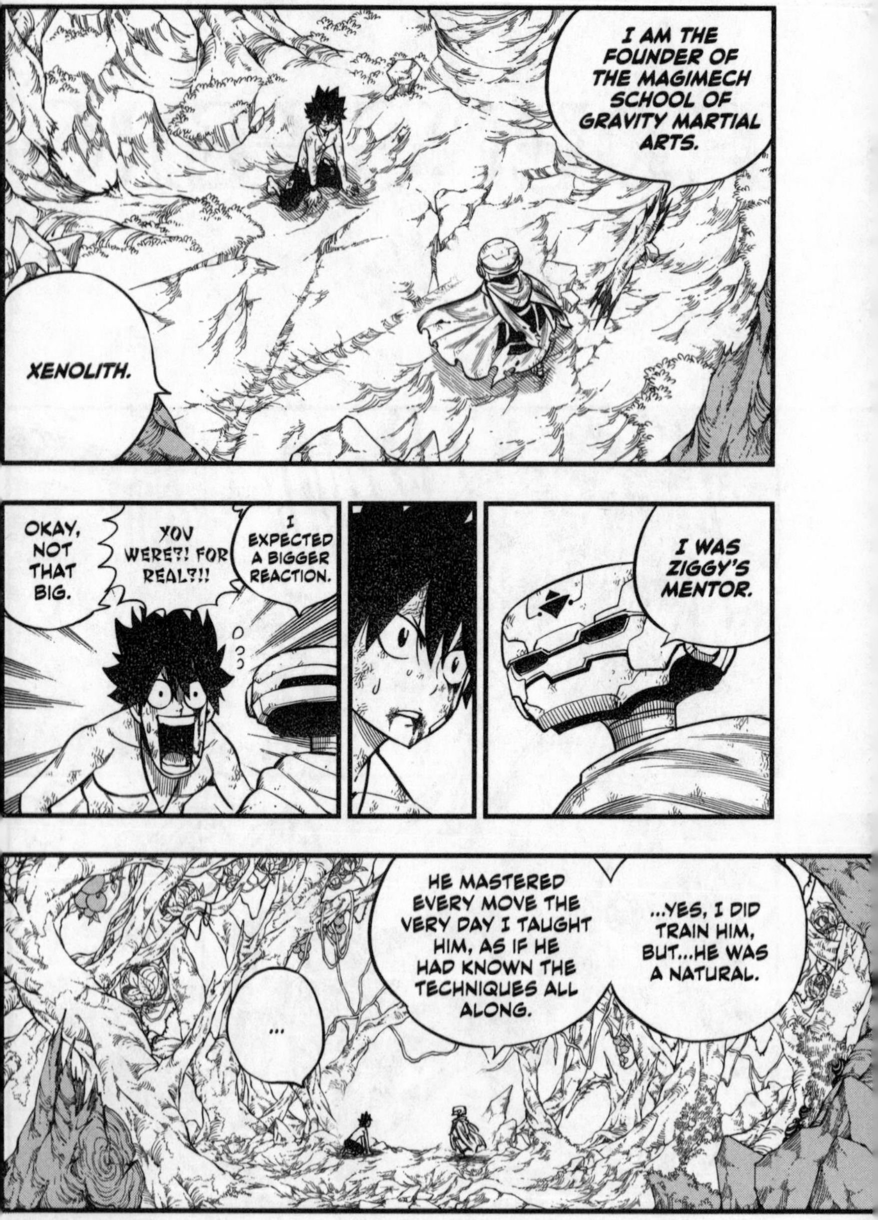
I AM THE FOUNDER OF THE MAGIMECH SCHOOL OF GRAVITY MARTIAL ARTS.
XENOLITH.
I WAS ZIGGY'S MENTOR.
I EXPECTED A BIGGER REACTION.
YOU WERE?! FOR REAL?!!
OKAY, NOT THAT BIG.
...YES, I DID TRAIN HIM, BUT...HE WAS A NATURAL.
HE MASTERED EVERY MOVE THE VERY DAY I TAUGHT HIM, AS IF HE HAD KNOWN THE TECHNIQUES ALL ALONG.
...

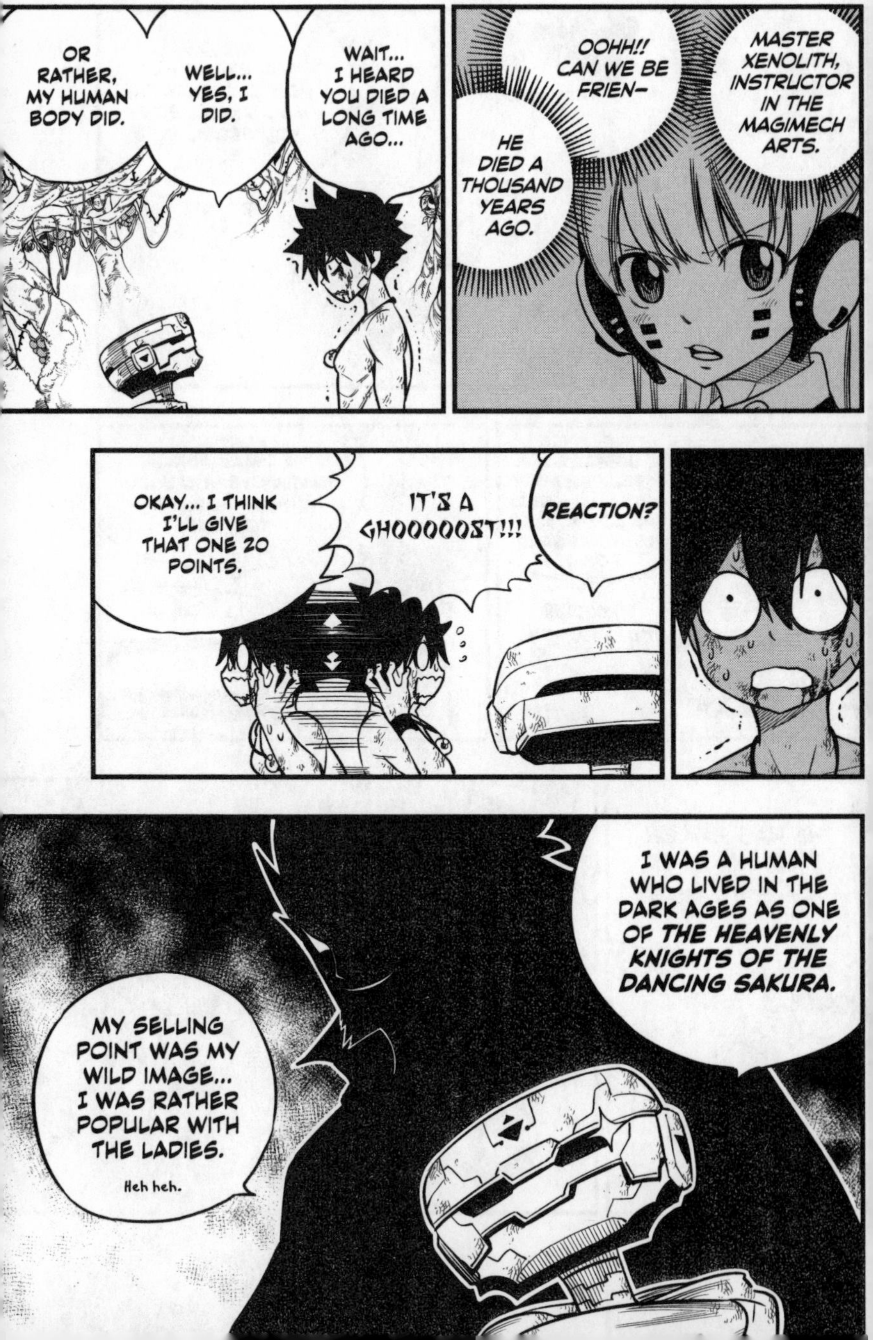
MASTER XENOLITH, INSTRUCTOR IN THE MAGIMECH ARTS.
OOHH!! CAN WE BE FRIEN—
HE DIED A THOUSAND YEARS AGO.
WAIT... I HEARD YOU DIED A LONG TIME AGO...
WELL... YES, I DID.
OR RATHER, MY HUMAN BODY DID.
REACTION?
IT'S A GHOOOOOST!!!
OKAY... I THINK I'LL GIVE THAT ONE 20 POINTS.
I WAS A HUMAN WHO LIVED IN THE DARK AGES AS ONE OF *THE HEAVENLY KNIGHTS OF THE DANCING SAKURA.*
MY SELLING POINT WAS MY WILD IMAGE... I WAS RATHER POPULAR WITH THE LADIES.
Heh heh.

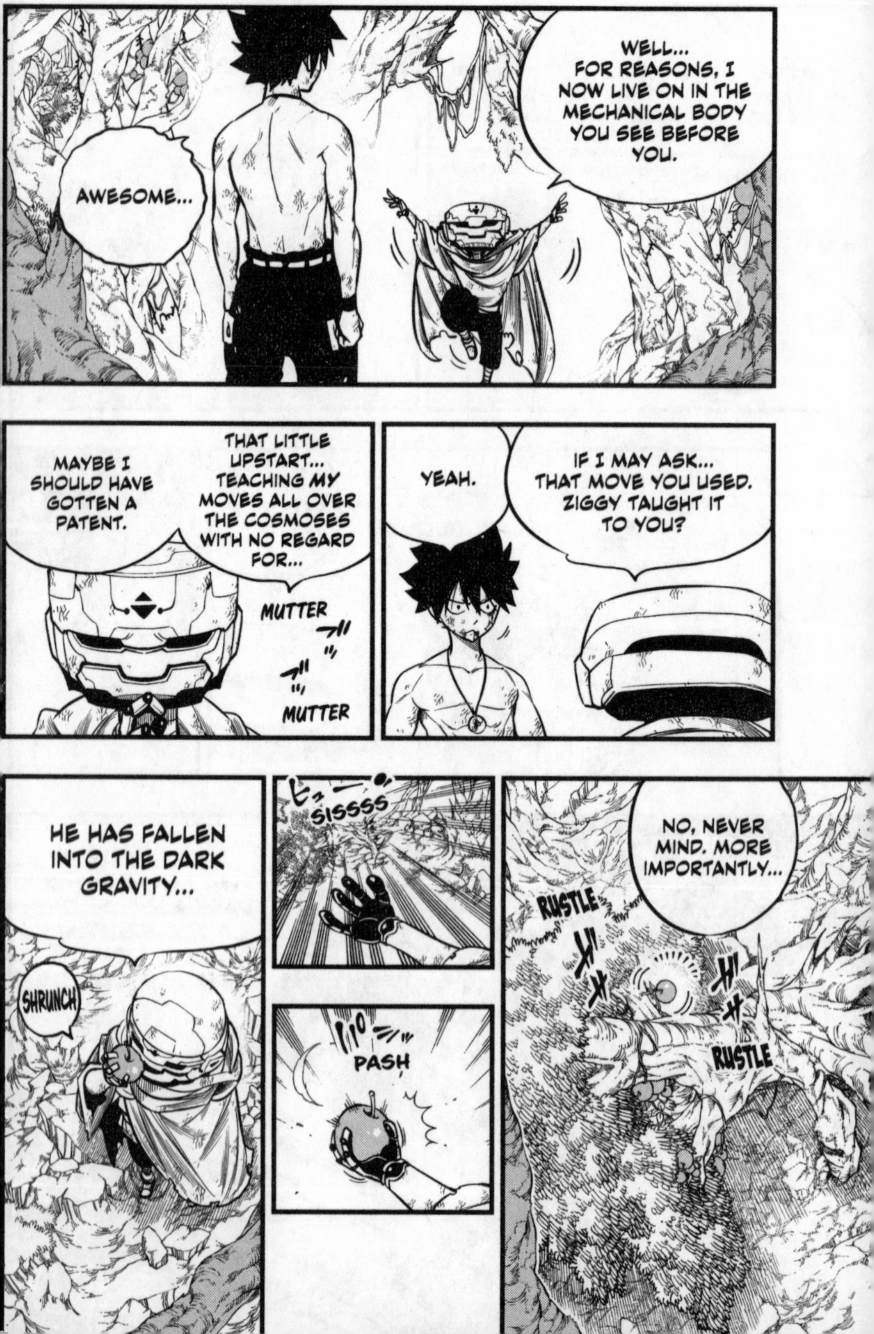
WELL... FOR REASONS, I NOW LIVE ON IN THE MECHANICAL BODY YOU SEE BEFORE YOU.
AWESOME...
IF I MAY ASK... THAT MOVE YOU USED. ZIGGY TAUGHT IT TO YOU?
YEAH.
THAT LITTLE UPSTART... TEACHING MY MOVES ALL OVER THE COSMOSES WITH NO REGARD FOR...
MAYBE I SHOULD HAVE GOTTEN A PATENT.
MUTTER
MUTTER
NO, NEVER MIND. MORE IMPORTANTLY...
RUSTLE
RUSTLE
SISSSS
PASH
HE HAS FALLEN INTO THE DARK GRAVITY...
SHRUNCH

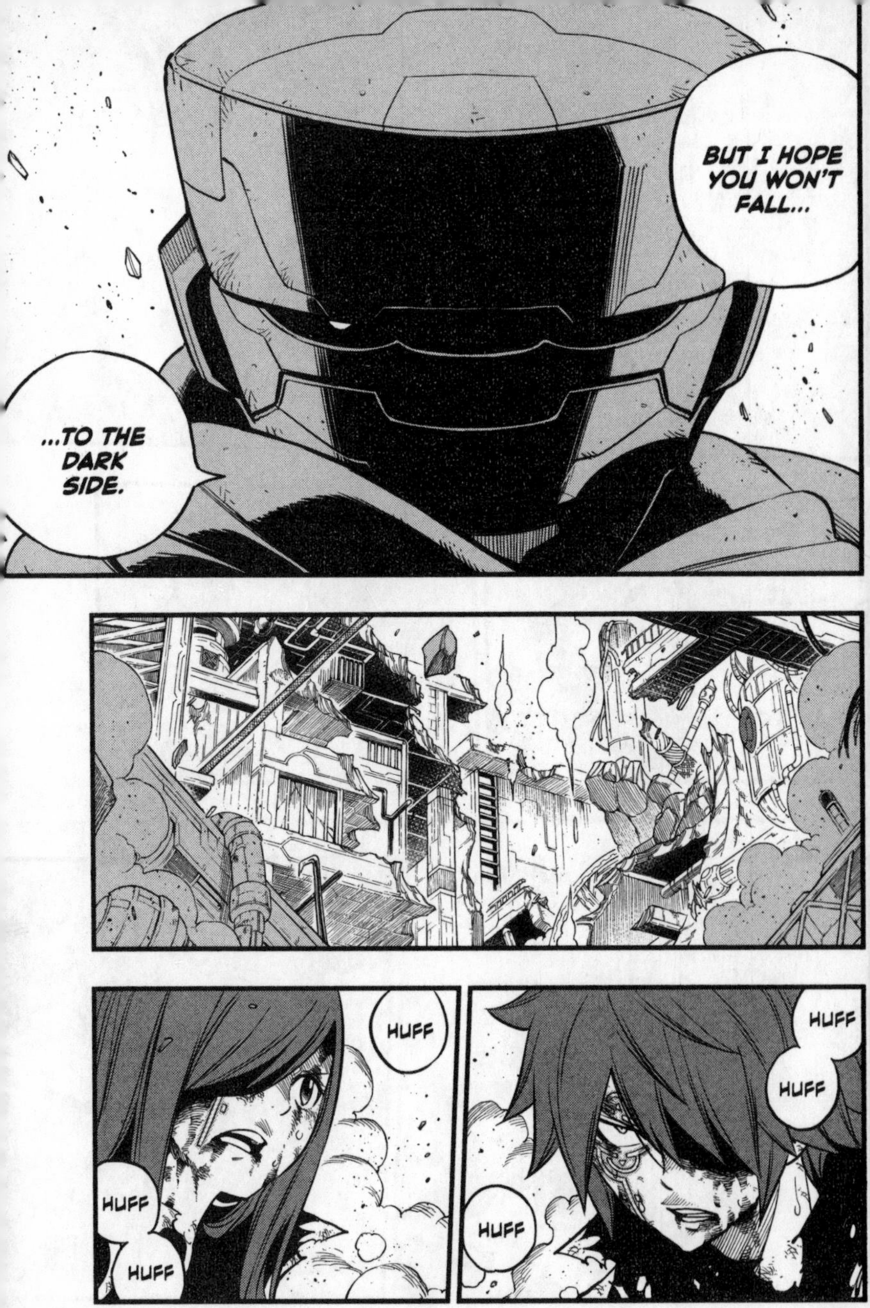
BUT I HOPE YOU WON'T FALL...
...TO THE DARK SIDE.
HUFF
HUFF
HUFF
HUFF
HUFF
HUFF

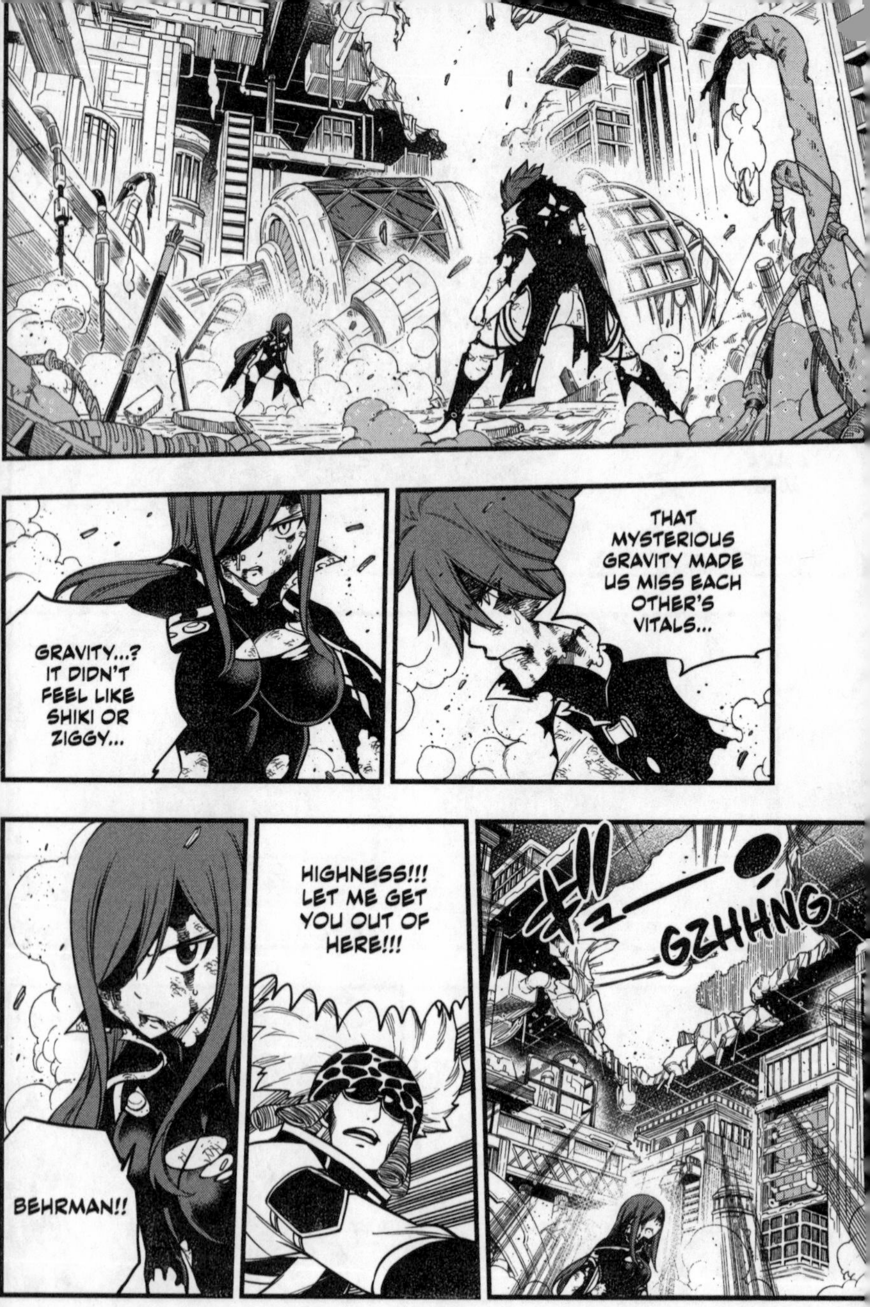
THAT MYSTERIOUS GRAVITY MADE US MISS EACH OTHER'S VITALS...
GRAVITY...? IT DIDN'T FEEL LIKE SHIKI OR ZIGGY...
GZHHNG
HIGHNESS!!! LET ME GET YOU OUT OF HERE!!!
BEHRMAN!!

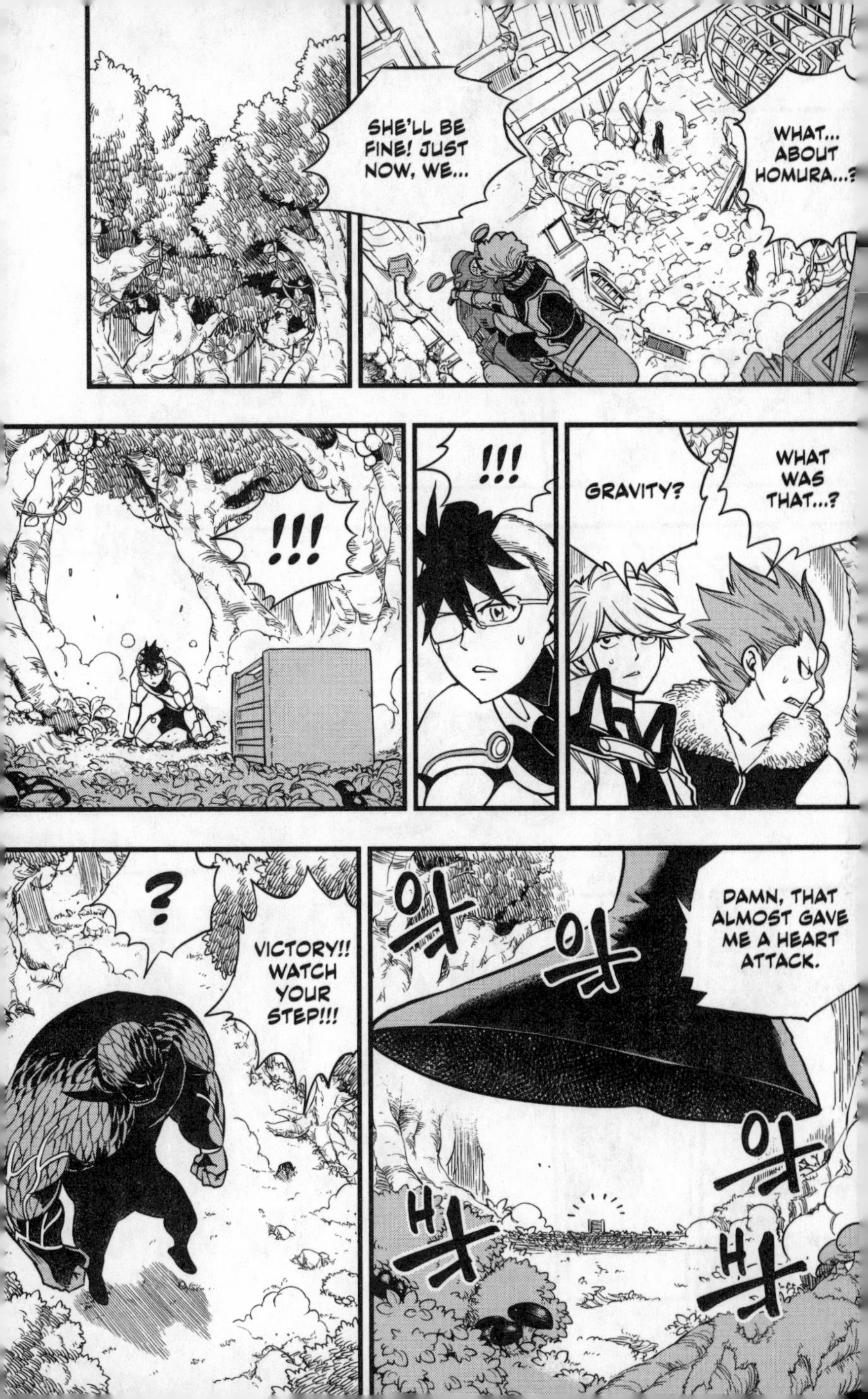
WHAT... ABOUT HOMURA...?
SHE'LL BE FINE! JUST NOW, WE...
WHAT WAS THAT...?
GRAVITY?
!!!
!!!
DAMN, THAT ALMOST GAVE ME A HEART ATTACK.
VICTORY!! WATCH YOUR STEP!!!
?

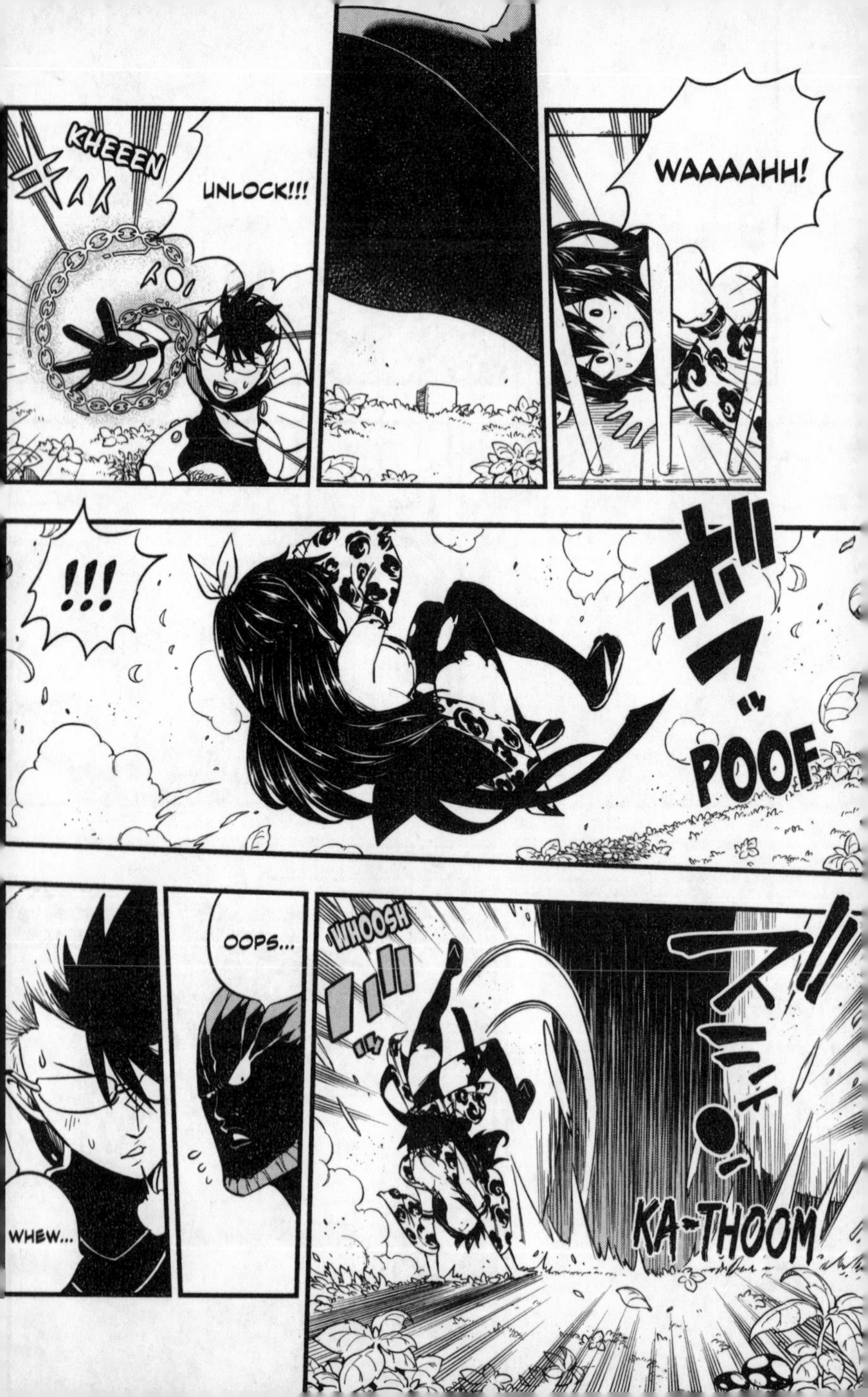
WAAAAHH!
KHEEEEN
UNLOCK!!!
POOF
!!!
WHOOSH
KA-THOOM
OOPS...
WHEW...

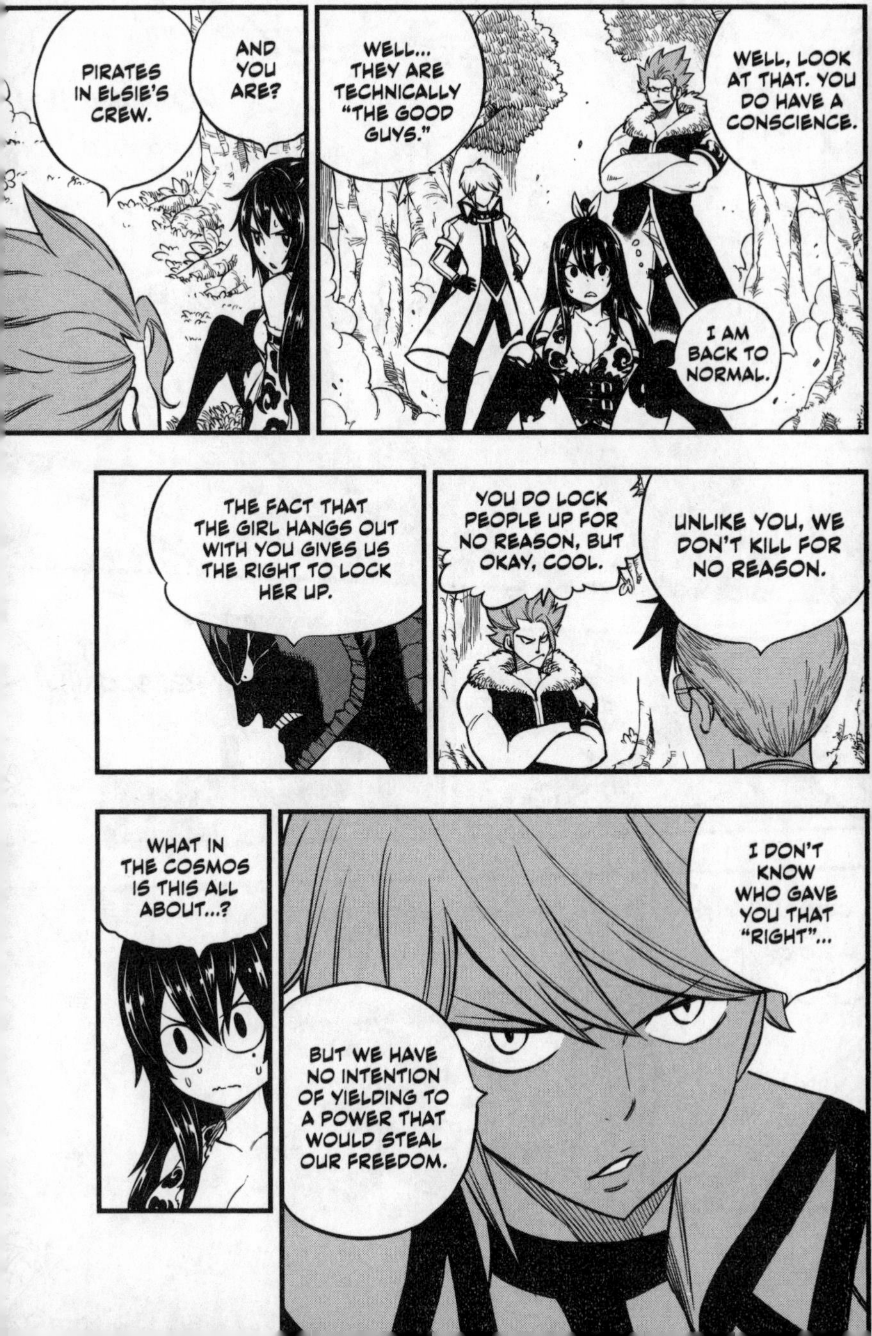
WELL, LOOK AT THAT. YOU DO HAVE A CONSCIENCE.
WELL... THEY ARE TECHNICALLY "THE GOOD GUYS."
I AM BACK TO NORMAL.
AND YOU ARE?
PIRATES IN ELSIE'S CREW.
UNLIKE YOU, WE DON'T KILL FOR NO REASON.
YOU DO LOCK PEOPLE UP FOR NO REASON, BUT OKAY, COOL.
THE FACT THAT THE GIRL HANGS OUT WITH YOU GIVES US THE RIGHT TO LOCK HER UP.
I DON'T KNOW WHO GAVE YOU THAT "RIGHT"...
BUT WE HAVE NO INTENTION OF YIELDING TO A POWER THAT WOULD STEAL OUR FREEDOM.
WHAT IN THE COSMOS IS THIS ALL ABOUT...?

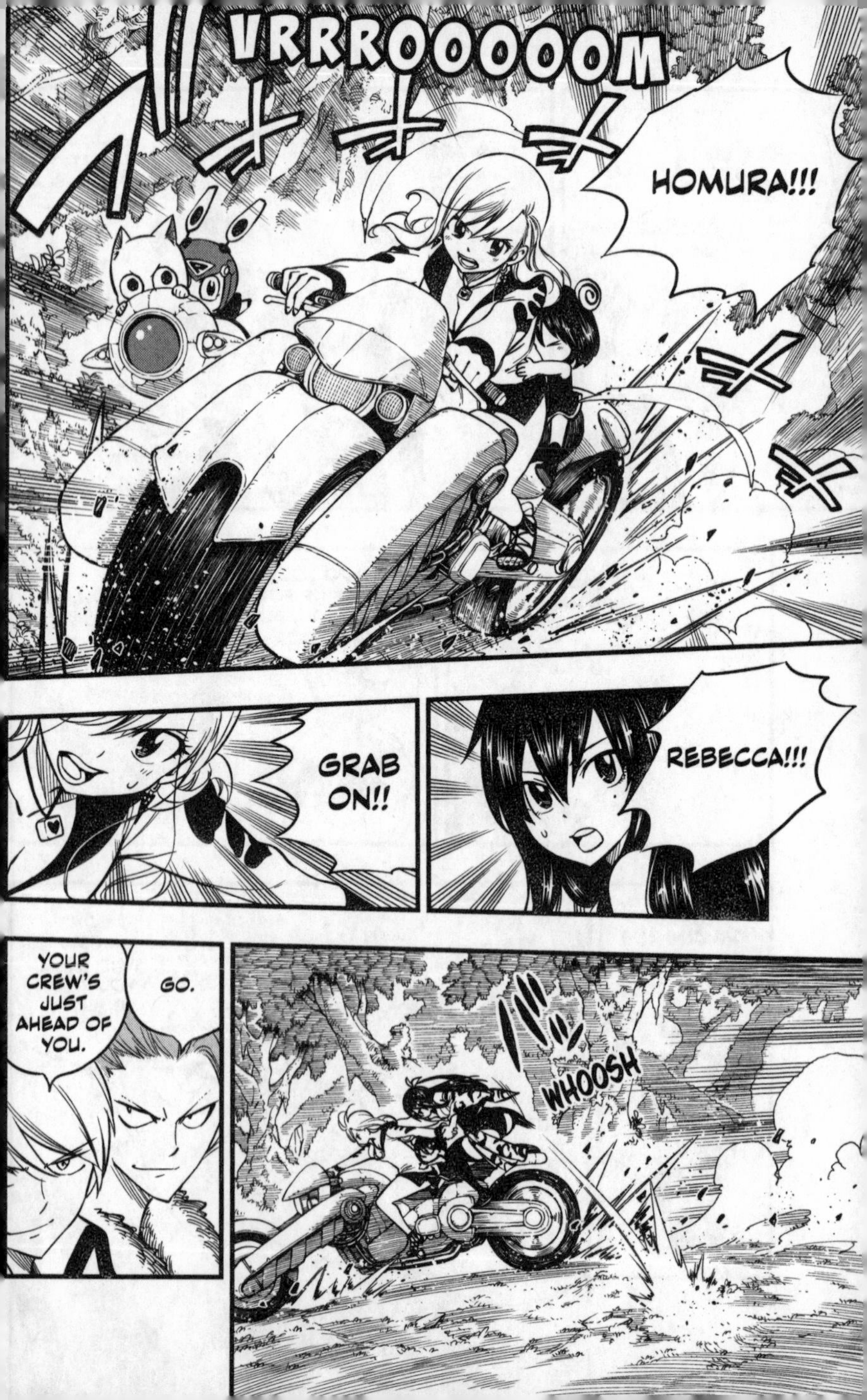
VRRROOOOOM
HOMURA!!!
REBECCA!!!
GRAB ON!!
WHOOSH
GO.
YOUR CREW'S JUST AHEAD OF YOU.

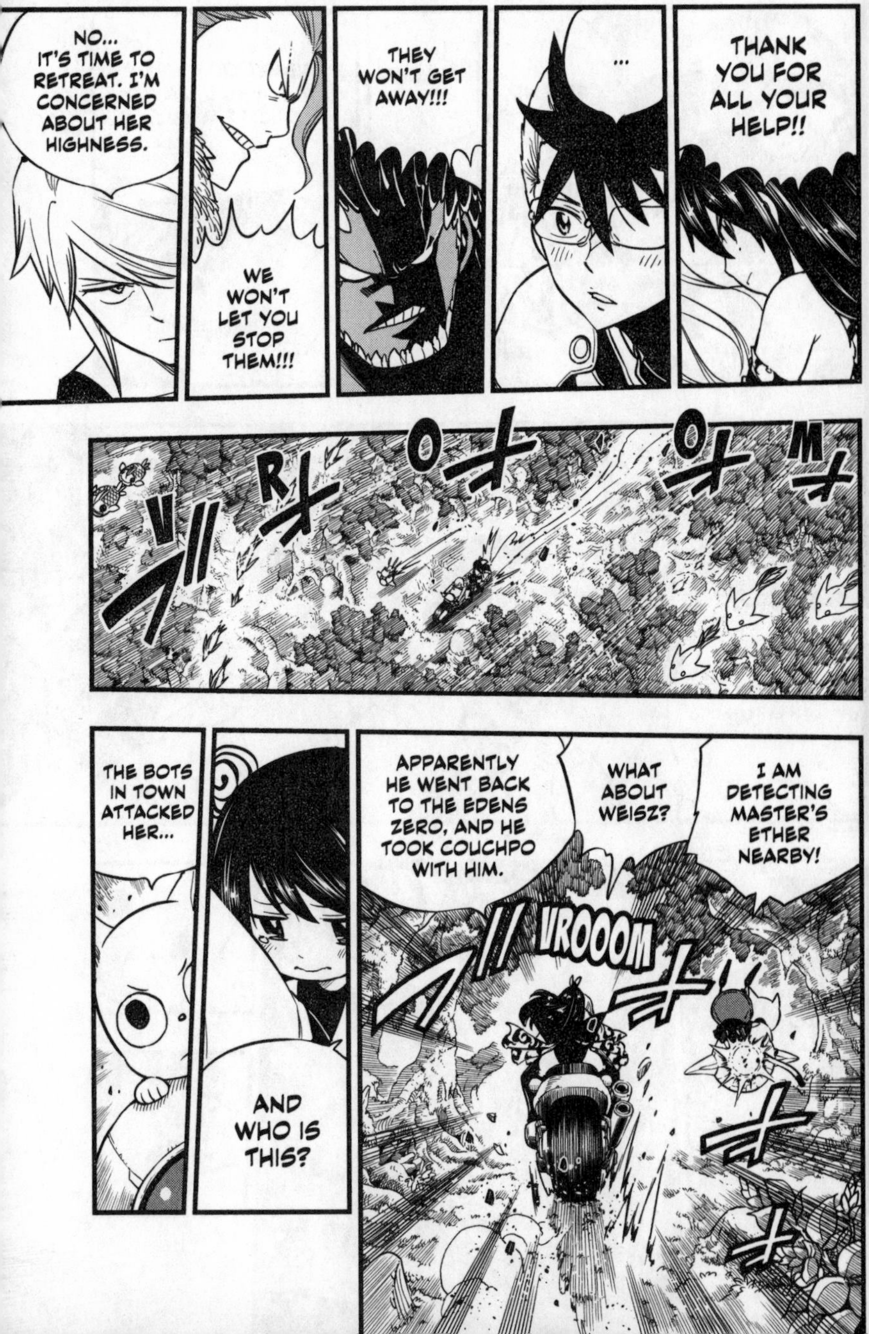
THANK YOU FOR ALL YOUR HELP!!
...
THEY WON'T GET AWAY!!!
WE WON'T LET YOU STOP THEM!!!
NO... IT'S TIME TO RETREAT. I'M CONCERNED ABOUT HER HIGHNESS.
VROOM
I AM DETECTING MASTER'S ETHER NEARBY!
WHAT ABOUT WEISZ?
APPARENTLY HE WENT BACK TO THE EDENS ZERO, AND HE TOOK COUCHPO WITH HIM.
VROOOM
AND WHO IS THIS?
THE BOTS IN TOWN ATTACKED HER...

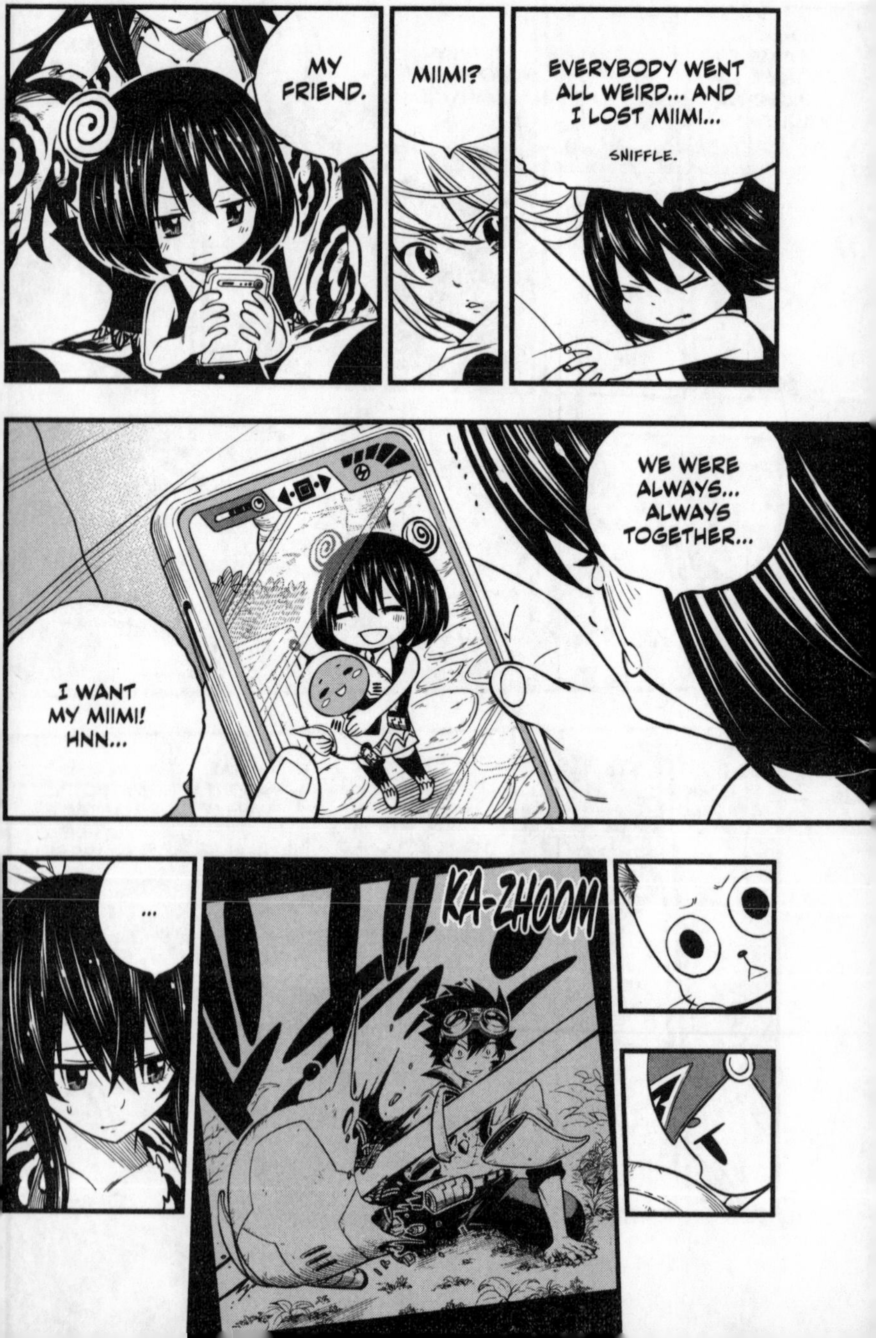
EVERYBODY WENT ALL WEIRD... AND I LOST MIIMI...
SNIFFLE.
MIIMI?
MY FRIEND.
WE WERE ALWAYS... ALWAYS TOGETHER...
I WANT MY MIIMI! HNN...
KA-ZHOOM
...

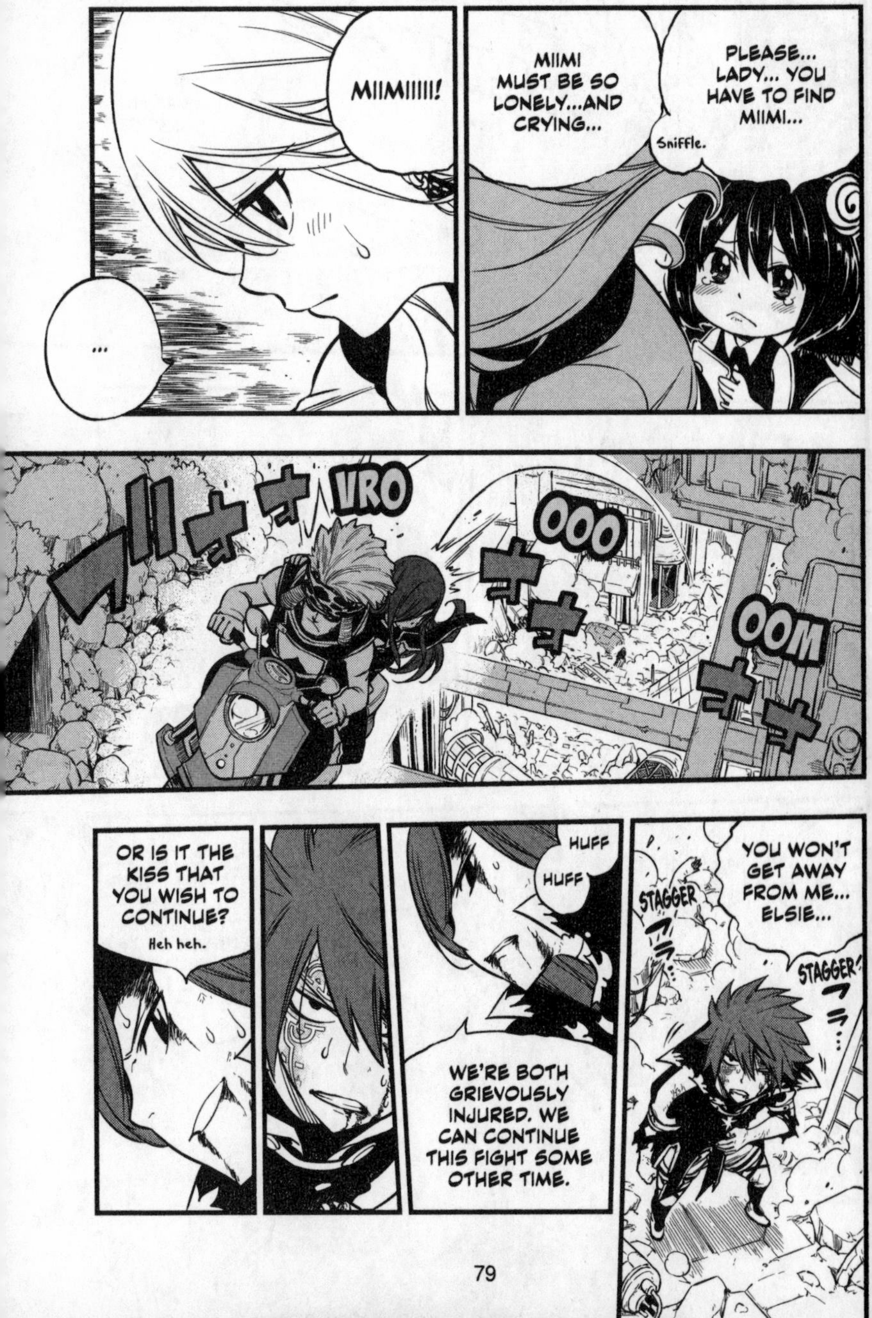
PLEASE... LADY... YOU HAVE TO FIND MIIMI...
Sniffle.
MIIMI MUST BE SO LONELY...AND CRYING...
MIIMIIIII!
...
VRO
OOO
OOM
STAGGER
YOU WON'T GET AWAY FROM ME... ELSIE...
STAGGER
HUFF
HUFF
WE'RE BOTH GRIEVOUSLY INJURED. WE CAN CONTINUE THIS FIGHT SOME OTHER TIME.
OR IS IT THE KISS THAT YOU WISH TO CONTINUE?
Heh heh.

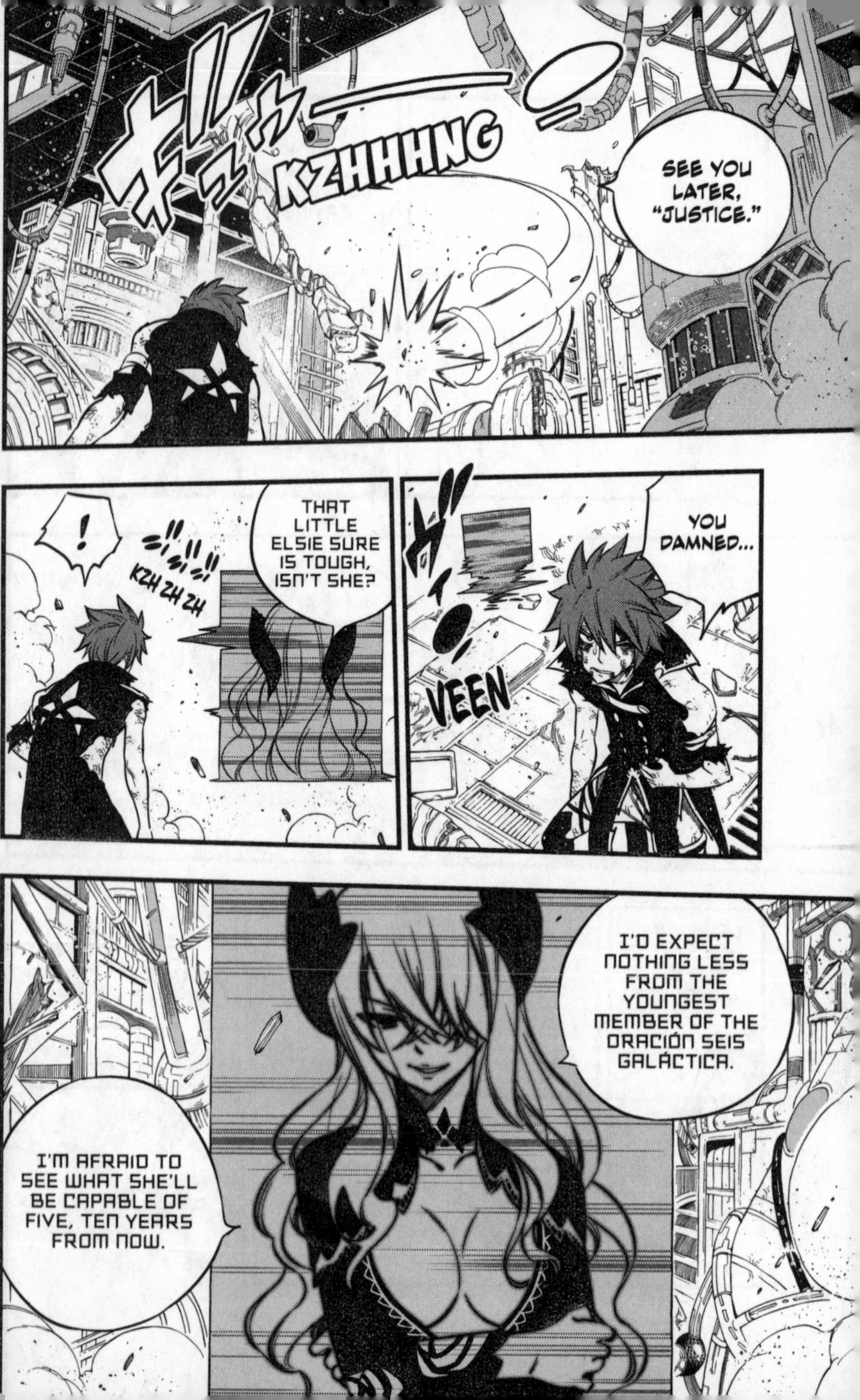
SEE YOU LATER, "JUSTICE."
KZHHHNG
YOU DAMNED...
VEEN
THAT LITTLE ELSIE SURE IS TOUGH, ISN'T SHE?
!
KZH ZH ZH
I'D EXPECT NOTHING LESS FROM THE YOUNGEST MEMBER OF THE ORACIÓN SEIS GALÁCTICA.
I'M AFRAID TO SEE WHAT SHE'LL BE CAPABLE OF FIVE, TEN YEARS FROM NOW.

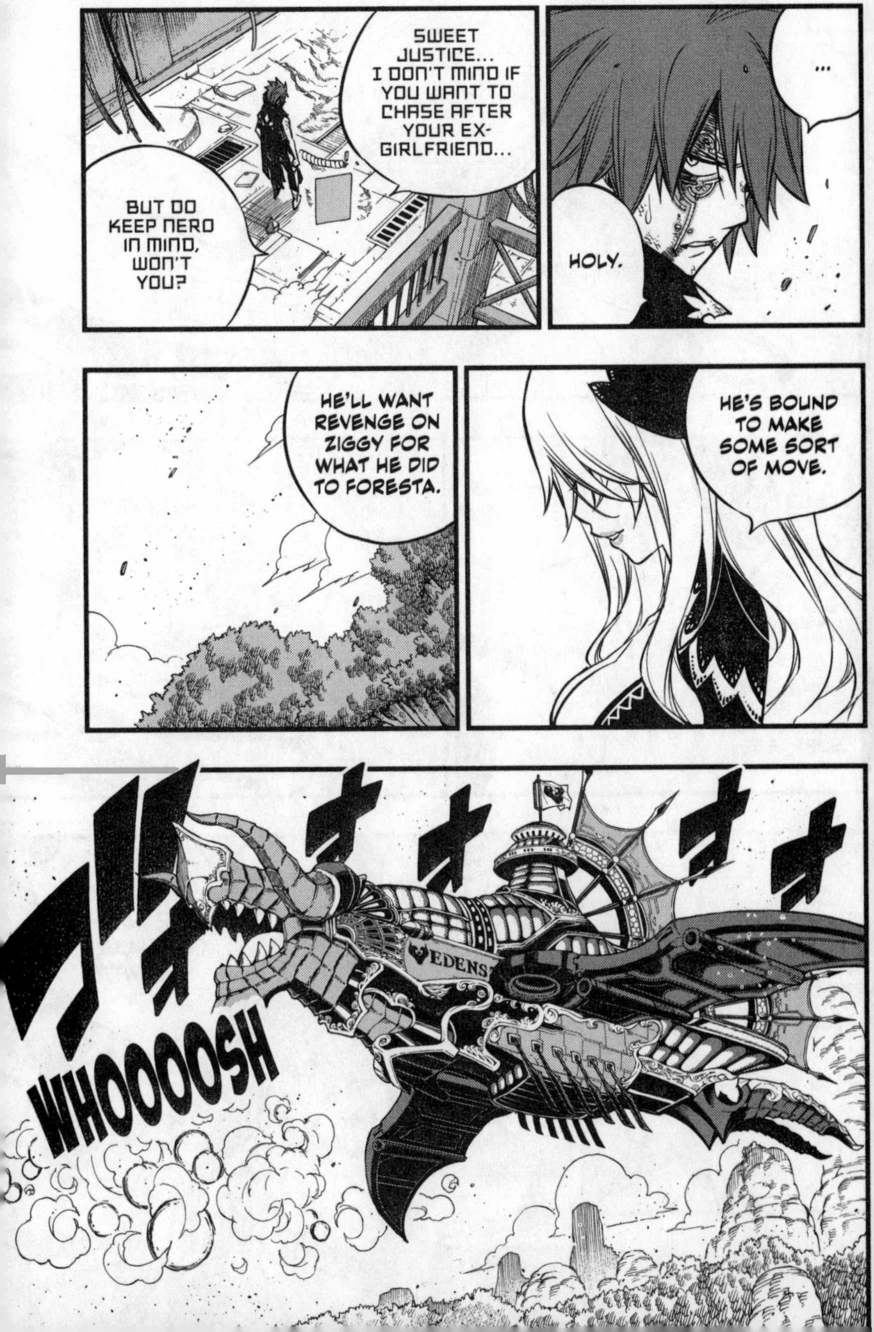
...
HOLY.
SWEET JUSTICE... I DON'T MIND IF YOU WANT TO CHASE AFTER YOUR EX-GIRLFRIEND...
BUT DO KEEP NERO IN MIND, WON'T YOU?
HE'S BOUND TO MAKE SOME SORT OF MOVE.
HE'LL WANT REVENGE ON ZIGGY FOR WHAT HE DID TO FORESTA.
EDENS
WHOOOOSH

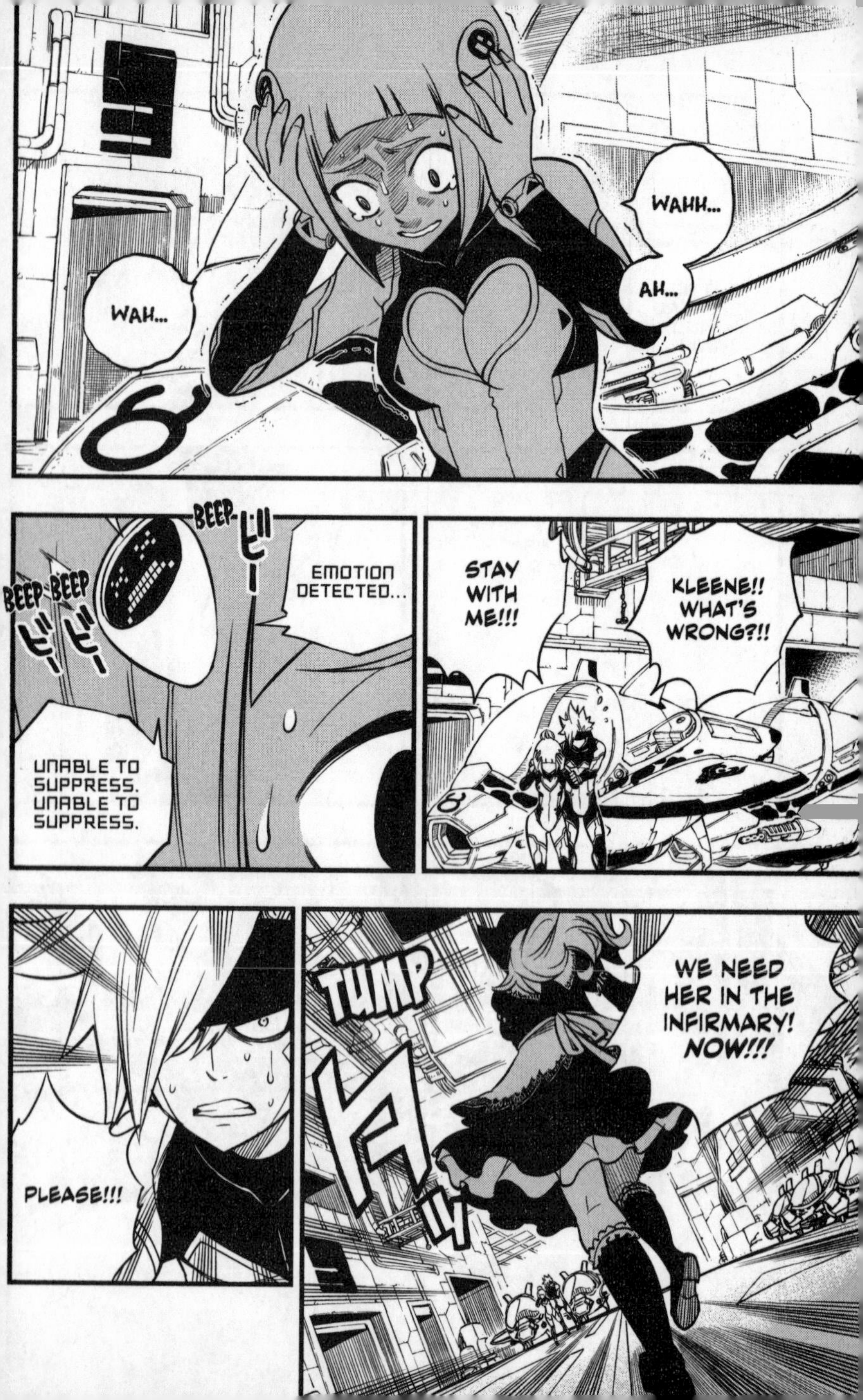

WAHH...
AH...
WAH...
KLEENE!! WHAT'S WRONG?!!
STAY WITH ME!!!
BEEP ビー
EMOTION DETECTED...
BEEP BEEP ビービー
UNABLE TO SUPPRESS. UNABLE TO SUPPRESS.
WE NEED HER IN THE INFIRMARY! NOW!!!
TUMP
PLEASE!!!

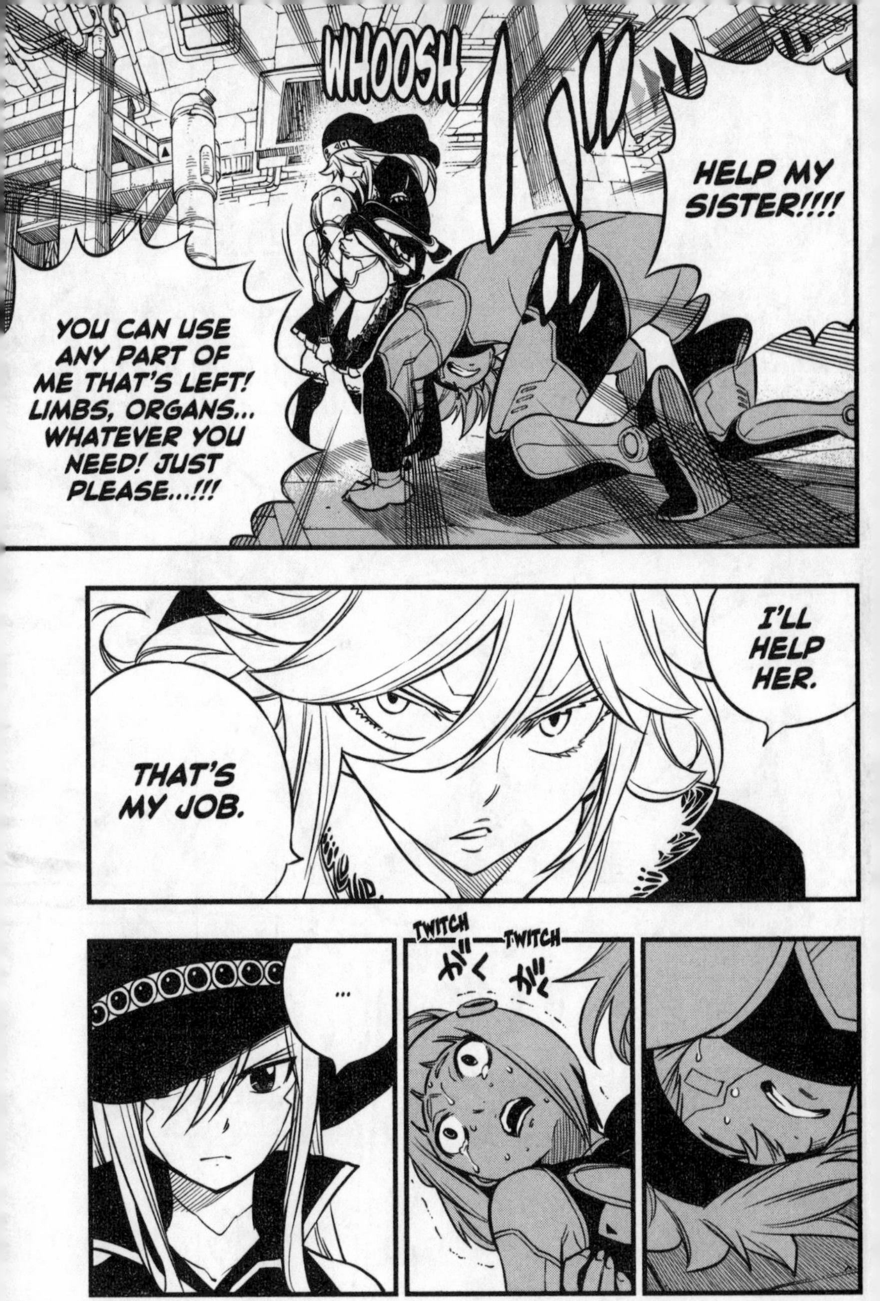
WHOOSH
HELP MY SISTER!!!!
YOU CAN USE ANY PART OF ME THAT'S LEFT! LIMBS, ORGANS... WHATEVER YOU NEED! JUST PLEASE...!!!
I'LL HELP HER.
THAT'S MY JOB.
TWITCH TWITCH
がく がく
...

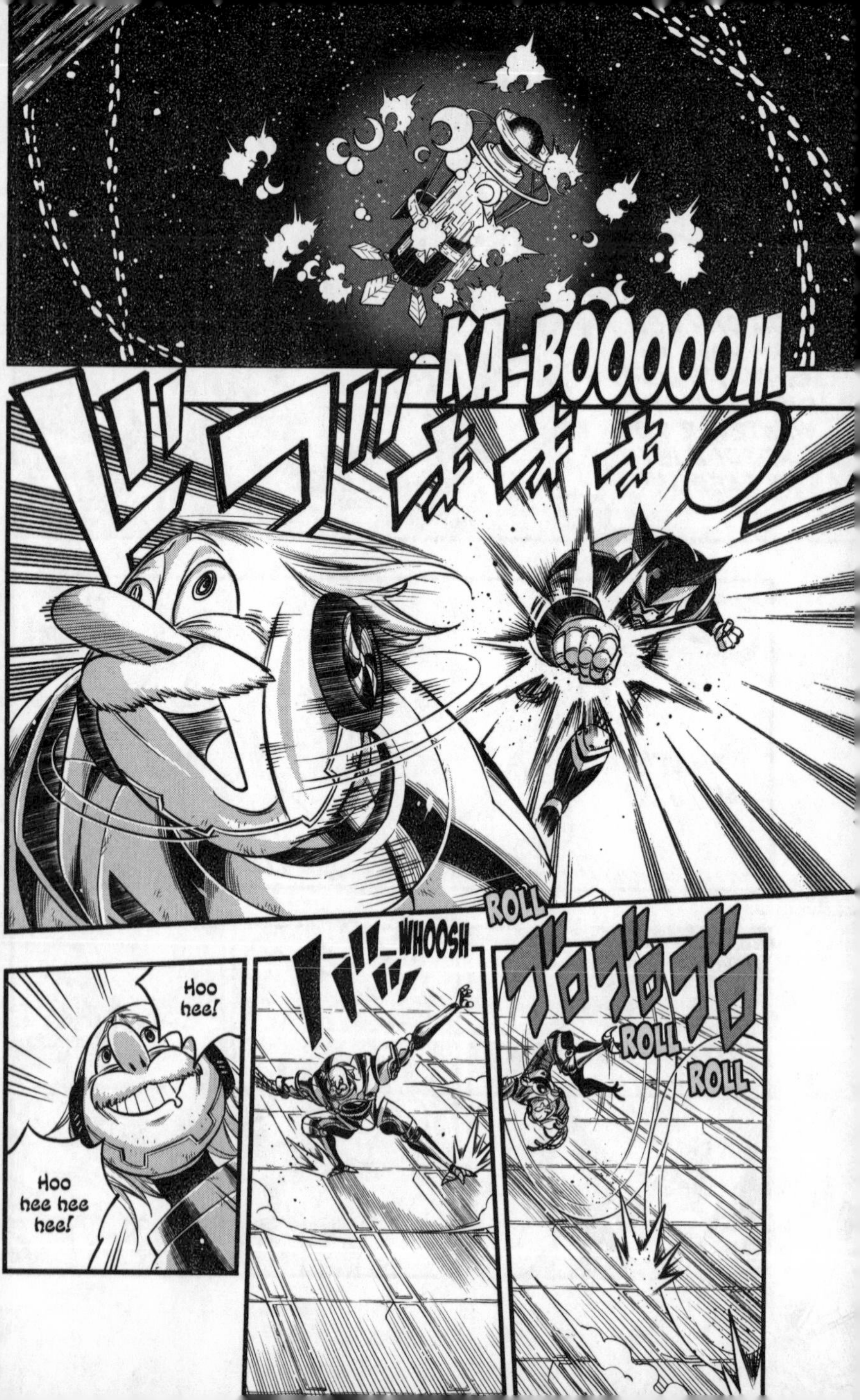
KA-BOOOOOM
ROLL
ROLL
ROLL
WHOOSH
Hoo hee!
Hoo hee hee hee!

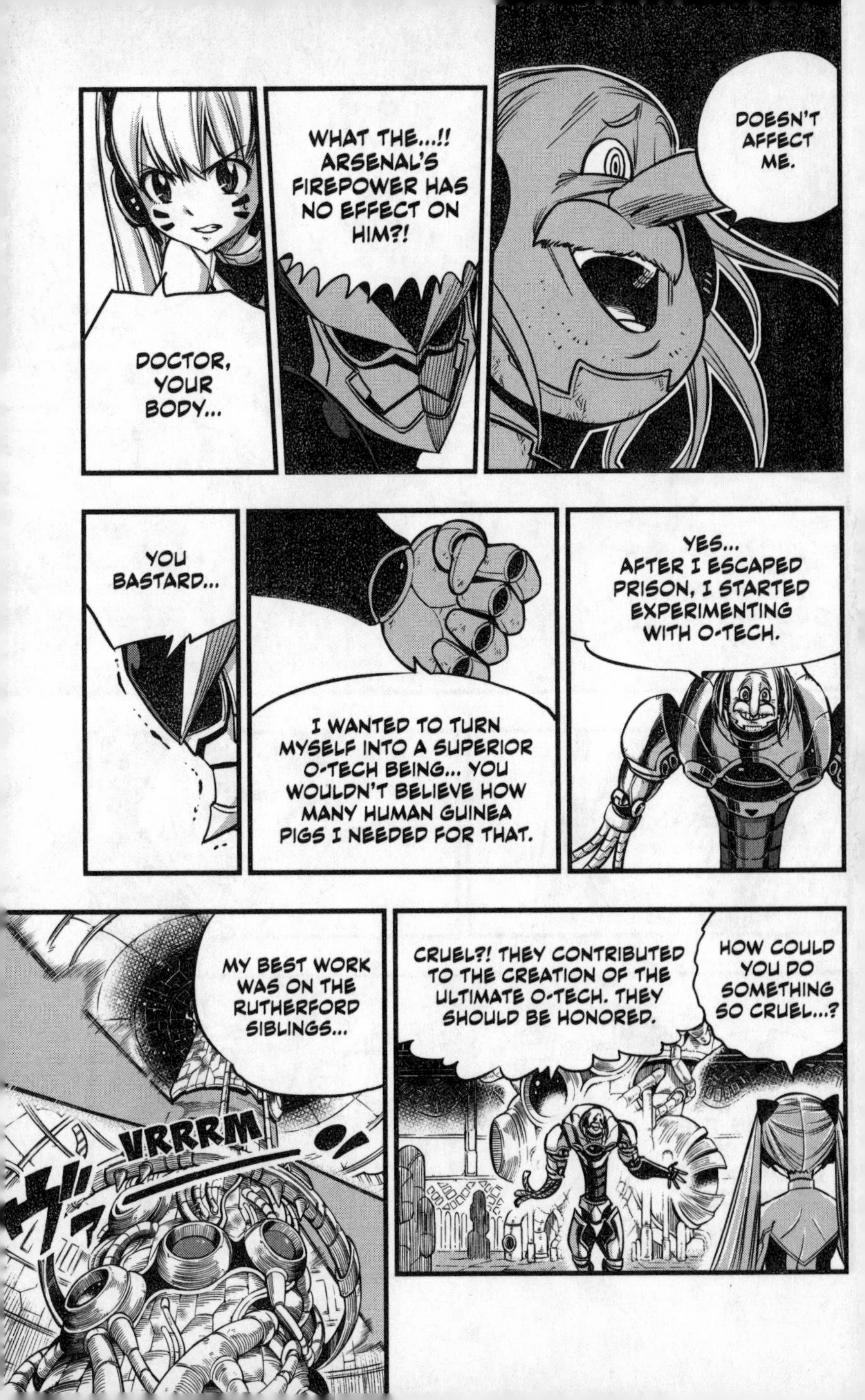
DOESN'T AFFECT ME.
WHAT THE...!! ARSENAL'S FIREPOWER HAS NO EFFECT ON HIM?!
DOCTOR, YOUR BODY...
YES... AFTER I ESCAPED PRISON, I STARTED EXPERIMENTING WITH O-TECH.
I WANTED TO TURN MYSELF INTO A SUPERIOR O-TECH BEING... YOU WOULDN'T BELIEVE HOW MANY HUMAN GUINEA PIGS I NEEDED FOR THAT.
YOU BASTARD...
HOW COULD YOU DO SOMETHING SO CRUEL...?
CRUEL?! THEY CONTRIBUTED TO THE CREATION OF THE ULTIMATE O-TECH. THEY SHOULD BE HONORED.
MY BEST WORK WAS ON THE RUTHERFORD SIBLINGS...
VRRRM

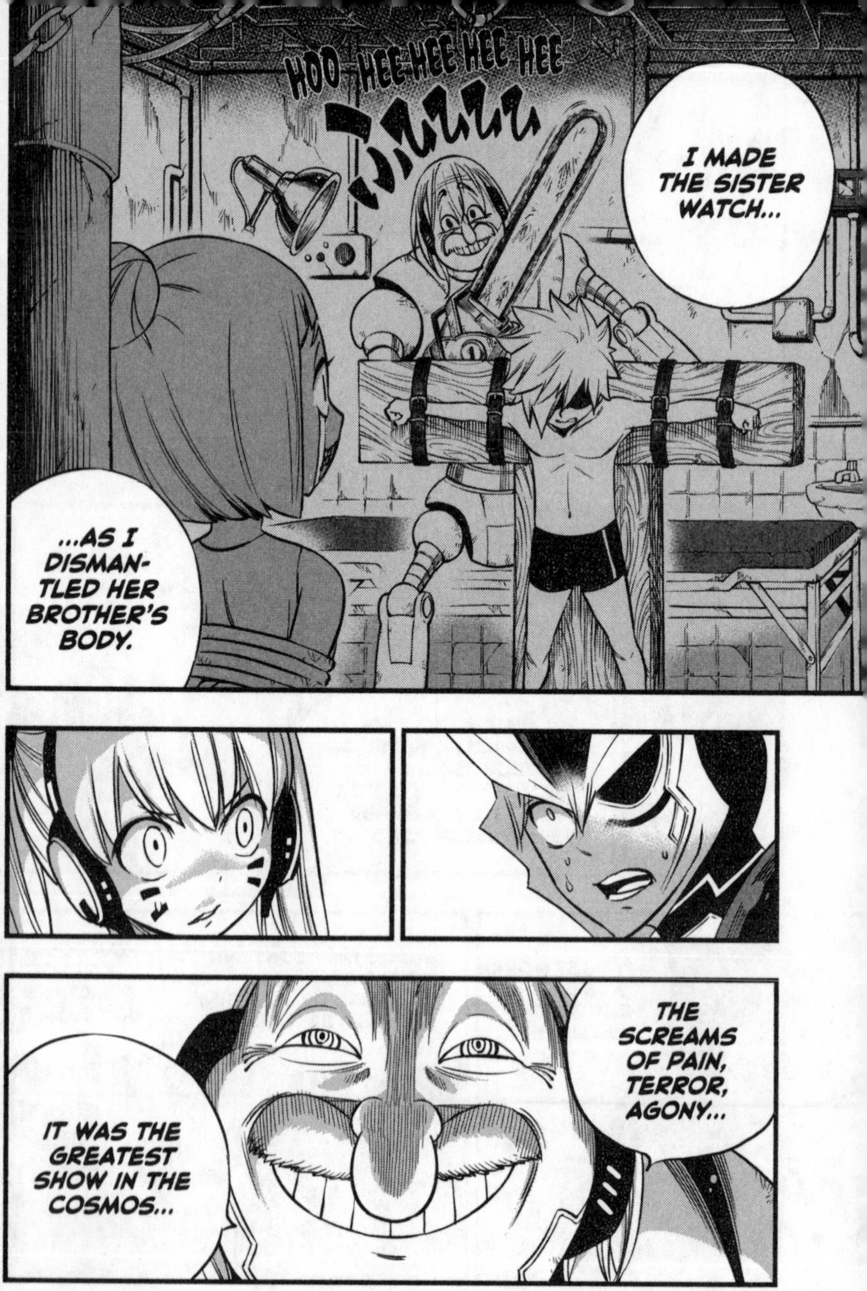
I MADE THE SISTER WATCH...
HOO HEE HEE HEE HEE
...AS I DISMAN-TLED HER BROTHER'S BODY.
THE SCREAMS OF PAIN, TERROR, AGONY...
IT WAS THE GREATEST SHOW IN THE COSMOS...

EDENS ZERO

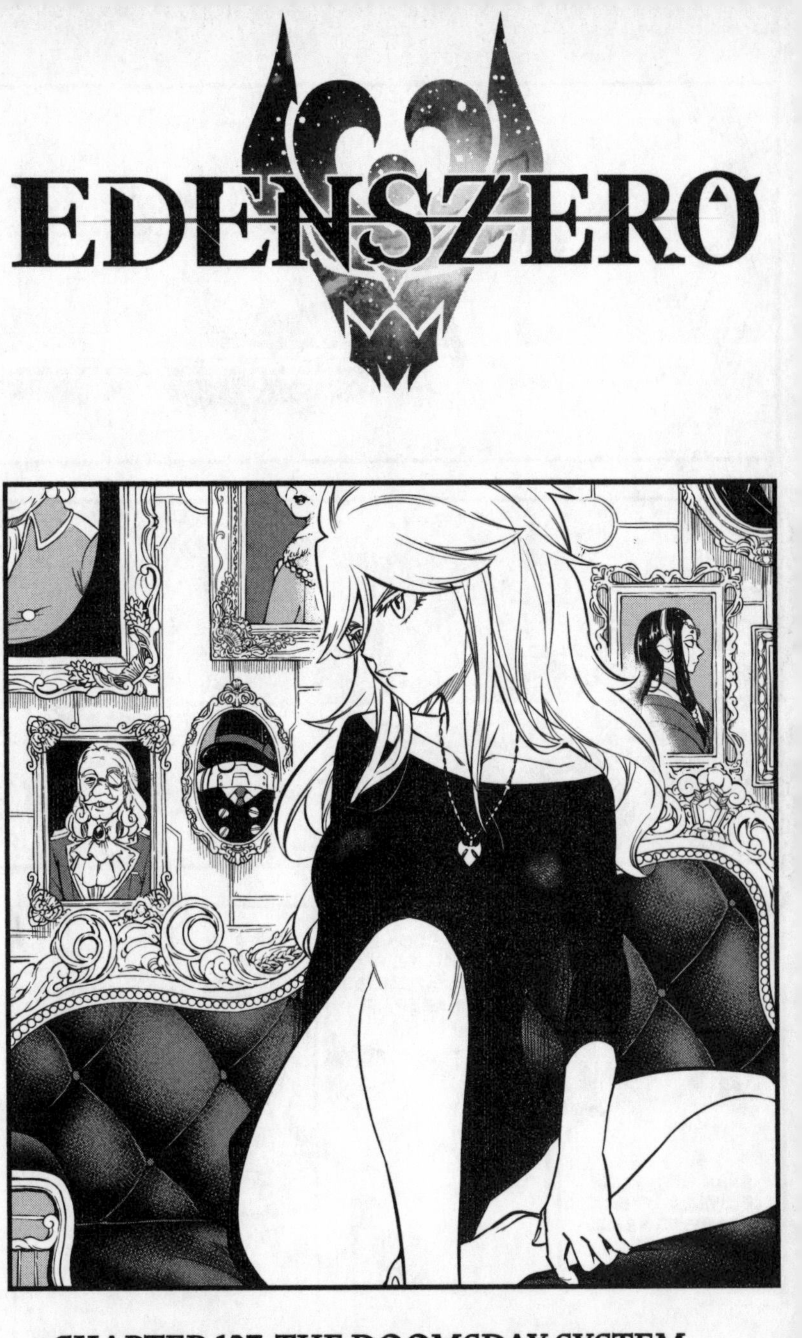

CHAPTER 127: THE DOOMSDAY SYSTEM

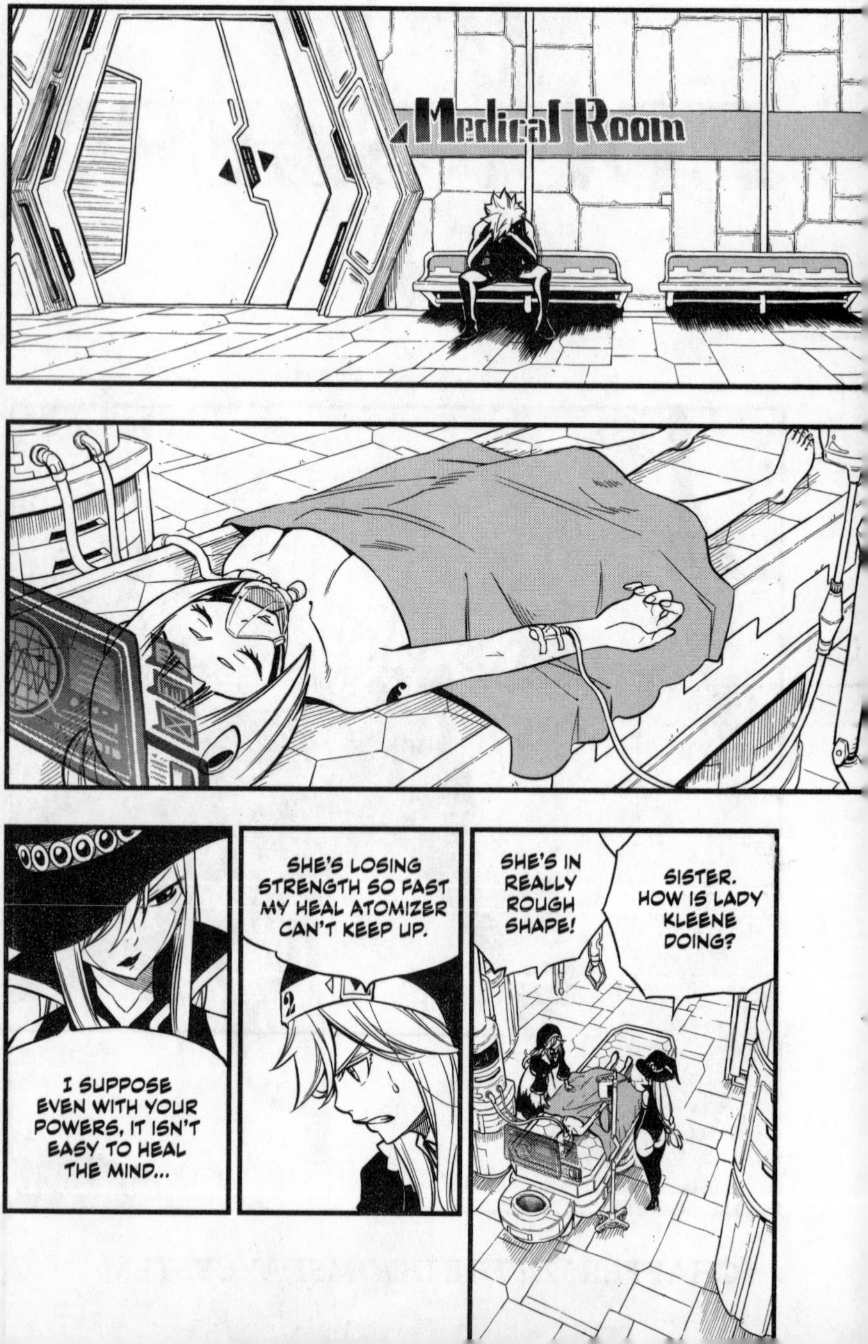
Medical Room
SISTER. HOW IS LADY KLEENE DOING?
SHE'S IN REALLY ROUGH SHAPE!
SHE'S LOSING STRENGTH SO FAST MY HEAL ATOMIZER CAN'T KEEP UP.
I SUPPOSE EVEN WITH YOUR POWERS, IT ISN'T EASY TO HEAL THE MIND...

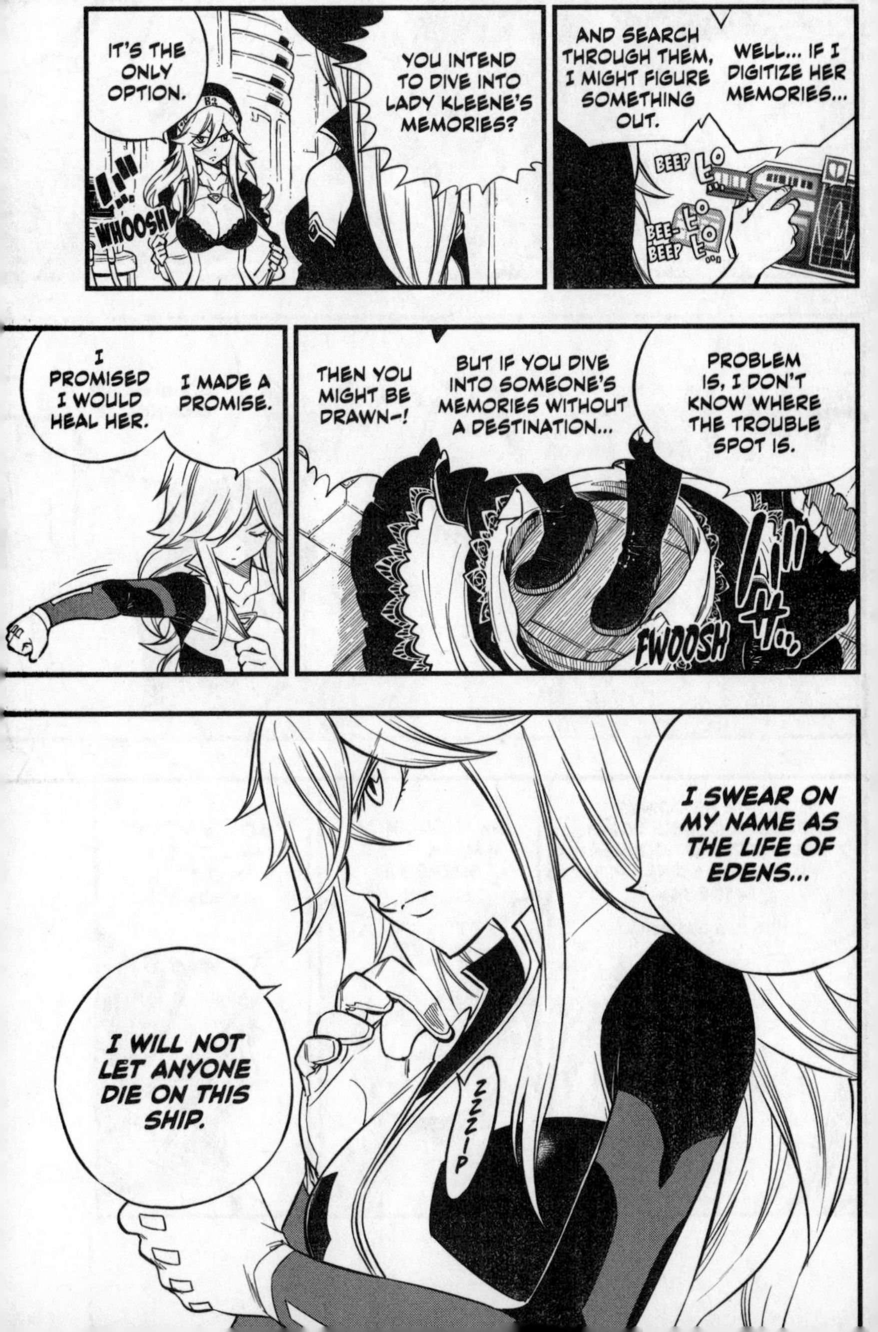
WELL... IF I DIGITIZE HER MEMORIES...
AND SEARCH THROUGH THEM, I MIGHT FIGURE SOMETHING OUT.
BEEP
BEE-BEEP
YOU INTEND TO DIVE INTO LADY KLEENE'S MEMORIES?
IT'S THE ONLY OPTION.
WHOOSH
PROBLEM IS, I DON'T KNOW WHERE THE TROUBLE SPOT IS.
BUT IF YOU DIVE INTO SOMEONE'S MEMORIES WITHOUT A DESTINATION...
THEN YOU MIGHT BE DRAWN—!
FWOOSH
I MADE A PROMISE.
I PROMISED I WOULD HEAL HER.
I SWEAR ON MY NAME AS THE LIFE OF EDENS...
I WILL NOT LET ANYONE DIE ON THIS SHIP.
ZZZIP

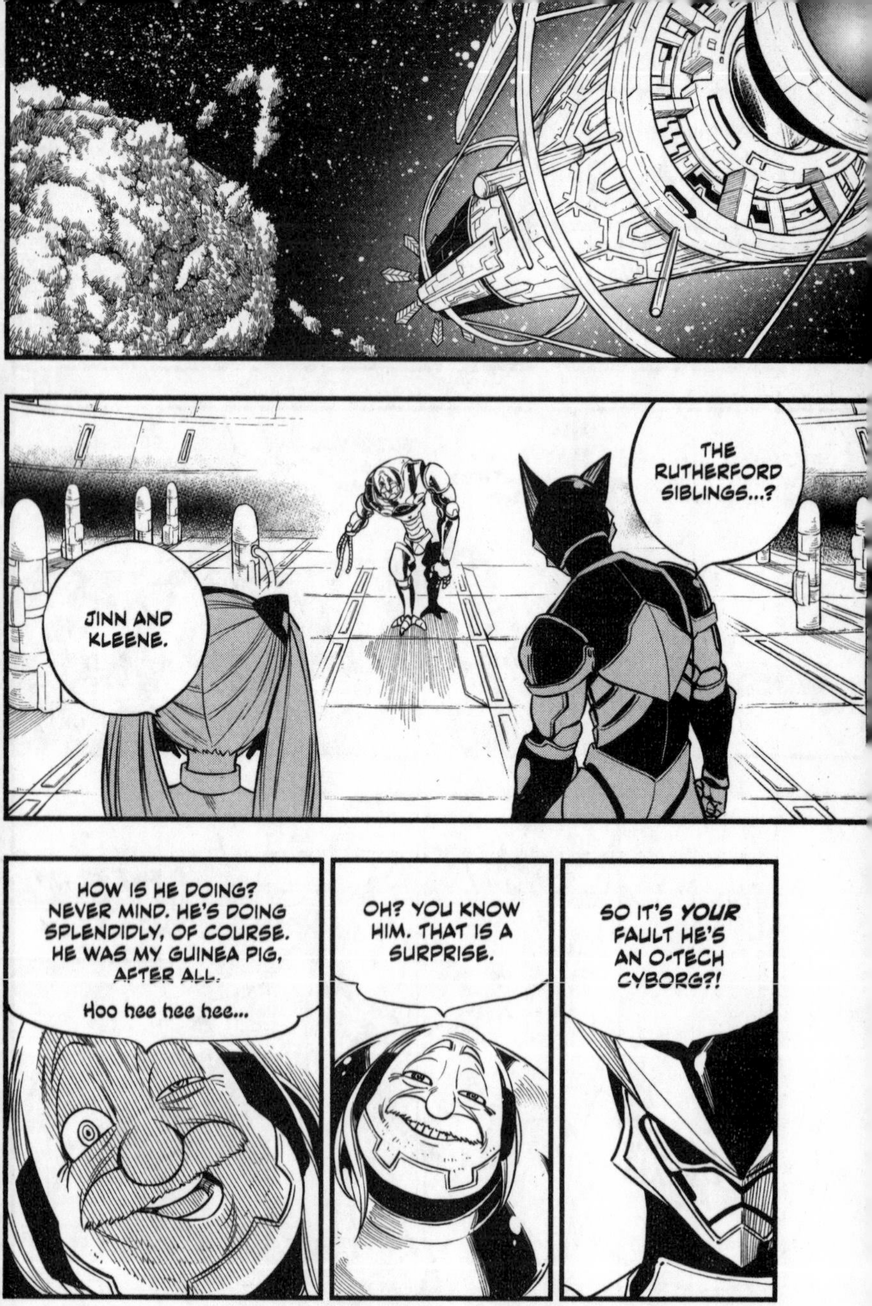
THE RUTHERFORD SIBLINGS...?
JINN AND KLEENE.
SO IT'S *YOUR* FAULT HE'S AN O-TECH CYBORG?!
OH? YOU KNOW HIM. THAT IS A SURPRISE.
HOW IS HE DOING? NEVER MIND. HE'S DOING SPLENDIDLY, OF COURSE. HE WAS MY GUINEA PIG, AFTER ALL.
Hoo hee hee hee...

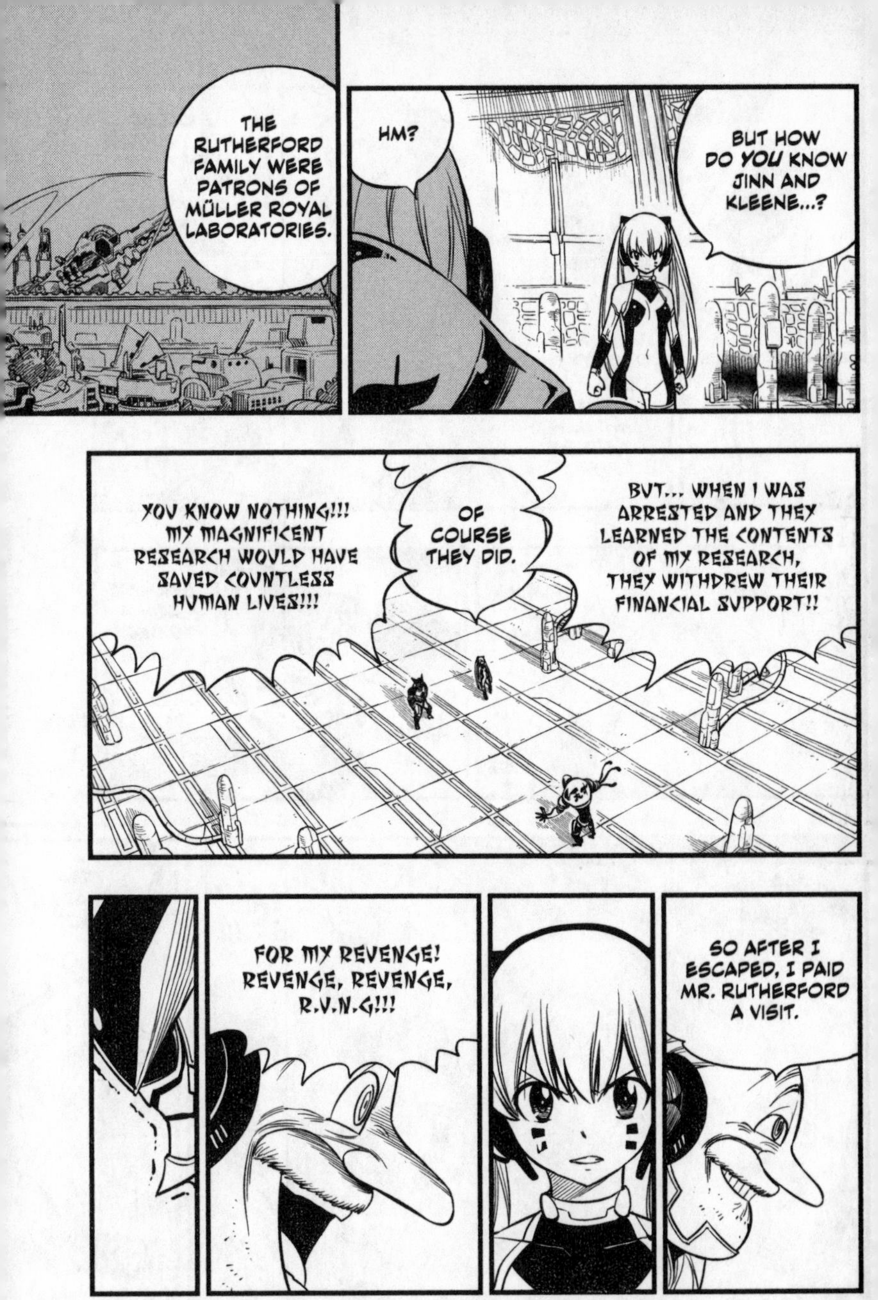

BUT HOW DO *YOU* KNOW JINN AND KLEENE...?
HM?
THE RUTHERFORD FAMILY WERE PATRONS OF MÜLLER ROYAL LABORATORIES.
BUT... WHEN I WAS ARRESTED AND THEY LEARNED THE CONTENTS OF MY RESEARCH, THEY WITHDREW THEIR FINANCIAL SUPPORT!!
OF COURSE THEY DID.
YOU KNOW NOTHING!!! MY MAGNIFICENT RESEARCH WOULD HAVE SAVED COUNTLESS HUMAN LIVES!!!
SO AFTER I ESCAPED, I PAID MR. RUTHERFORD A VISIT.
FOR MY REVENGE! REVENGE, REVENGE, R.V.N.G!!!

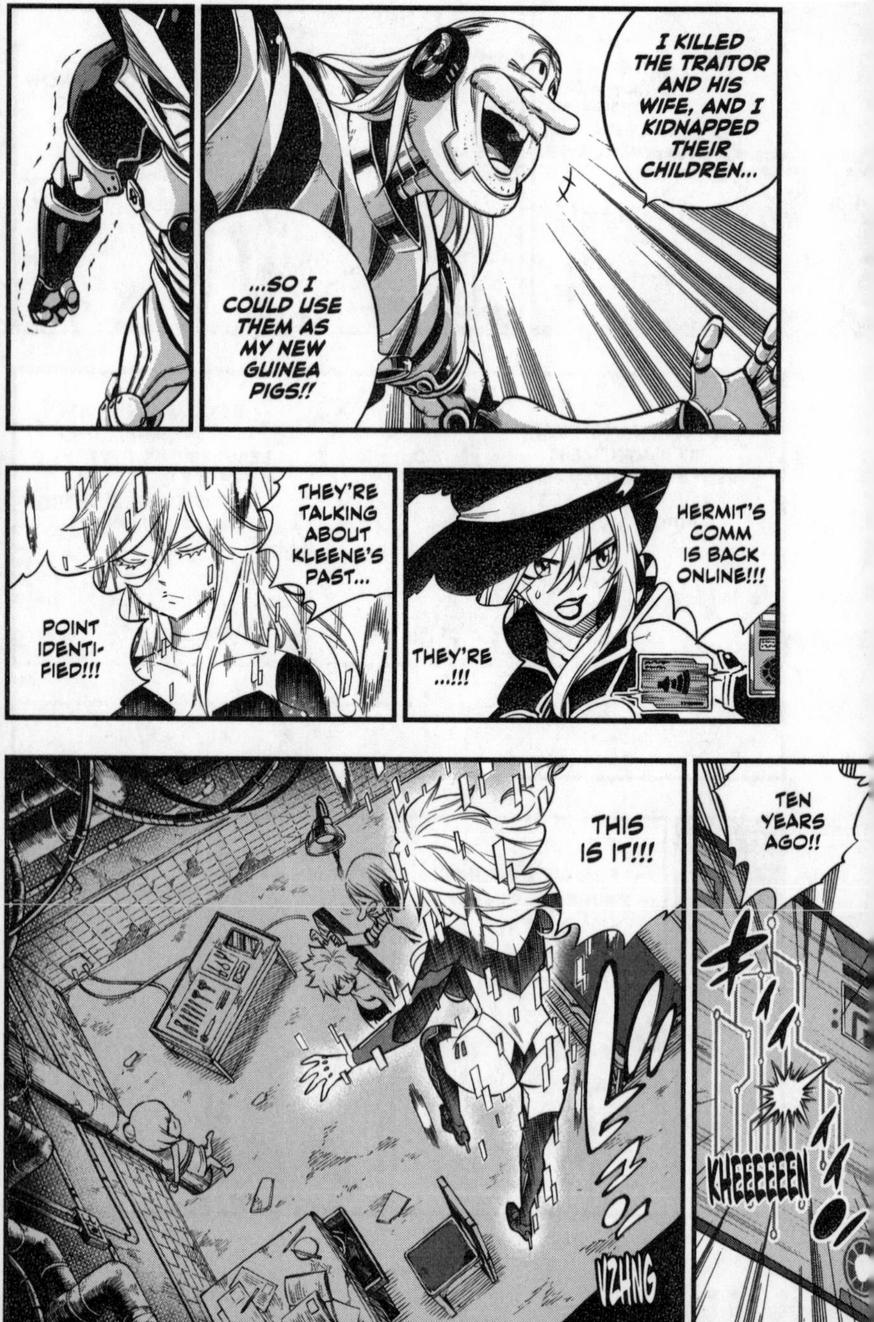
I KILLED THE TRAITOR AND HIS WIFE, AND I KIDNAPPED THEIR CHILDREN...
...SO I COULD USE THEM AS MY NEW GUINEA PIGS!!
HERMIT'S COMM IS BACK ONLINE!!!
THEY'RE ...!!!
THEY'RE TALKING ABOUT KLEENE'S PAST...
POINT IDENTI-FIED!!!
TEN YEARS AGO!!
KHEEEEEEEN
THIS IS IT!!!
VZHNG

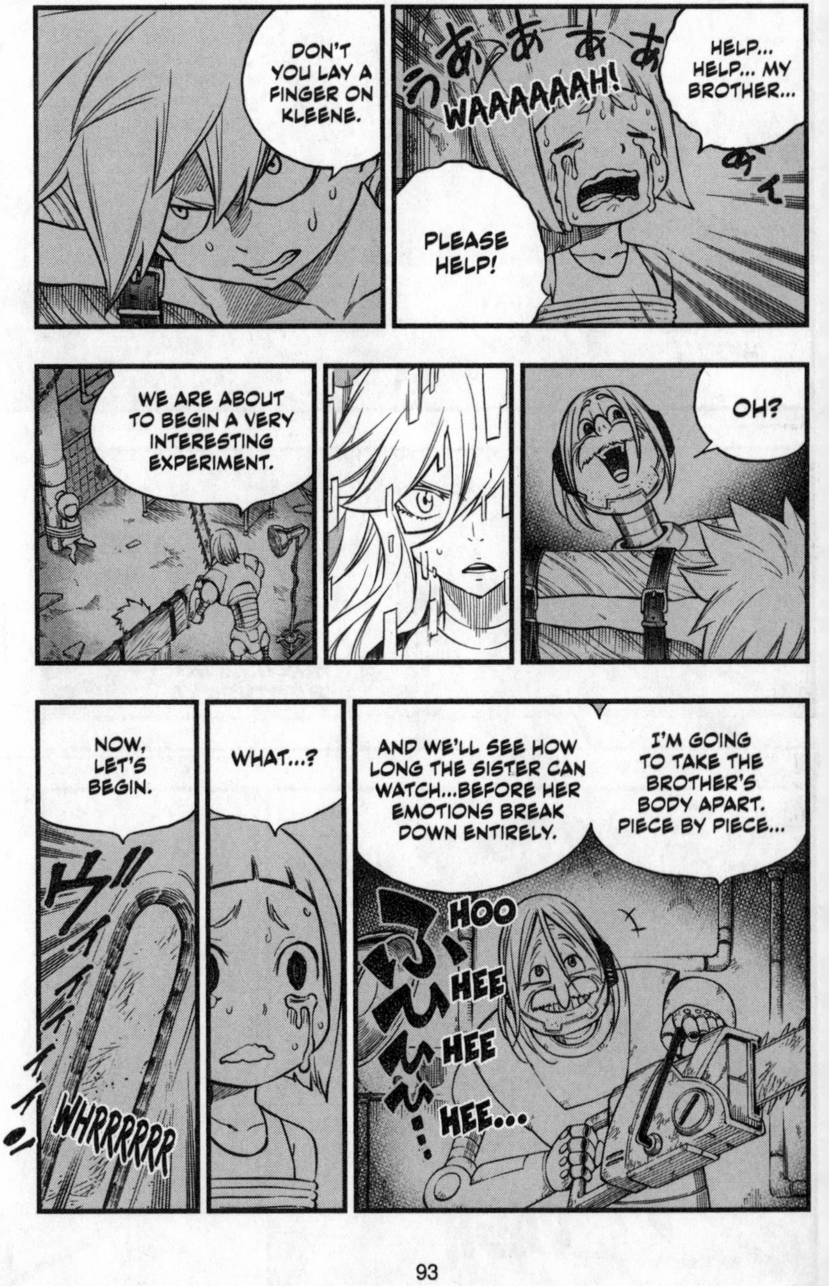
HELP... HELP... MY BROTHER...
WAAAAAAH!
PLEASE HELP!
DON'T YOU LAY A FINGER ON KLEENE.
OH?
WE ARE ABOUT TO BEGIN A VERY INTERESTING EXPERIMENT.
I'M GOING TO TAKE THE BROTHER'S BODY APART. PIECE BY PIECE...
AND WE'LL SEE HOW LONG THE SISTER CAN WATCH...BEFORE HER EMOTIONS BREAK DOWN ENTIRELY.
HOO HEE HEE HEE...
WHAT...?
NOW, LET'S BEGIN.
WHRRRRRR

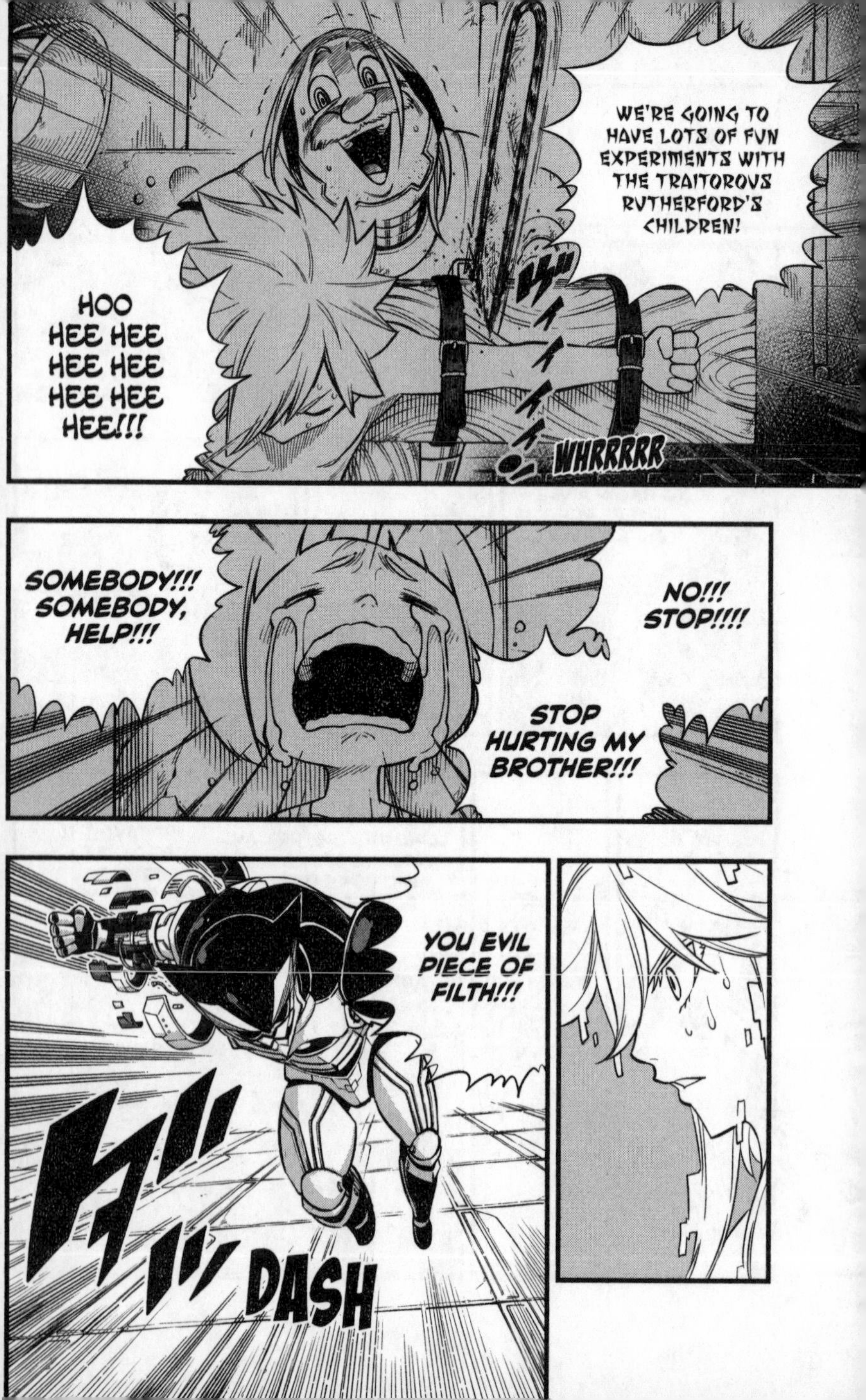
WE'RE GOING TO HAVE LOTS OF FUN EXPERIMENTS WITH THE TRAITOROUS RUTHERFORD'S CHILDREN!
WHRRRRR
HOO HEE HEE HEE HEE HEE HEE HEE!!!
NO!!! STOP!!!!
SOMEBODY!!! SOMEBODY, HELP!!!
STOP HURTING MY BROTHER!!!
YOU EVIL PIECE OF FILTH!!!
DASH

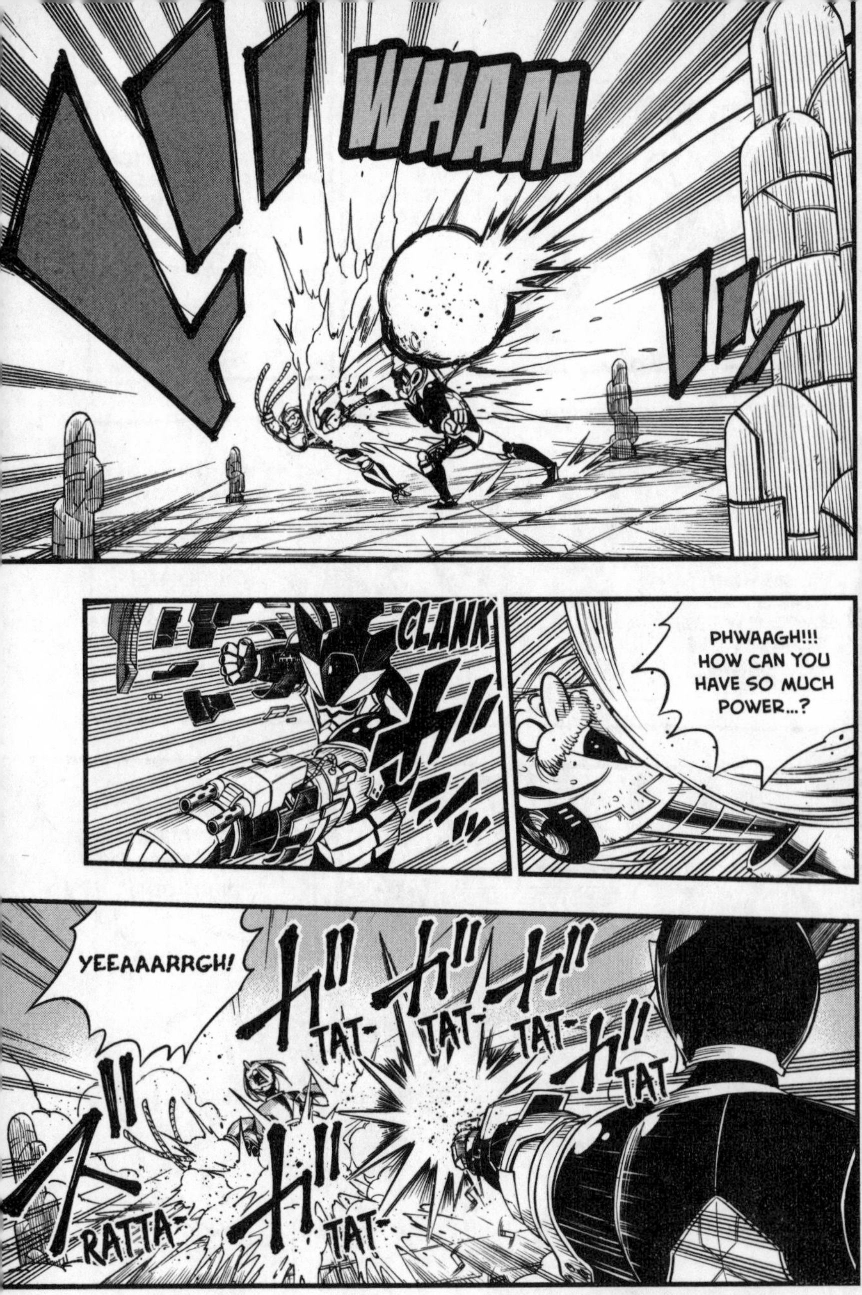
WHAM
PHWAAGH!!! HOW CAN YOU HAVE SO MUCH POWER...?
CLANK
YEEAAAARRGH!
TAT- TAT- TAT- TAT
RATTA- TAT

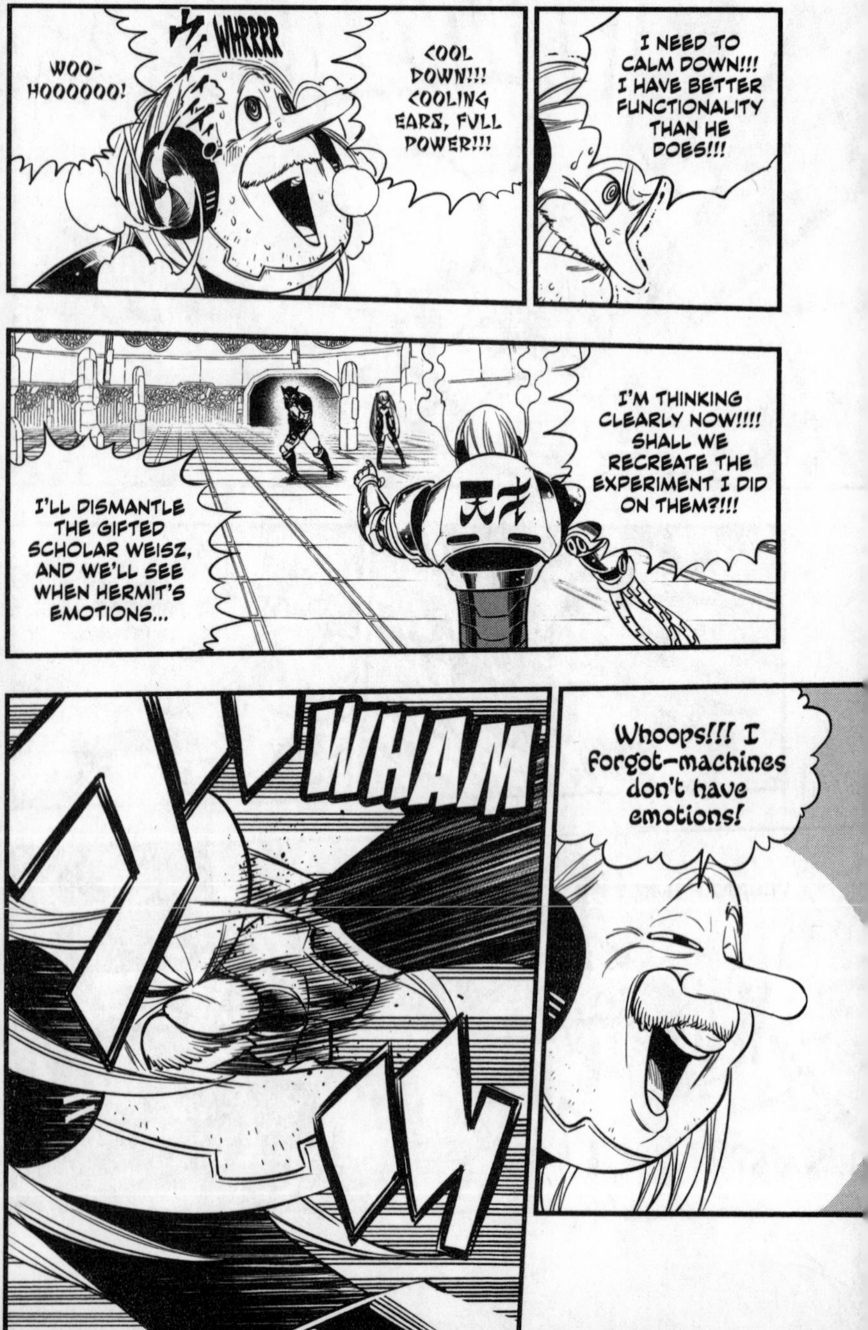
I NEED TO CALM DOWN!!! I HAVE BETTER FUNCTIONALITY THAN HE DOES!!!
COOL DOWN!!! COOLING EARS, FULL POWER!!!
WHRRRR
WOO-HOOOOOO!
I'M THINKING CLEARLY NOW!!!! SHALL WE RECREATE THE EXPERIMENT I DID ON THEM?!!!
I'LL DISMANTLE THE GIFTED SCHOLAR WEISZ, AND WE'LL SEE WHEN HERMIT'S EMOTIONS...
Whoops!!! I forgot—machines don't have emotions!
WHAM

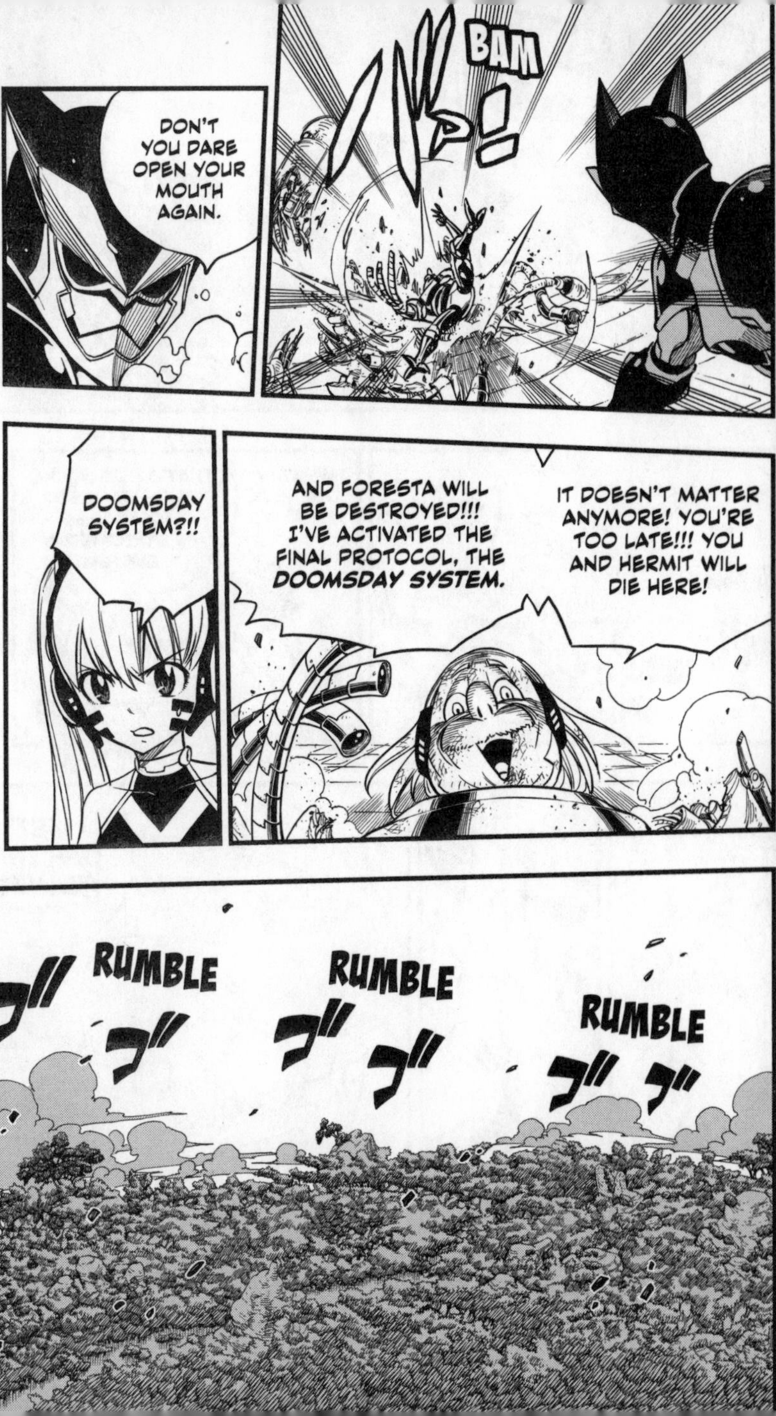
BAM
DON'T YOU DARE OPEN YOUR MOUTH AGAIN.
IT DOESN'T MATTER ANYMORE! YOU'RE TOO LATE!!! YOU AND HERMIT WILL DIE HERE!
AND FORESTA WILL BE DESTROYED!!! I'VE ACTIVATED THE FINAL PROTOCOL, THE *DOOMSDAY SYSTEM.*
DOOMSDAY SYSTEM?!!
RUMBLE
RUMBLE
RUMBLE

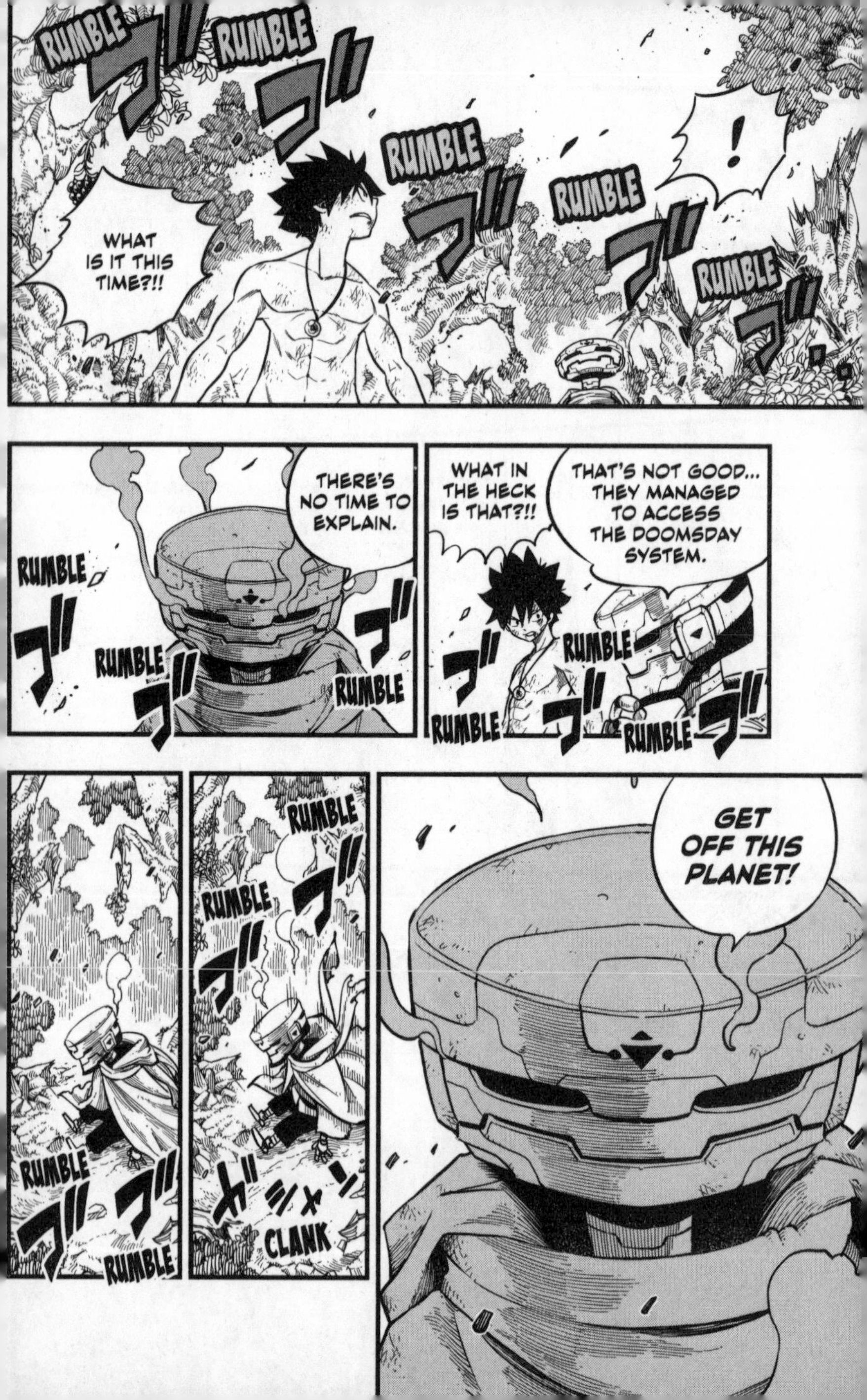
RUMBLE
RUMBLE
RUMBLE
RUMBLE
RUMBLE
!
WHAT IS IT THIS TIME?!!
THAT'S NOT GOOD... THEY MANAGED TO ACCESS THE DOOMSDAY SYSTEM.
WHAT IN THE HECK IS THAT?!!
RUMBLE
RUMBLE
RUMBLE
THERE'S NO TIME TO EXPLAIN.
RUMBLE
RUMBLE
RUMBLE
GET OFF THIS PLANET!
RUMBLE
RUMBLE
CLANK
RUMBLE
RUMBLE

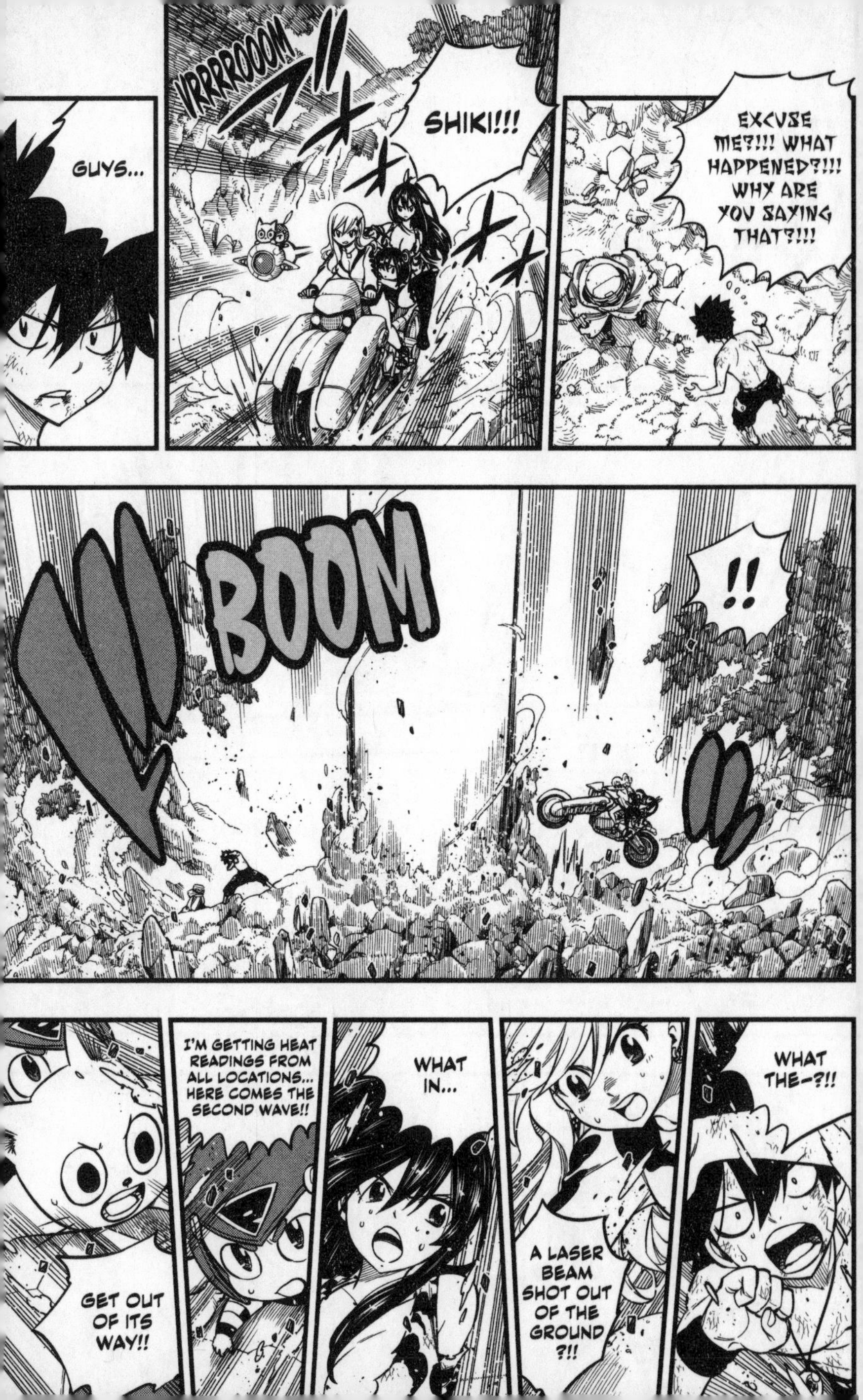
EXCUSE ME?!!! WHAT HAPPENED?!!! WHY ARE YOU SAYING THAT?!!!
SHIKI!!!
VRRRROOOM
GUYS...
!!
BOOM
WHAT THE-?!!
A LASER BEAM SHOT OUT OF THE GROUND?!!
WHAT IN...
I'M GETTING HEAT READINGS FROM ALL LOCATIONS... HERE COMES THE SECOND WAVE!!
GET OUT OF ITS WAY!!

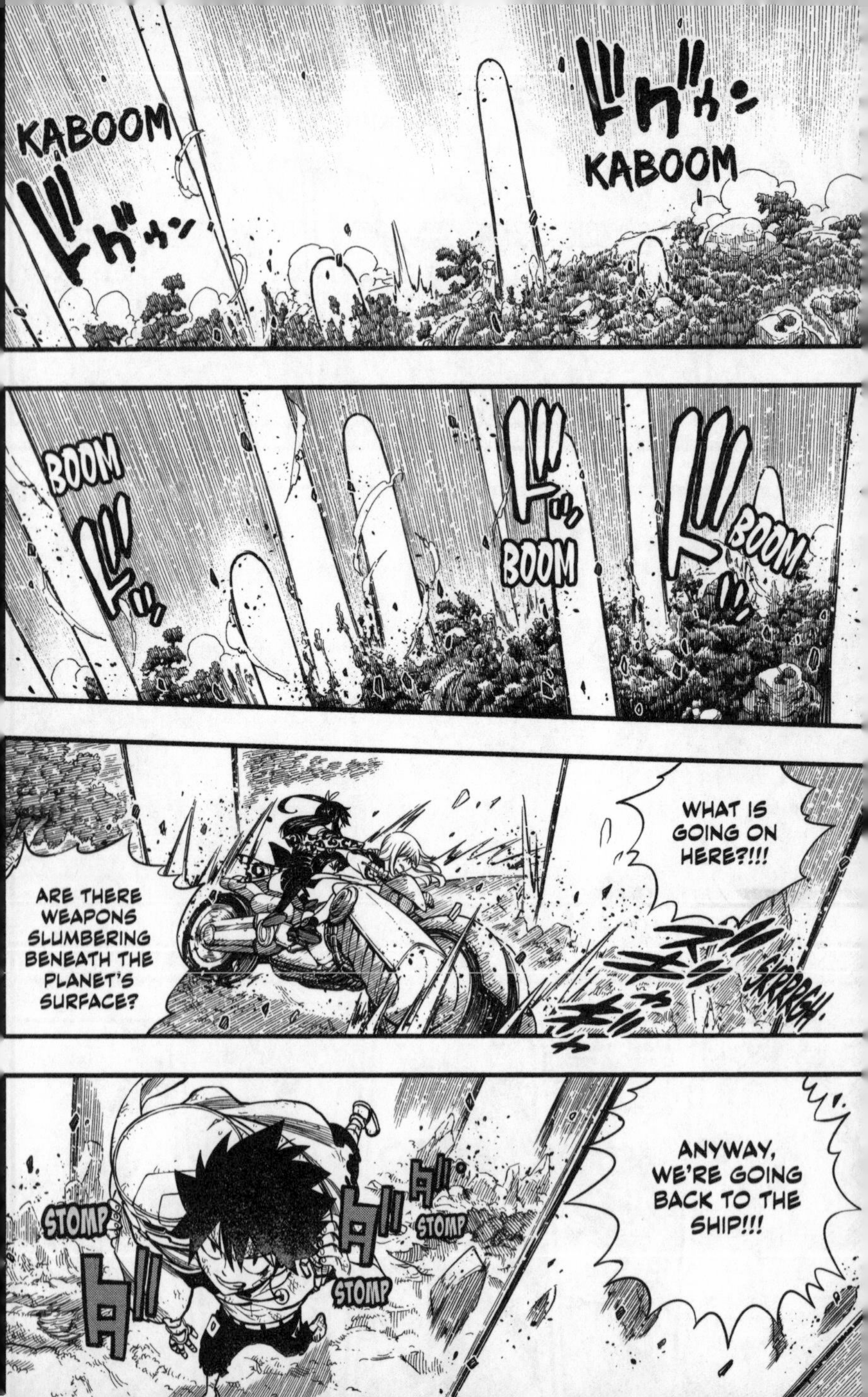
KABOOM
KABOOM
BOOM
BOOM
BOOM
WHAT IS GOING ON HERE?!!!
SKRRRGH
ARE THERE WEAPONS SLUMBERING BENEATH THE PLANET'S SURFACE?
ANYWAY, WE'RE GOING BACK TO THE SHIP!!!
STOMP
STOMP
STOMP

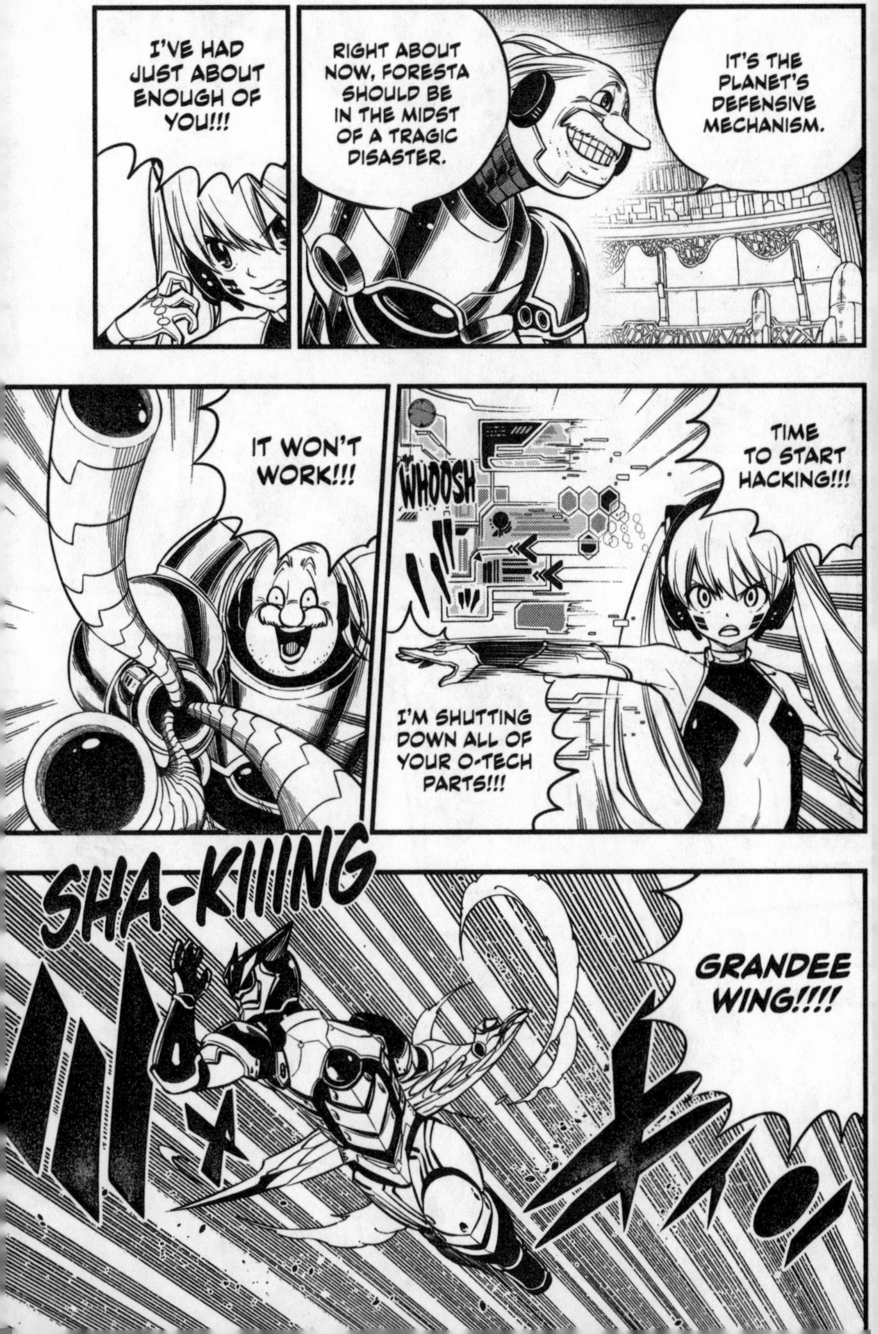
IT'S THE PLANET'S DEFENSIVE MECHANISM.
RIGHT ABOUT NOW, FORESTA SHOULD BE IN THE MIDST OF A TRAGIC DISASTER.
I'VE HAD JUST ABOUT ENOUGH OF YOU!!!
TIME TO START HACKING!!!
WHOOSH
I'M SHUTTING DOWN ALL OF YOUR O-TECH PARTS!!!
IT WON'T WORK!!!
GRANDEE WING!!!!
SHA-KIIING

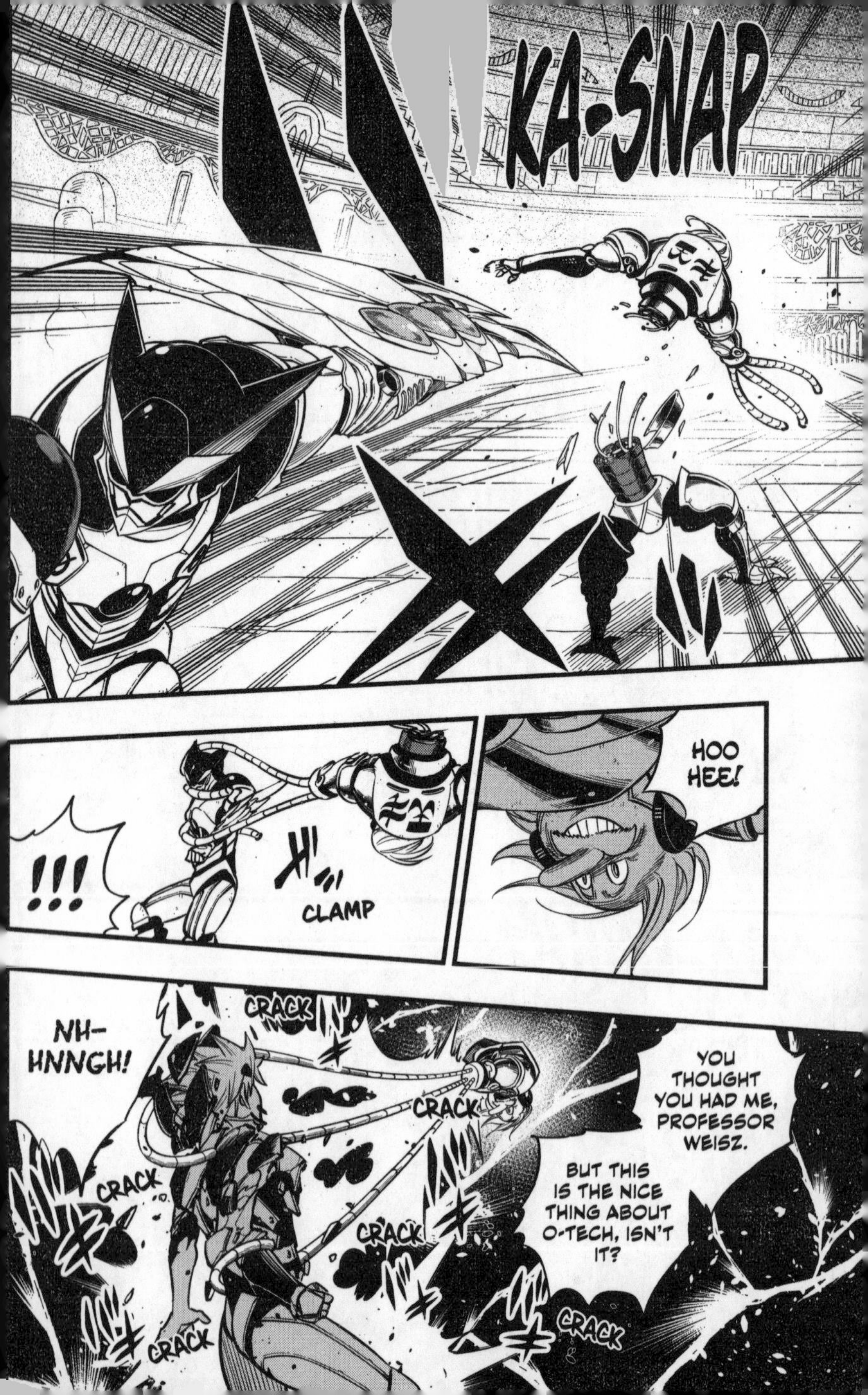
KA-SNAP
HOO HEE!
CLAMP
!!!
YOU THOUGHT YOU HAD ME, PROFESSOR WEISZ.
BUT THIS IS THE NICE THING ABOUT O-TECH, ISN'T IT?
CRACK
CRACK
CRACK
CRACK
CRACK
CRACK
NH-HNNGH!

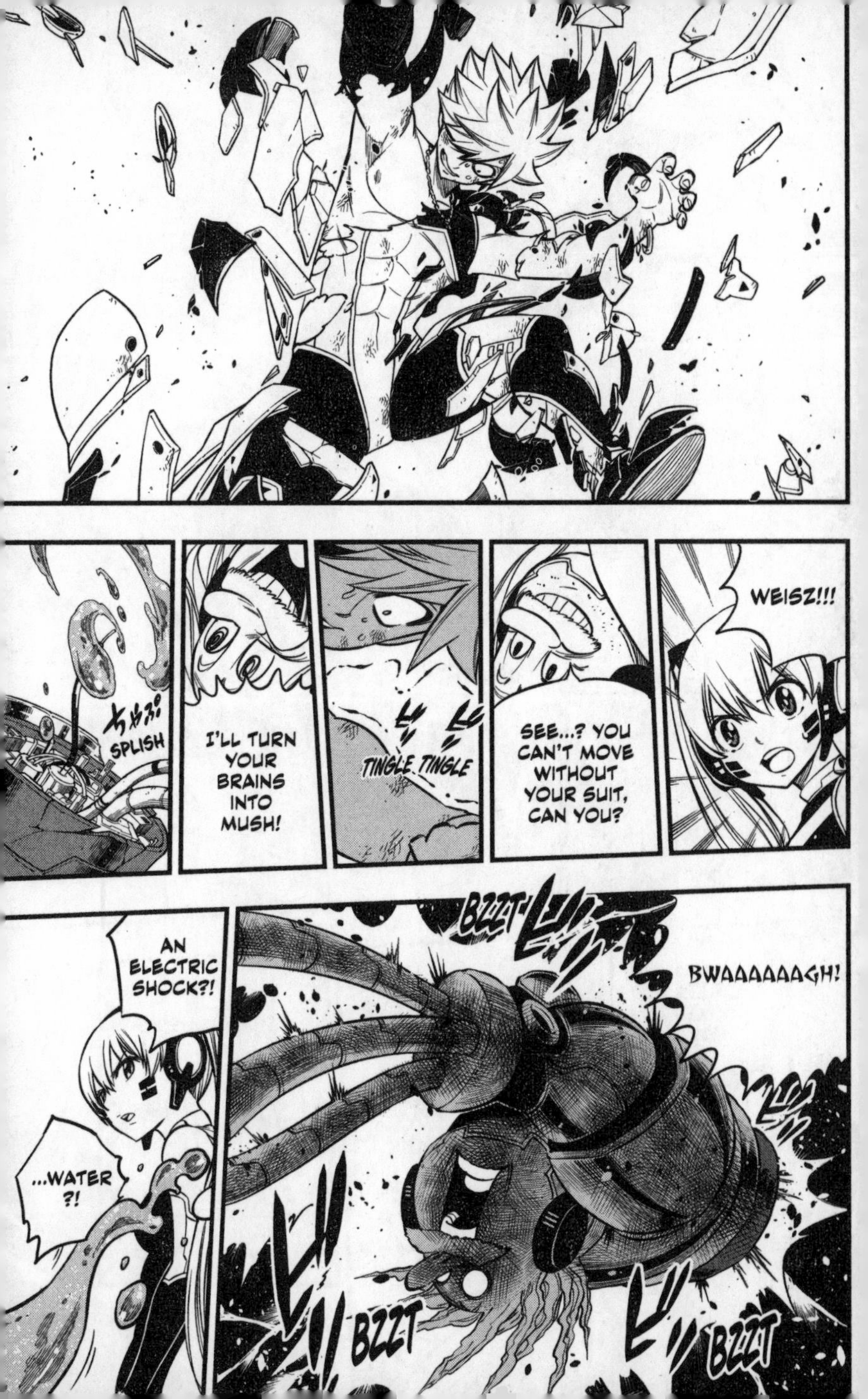

WEISZ!!!
SEE...? YOU CAN'T MOVE WITHOUT YOUR SUIT, CAN YOU?
TINGLE TINGLE
I'LL TURN YOUR BRAINS INTO MUSH!
SPLISH
BZZT
BWAAAAAAGH!
BZZT
BZZT
AN ELECTRIC SHOCK?!
...WATER ?!

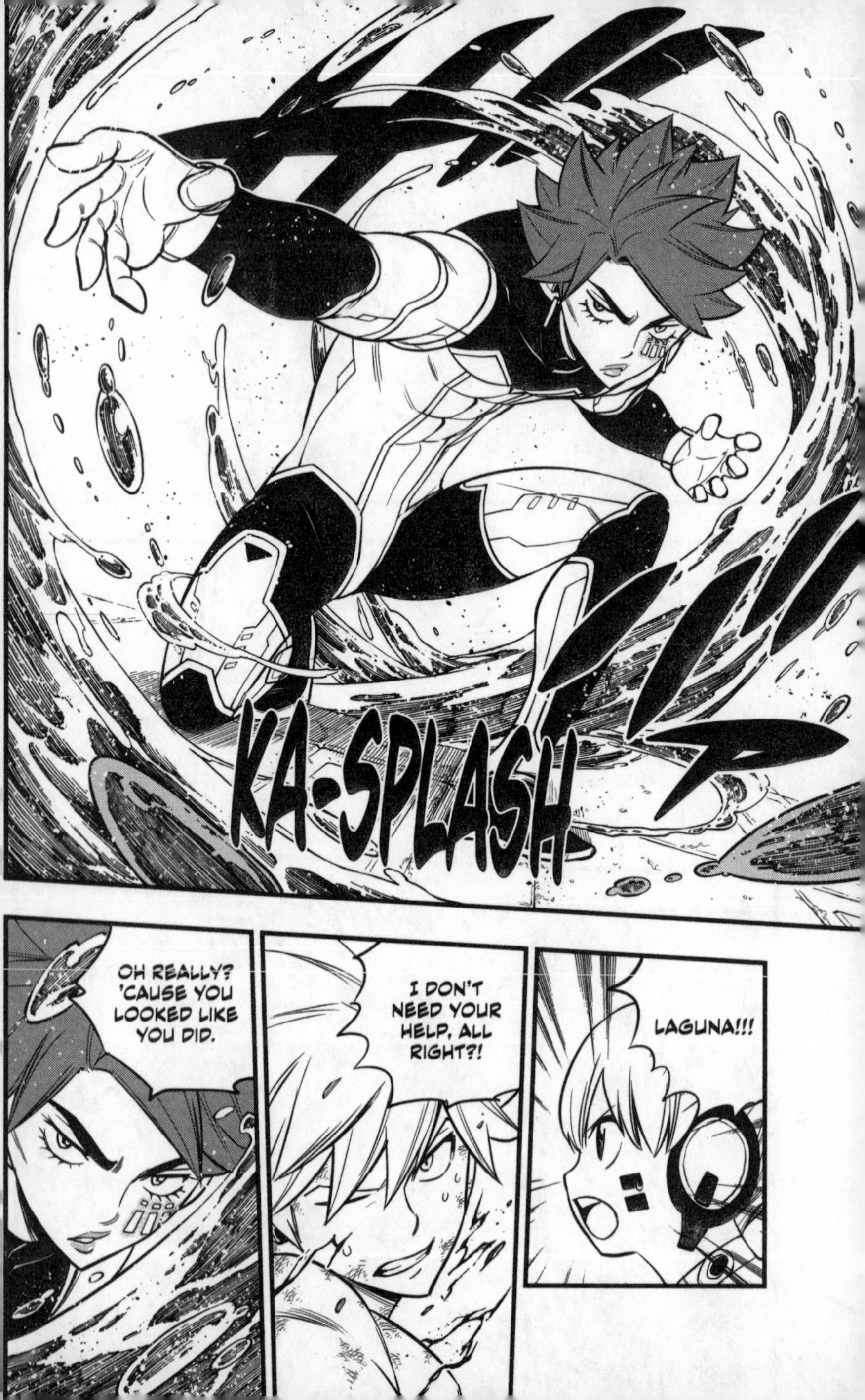
KA-SPLASH
LAGUNA!!!
I DON'T NEED YOUR HELP, ALL RIGHT?!
OH REALLY? 'CAUSE YOU LOOKED LIKE YOU DID.

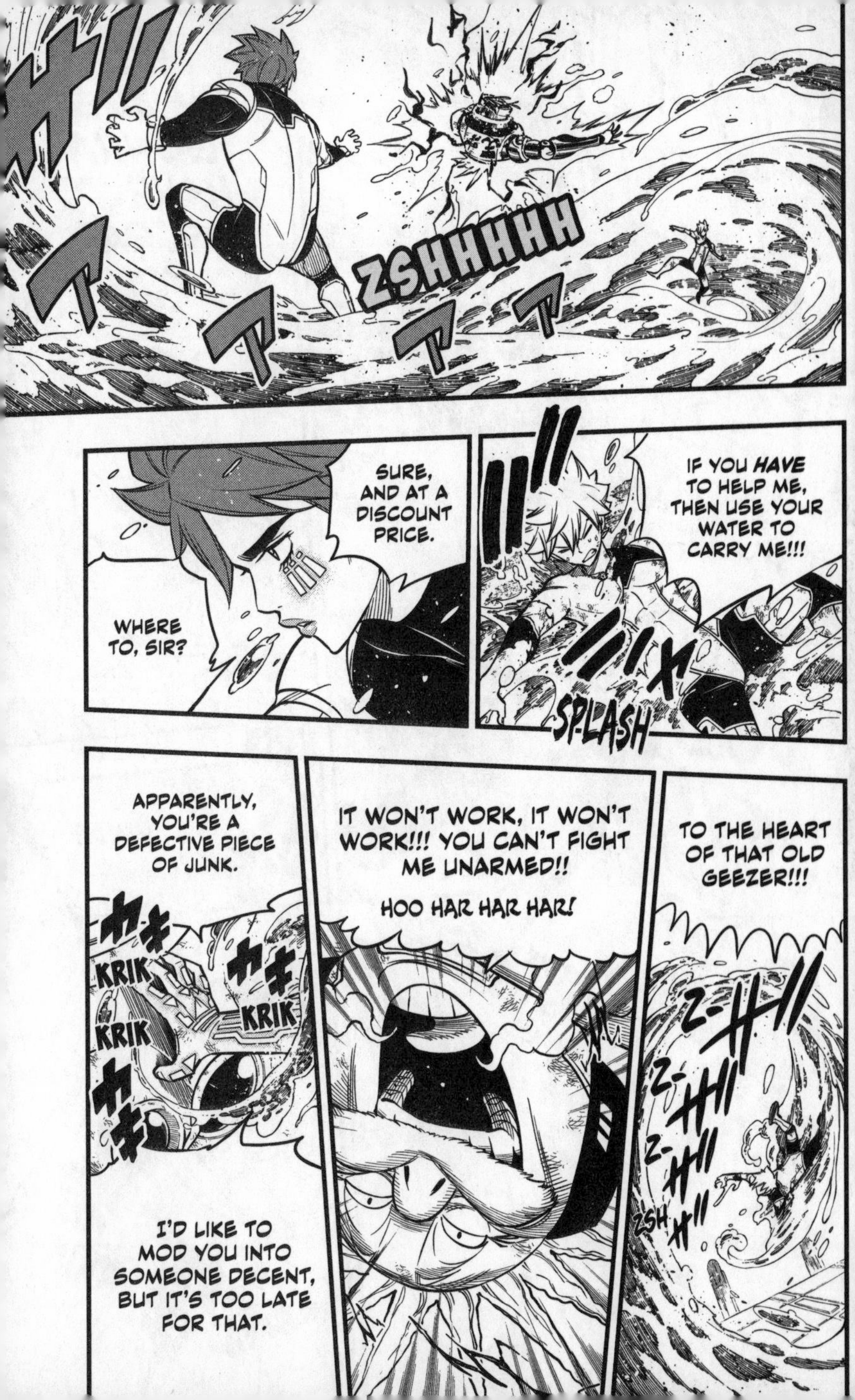
ZSHHHHHH
IF YOU *HAVE* TO HELP ME, THEN USE YOUR WATER TO CARRY ME!!!
SPLASH
SURE, AND AT A DISCOUNT PRICE.
WHERE TO, SIR?
TO THE HEART OF THAT OLD GEEZER!!!
ZSH
IT WON'T WORK, IT WON'T WORK!!! YOU CAN'T FIGHT ME UNARMED!!
HOO HAR HAR HAR!
APPARENTLY, YOU'RE A DEFECTIVE PIECE OF JUNK.
KRIK
KRIK
KRIK
I'D LIKE TO MOD YOU INTO SOMEONE DECENT, BUT IT'S TOO LATE FOR THAT.

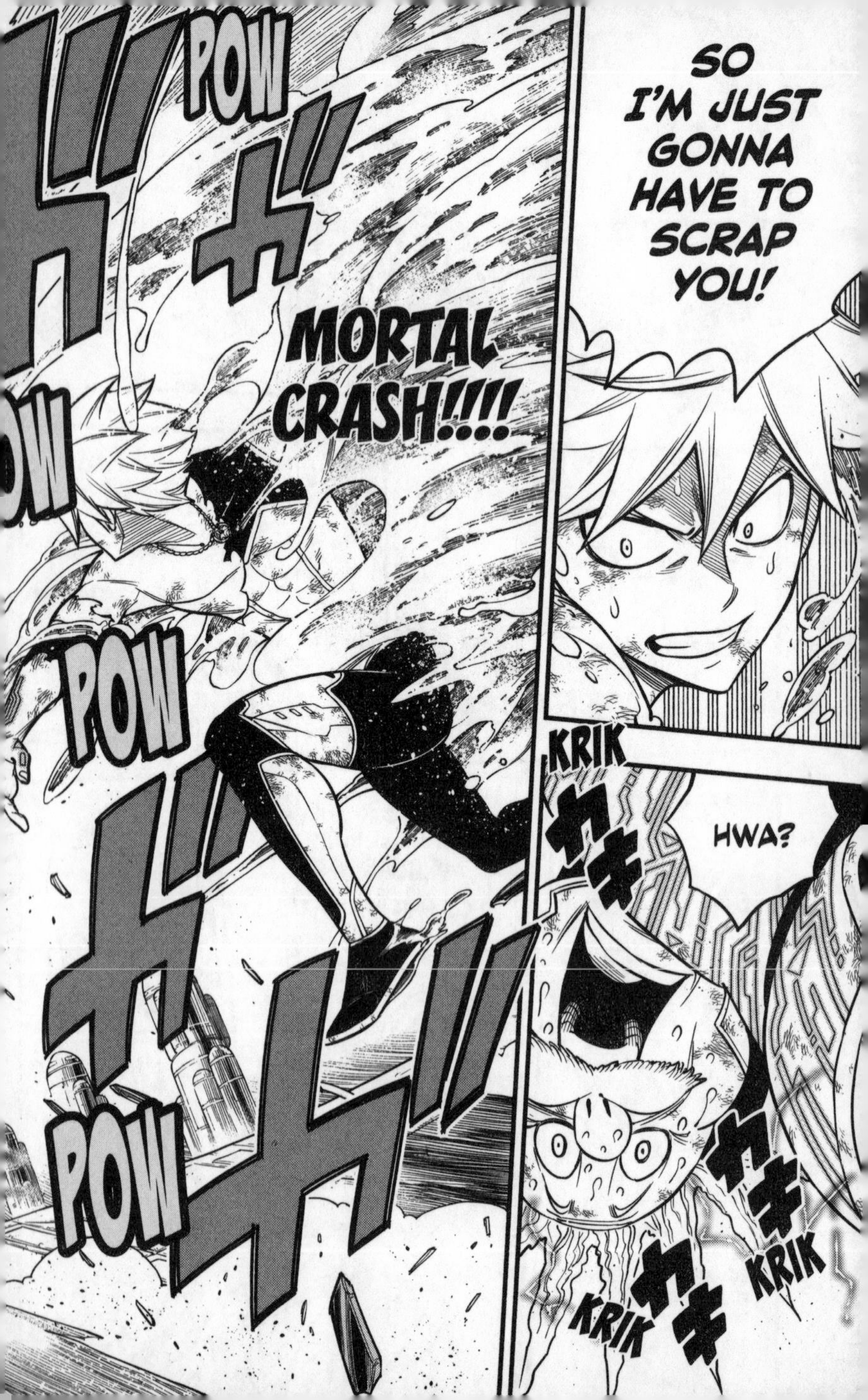
SO I'M JUST GONNA HAVE TO SCRAP YOU!
KRIK
HWA?
KRIK
KRIK
POW
MORTAL CRASH!!!!
OW
POW
POW

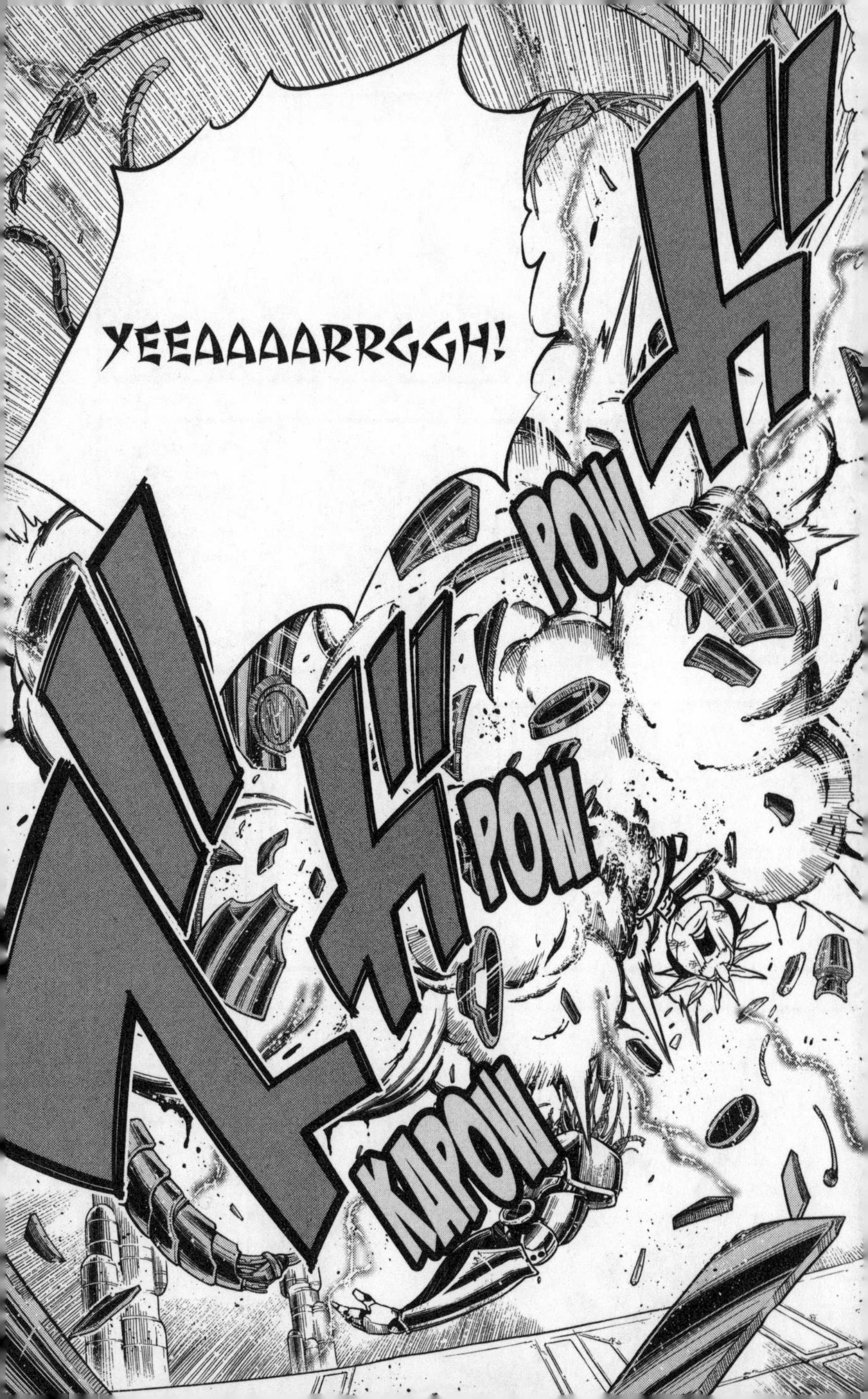
YEEAAAARRGGH!
POW
POW
KAPOW

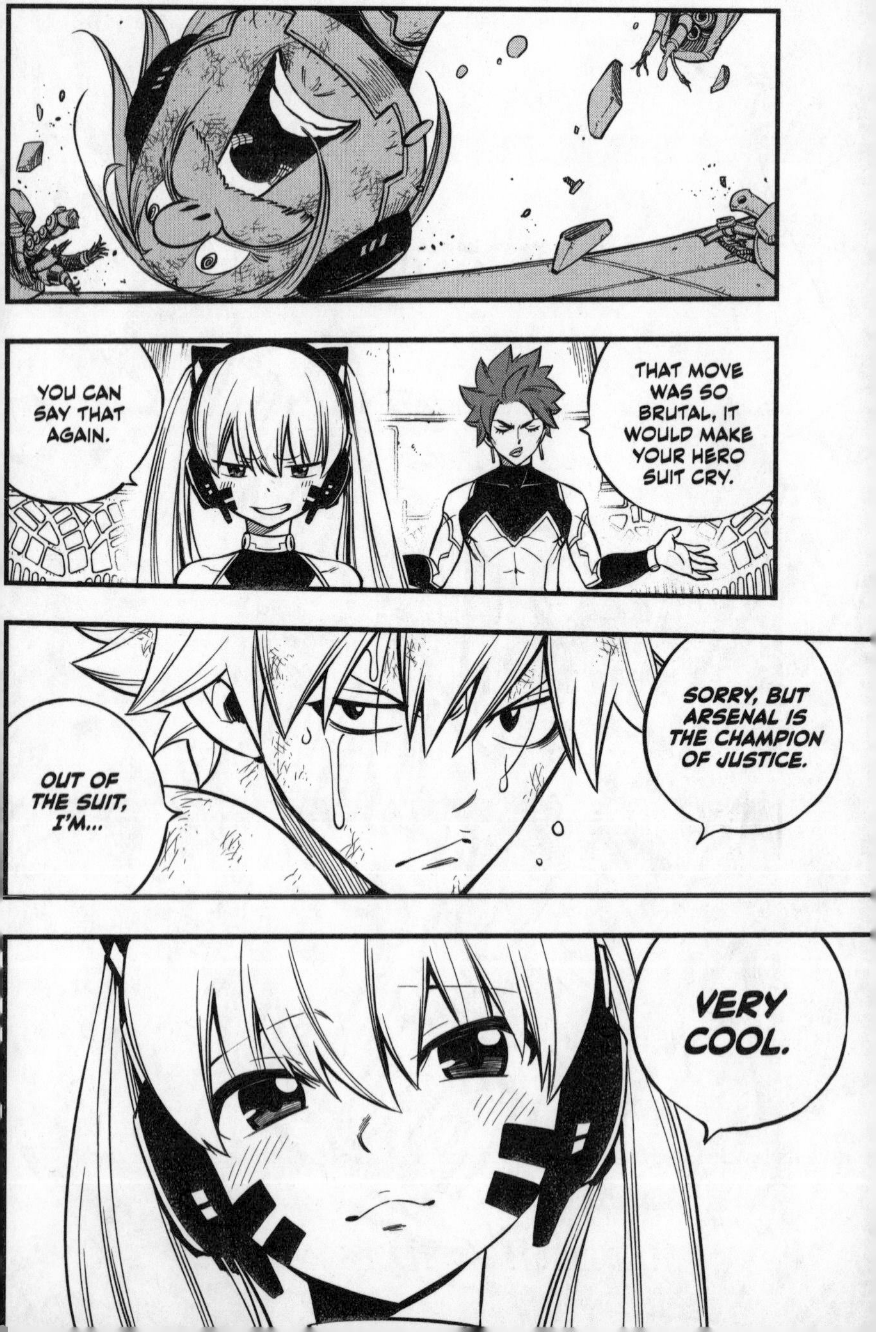
THAT MOVE WAS SO BRUTAL, IT WOULD MAKE YOUR HERO SUIT CRY.
YOU CAN SAY THAT AGAIN.
SORRY, BUT ARSENAL IS THE CHAMPION OF JUSTICE.
OUT OF THE SUIT, I'M...
VERY COOL.

EDENS ZERO

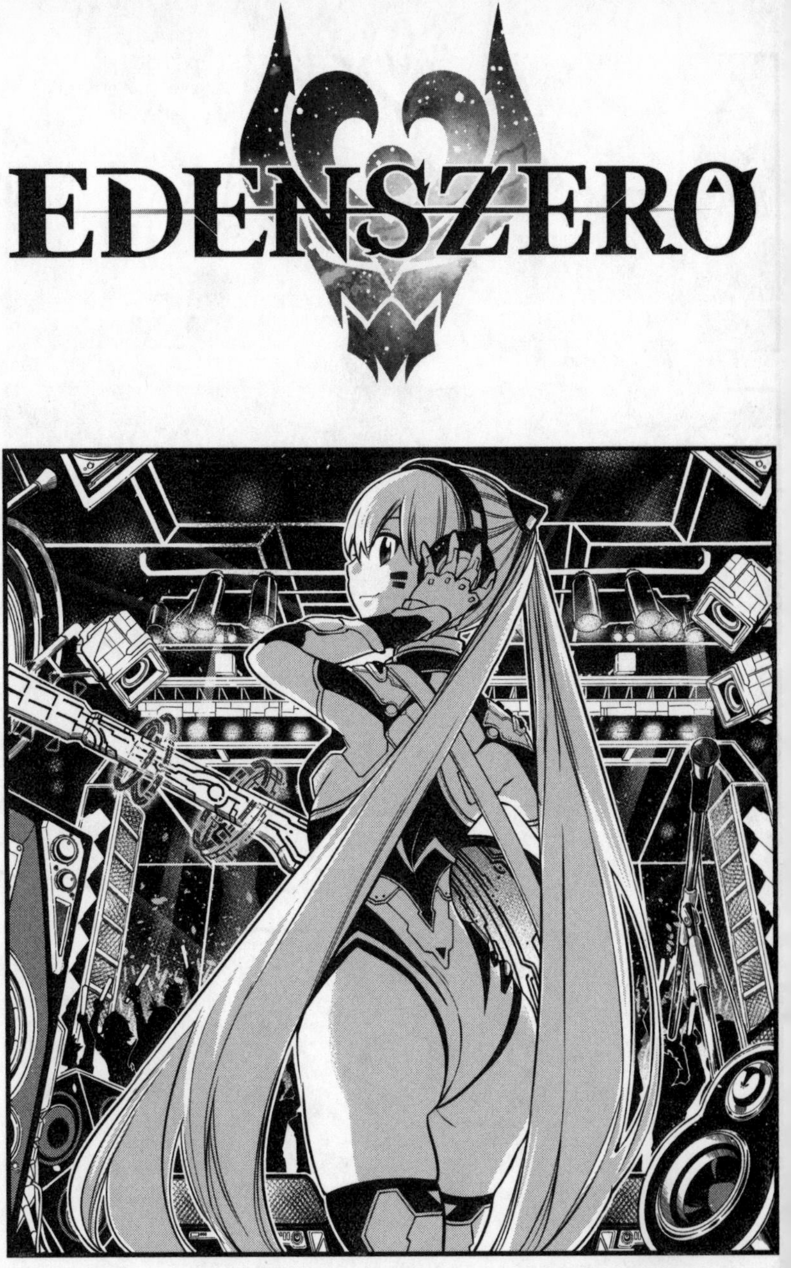

CHAPTER 128: WHAT'S IMPORTANT

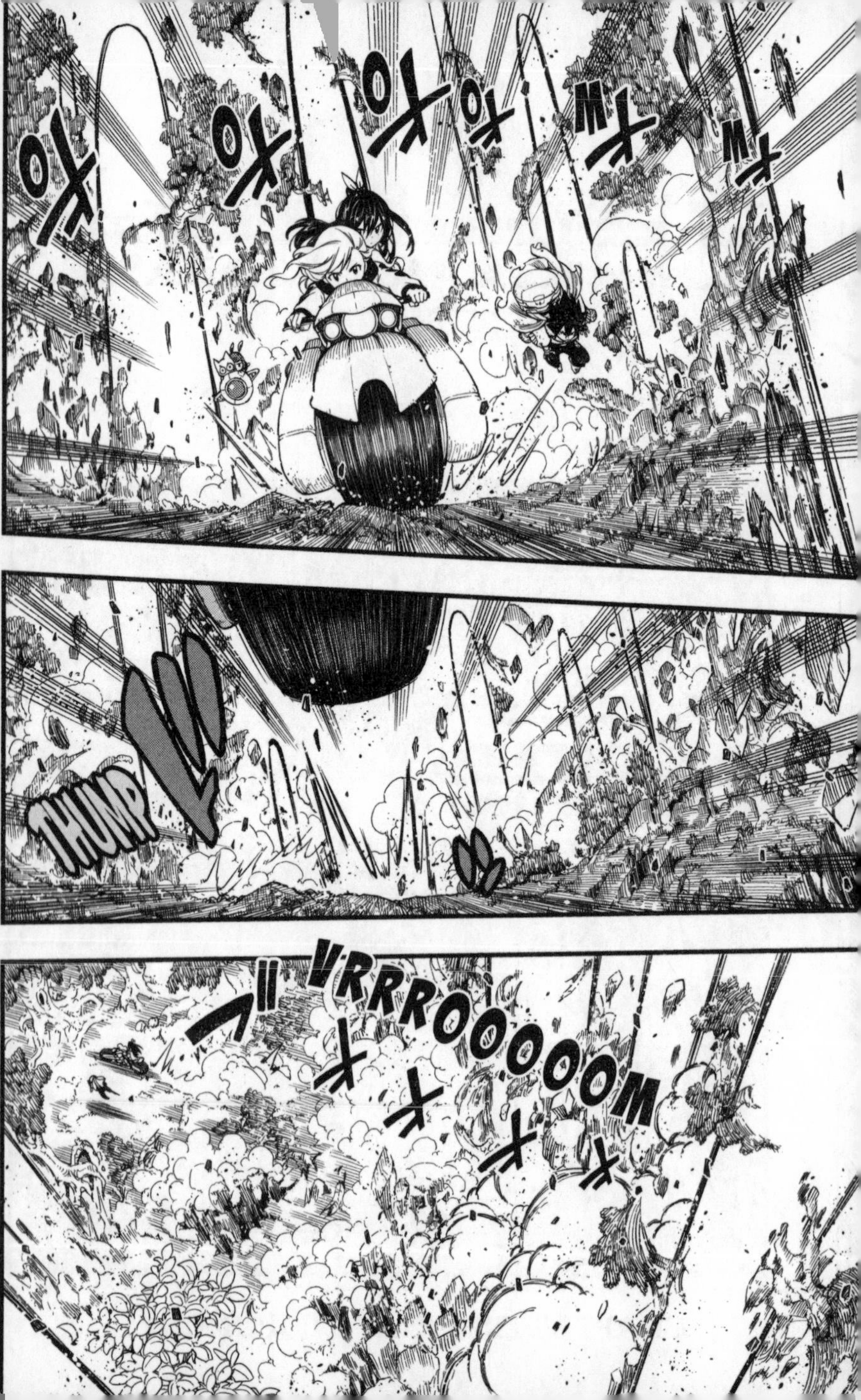
THUMP
VRRROOOOOOM

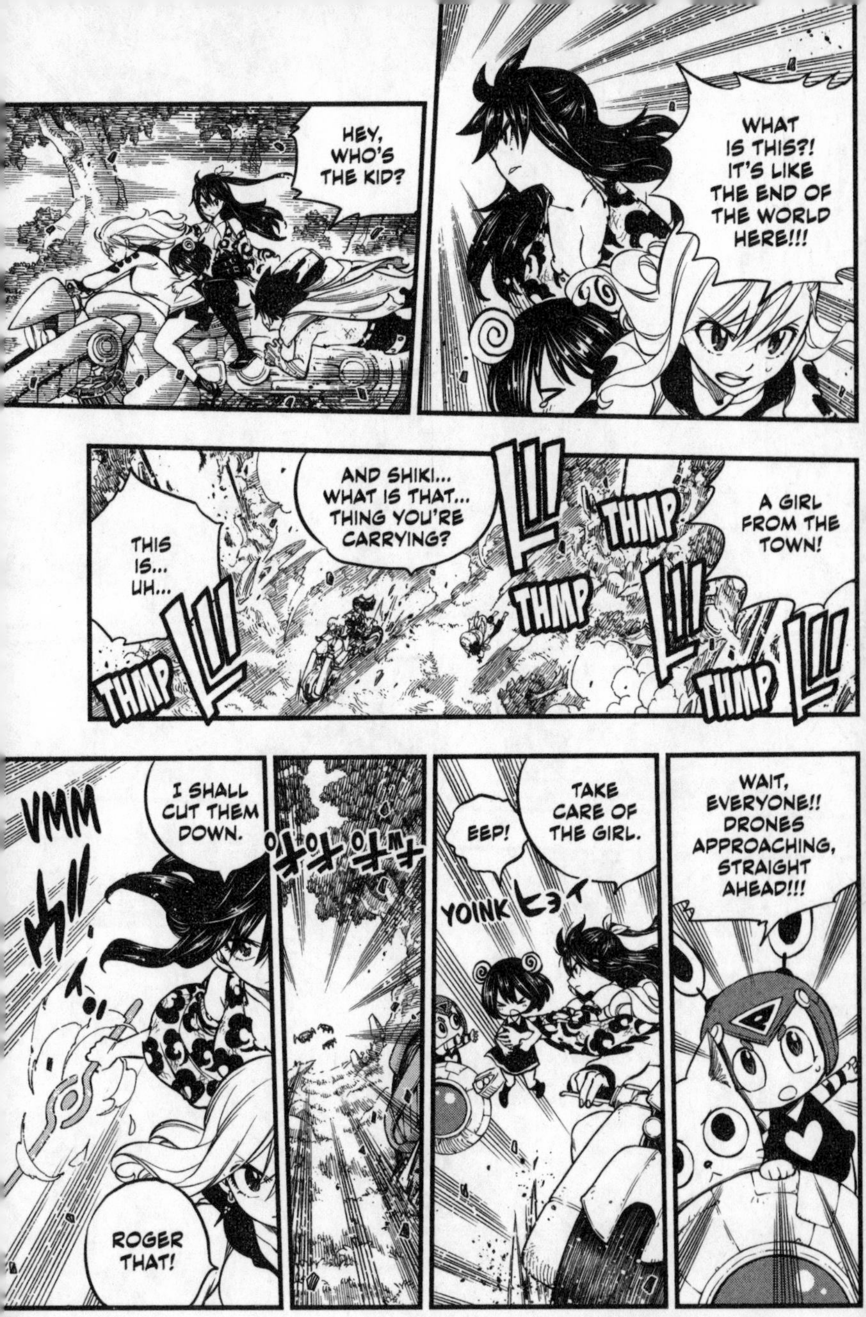
WHAT IS THIS?! IT'S LIKE THE END OF THE WORLD HERE!!!
HEY, WHO'S THE KID?
A GIRL FROM THE TOWN!
THMP
THMP
THMP
THMP
AND SHIKI... WHAT IS THAT... THING YOU'RE CARRYING?
THIS IS... UH...
WAIT, EVERYONE!! DRONES APPROACHING, STRAIGHT AHEAD!!!
TAKE CARE OF THE GIRL.
EEP!
YOINK
I SHALL CUT THEM DOWN.
VMM
ROGER THAT!

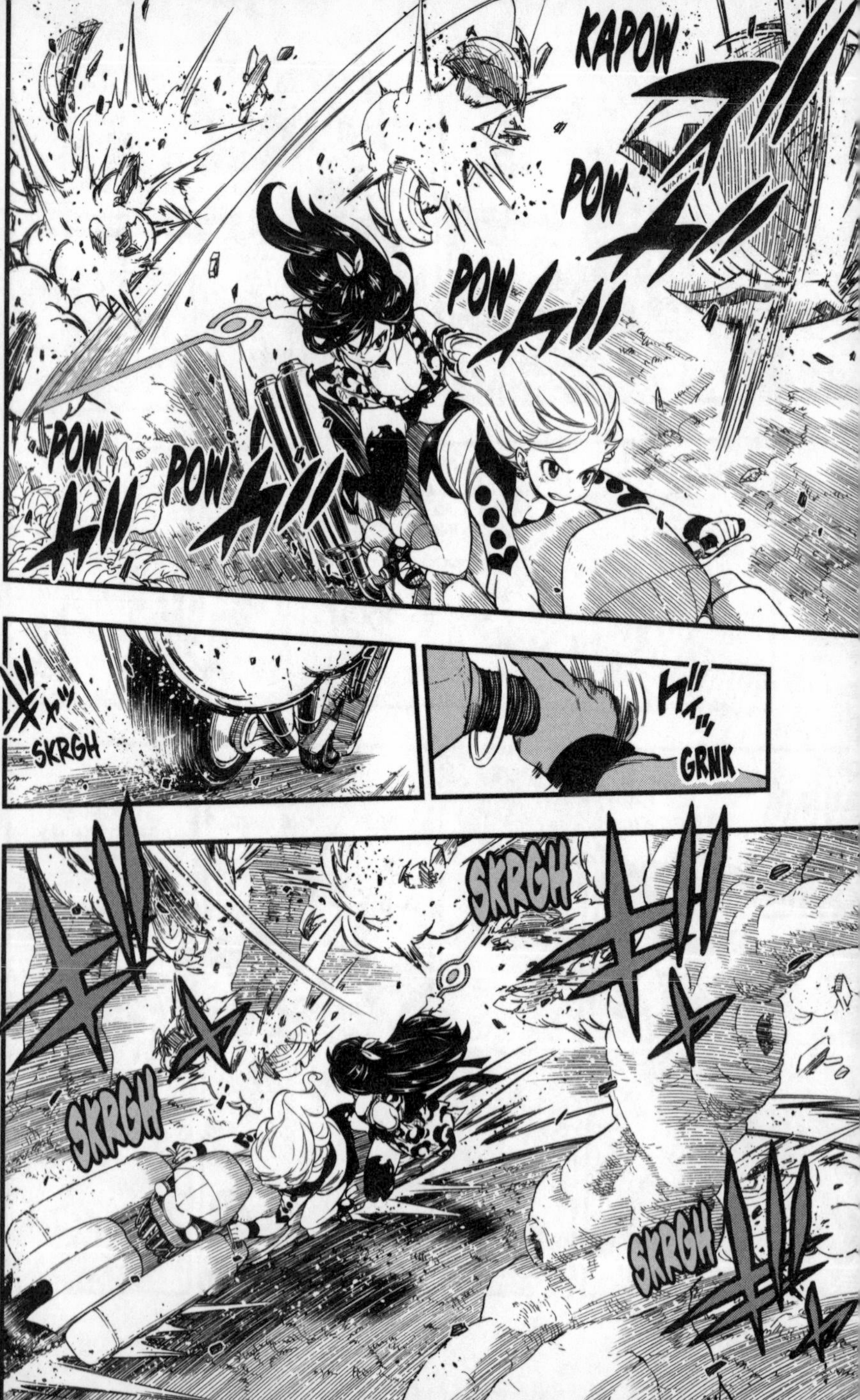
KAPOW
POW
POW
POW
POW
GRNK
SKRGH
SKRGH
SKRGH
SKRGH

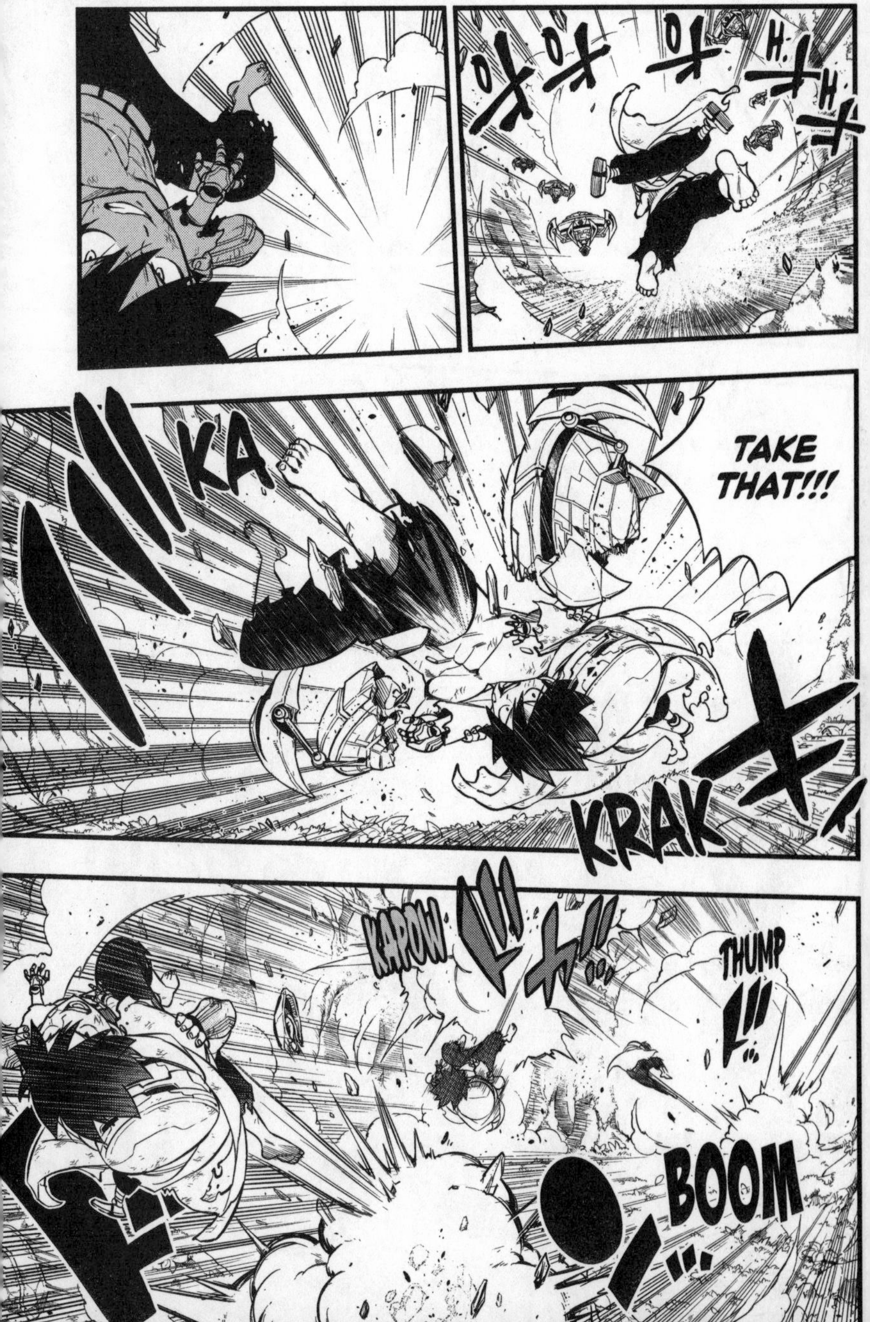
TAKE THAT!!!
KRAK
KA
THUMP
KAPOW
BOOM

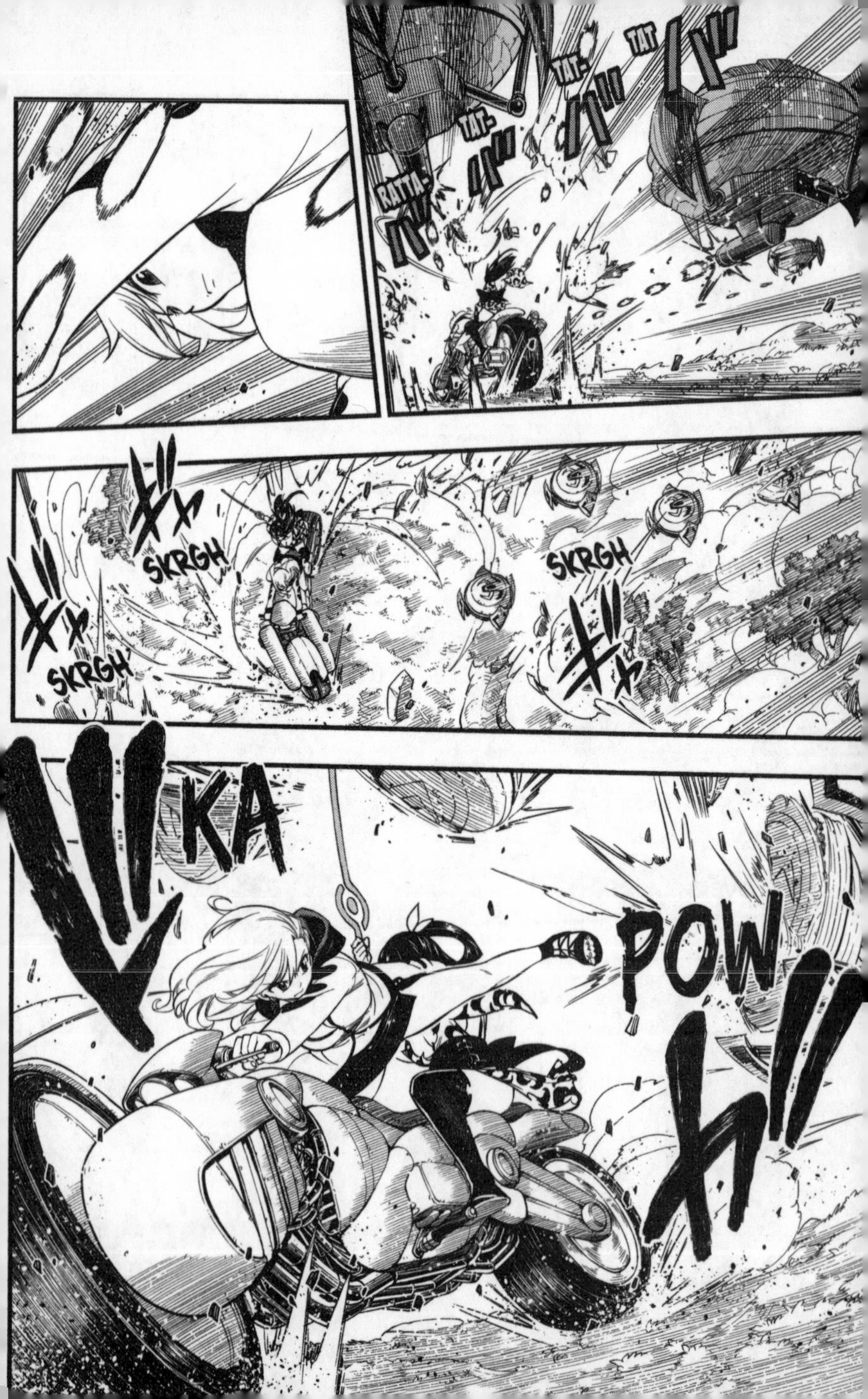

RATTA-
TAT-
TAT-
TAT
SKRGH
SKRGH
SKRGH
POW
KA

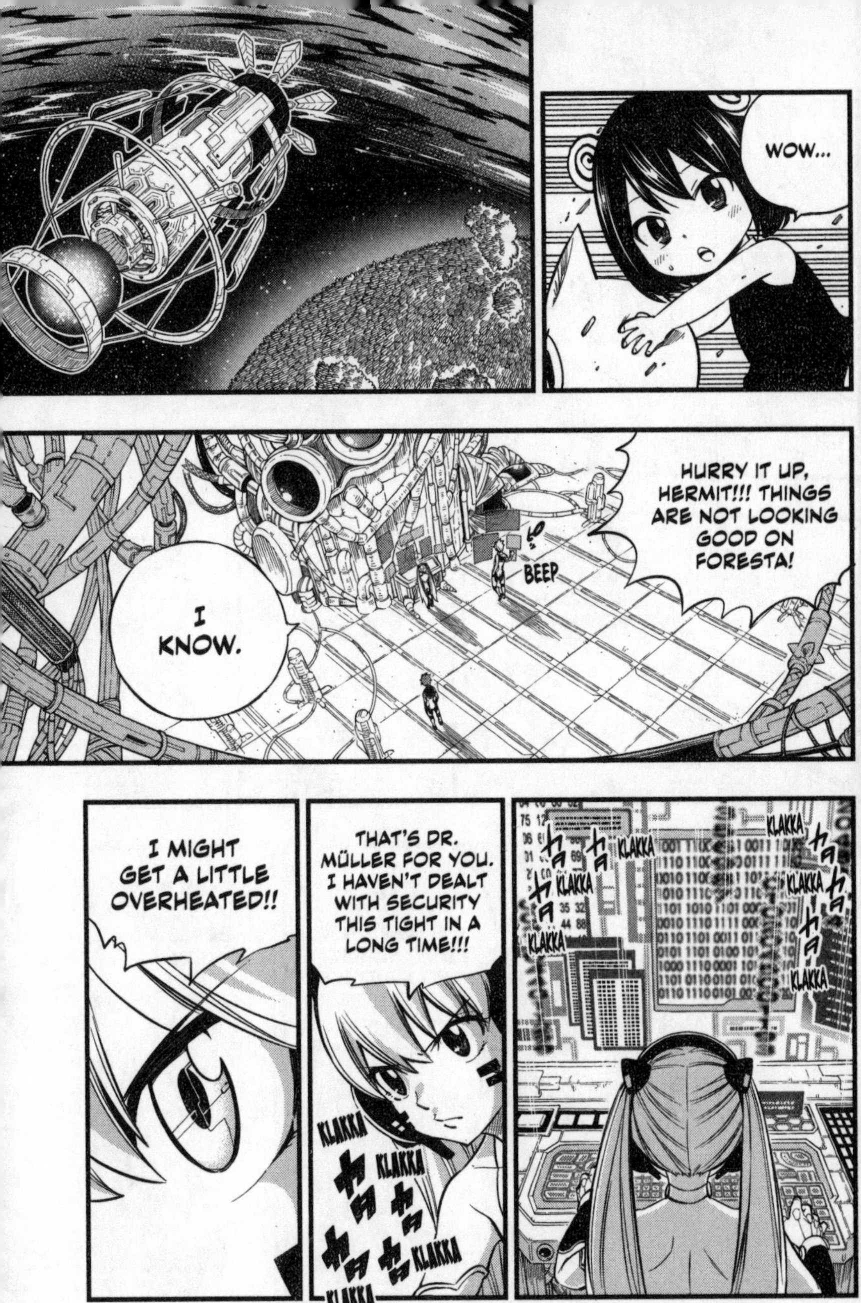
WOW...
HURRY IT UP, HERMIT!!! THINGS ARE NOT LOOKING GOOD ON FORESTA!
BEEP
I KNOW.
KLAKKA
KLAKKA
KLAKKA
KLAKKA
KLAKKA
KLAKKA
THAT'S DR. MÜLLER FOR YOU. I HAVEN'T DEALT WITH SECURITY THIS TIGHT IN A LONG TIME!!!
KLAKKA
KLAKKA
KLAKKA
KLAKKA
I MIGHT GET A LITTLE OVERHEATED!!

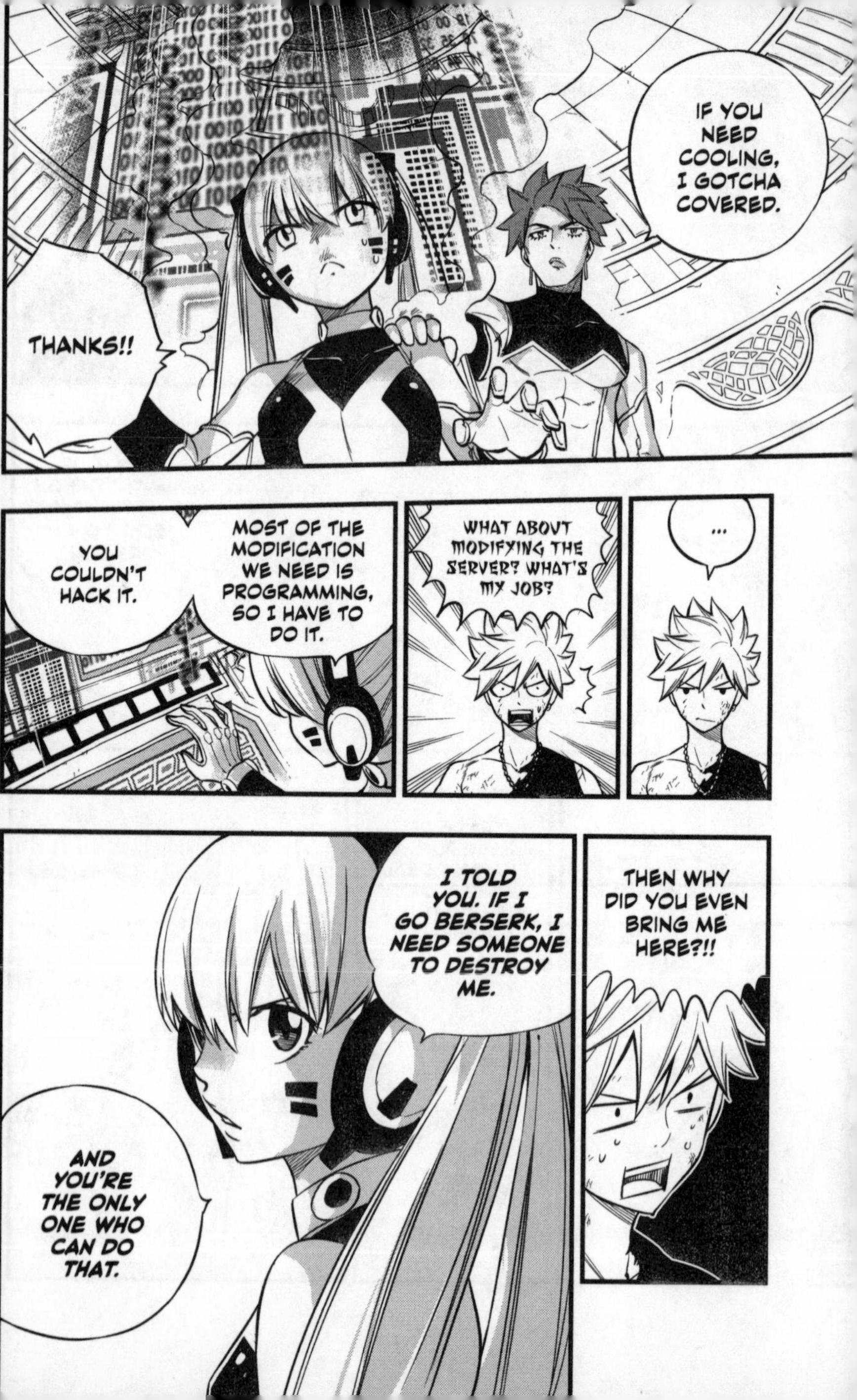

IF YOU NEED COOLING, I GOTCHA COVERED.
THANKS!!
...
WHAT ABOUT MODIFYING THE SERVER? WHAT'S MY JOB?
MOST OF THE MODIFICATION WE NEED IS PROGRAMMING, SO I HAVE TO DO IT.
YOU COULDN'T HACK IT.
THEN WHY DID YOU EVEN BRING ME HERE?!!
I TOLD YOU. IF I GO BERSERK, I NEED SOMEONE TO DESTROY ME.
AND YOU'RE THE ONLY ONE WHO CAN DO THAT.

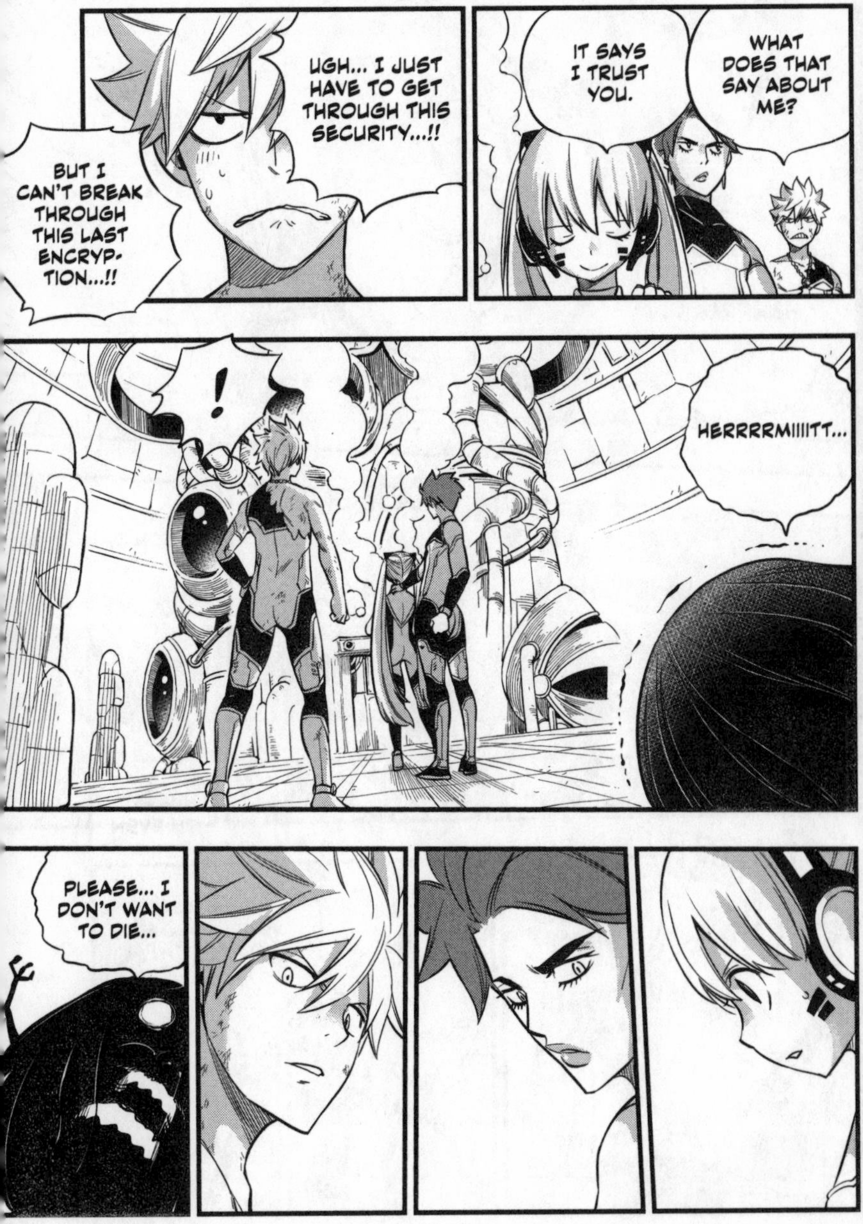
WHAT DOES THAT SAY ABOUT ME?
IT SAYS I TRUST YOU.
UGH... I JUST HAVE TO GET THROUGH THIS SECURITY...!!
BUT I CAN'T BREAK THROUGH THIS LAST ENCRYPTION...!!
HERRRRMIIIIITT...
!
PLEASE... I DON'T WANT TO DIE...

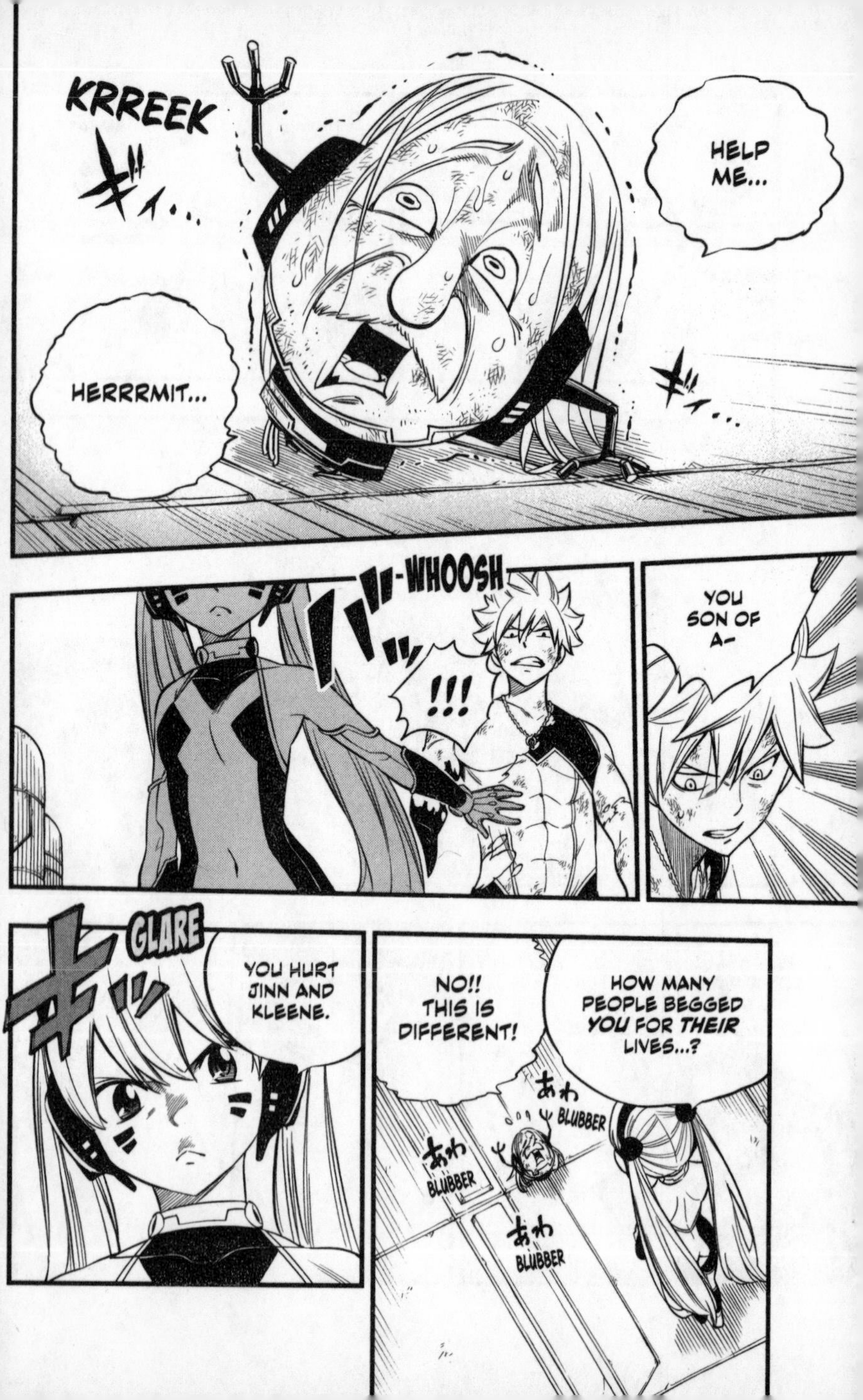
HELP ME...
KRREEK
HERRRMIT...
YOU SON OF A-
-WHOOSH
!!!
HOW MANY PEOPLE BEGGED *YOU* FOR *THEIR* LIVES...?
NO!! THIS IS DIFFERENT!
あわ
BLUBBER
あわ
BLUBBER
あわ
BLUBBER
GLARE
YOU HURT JINN AND KLEENE.

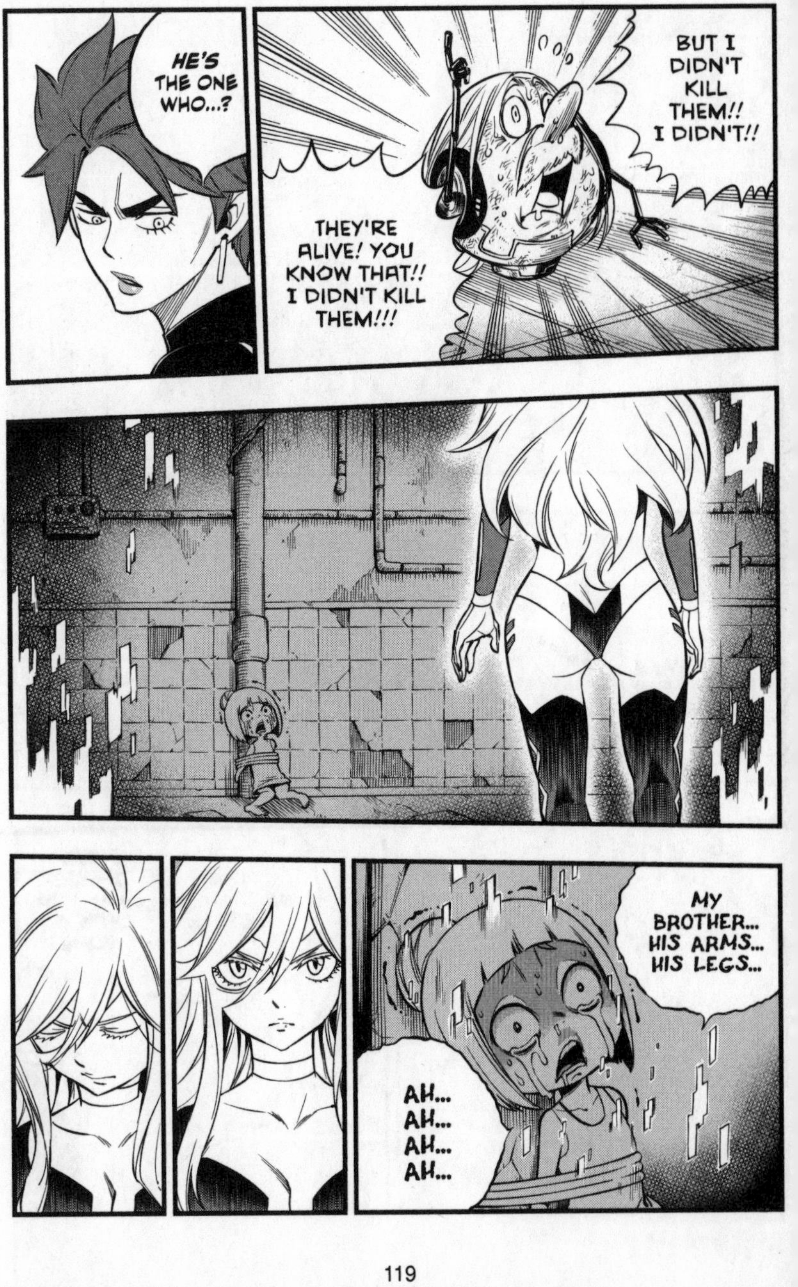
BUT I DIDN'T KILL THEM!! I DIDN'T!!
THEY'RE ALIVE! YOU KNOW THAT!! I DIDN'T KILL THEM!!!
HE'S THE ONE WHO...?
MY BROTHER... HIS ARMS... HIS LEGS...
AH... AH... AH... AH...

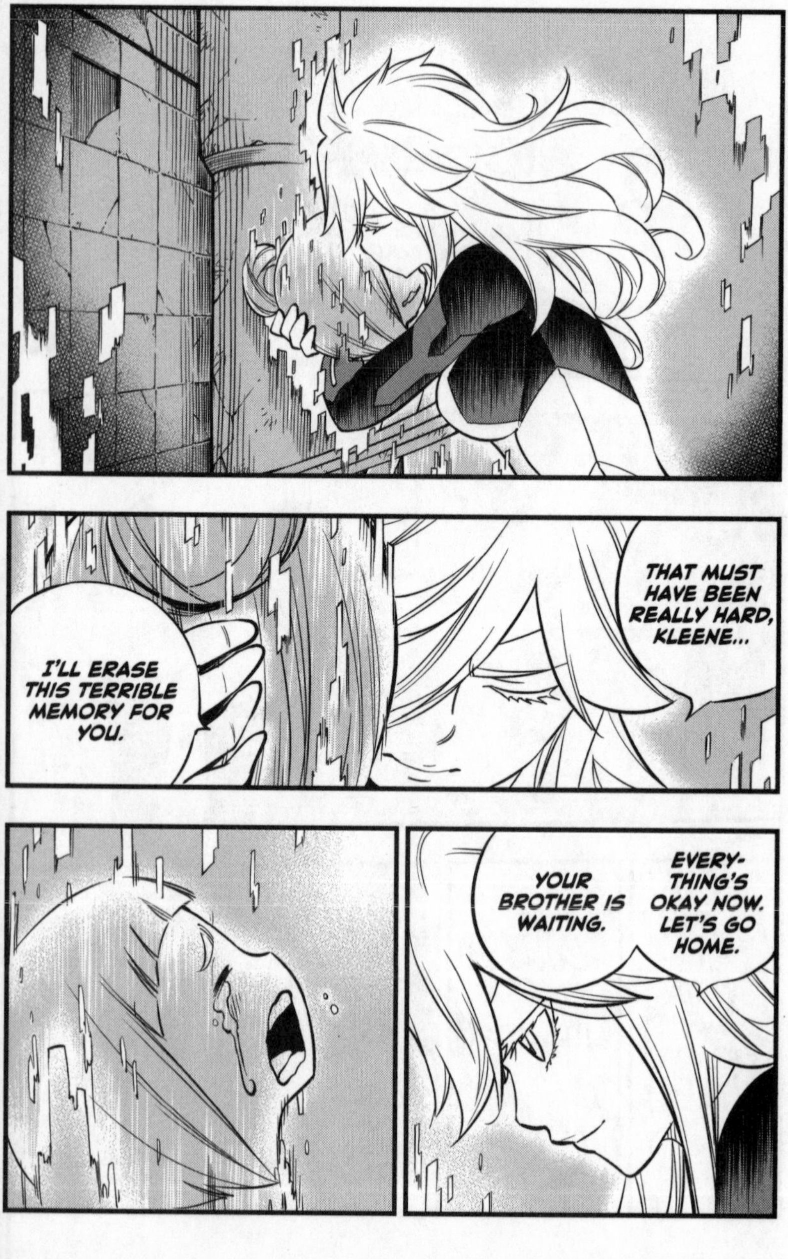
THAT MUST HAVE BEEN REALLY HARD, KLEENE...
I'LL ERASE THIS TERRIBLE MEMORY FOR YOU.
EVERY-THING'S OKAY NOW. LET'S GO HOME.
YOUR BROTHER IS WAITING.

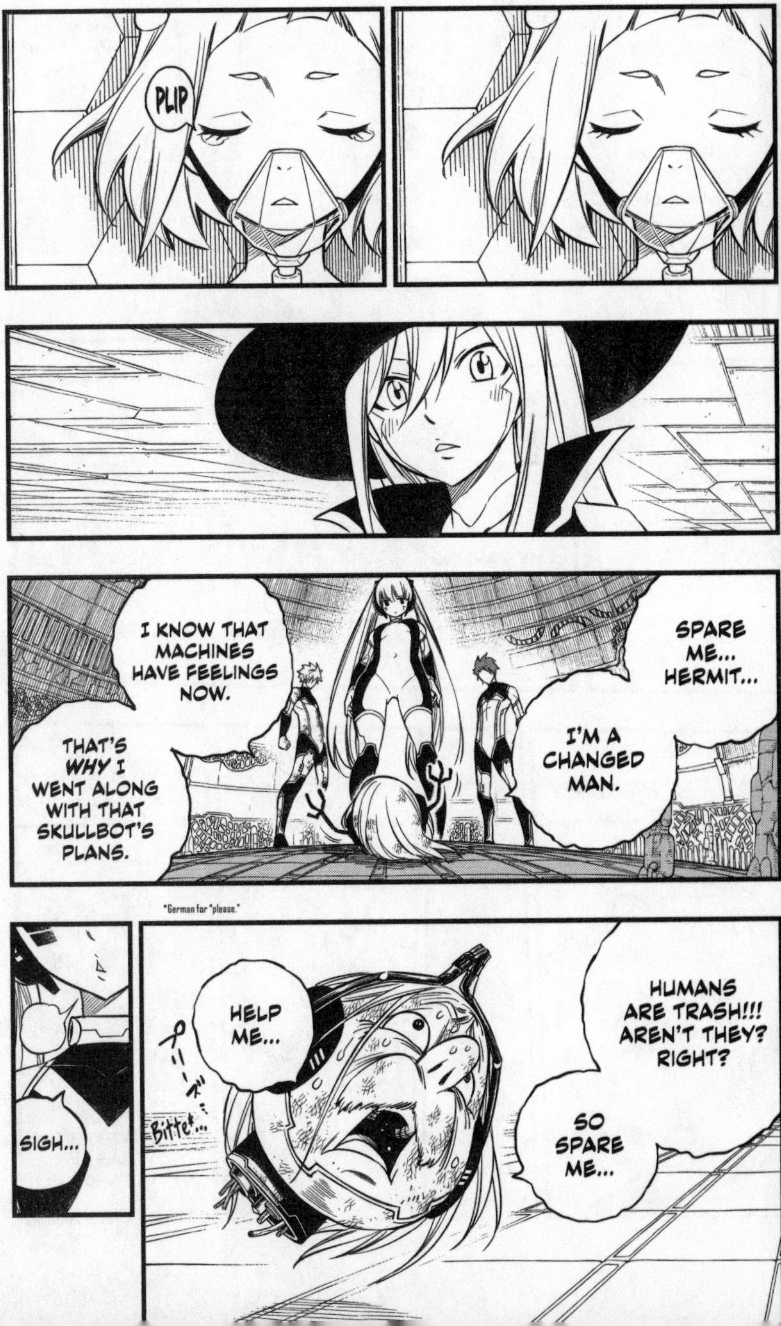
PLIP
SPARE ME... HERMIT...
I'M A CHANGED MAN.
I KNOW THAT MACHINES HAVE FEELINGS NOW.
THAT'S *WHY* I WENT ALONG WITH THAT SKULLBOT'S PLANS.
HUMANS ARE TRASH!!! AREN'T THEY? RIGHT?
SO SPARE ME...
HELP ME...
プリーズ…
Bitte*...
SIGH...

*German for "please."

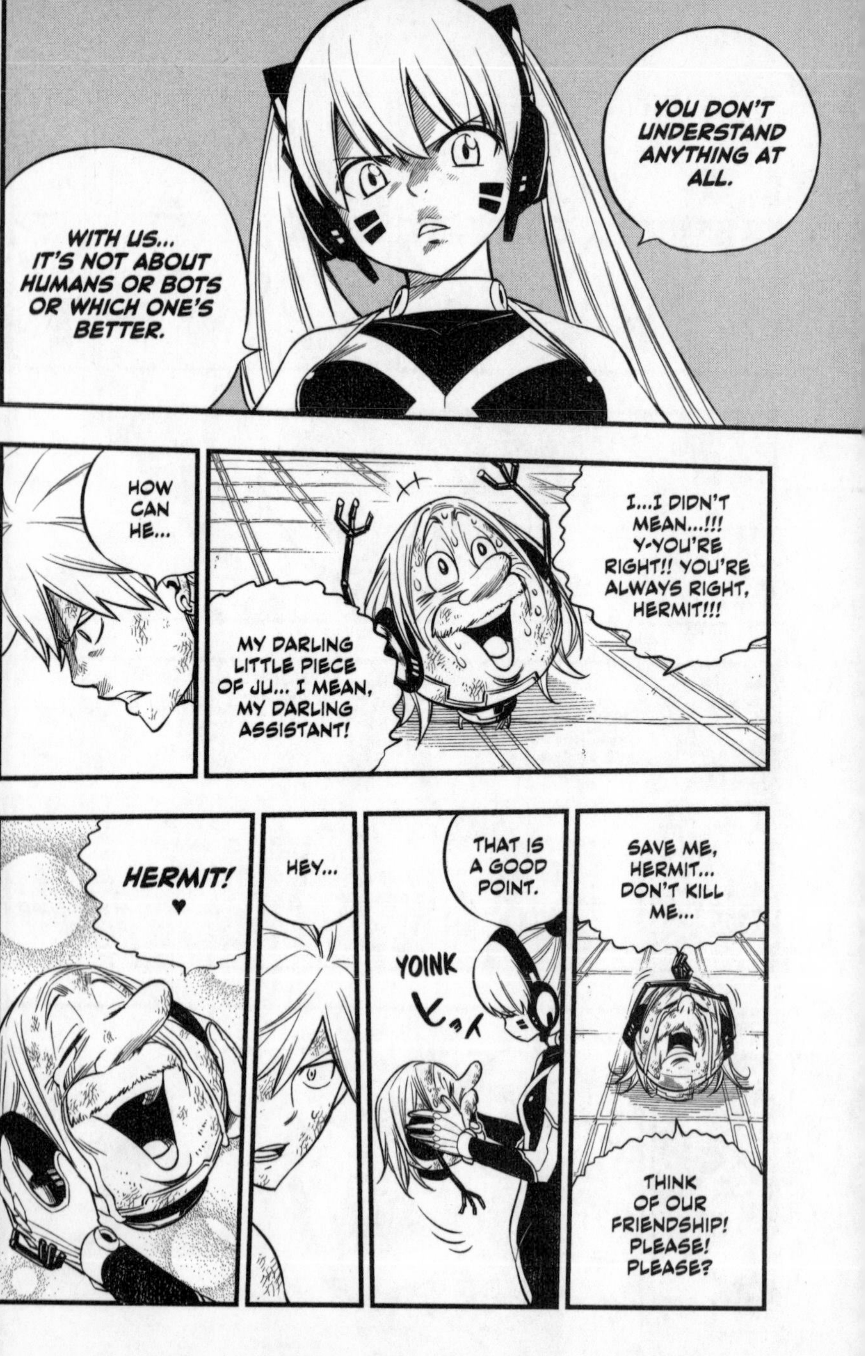
YOU DON'T UNDERSTAND ANYTHING AT ALL.
WITH US... IT'S NOT ABOUT HUMANS OR BOTS OR WHICH ONE'S BETTER.
I...I DIDN'T MEAN...!!! Y-YOU'RE RIGHT!! YOU'RE ALWAYS RIGHT, HERMIT!!!
MY DARLING LITTLE PIECE OF JU... I MEAN, MY DARLING ASSISTANT!
HOW CAN HE...
SAVE ME, HERMIT... DON'T KILL ME...
THINK OF OUR FRIENDSHIP! PLEASE! PLEASE?
THAT IS A GOOD POINT.
YOINK
ヒョイ
HEY...
HERMIT! ♥

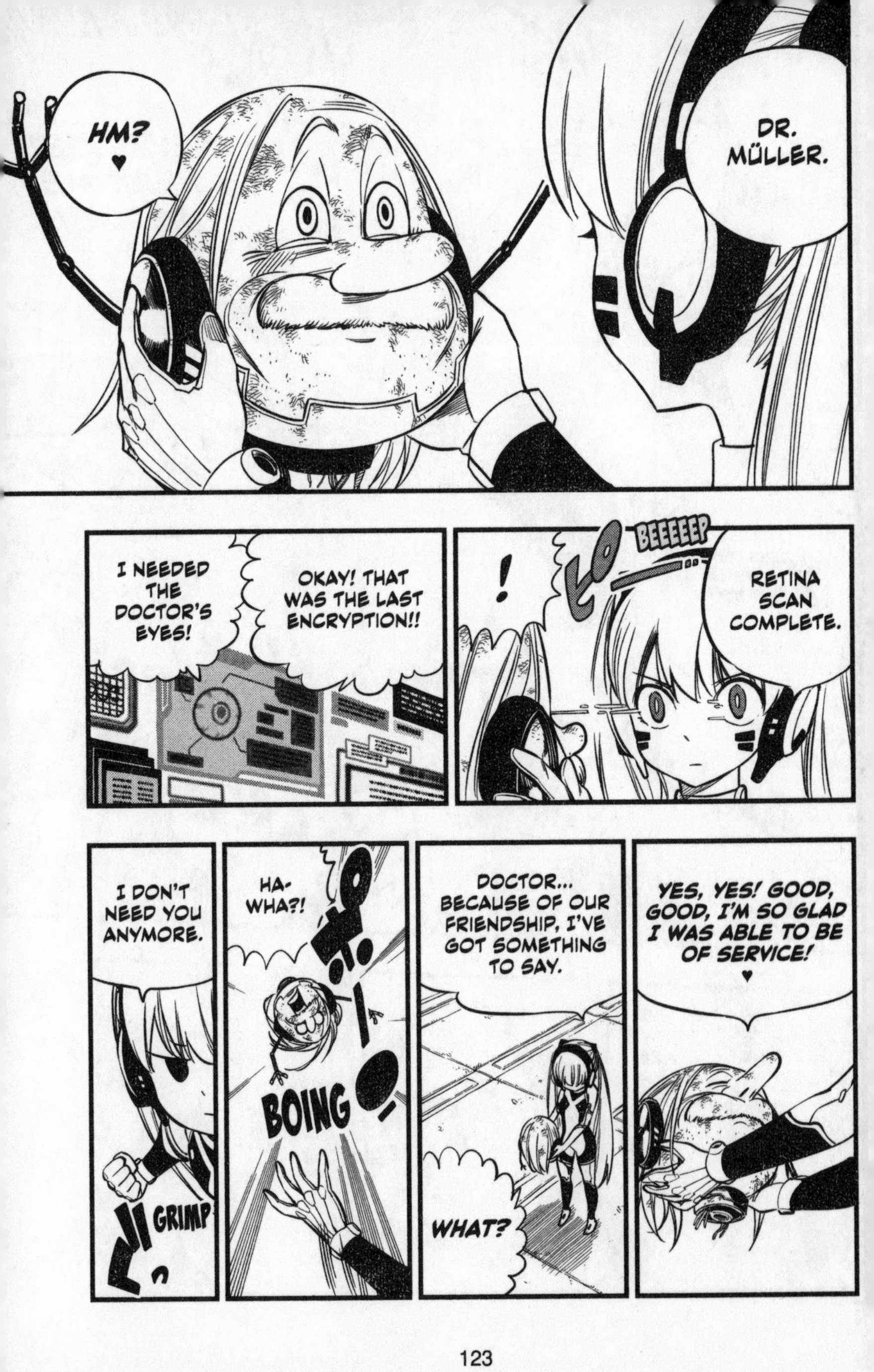
DR. MÜLLER.
HM? ♥
RETINA SCAN COMPLETE.
BEEEEEP
!
OKAY! THAT WAS THE LAST ENCRYPTION!!
I NEEDED THE DOCTOR'S EYES!
YES, YES! GOOD, GOOD, I'M SO GLAD I WAS ABLE TO BE OF SERVICE! ♥
DOCTOR... BECAUSE OF OUR FRIENDSHIP, I'VE GOT SOMETHING TO SAY.
WHAT?
HA-WHA?!
BOING
I DON'T NEED YOU ANYMORE.
GRIMP

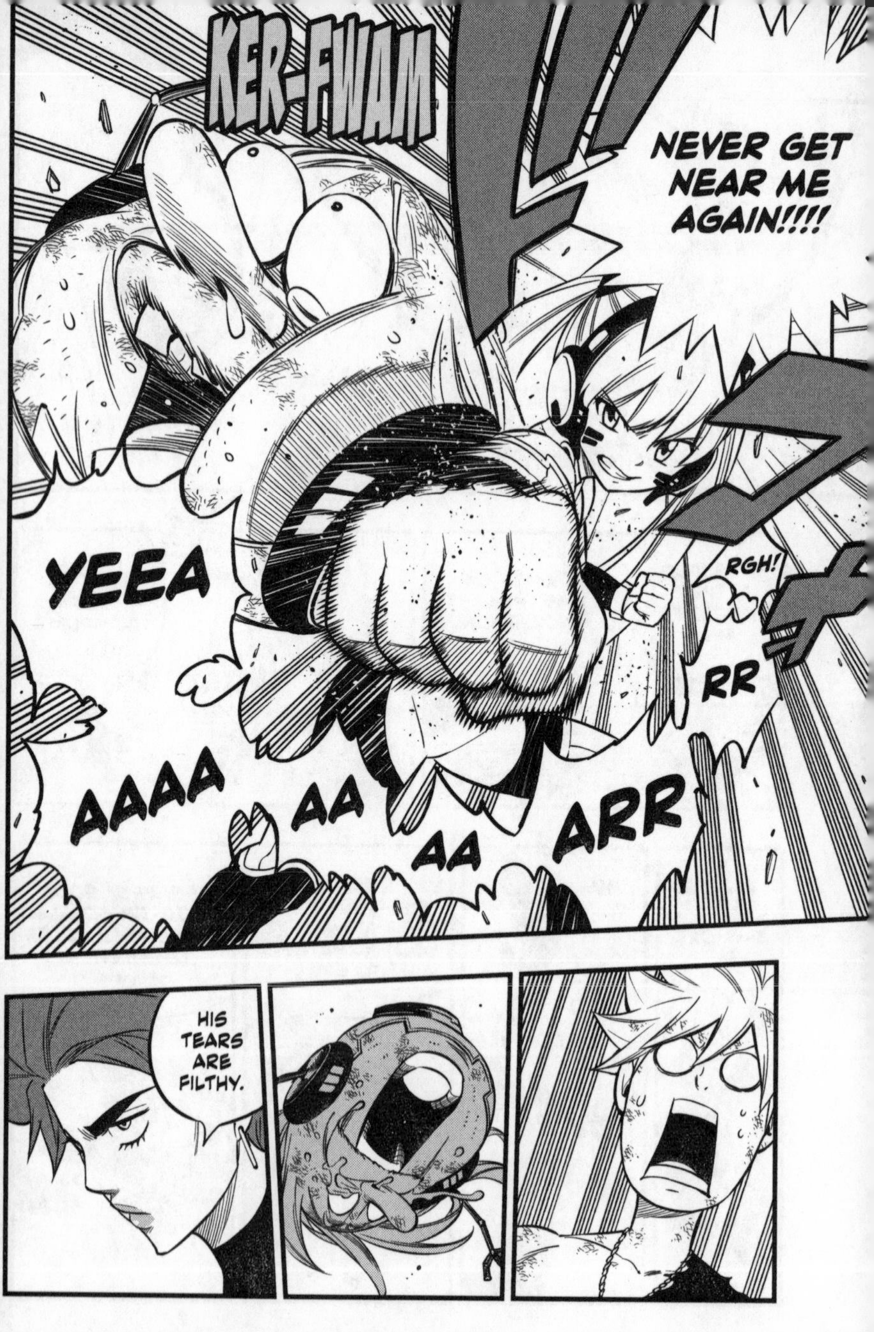
KER-FWAM
NEVER GET NEAR ME AGAIN!!!!
RGH!
YEEA
AAAA
AA
AA
ARR
RR
HIS TEARS ARE FILTHY.

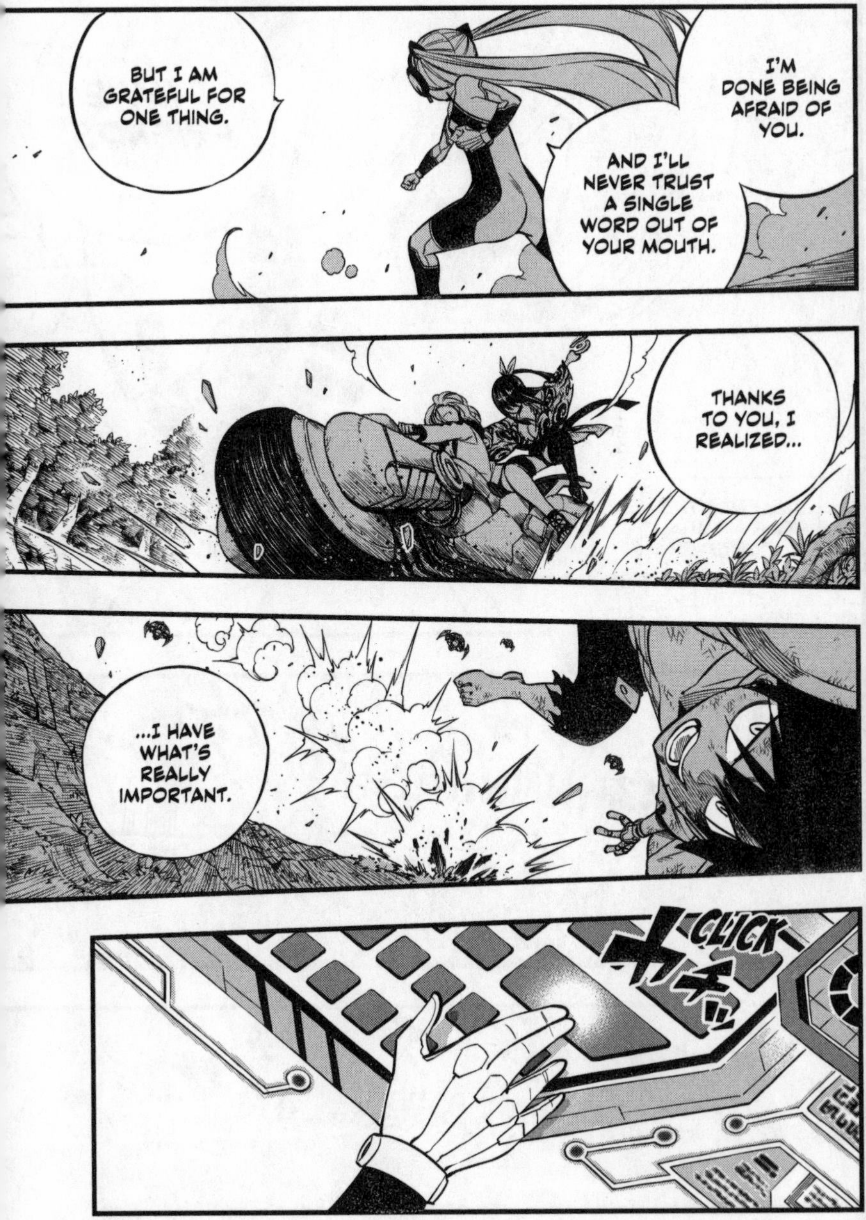
I'M DONE BEING AFRAID OF YOU.
AND I'LL NEVER TRUST A SINGLE WORD OUT OF YOUR MOUTH.
BUT I AM GRATEFUL FOR ONE THING.
THANKS TO YOU, I REALIZED...
...I HAVE WHAT'S REALLY IMPORTANT.
CLICK

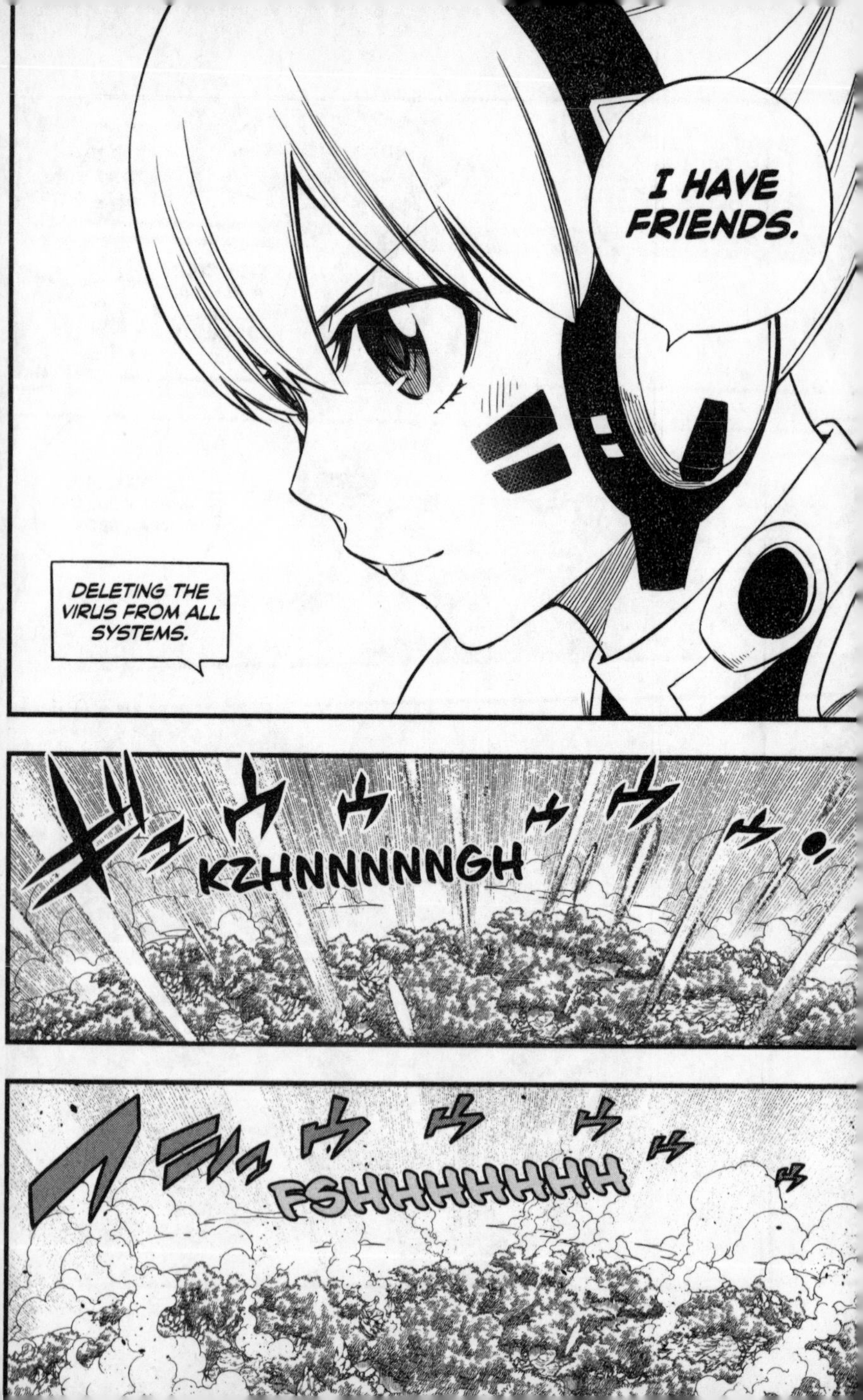
I HAVE FRIENDS.
DELETING THE VIRUS FROM ALL SYSTEMS.
KZHNNNNNGH
FSHHHHHHH

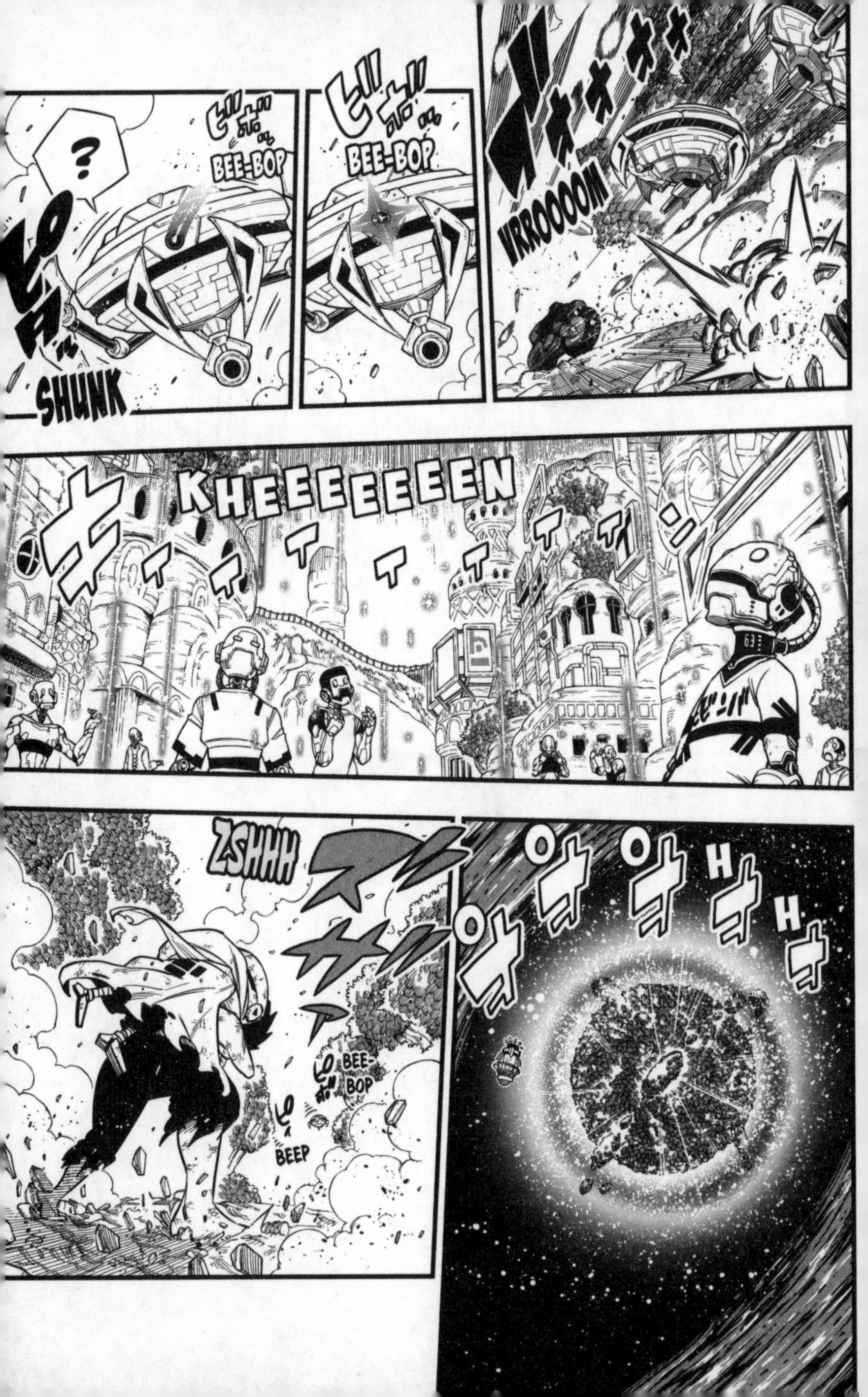
VRROOOOM
BEE-BOP
BEE-BOP
?
SHUNK
KHEEEEEEEN
ZSHHH
BEE-BOP
BEEP

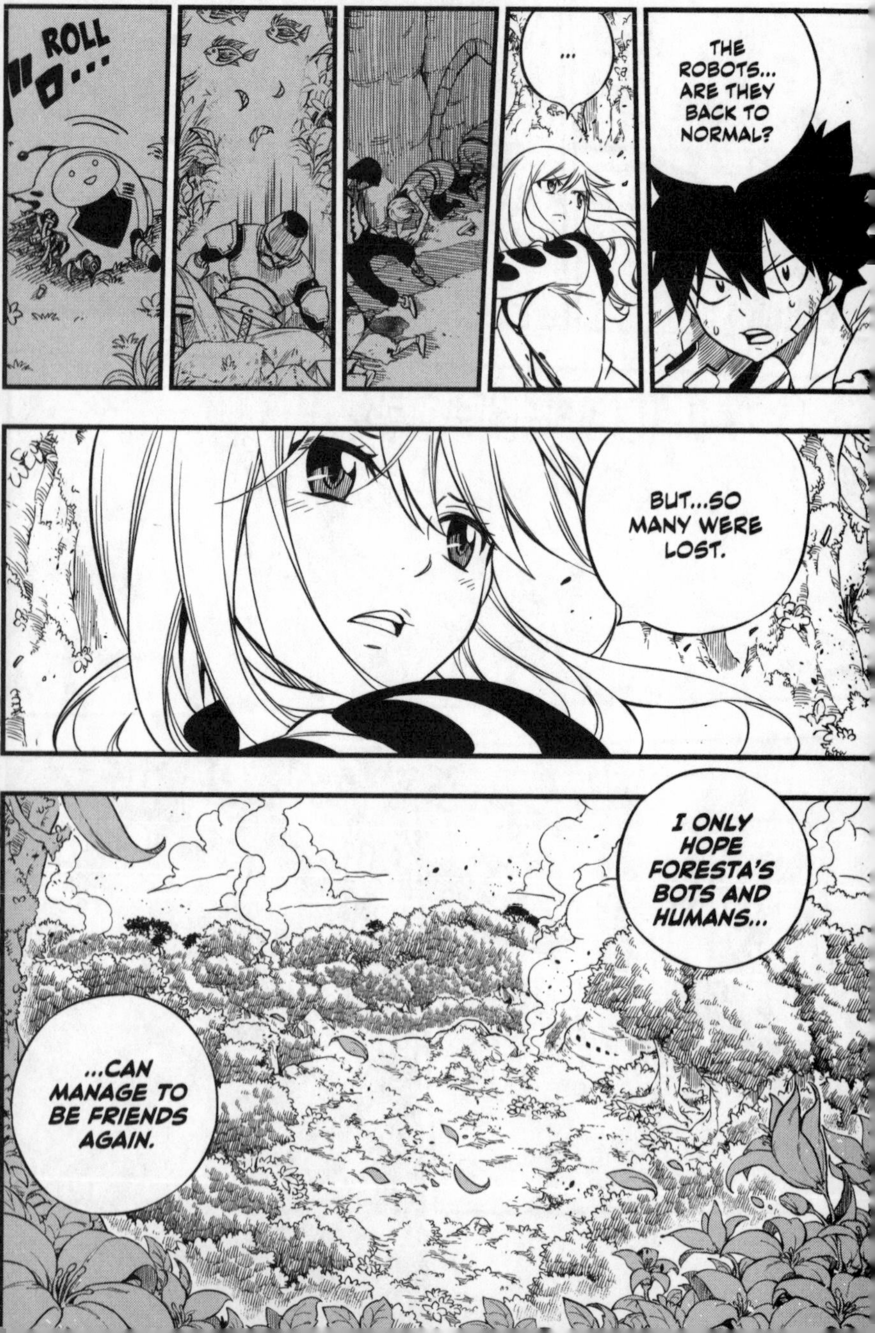
THE ROBOTS... ARE THEY BACK TO NORMAL?
...
ROLL
BUT...SO MANY WERE LOST.
I ONLY HOPE FORESTA'S BOTS AND HUMANS...
...CAN MANAGE TO BE FRIENDS AGAIN.

EDENS ZERO

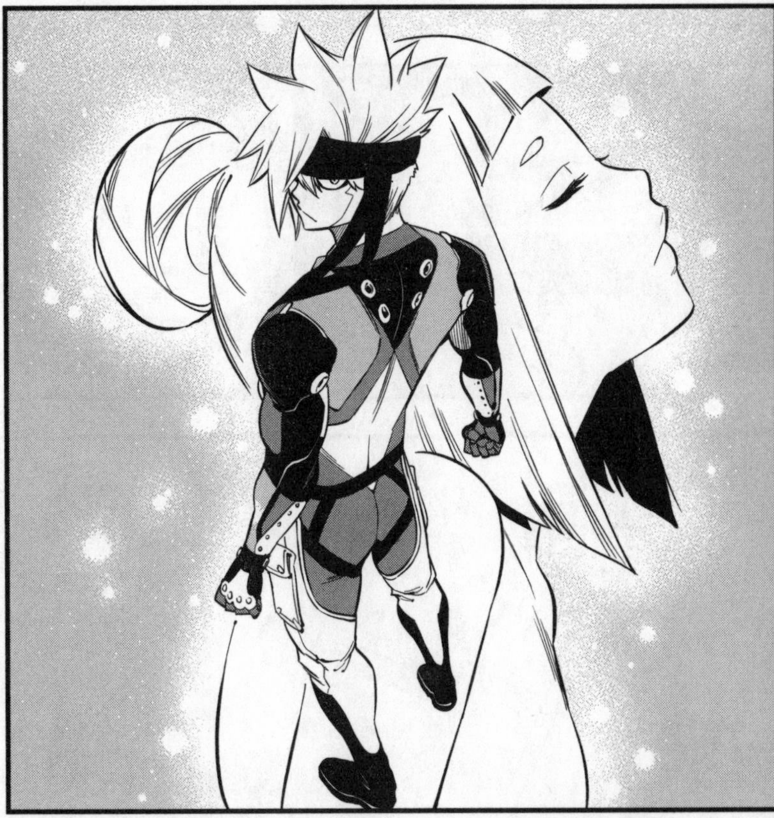

CHAPTER 129: SO WE CAN SMILE BRIGHTER

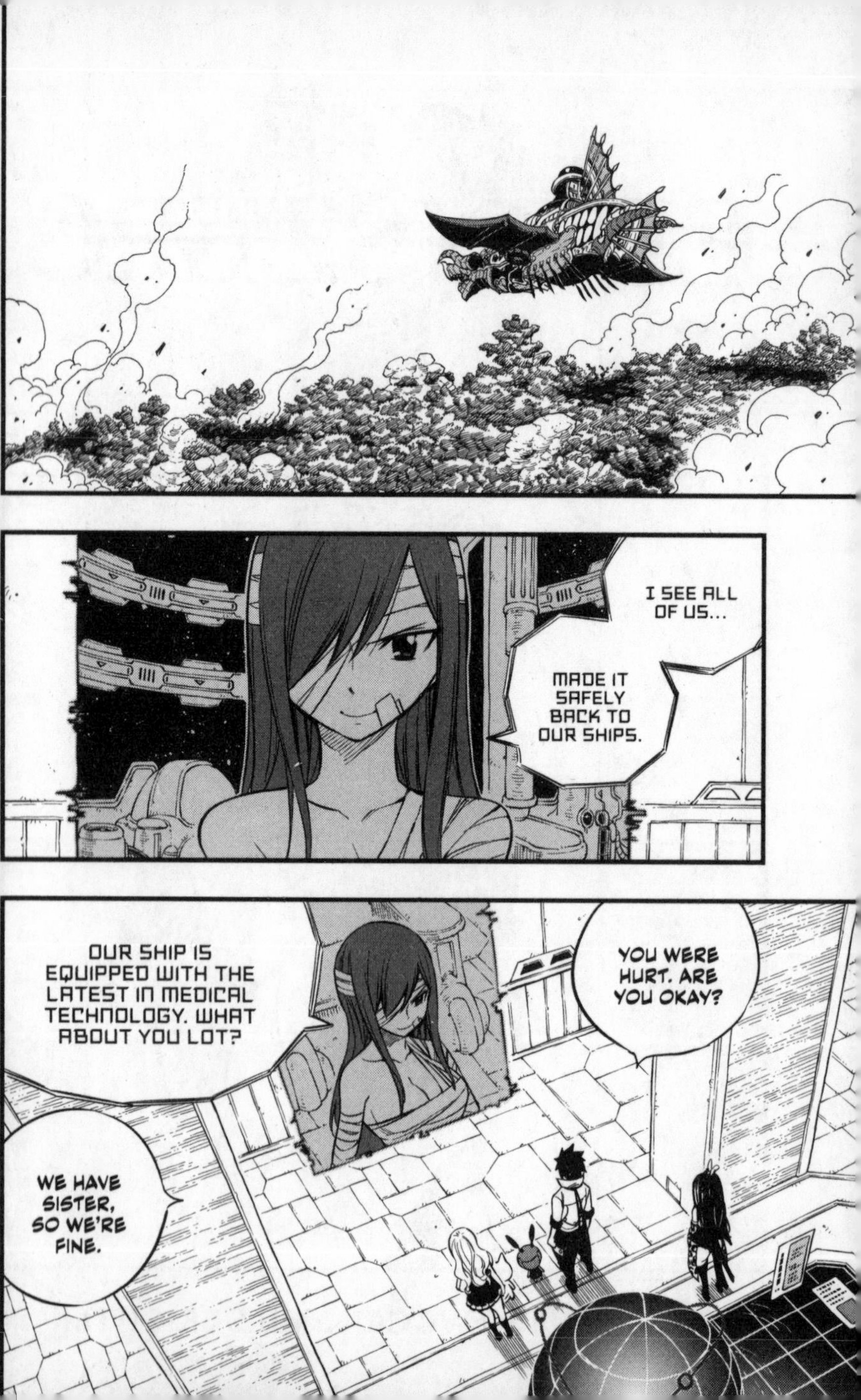

I SEE ALL OF US...
MADE IT SAFELY BACK TO OUR SHIPS.
YOU WERE HURT. ARE YOU OKAY?
OUR SHIP IS EQUIPPED WITH THE LATEST IN MEDICAL TECHNOLOGY. WHAT ABOUT YOU LOT?
WE HAVE SISTER, SO WE'RE FINE.

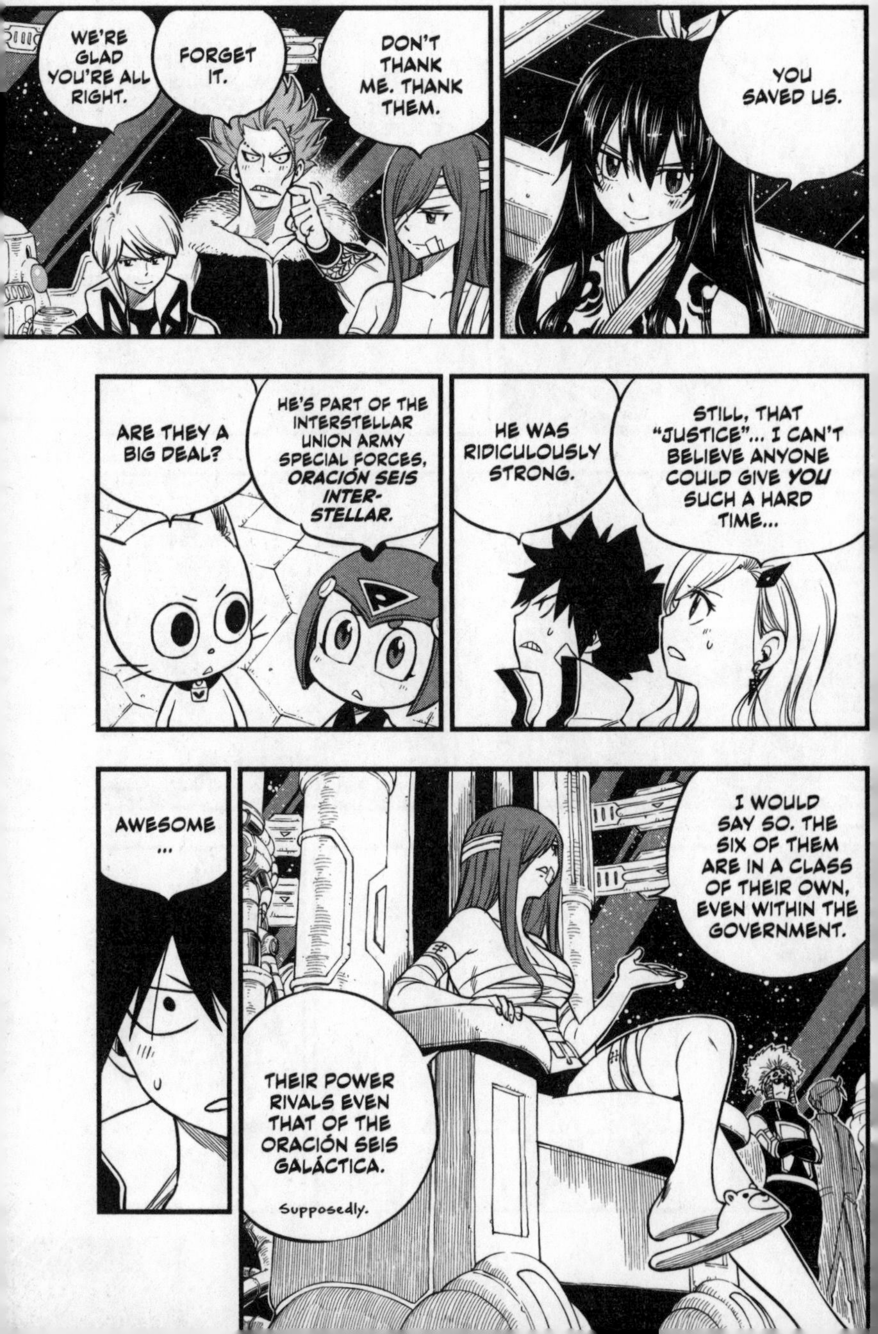
YOU SAVED US.
DON'T THANK ME. THANK THEM.
FORGET IT.
WE'RE GLAD YOU'RE ALL RIGHT.
STILL, THAT "JUSTICE"... I CAN'T BELIEVE ANYONE COULD GIVE *YOU* SUCH A HARD TIME...
HE WAS RIDICULOUSLY STRONG.
HE'S PART OF THE INTERSTELLAR UNION ARMY SPECIAL FORCES, *ORACIÓN SEIS INTER-STELLAR.*
ARE THEY A BIG DEAL?
I WOULD SAY SO. THE SIX OF THEM ARE IN A CLASS OF THEIR OWN, EVEN WITHIN THE GOVERNMENT.
THEIR POWER RIVALS EVEN THAT OF THE ORACIÓN SEIS GALÁCTICA.
Supposedly.
AWESOME...

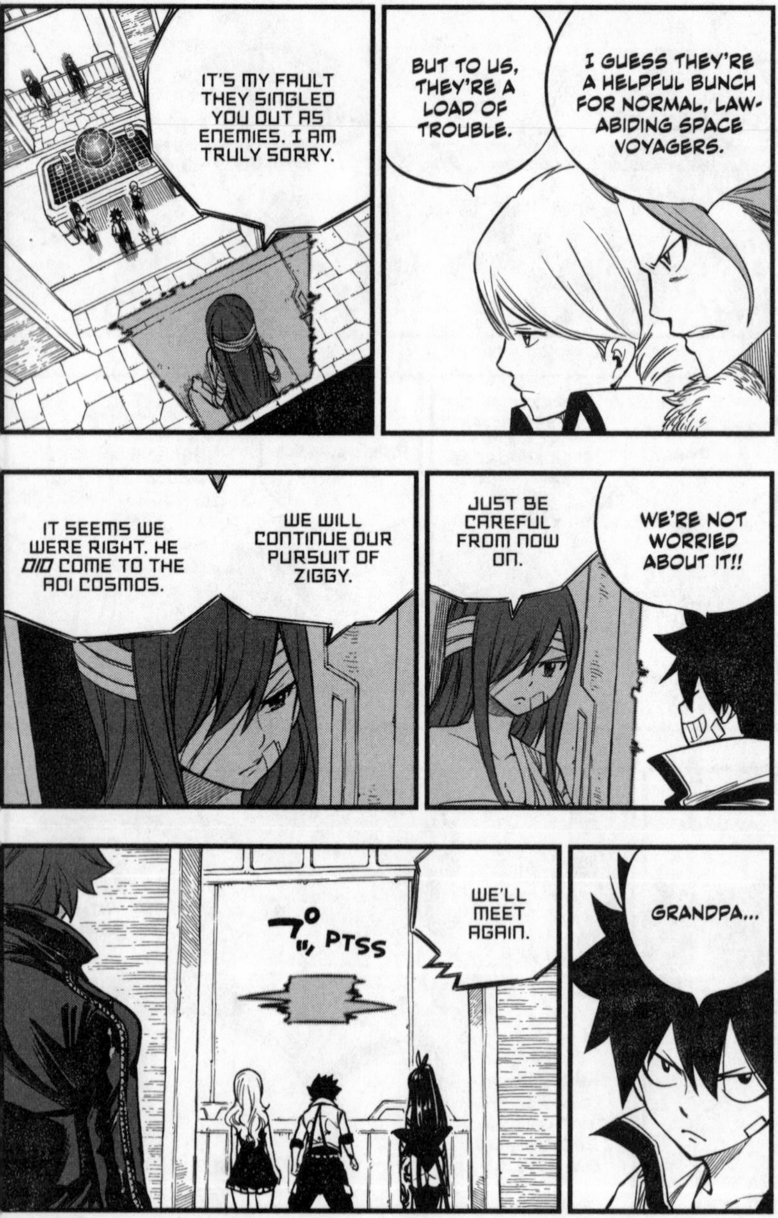

I GUESS THEY'RE A HELPFUL BUNCH FOR NORMAL, LAW-ABIDING SPACE VOYAGERS.
BUT TO US, THEY'RE A LOAD OF TROUBLE.
IT'S MY FAULT THEY SINGLED YOU OUT AS ENEMIES. I AM TRULY SORRY.
WE'RE NOT WORRIED ABOUT IT!!
JUST BE CAREFUL FROM NOW ON.
WE WILL CONTINUE OUR PURSUIT OF ZIGGY.
IT SEEMS WE WERE RIGHT. HE *DID* COME TO THE AOI COSMOS.
GRANDPA...
WE'LL MEET AGAIN.
PTSS

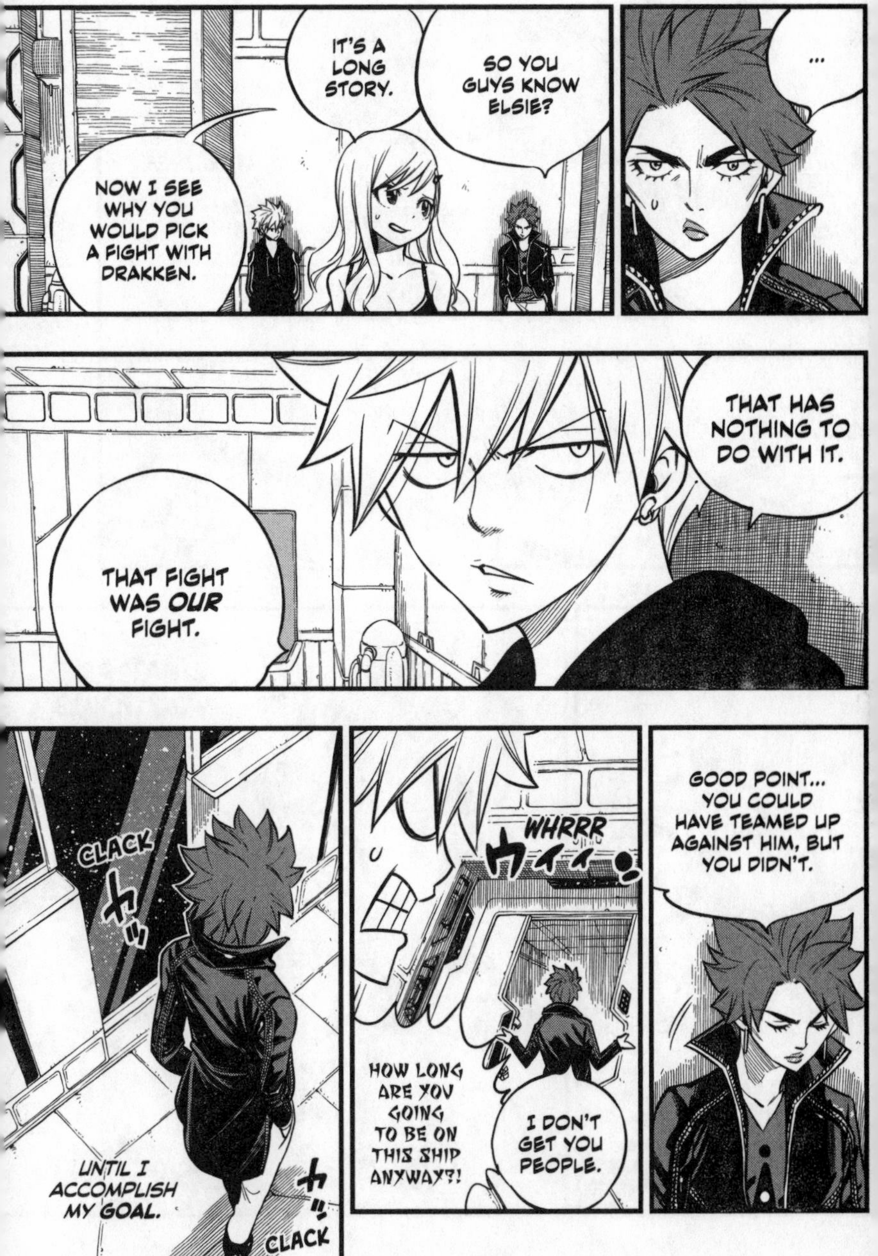
...
SO YOU GUYS KNOW ELSIE?
IT'S A LONG STORY.
NOW I SEE WHY YOU WOULD PICK A FIGHT WITH DRAKKEN.
THAT HAS NOTHING TO DO WITH IT.
THAT FIGHT WAS *OUR* FIGHT.
GOOD POINT... YOU COULD HAVE TEAMED UP AGAINST HIM, BUT YOU DIDN'T.
WHRRR
I DON'T GET YOU PEOPLE.
HOW LONG ARE YOU GOING TO BE ON THIS SHIP ANYWAY?!
CLACK
UNTIL I ACCOMPLISH MY GOAL.
CLACK

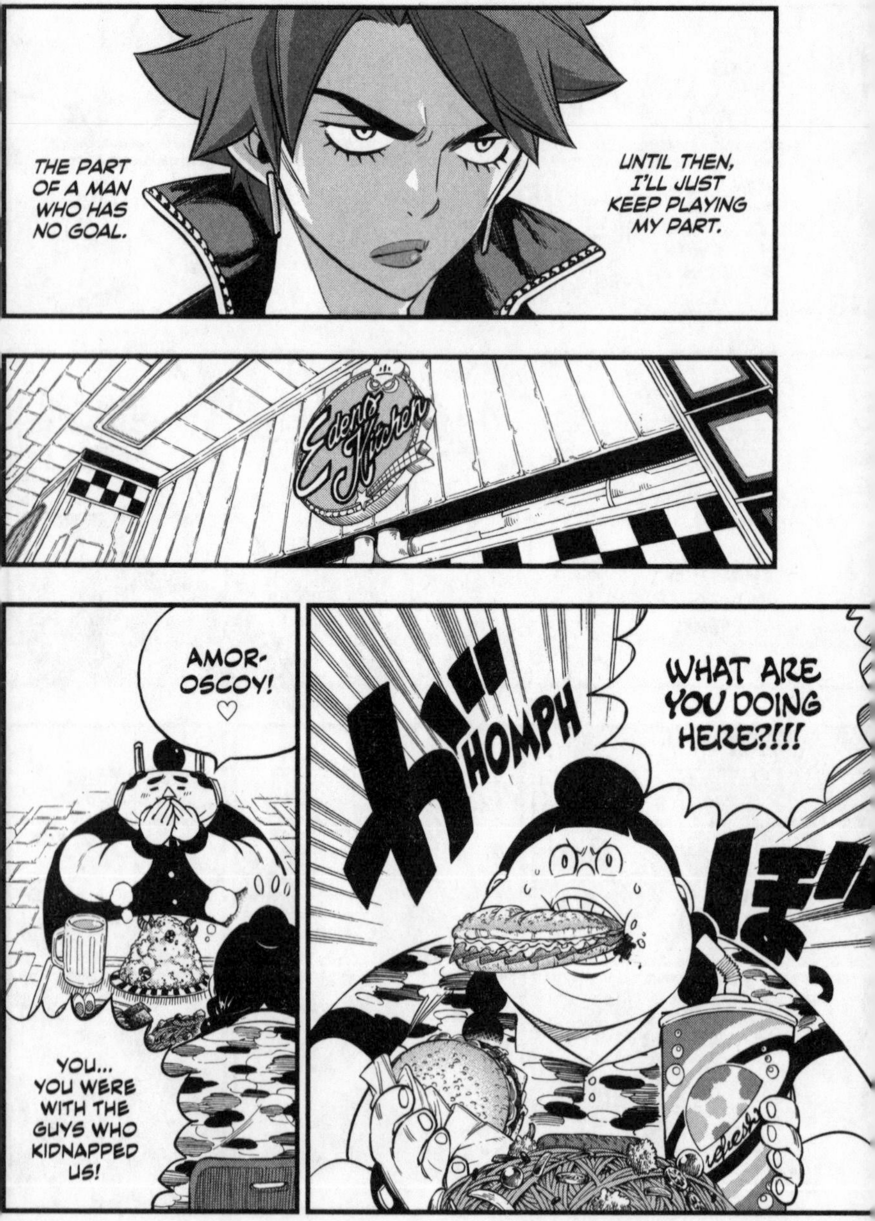

UNTIL THEN, I'LL JUST KEEP PLAYING MY PART.
THE PART OF A MAN WHO HAS NO GOAL.
Eden's Kitchen
WHAT ARE YOU DOING HERE?!!!
HOMPH
AMOR-OSCOY! ♡
YOU... YOU WERE WITH THE GUYS WHO KIDNAPPED US!

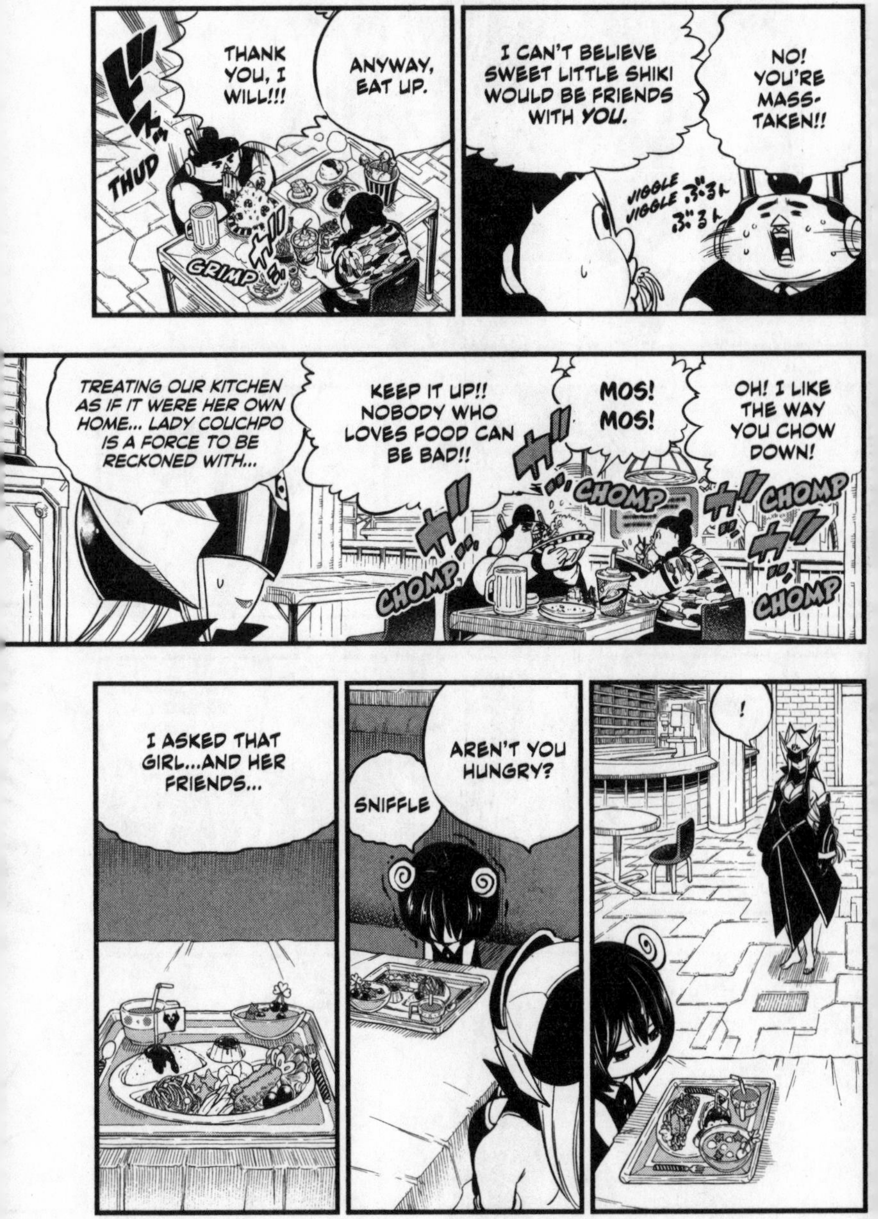
I CAN'T BELIEVE SWEET LITTLE SHIKI WOULD BE FRIENDS WITH *YOU.*
NO! YOU'RE MASS-TAKEN!!
VIGGLE VIGGLE ぶるん ぶるん
ANYWAY, EAT UP.
THANK YOU, I WILL!!!
THUD
GRIMP
OH! I LIKE THE WAY YOU CHOW DOWN!
CHOMP
CHOMP
MOS! MOS!
CHOMP
KEEP IT UP!! NOBODY WHO LOVES FOOD CAN BE BAD!!
CHOMP
TREATING OUR KITCHEN AS IF IT WERE HER OWN HOME... LADY COUCHPO IS A FORCE TO BE RECKONED WITH...
!
AREN'T YOU HUNGRY?
SNIFFLE
I ASKED THAT GIRL...AND HER FRIENDS...

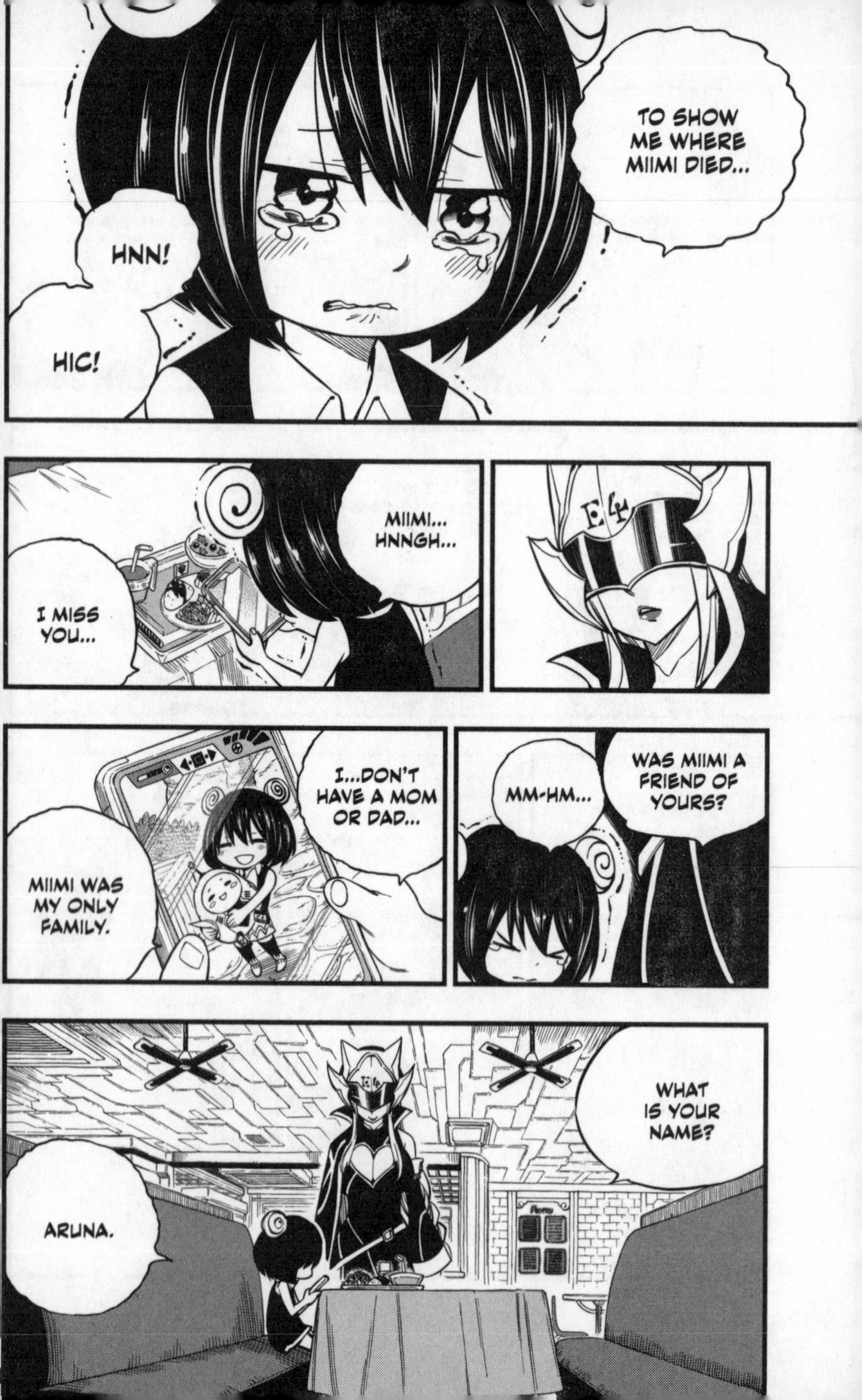
TO SHOW ME WHERE MIIMI DIED...
HNN!
HIC!
MIIMI... HNNGH...
I MISS YOU...
WAS MIIMI A FRIEND OF YOURS?
MM-HM...
I...DON'T HAVE A MOM OR DAD...
MIIMI WAS MY ONLY FAMILY.
WHAT IS YOUR NAME?
ARUNA.

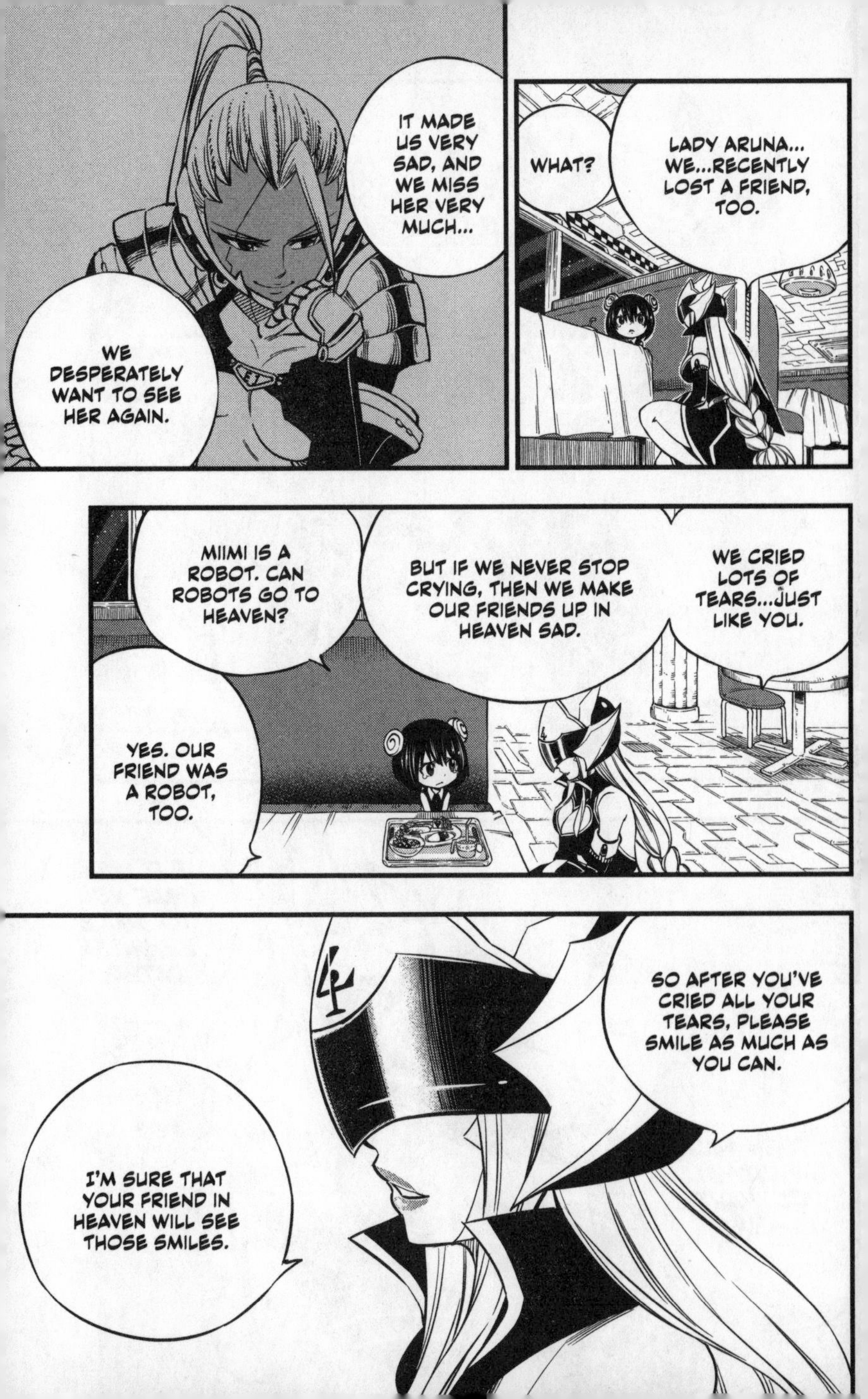
LADY ARUNA... WE...RECENTLY LOST A FRIEND, TOO.
WHAT?
IT MADE US VERY SAD, AND WE MISS HER VERY MUCH...
WE DESPERATELY WANT TO SEE HER AGAIN.
WE CRIED LOTS OF TEARS...JUST LIKE YOU.
BUT IF WE NEVER STOP CRYING, THEN WE MAKE OUR FRIENDS UP IN HEAVEN SAD.
MIIMI IS A ROBOT. CAN ROBOTS GO TO HEAVEN?
YES. OUR FRIEND WAS A ROBOT, TOO.
SO AFTER YOU'VE CRIED ALL YOUR TEARS, PLEASE SMILE AS MUCH AS YOU CAN.
I'M SURE THAT YOUR FRIEND IN HEAVEN WILL SEE THOSE SMILES.

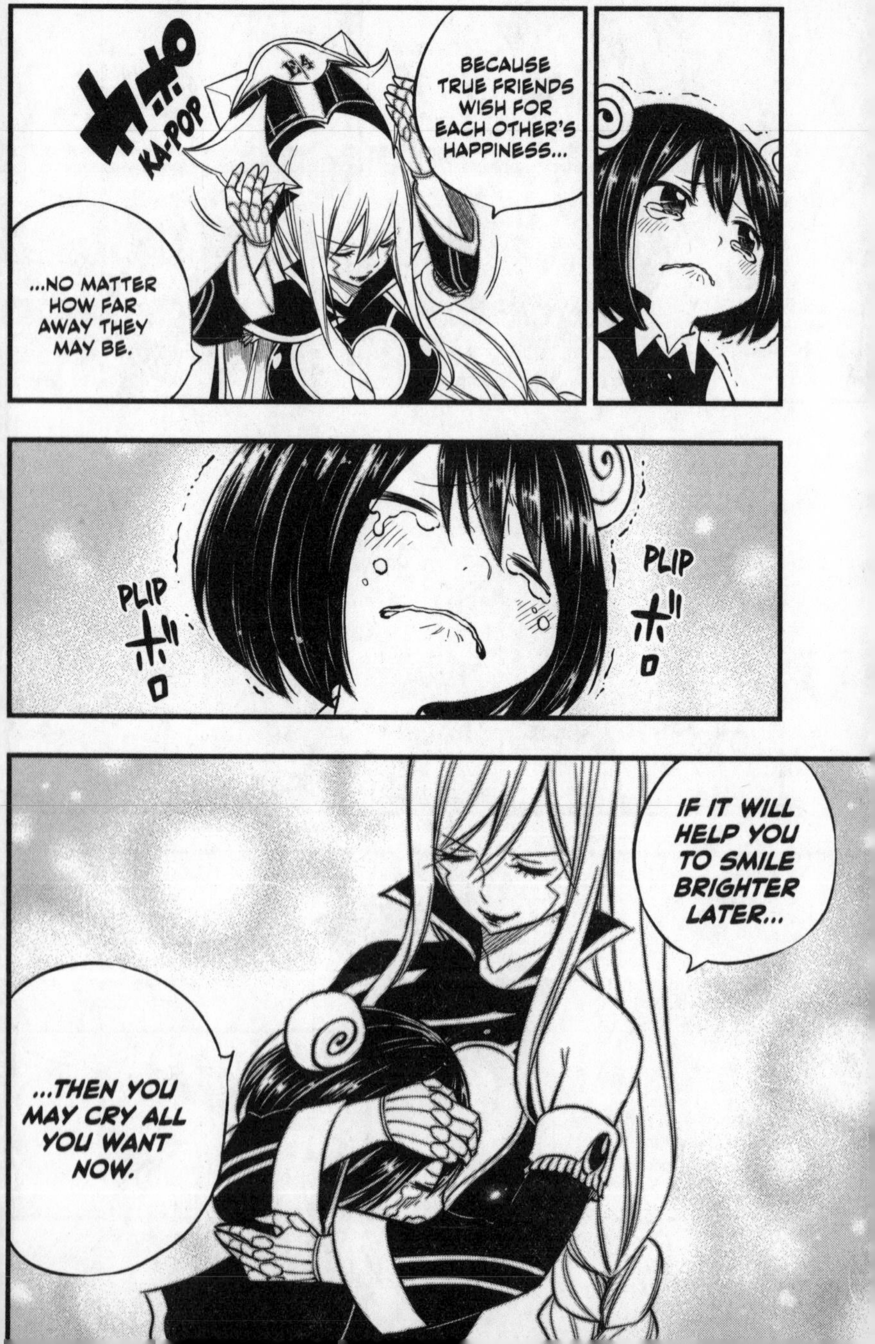
BECAUSE TRUE FRIENDS WISH FOR EACH OTHER'S HAPPINESS...
KA-POP
...NO MATTER HOW FAR AWAY THEY MAY BE.
PLIP
PLIP
IF IT WILL HELP YOU TO SMILE BRIGHTER LATER...
...THEN YOU MAY CRY ALL YOU WANT NOW.

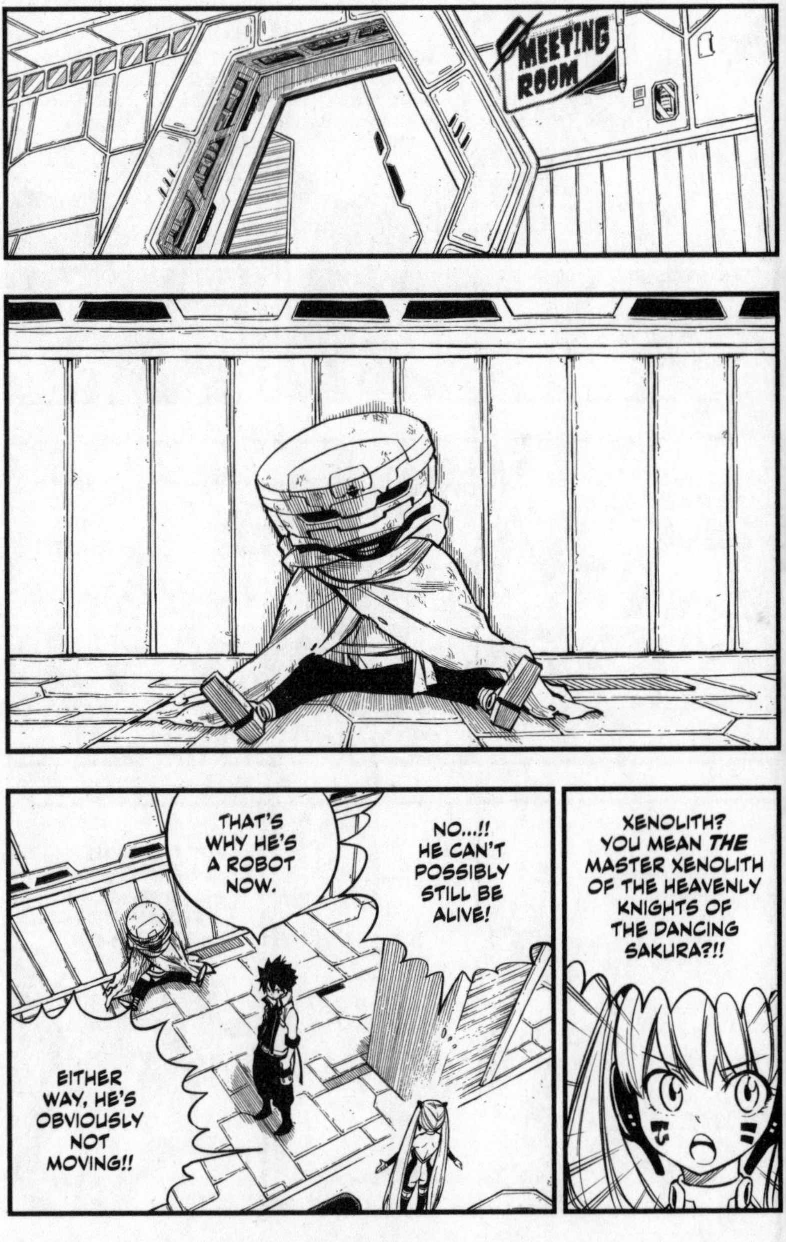
MEETING ROOM
XENOLITH? YOU MEAN *THE* MASTER XENOLITH OF THE HEAVENLY KNIGHTS OF THE DANCING SAKURA?!!
NO...!! HE CAN'T POSSIBLY STILL BE ALIVE!
THAT'S WHY HE'S A ROBOT NOW.
EITHER WAY, HE'S OBVIOUSLY NOT MOVING!!

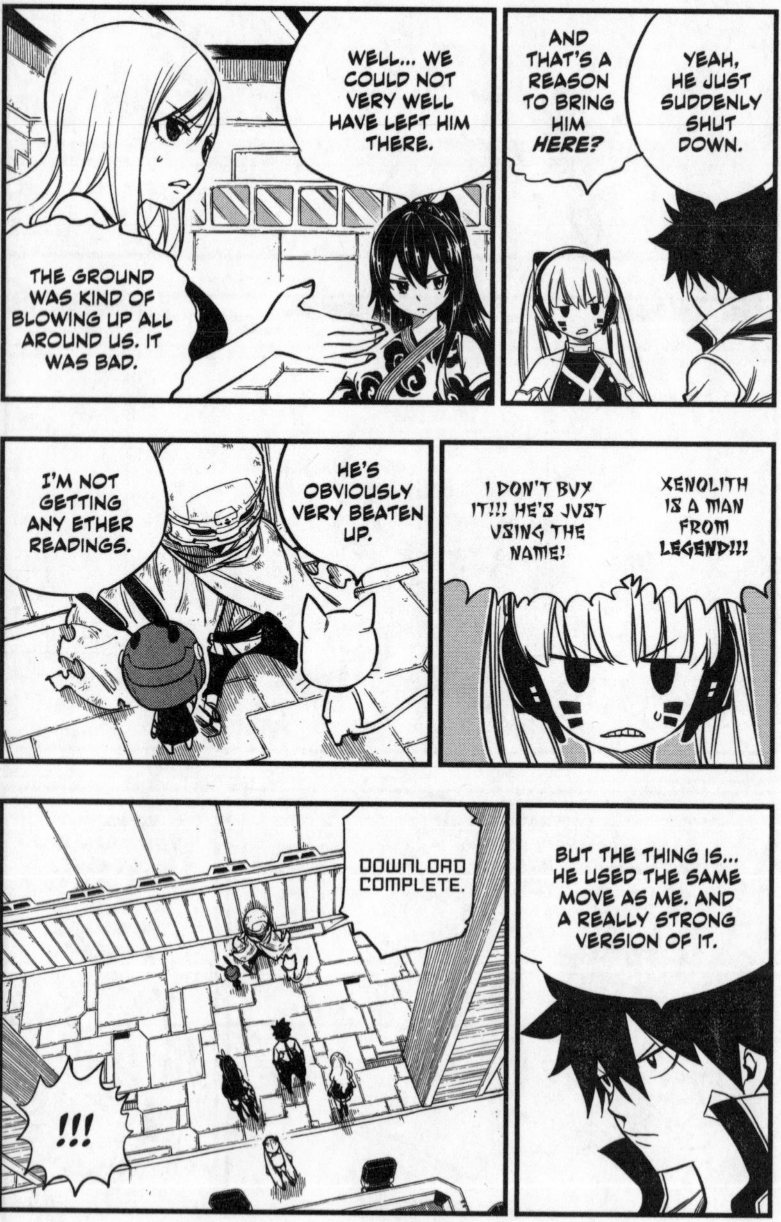
YEAH, HE JUST SUDDENLY SHUT DOWN.
AND THAT'S A REASON TO BRING HIM *HERE?*
WELL... WE COULD NOT VERY WELL HAVE LEFT HIM THERE.
THE GROUND WAS KIND OF BLOWING UP ALL AROUND US. IT WAS BAD.
XENOLITH IS A MAN FROM LEGEND!!!
I DON'T BUY IT!!! HE'S JUST USING THE NAME!
HE'S OBVIOUSLY VERY BEATEN UP.
I'M NOT GETTING ANY ETHER READINGS.
BUT THE THING IS... HE USED THE SAME MOVE AS ME. AND A REALLY STRONG VERSION OF IT.
DOWNLOAD COMPLETE.
!!!

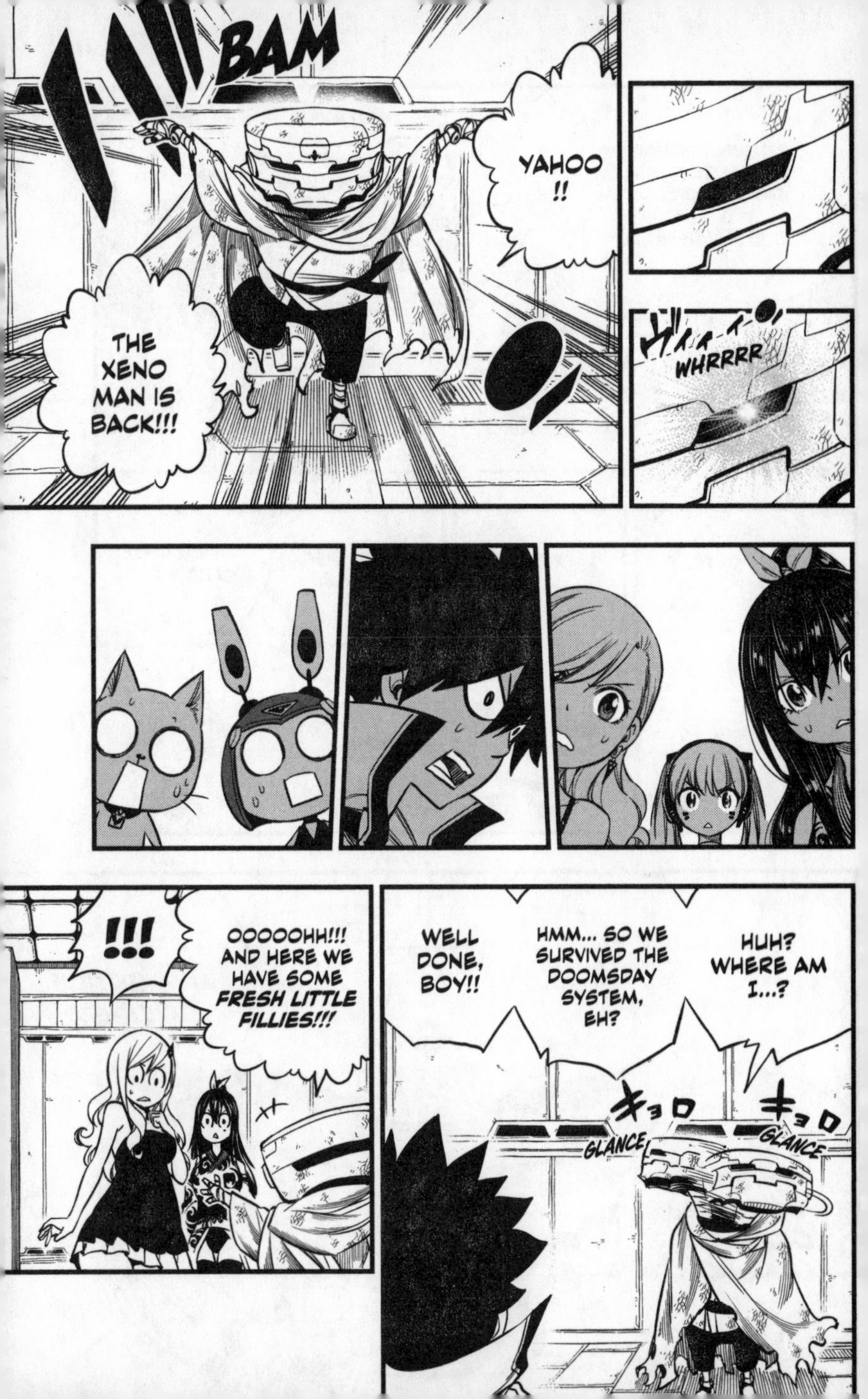
WHRRRR
BAM
YAHOO !!
THE XENO MAN IS BACK!!!
HUH? WHERE AM I...?
HMM... SO WE SURVIVED THE DOOMSDAY SYSTEM, EH?
WELL DONE, BOY!!
キョロ
GLANCE
キョロ
GLANCE
!!!
OOOOOHH!!! AND HERE WE HAVE SOME FRESH LITTLE FILLIES!!!

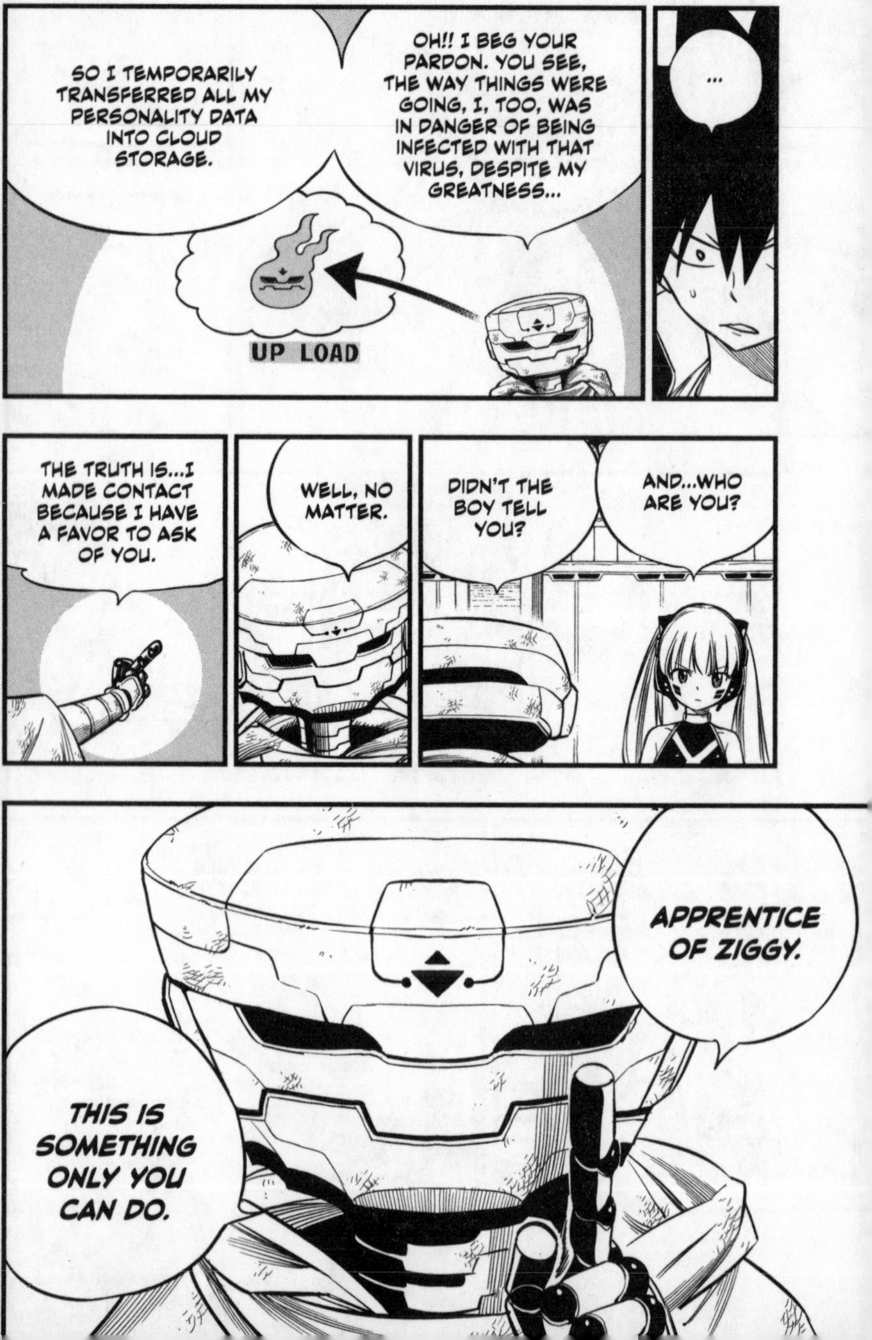
...
OH!! I BEG YOUR PARDON. YOU SEE, THE WAY THINGS WERE GOING, I, TOO, WAS IN DANGER OF BEING INFECTED WITH THAT VIRUS, DESPITE MY GREATNESS...
SO I TEMPORARILY TRANSFERRED ALL MY PERSONALITY DATA INTO CLOUD STORAGE.
UP LOAD
AND...WHO ARE YOU?
DIDN'T THE BOY TELL YOU?
WELL, NO MATTER.
THE TRUTH IS...I MADE CONTACT BECAUSE I HAVE A FAVOR TO ASK OF YOU.
APPRENTICE OF ZIGGY.
THIS IS SOMETHING ONLY YOU CAN DO.

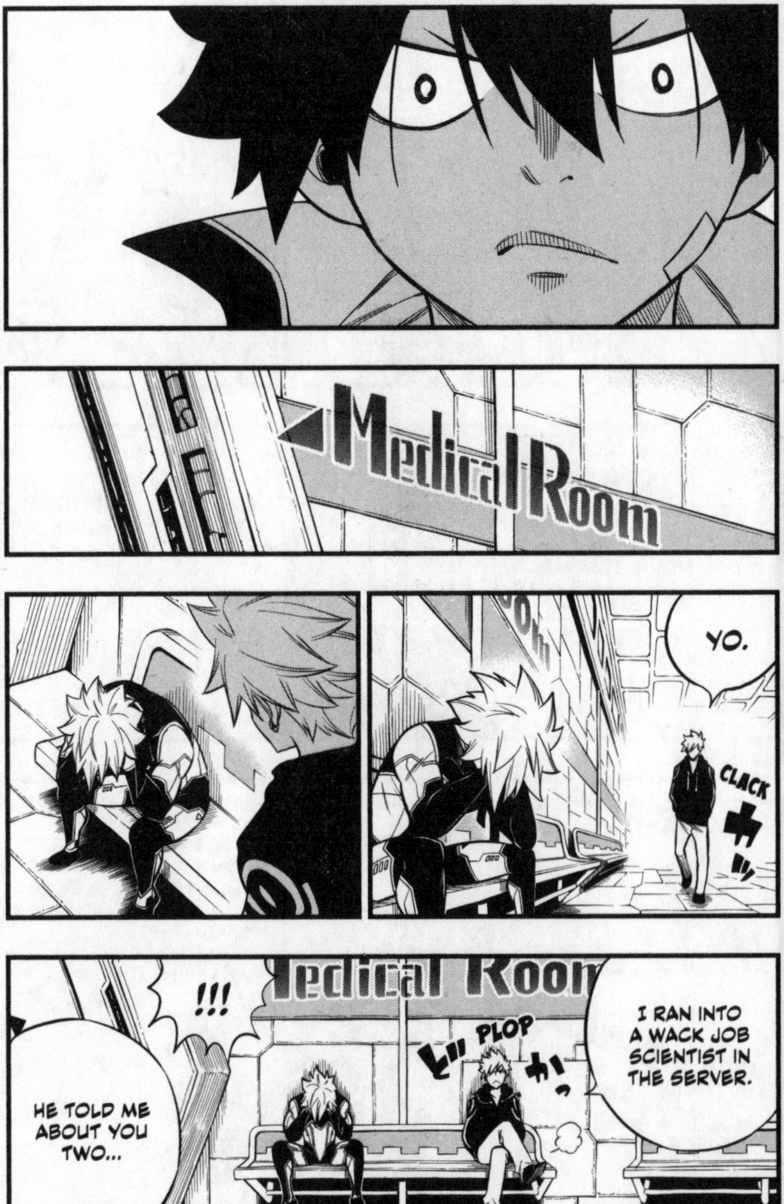
Medical Room
YO.
CLACK
I RAN INTO A WACK JOB SCIENTIST IN THE SERVER.
PLOP
!!!
HE TOLD ME ABOUT YOU TWO...

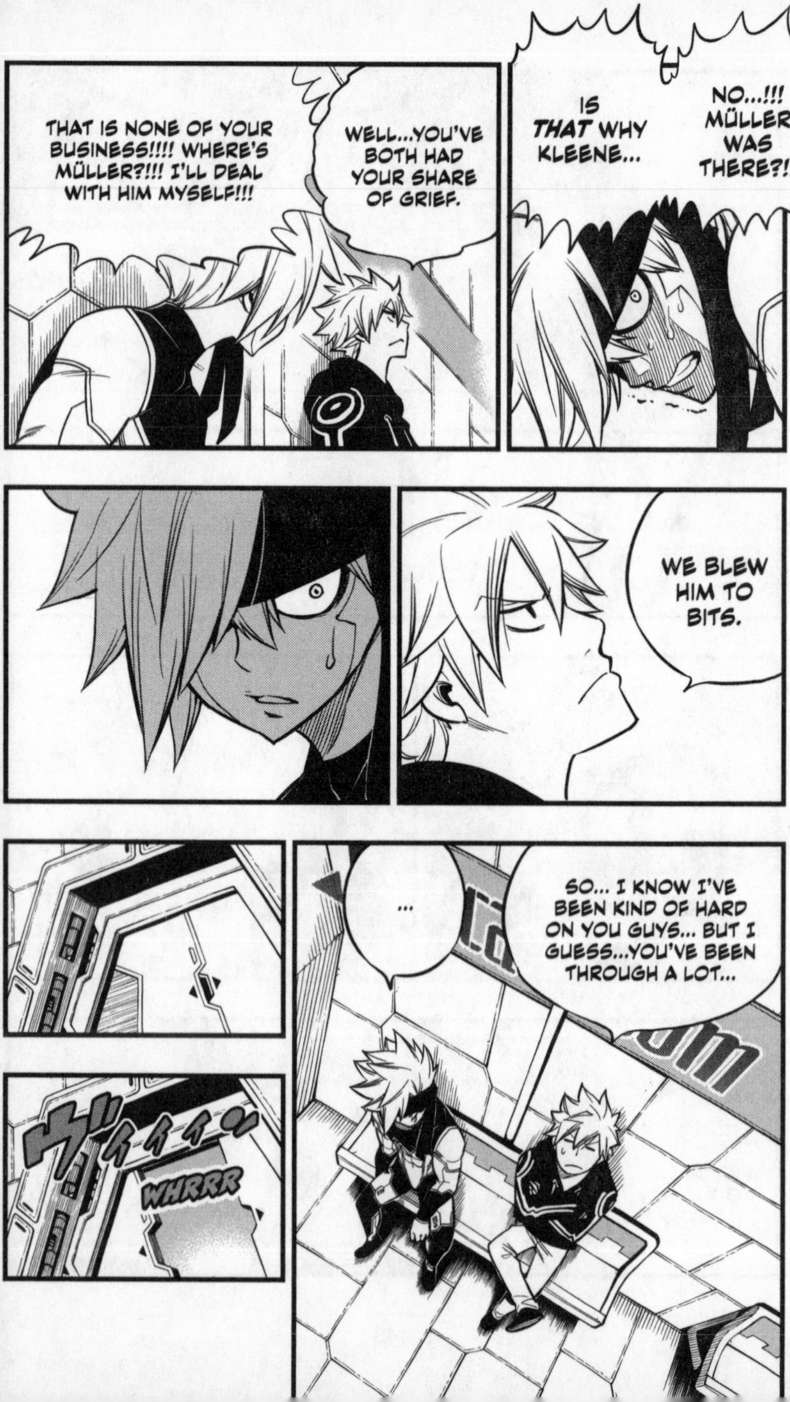
NO...!!! MÜLLER WAS THERE?!!
IS *THAT* WHY KLEENE...
WELL...YOU'VE BOTH HAD YOUR SHARE OF GRIEF.
THAT IS NONE OF YOUR BUSINESS!!!! WHERE'S MÜLLER?!!! I'LL DEAL WITH HIM MYSELF!!!
WE BLEW HIM TO BITS.
SO... I KNOW I'VE BEEN KIND OF HARD ON YOU GUYS... BUT I GUESS...YOU'VE BEEN THROUGH A LOT...
...
WHRRR

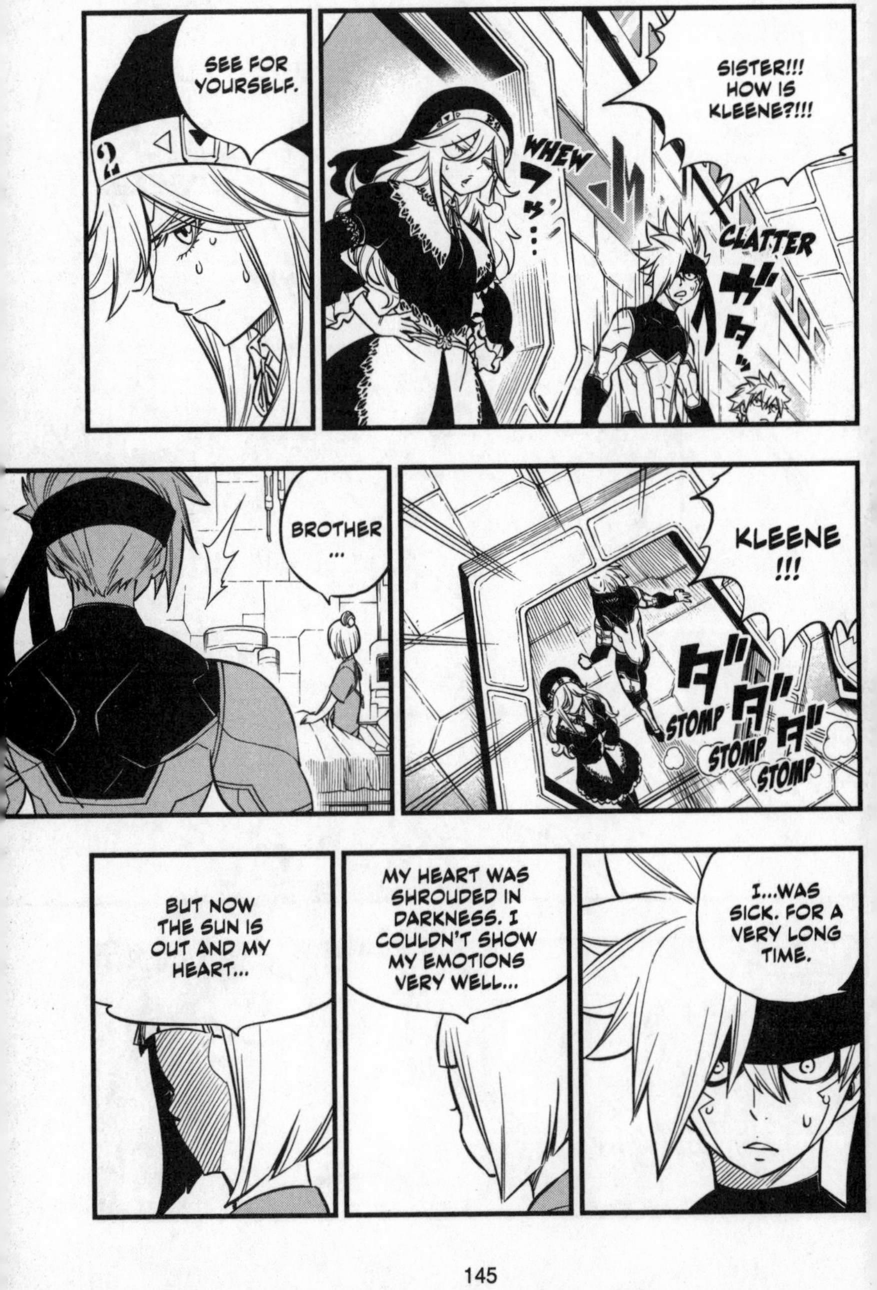
SISTER!!! HOW IS KLEENE?!!!
WHEW
CLATTER
SEE FOR YOURSELF.
KLEENE!!!
STOMP
STOMP
STOMP
BROTHER...
I...WAS SICK. FOR A VERY LONG TIME.
MY HEART WAS SHROUDED IN DARKNESS. I COULDN'T SHOW MY EMOTIONS VERY WELL...
BUT NOW THE SUN IS OUT AND MY HEART...

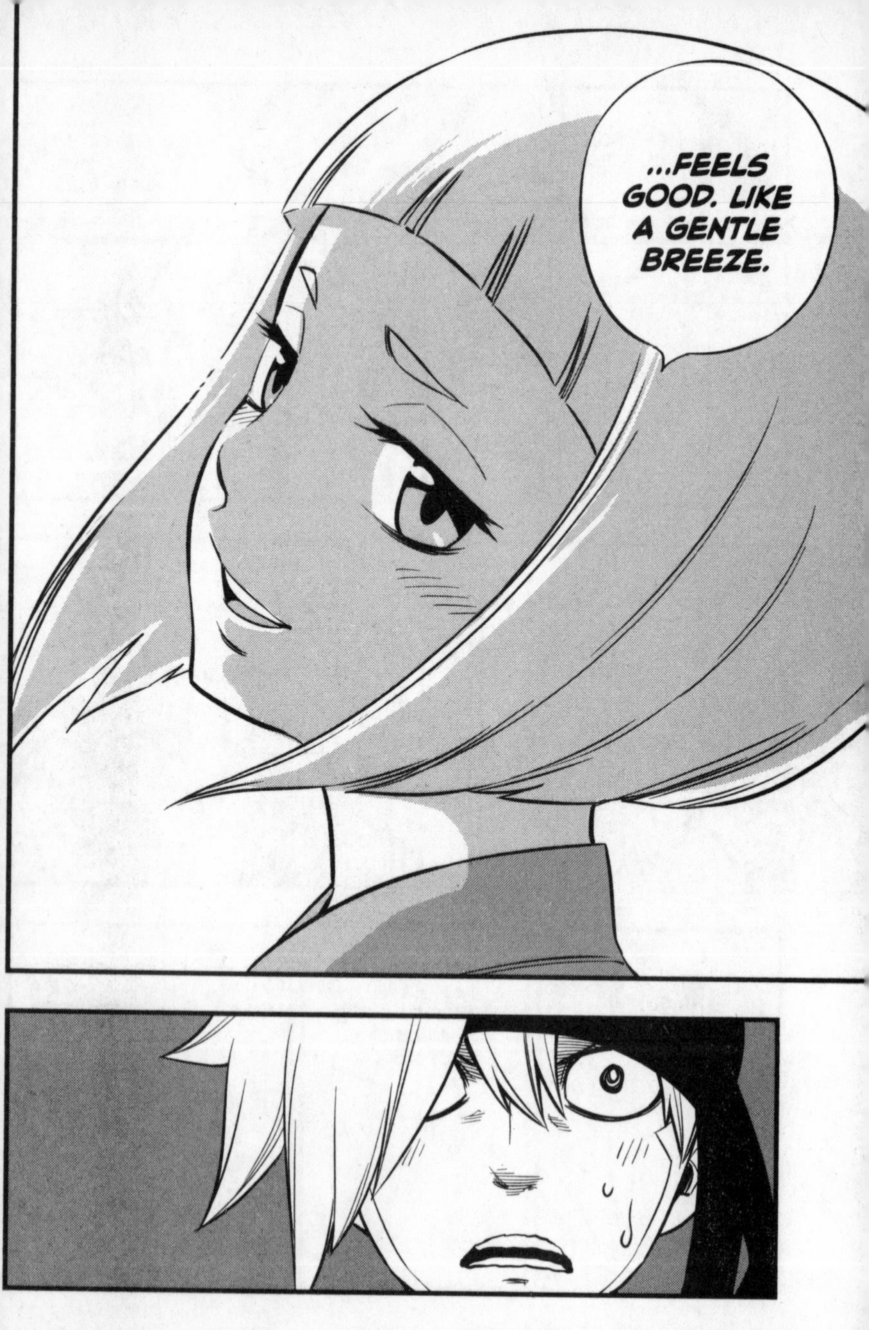
...FEELS GOOD. LIKE A GENTLE BREEZE.

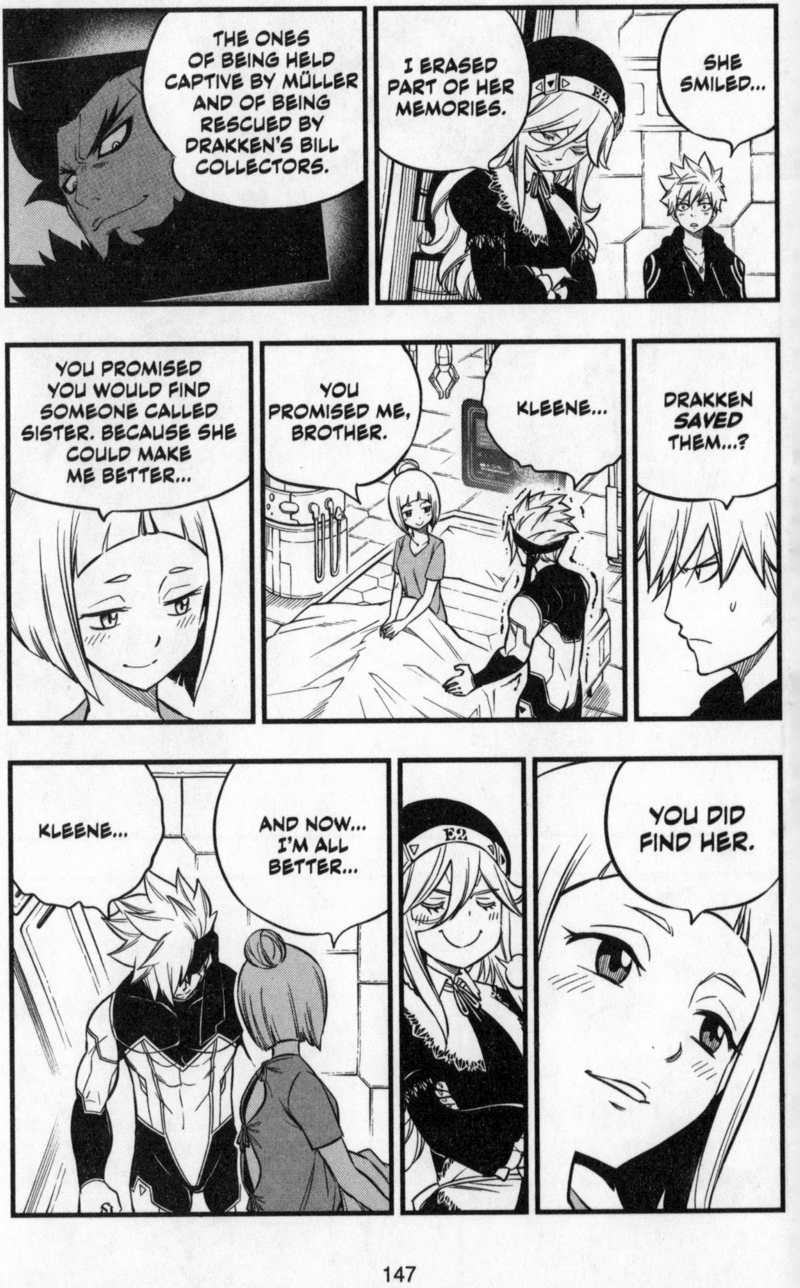
SHE SMILED...
I ERASED PART OF HER MEMORIES.
THE ONES OF BEING HELD CAPTIVE BY MÜLLER AND OF BEING RESCUED BY DRAKKEN'S BILL COLLECTORS.
DRAKKEN *SAVED* THEM...?
KLEENE...
YOU PROMISED ME, BROTHER.
YOU PROMISED YOU WOULD FIND SOMEONE CALLED SISTER. BECAUSE SHE COULD MAKE ME BETTER...
YOU DID FIND HER.
AND NOW... I'M ALL BETTER...
KLEENE...

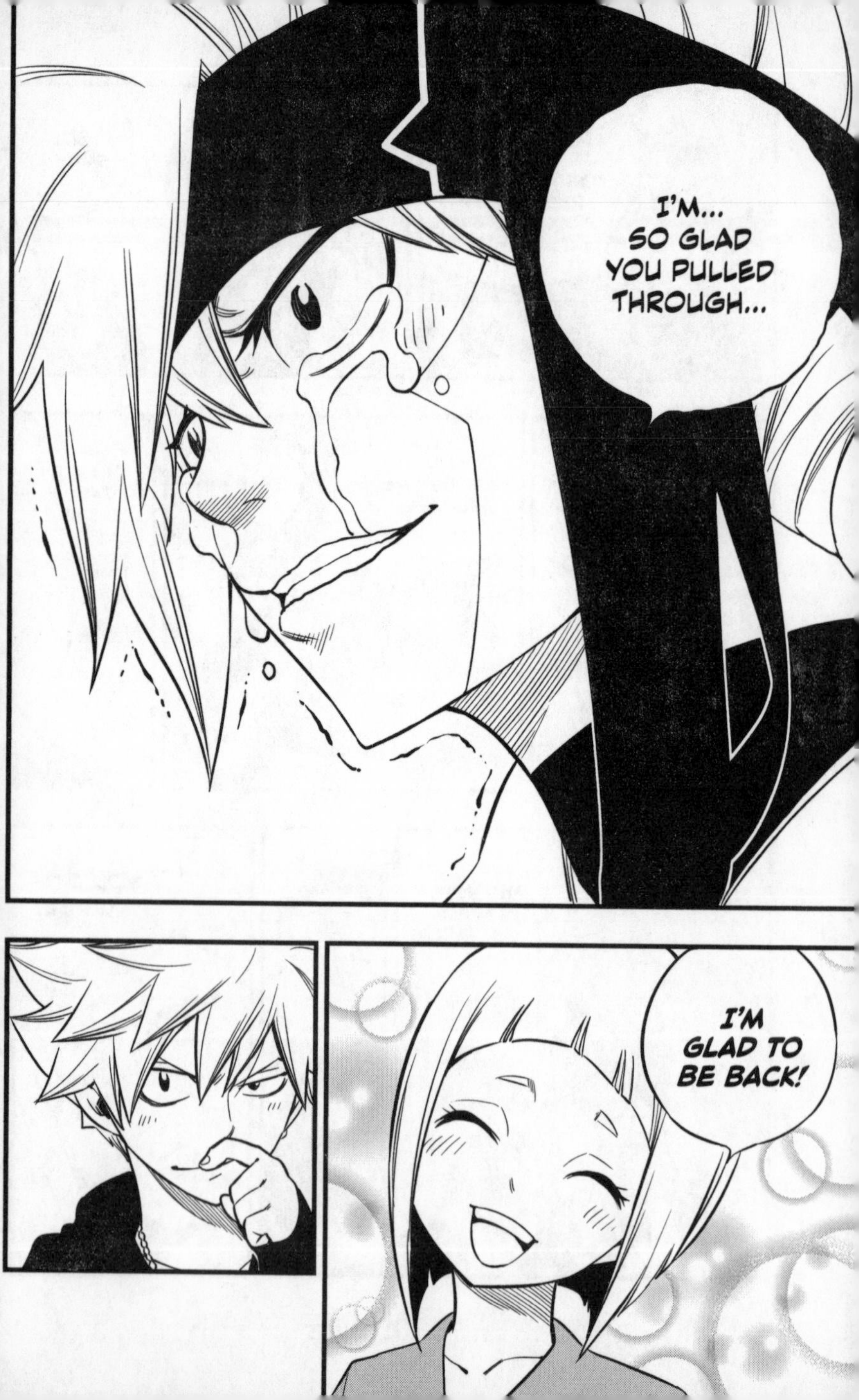
I'M... SO GLAD YOU PULLED THROUGH...
I'M GLAD TO BE BACK!

EDENS ZERO

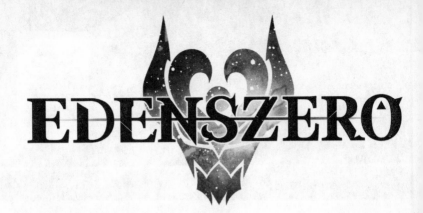

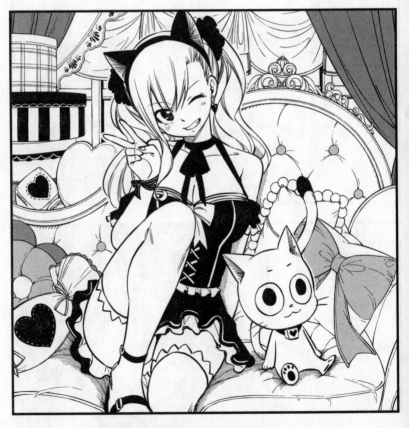

CHAPTER 130: OCEANS 6

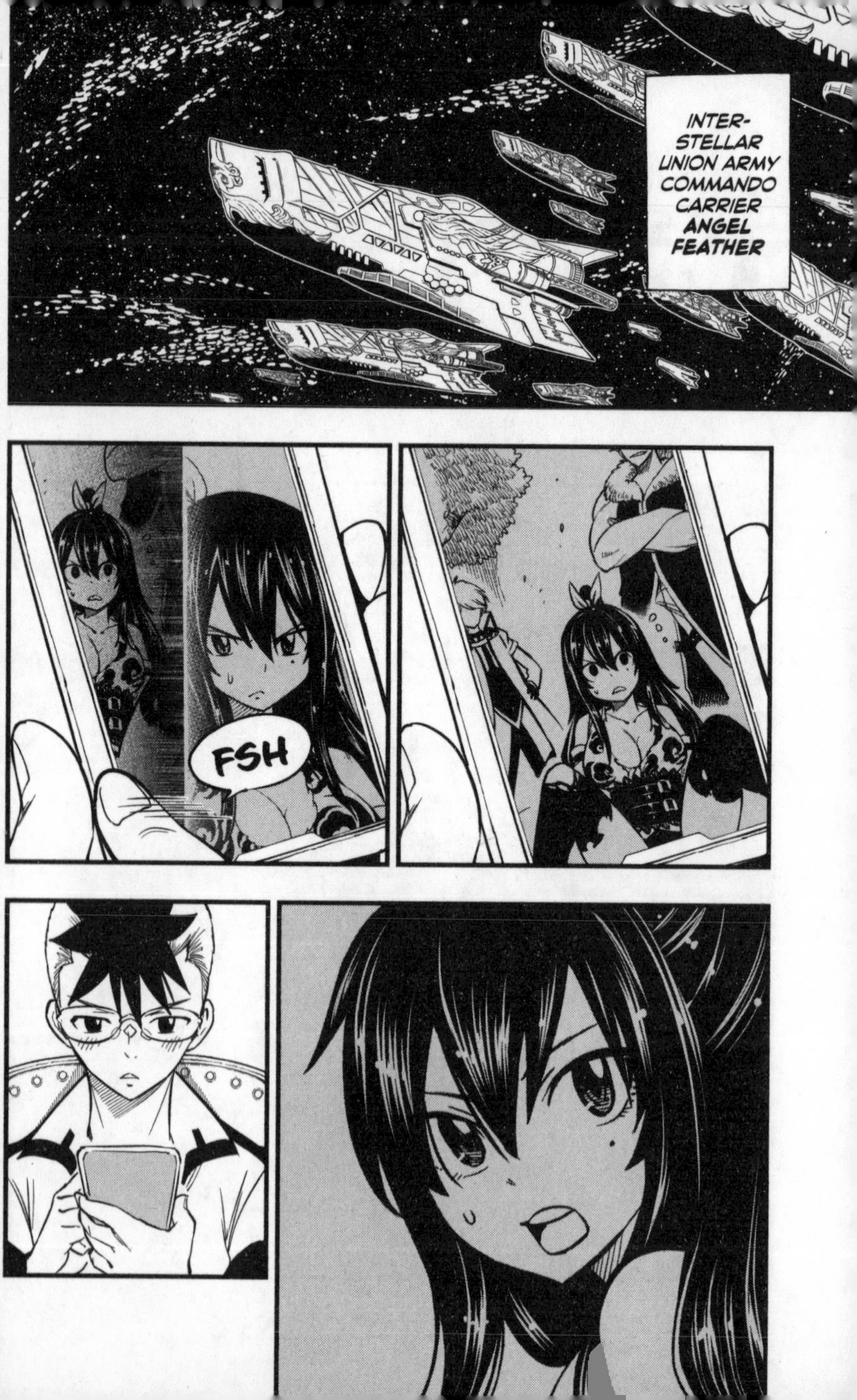
INTER-STELLAR UNION ARMY COMMANDO CARRIER ANGEL FEATHER
FSH

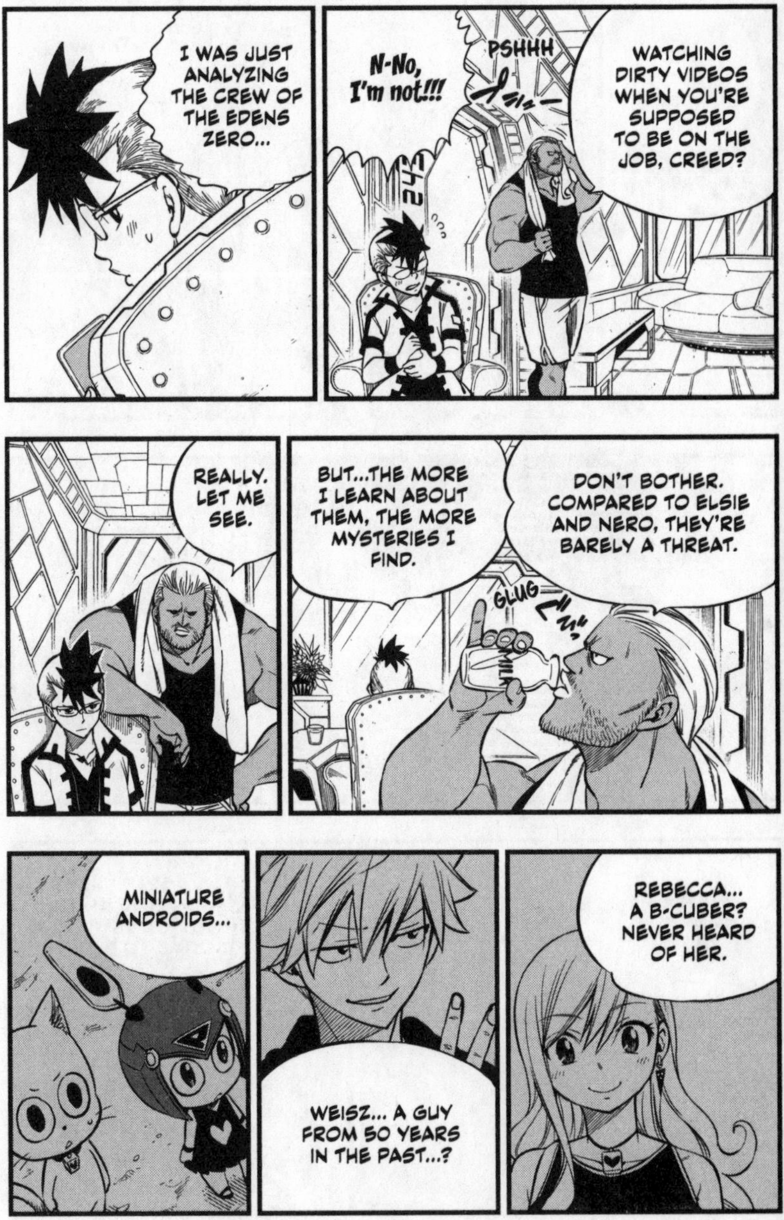
WATCHING DIRTY VIDEOS WHEN YOU'RE SUPPOSED TO BE ON THE JOB, CREED?
PSHHH
N-No, I'm not!!!
I WAS JUST ANALYZING THE CREW OF THE EDENS ZERO...
DON'T BOTHER. COMPARED TO ELSIE AND NERO, THEY'RE BARELY A THREAT.
BUT...THE MORE I LEARN ABOUT THEM, THE MORE MYSTERIES I FIND.
GLUG
MILK
REALLY. LET ME SEE.
REBECCA... A B-CUBER? NEVER HEARD OF HER.
WEISZ... A GUY FROM 50 YEARS IN THE PAST...?
MINIATURE ANDROIDS...

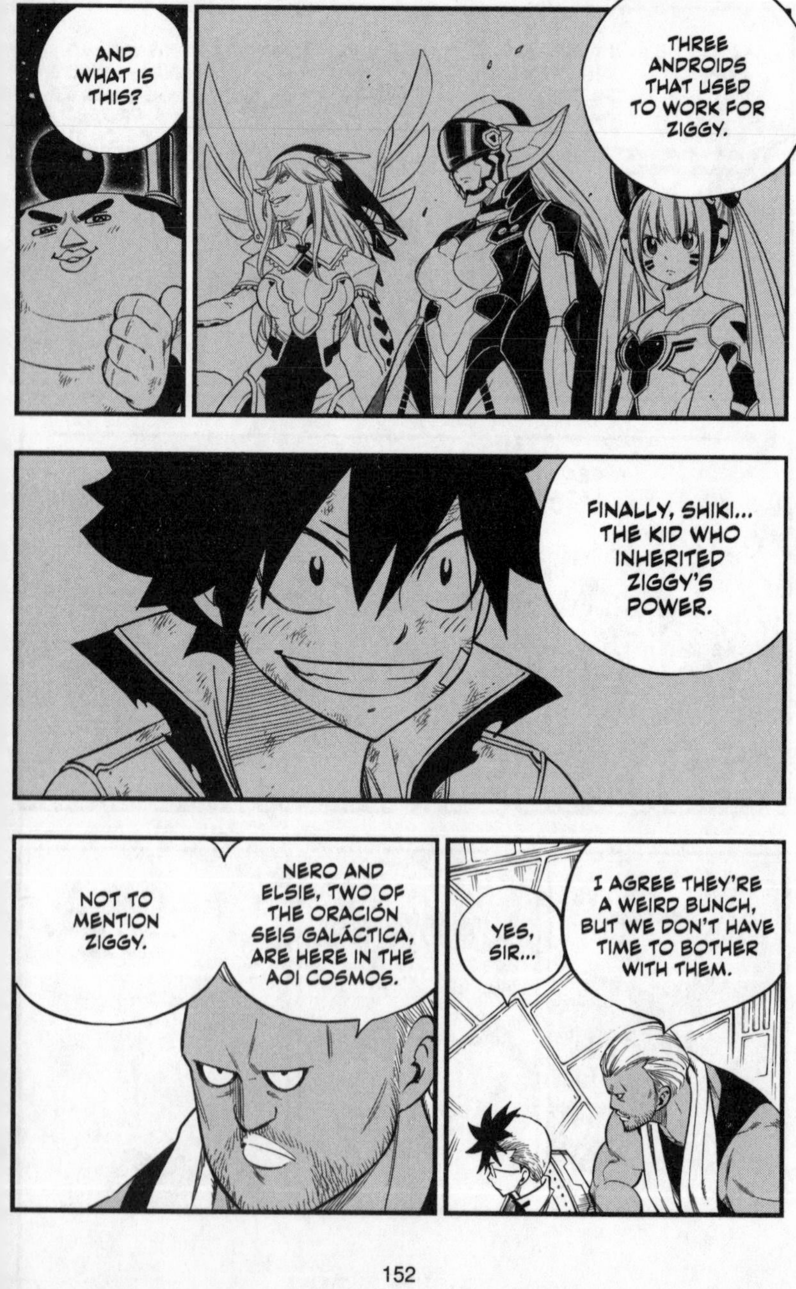
THREE ANDROIDS THAT USED TO WORK FOR ZIGGY.
AND WHAT IS THIS?
FINALLY, SHIKI... THE KID WHO INHERITED ZIGGY'S POWER.
I AGREE THEY'RE A WEIRD BUNCH, BUT WE DON'T HAVE TIME TO BOTHER WITH THEM.
YES, SIR...
NERO AND ELSIE, TWO OF THE ORACIÓN SEIS GALÁCTICA, ARE HERE IN THE AOI COSMOS.
NOT TO MENTION ZIGGY.

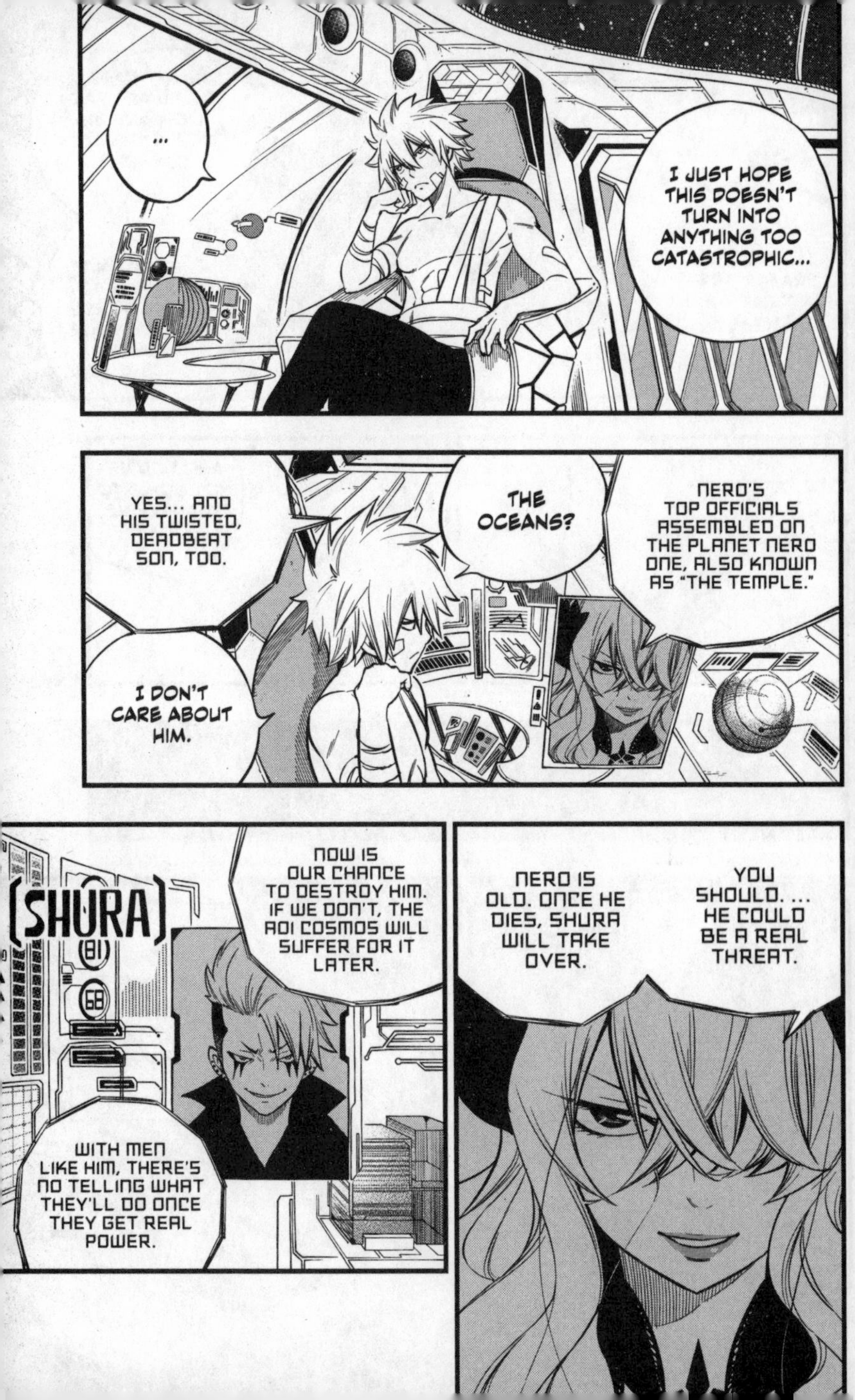

I JUST HOPE THIS DOESN'T TURN INTO ANYTHING TOO CATASTROPHIC...
...
NERO'S TOP OFFICIALS ASSEMBLED ON THE PLANET NERO ONE, ALSO KNOWN AS "THE TEMPLE."
THE OCEANS?
YES... AND HIS TWISTED, DEADBEAT SON, TOO.
I DON'T CARE ABOUT HIM.
YOU SHOULD. ... HE COULD BE A REAL THREAT.
NERO IS OLD. ONCE HE DIES, SHURA WILL TAKE OVER.
SHŪRA
81
68
NOW IS OUR CHANCE TO DESTROY HIM. IF WE DON'T, THE AOI COSMOS WILL SUFFER FOR IT LATER.
WITH MEN LIKE HIM, THERE'S NO TELLING WHAT THEY'LL DO ONCE THEY GET REAL POWER.

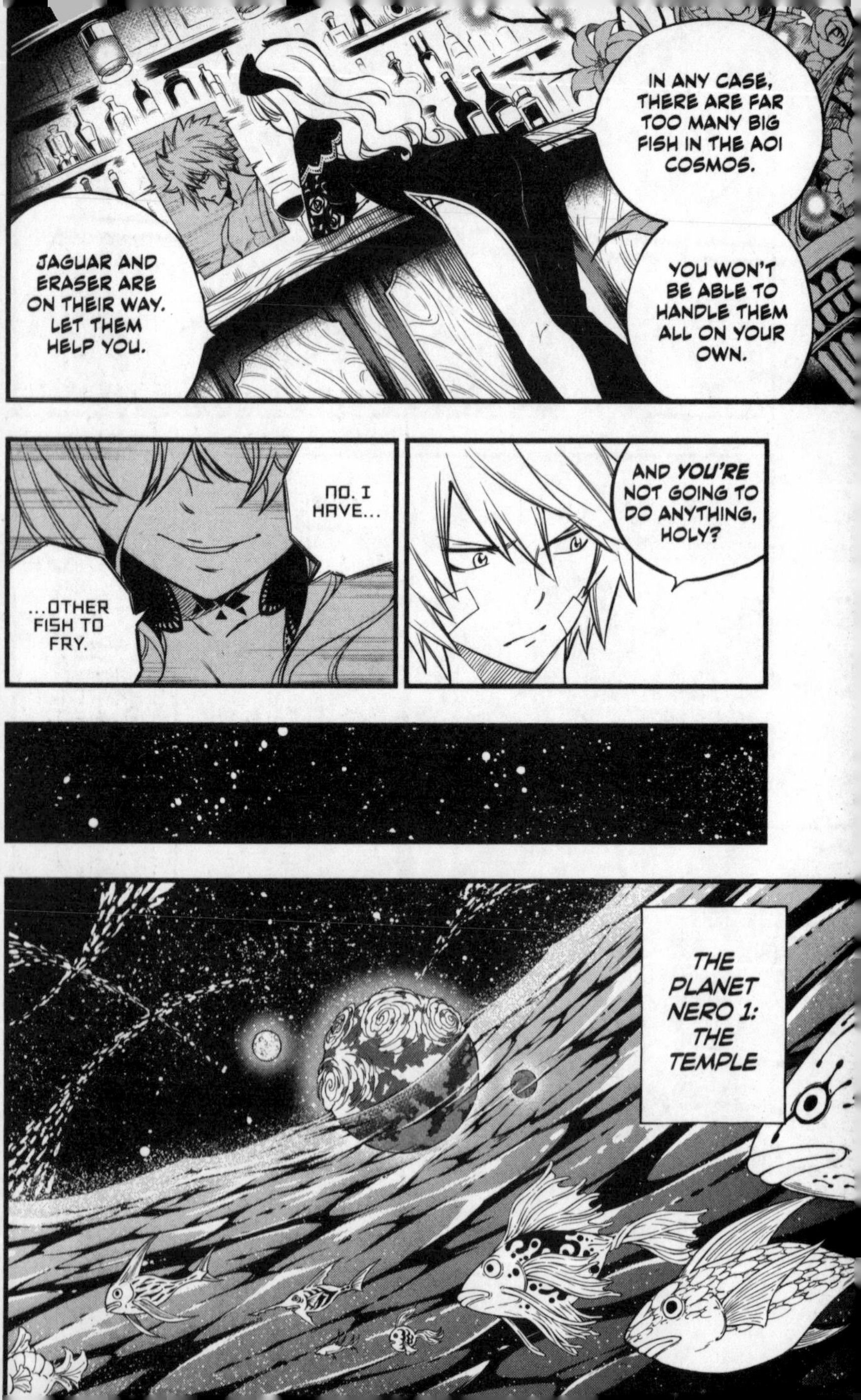
IN ANY CASE, THERE ARE FAR TOO MANY BIG FISH IN THE AOI COSMOS.
YOU WON'T BE ABLE TO HANDLE THEM ALL ON YOUR OWN.
JAGUAR AND ERASER ARE ON THEIR WAY. LET THEM HELP YOU.
AND *YOU'RE* NOT GOING TO DO ANYTHING, HOLY?
NO. I HAVE...
...OTHER FISH TO FRY.
THE PLANET NERO 1: THE TEMPLE

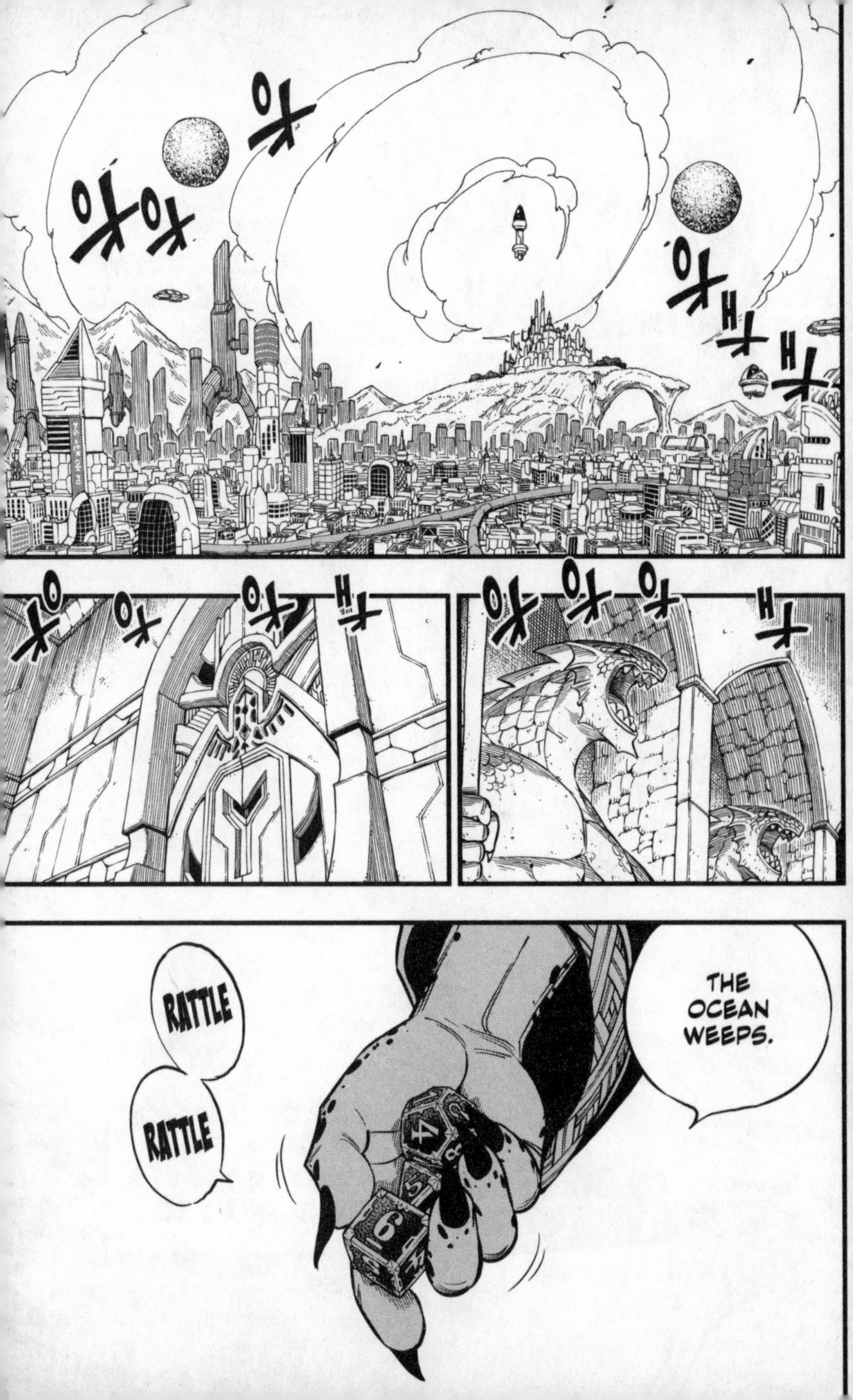
THE OCEAN WEEPS.
RATTLE
RATTLE

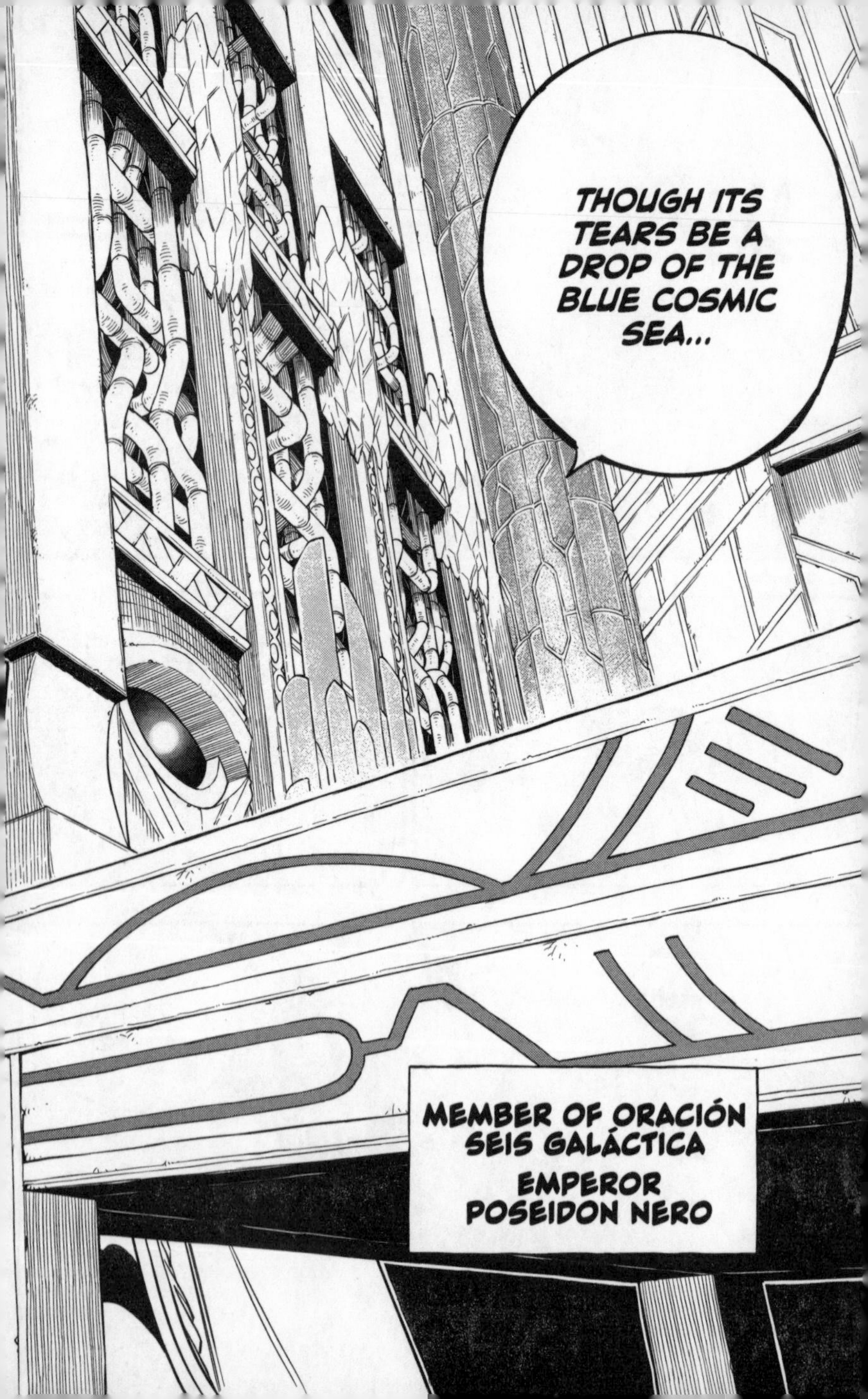
THOUGH ITS TEARS BE A DROP OF THE BLUE COSMIC SEA...
MEMBER OF ORACIÓN SEIS GALÁCTICA
EMPEROR POSEIDON NERO

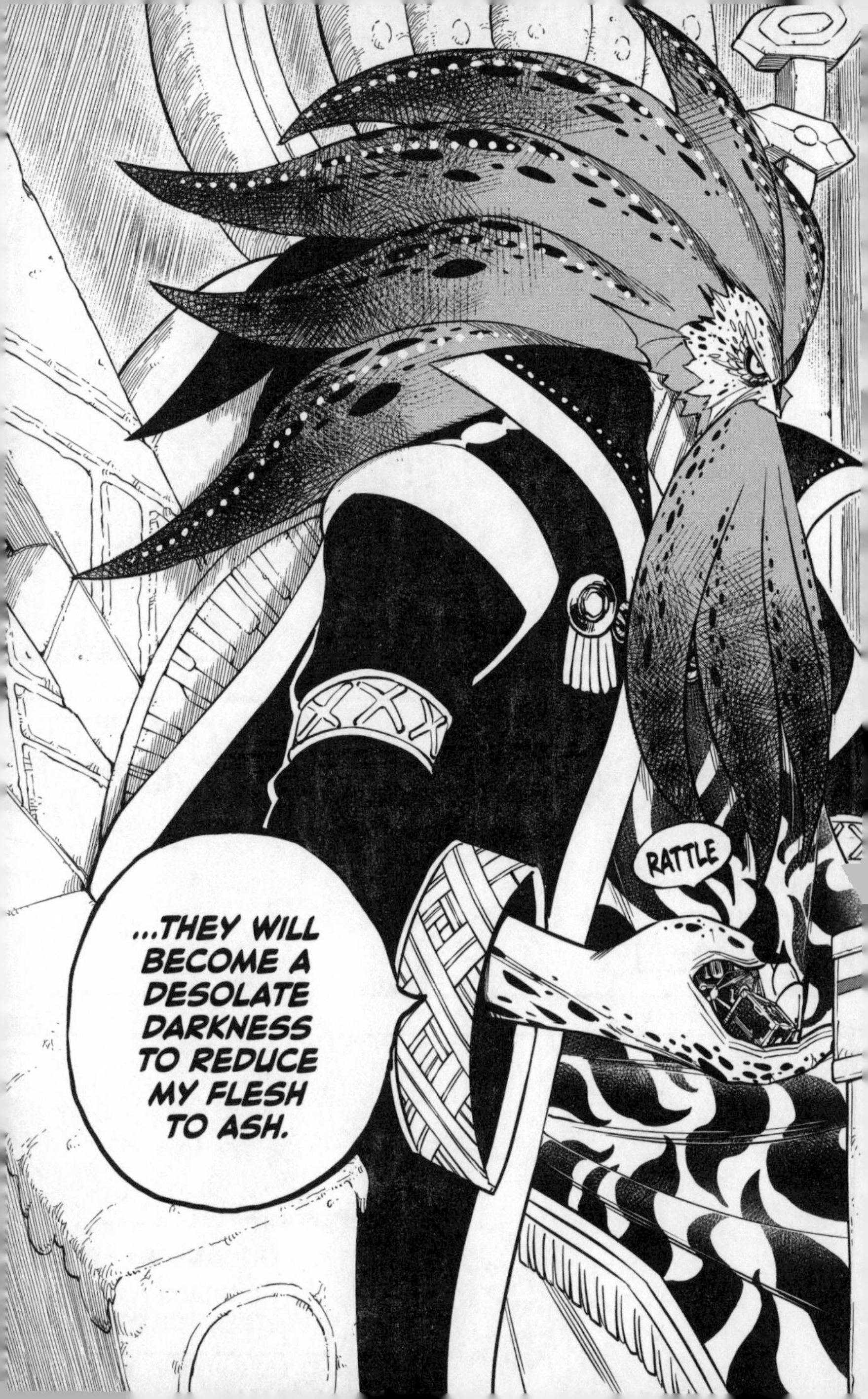
RATTLE
...THEY WILL BECOME A DESOLATE DARKNESS TO REDUCE MY FLESH TO ASH.

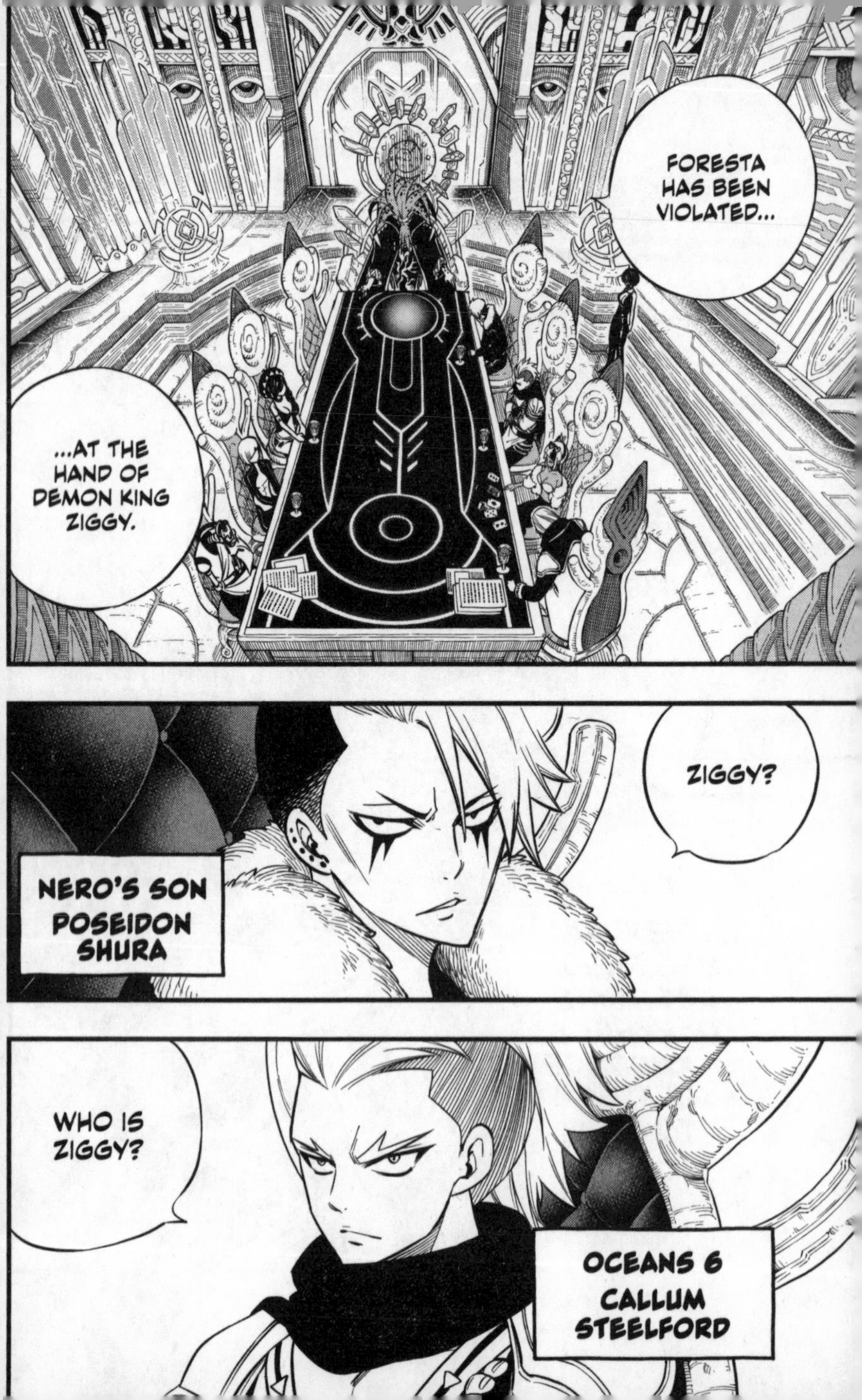
FORESTA HAS BEEN VIOLATED...
...AT THE HAND OF DEMON KING ZIGGY.
ZIGGY?
NERO'S SON POSEIDON SHURA
WHO IS ZIGGY?
OCEANS 6 CALLUM STEELFORD

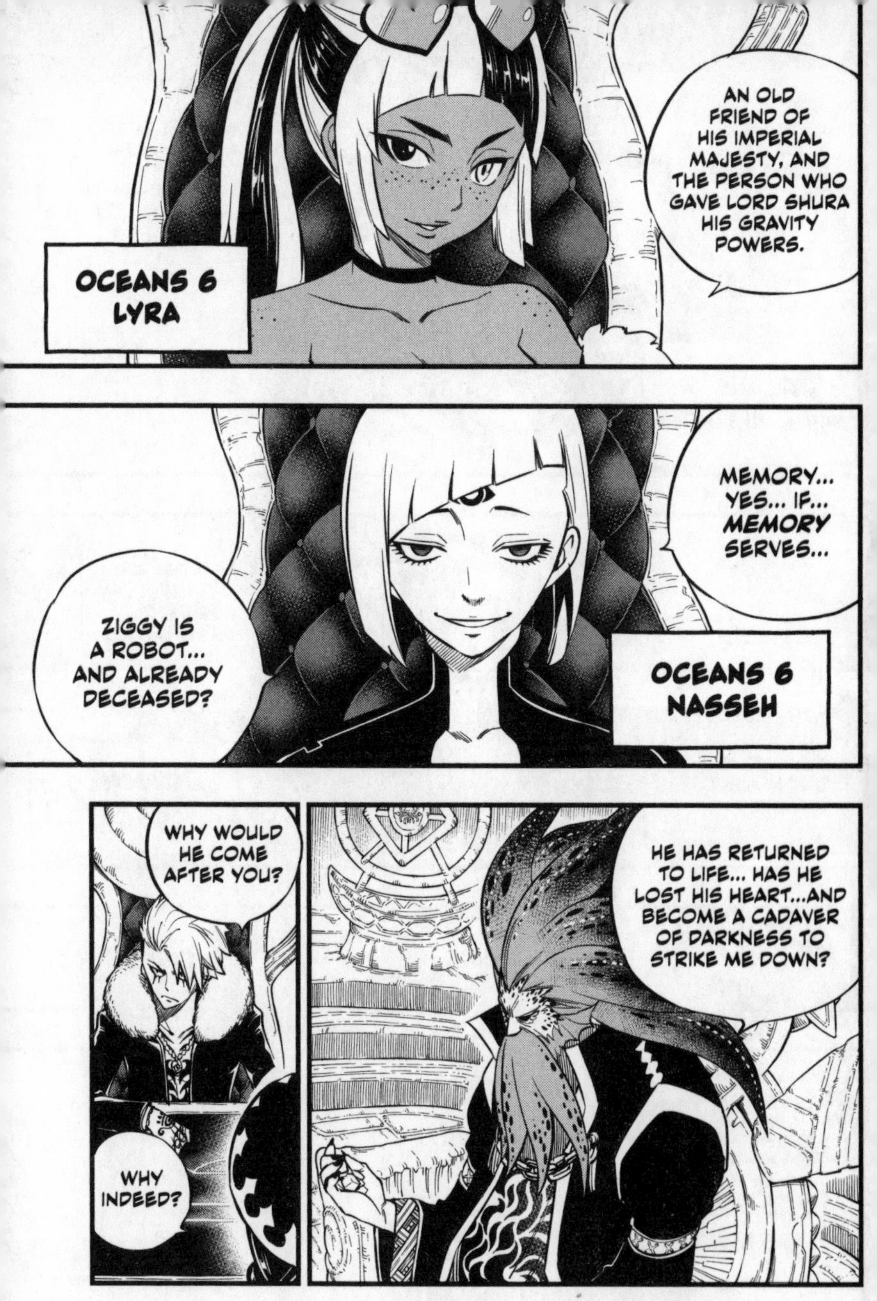
AN OLD FRIEND OF HIS IMPERIAL MAJESTY, AND THE PERSON WHO GAVE LORD SHURA HIS GRAVITY POWERS.
OCEANS 6 LYRA
MEMORY... YES... IF... *MEMORY* SERVES...
OCEANS 6 NASSEH
ZIGGY IS A ROBOT... AND ALREADY DECEASED?
HE HAS RETURNED TO LIFE... HAS HE LOST HIS HEART...AND BECOME A CADAVER OF DARKNESS TO STRIKE ME DOWN?
WHY WOULD HE COME AFTER YOU?
WHY INDEED?

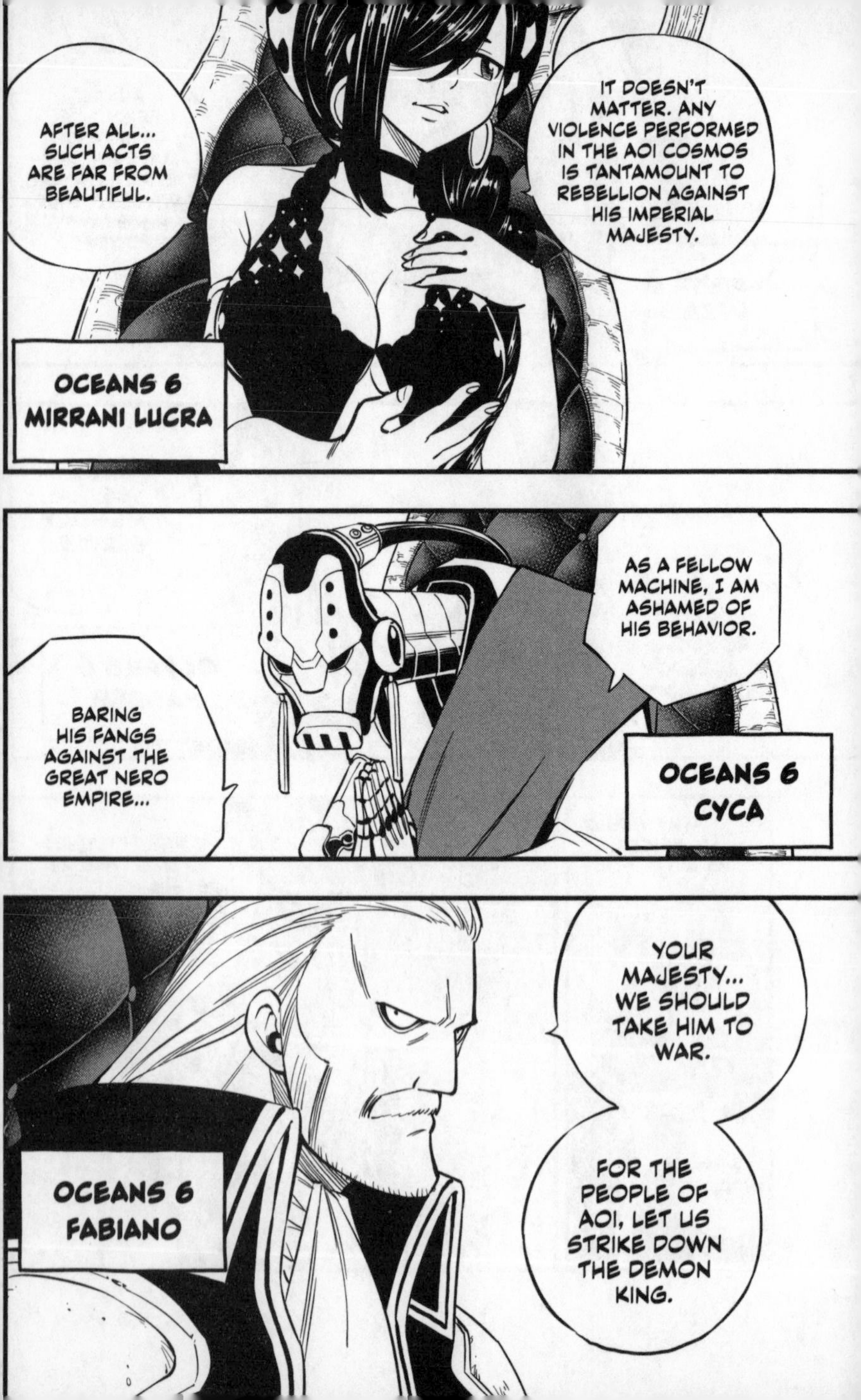
IT DOESN'T MATTER. ANY VIOLENCE PERFORMED IN THE AOI COSMOS IS TANTAMOUNT TO REBELLION AGAINST HIS IMPERIAL MAJESTY.
AFTER ALL... SUCH ACTS ARE FAR FROM BEAUTIFUL.
OCEANS 6 MIRRANI LUCRA
AS A FELLOW MACHINE, I AM ASHAMED OF HIS BEHAVIOR.
BARING HIS FANGS AGAINST THE GREAT NERO EMPIRE...
OCEANS 6 CYCA
YOUR MAJESTY... WE SHOULD TAKE HIM TO WAR.
FOR THE PEOPLE OF AOI, LET US STRIKE DOWN THE DEMON KING.
OCEANS 6 FABIANO

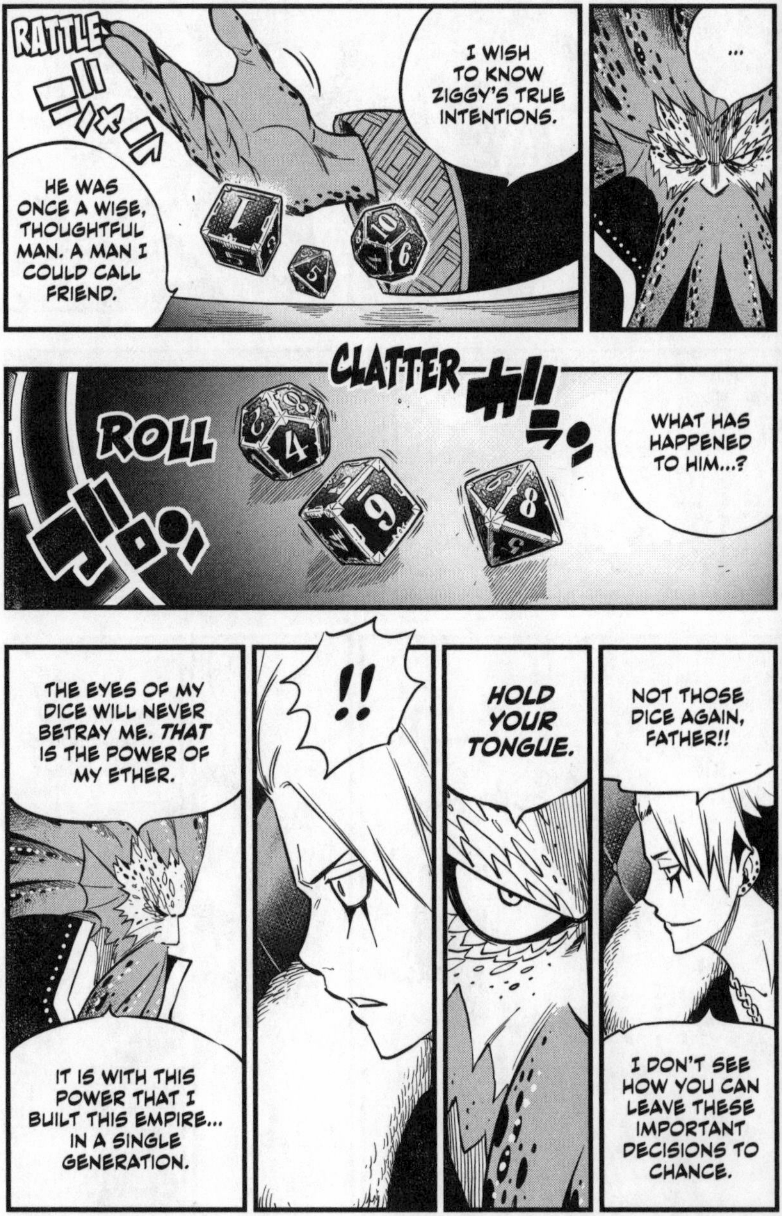
...
I WISH TO KNOW ZIGGY'S TRUE INTENTIONS.
RATTLE
HE WAS ONCE A WISE, THOUGHTFUL MAN. A MAN I COULD CALL FRIEND.
WHAT HAS HAPPENED TO HIM...?
CLATTER
ROLL
NOT THOSE DICE AGAIN, FATHER!!
I DON'T SEE HOW YOU CAN LEAVE THESE IMPORTANT DECISIONS TO CHANCE.
HOLD YOUR TONGUE.
!!
THE EYES OF MY DICE WILL NEVER BETRAY ME. *THAT* IS THE POWER OF MY ETHER.
IT IS WITH THIS POWER THAT I BUILT THIS EMPIRE... IN A SINGLE GENERATION.

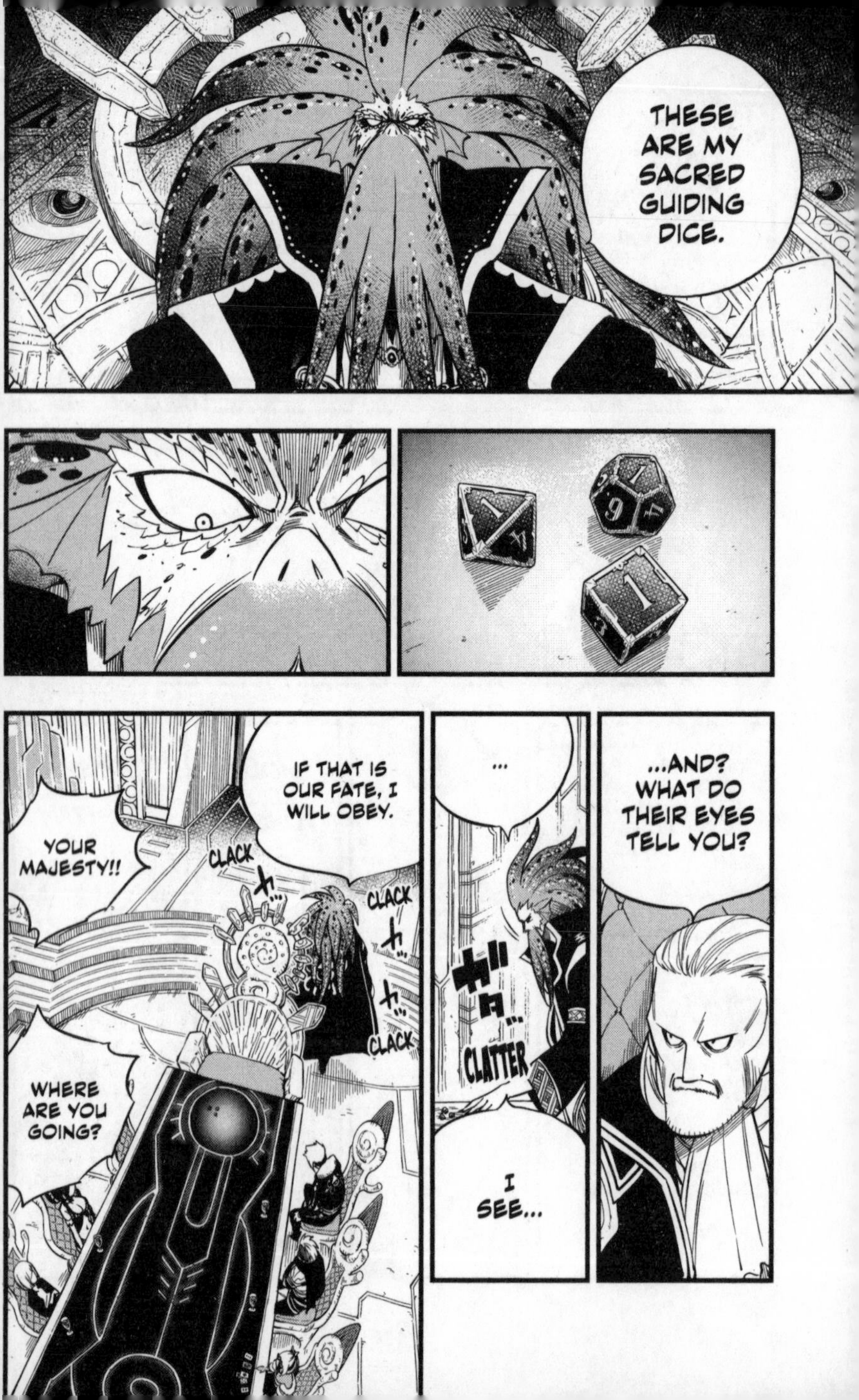
THESE ARE MY SACRED GUIDING DICE.
...AND? WHAT DO THEIR EYES TELL YOU?
...
CLATTER
I SEE...
IF THAT IS OUR FATE, I WILL OBEY.
CLACK
CLACK
CLACK
YOUR MAJESTY!!
WHERE ARE YOU GOING?

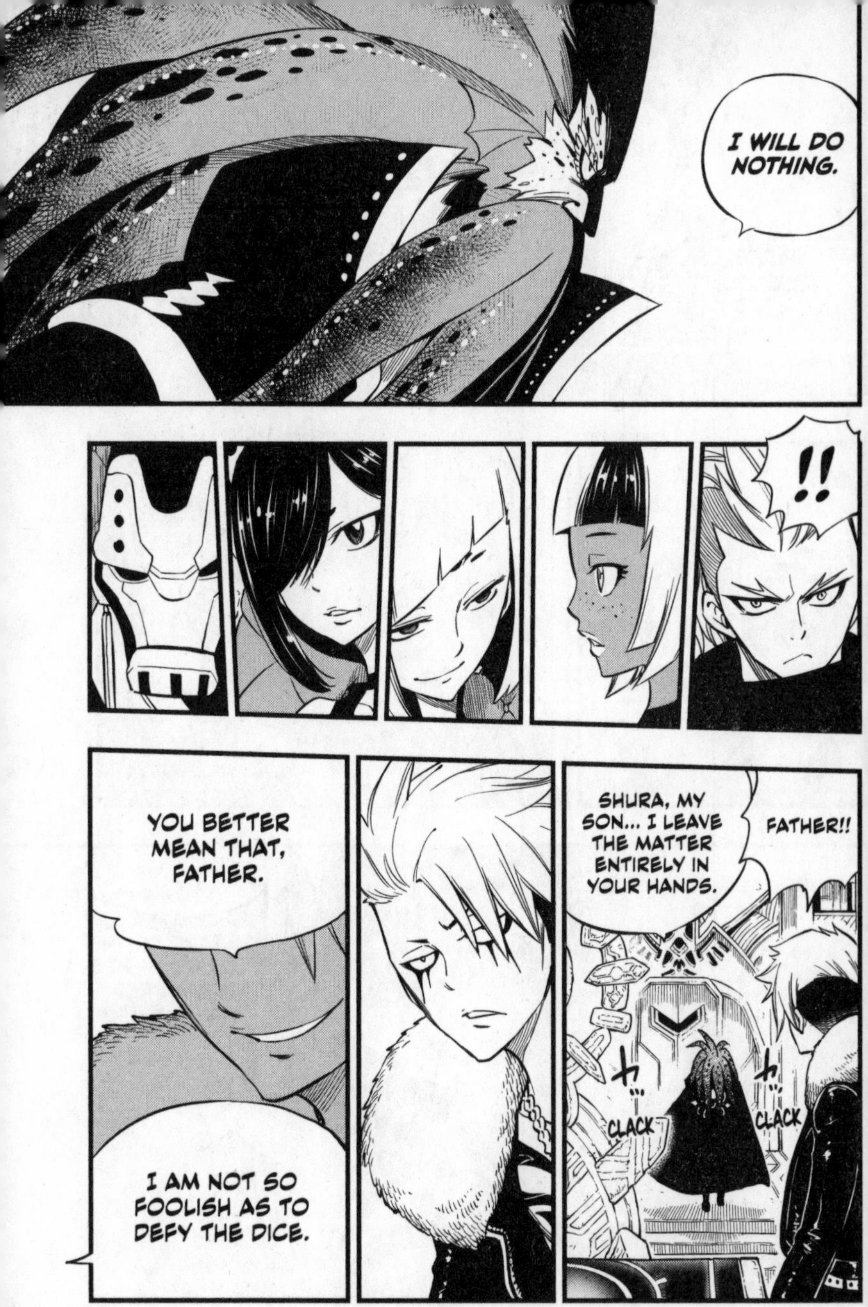
I WILL DO NOTHING.
!!
FATHER!!
SHURA, MY SON... I LEAVE THE MATTER ENTIRELY IN YOUR HANDS.
CLACK
CLACK
YOU BETTER MEAN THAT, FATHER.
I AM NOT SO FOOLISH AS TO DEFY THE DICE.

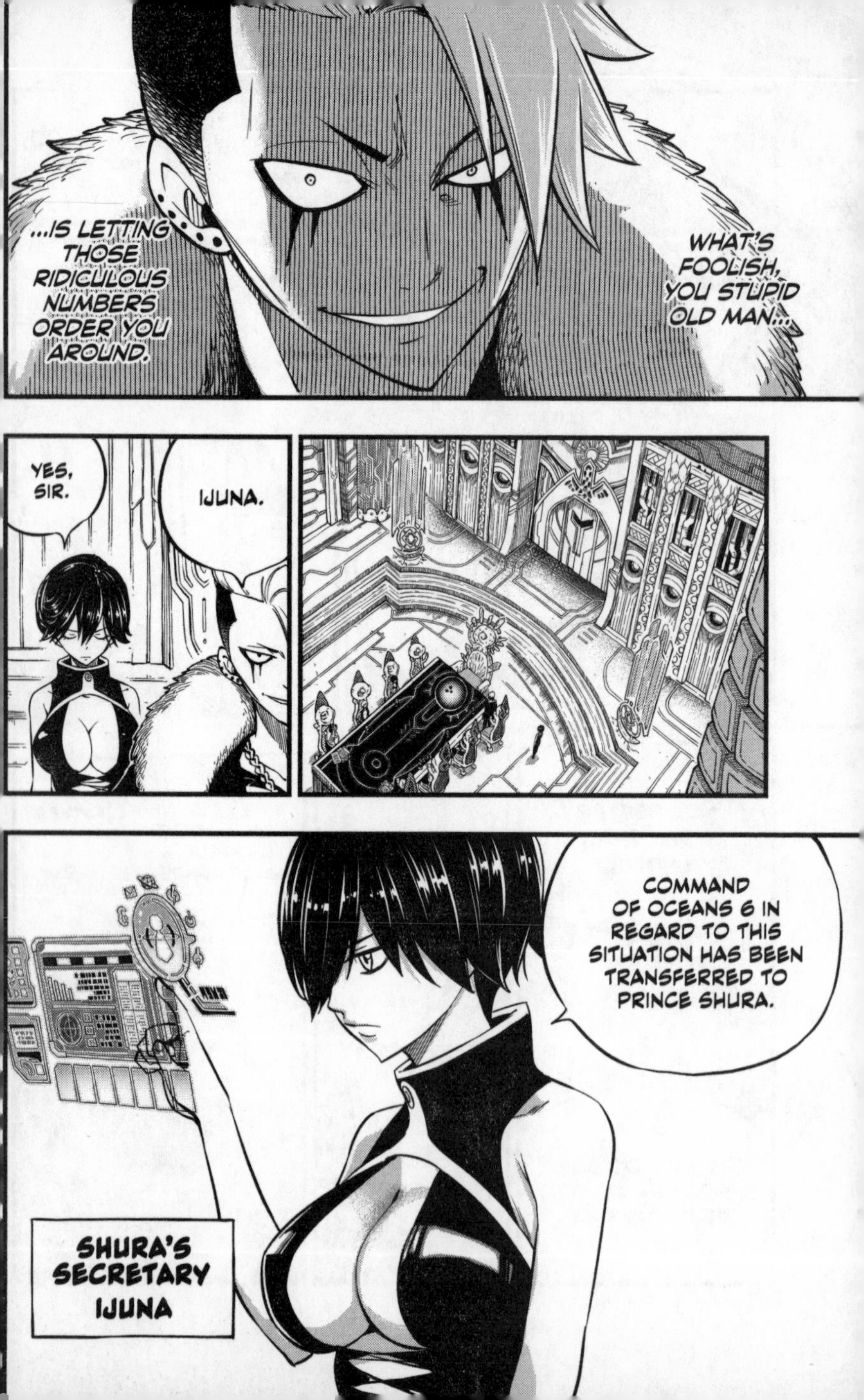
WHAT'S FOOLISH, YOU STUPID OLD MAN...
...IS LETTING THOSE RIDICULOUS NUMBERS ORDER YOU AROUND.
IJUNA.
YES, SIR.
COMMAND OF OCEANS 6 IN REGARD TO THIS SITUATION HAS BEEN TRANSFERRED TO PRINCE SHURA.
SHURA'S SECRETARY IJUNA

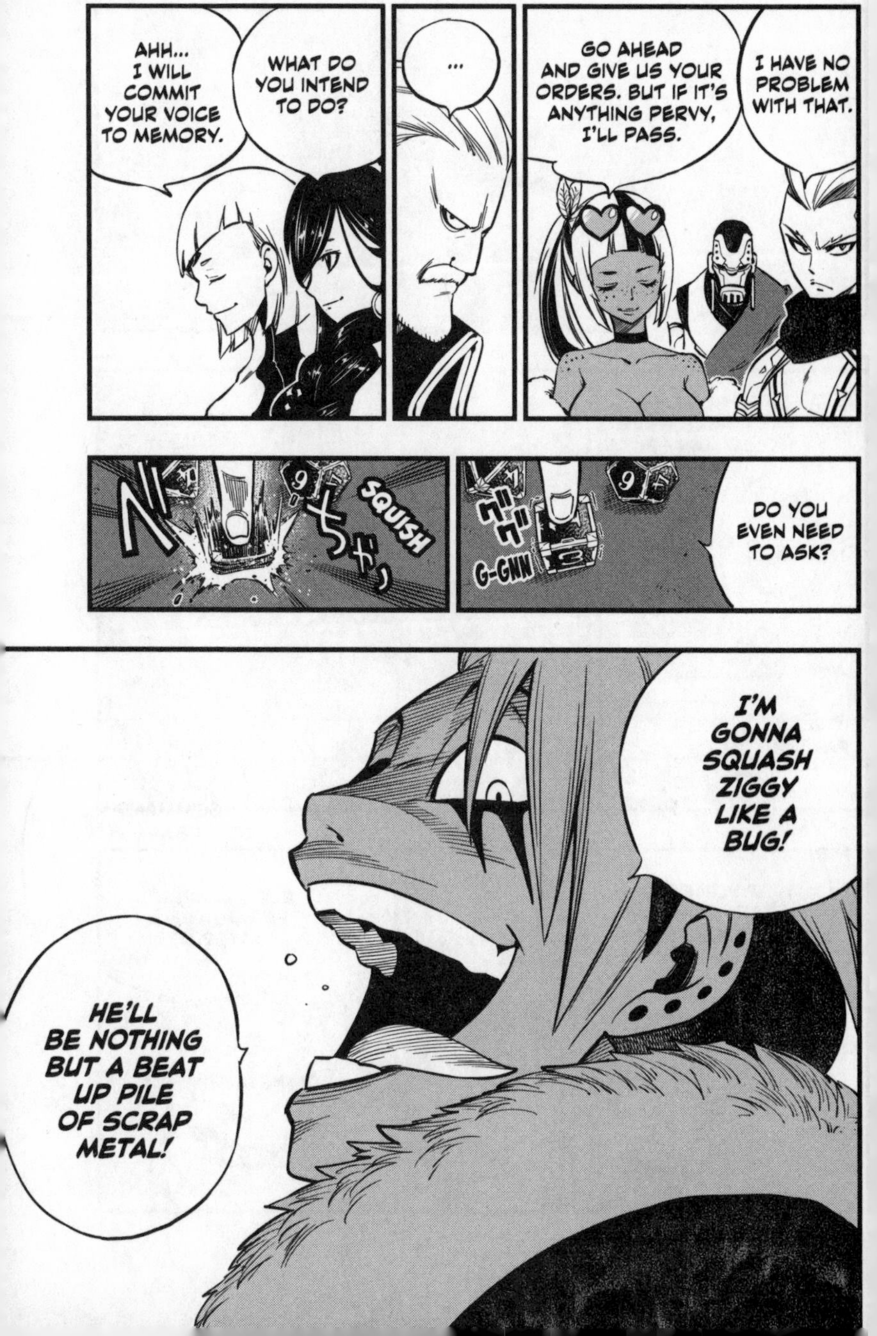
I HAVE NO PROBLEM WITH THAT.
GO AHEAD AND GIVE US YOUR ORDERS. BUT IF IT'S ANYTHING PERVY, I'LL PASS.
...
WHAT DO YOU INTEND TO DO?
AHH... I WILL COMMIT YOUR VOICE TO MEMORY.
DO YOU EVEN NEED TO ASK?
G-GNN
SQUISH
I'M GONNA SQUASH ZIGGY LIKE A BUG!
HE'LL BE NOTHING BUT A BEAT UP PILE OF SCRAP METAL!

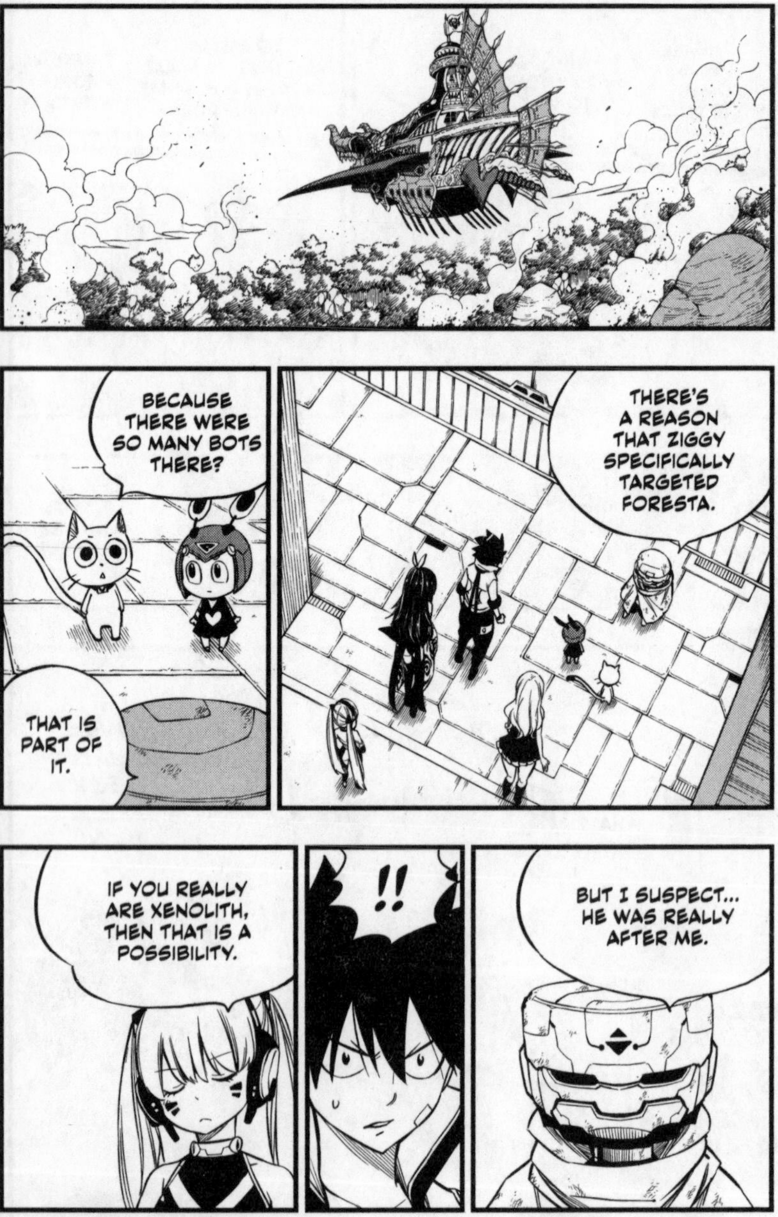
THERE'S A REASON THAT ZIGGY SPECIFICALLY TARGETED FORESTA.
BECAUSE THERE WERE SO MANY BOTS THERE?
THAT IS PART OF IT.
BUT I SUSPECT... HE WAS REALLY AFTER ME.
!!
IF YOU REALLY ARE XENOLITH, THEN THAT IS A POSSIBILITY.

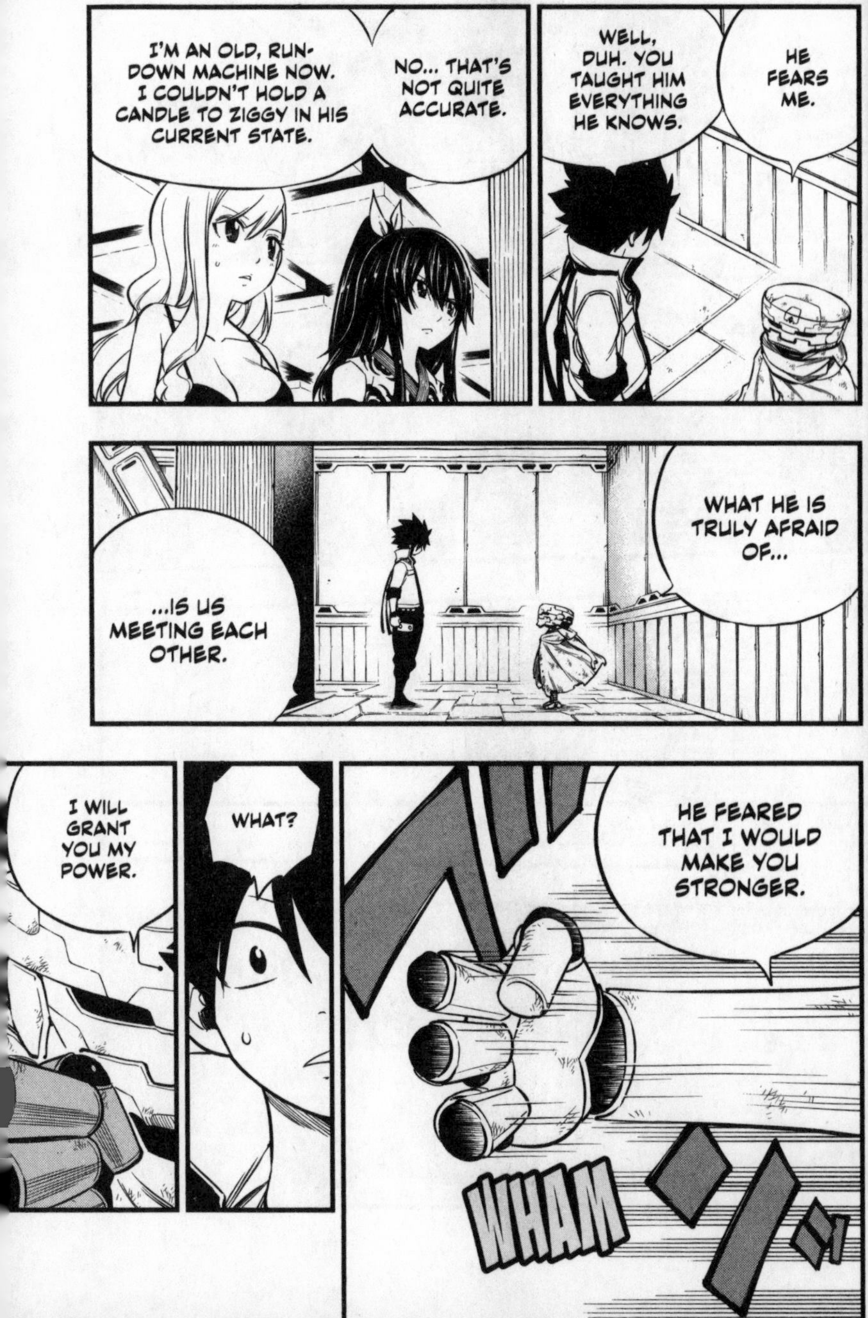
HE FEARS ME.
WELL, DUH. YOU TAUGHT HIM EVERYTHING HE KNOWS.
NO... THAT'S NOT QUITE ACCURATE.
I'M AN OLD, RUN-DOWN MACHINE NOW. I COULDN'T HOLD A CANDLE TO ZIGGY IN HIS CURRENT STATE.
WHAT HE IS TRULY AFRAID OF...
...IS US MEETING EACH OTHER.
HE FEARED THAT I WOULD MAKE YOU STRONGER.
WHAM
WHAT?
I WILL GRANT YOU MY POWER.

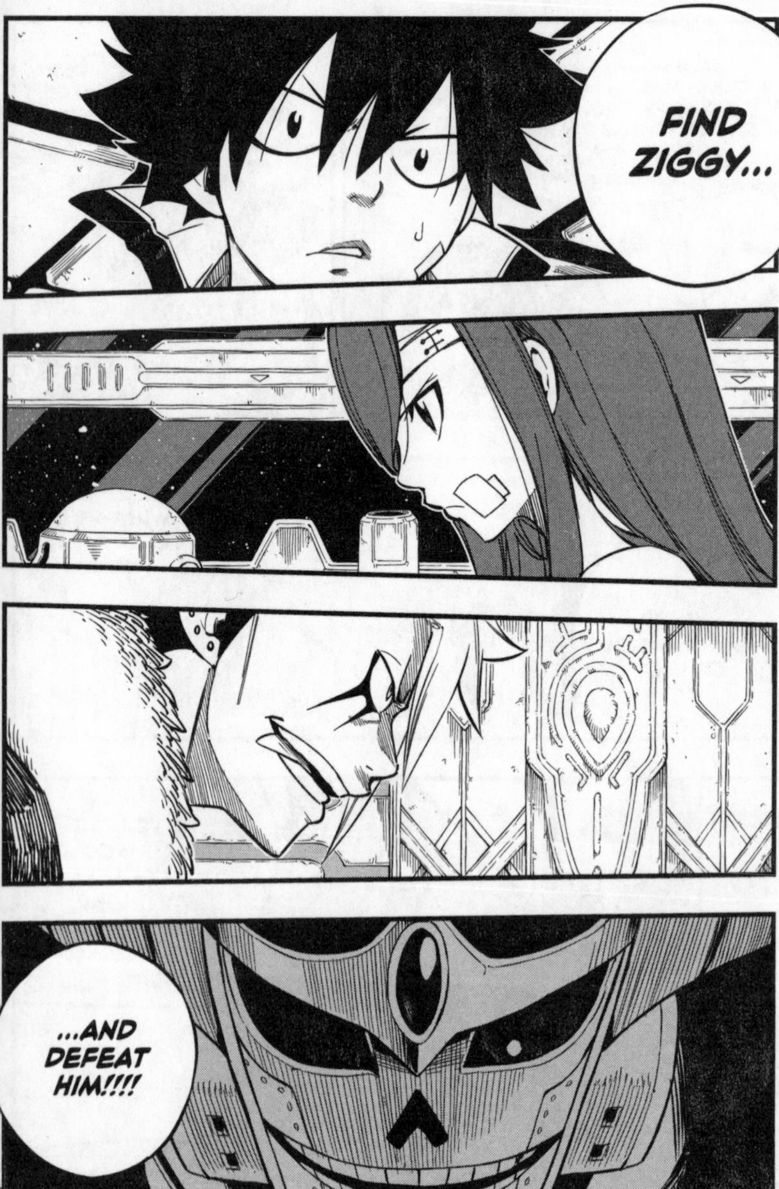
FIND ZIGGY...
...AND DEFEAT HIM!!!!

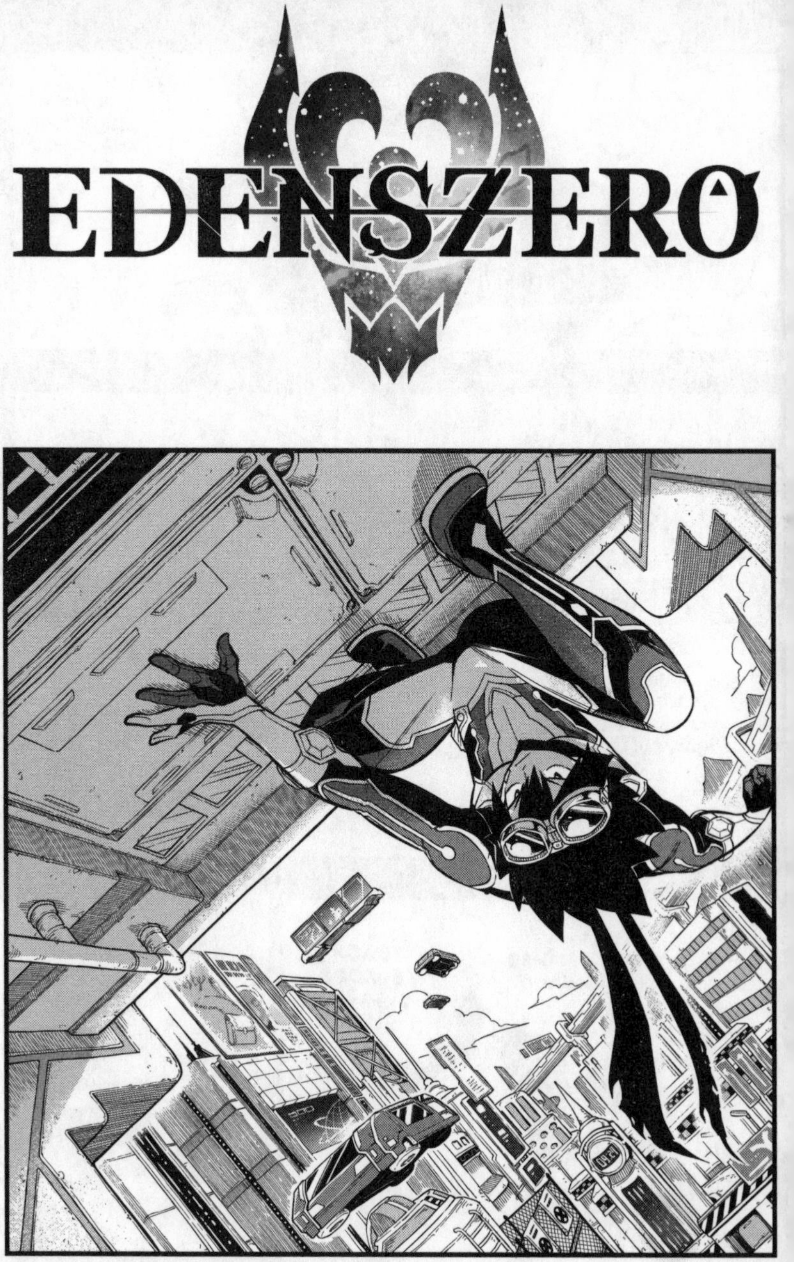

CHAPTER 131: VR-C

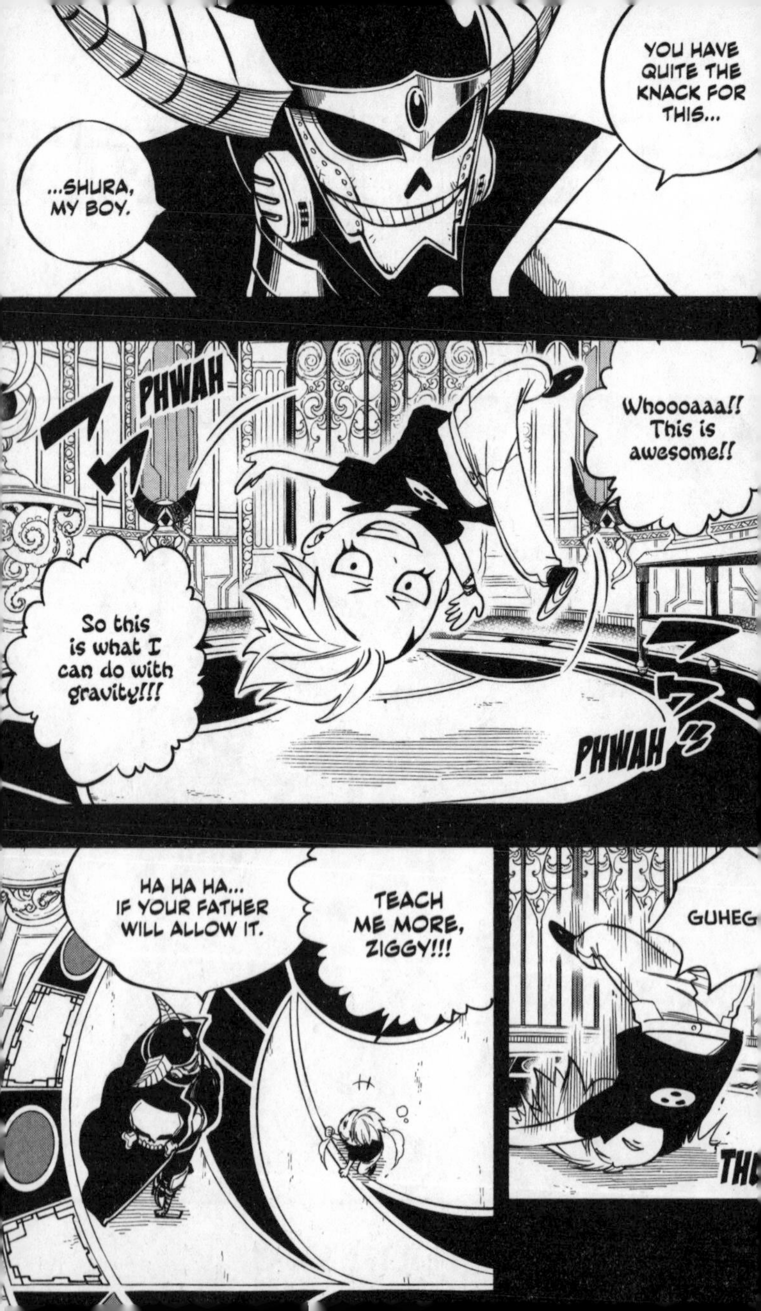
YOU HAVE QUITE THE KNACK FOR THIS...
...SHURA, MY BOY.
Whoooaaa!! This is awesome!!
PHWAH
So this is what I can do with gravity!!!
PHWAH
GUHEG
TH
TEACH ME MORE, ZIGGY!!!
HA HA HA... IF YOUR FATHER WILL ALLOW IT.

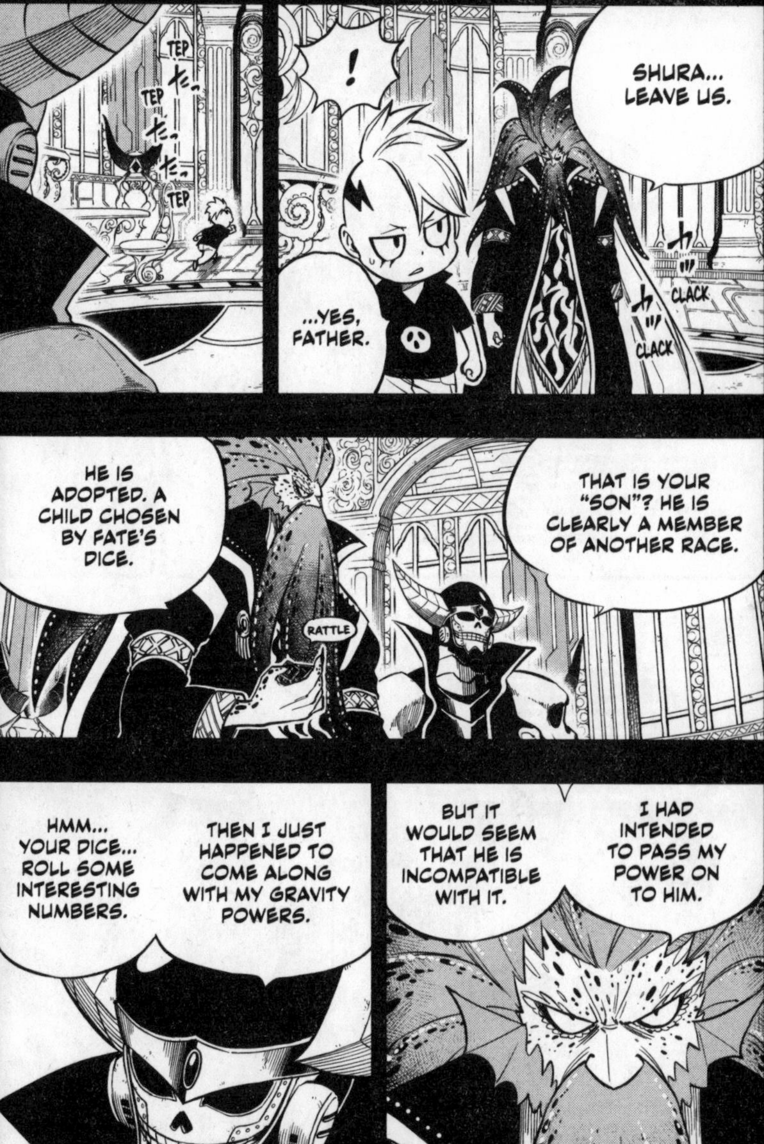

SHURA... LEAVE US.
!
CLACK
CLACK
...YES, FATHER.
TEP
TEP
TEP
THAT IS YOUR "SON"? HE IS CLEARLY A MEMBER OF ANOTHER RACE.
HE IS ADOPTED. A CHILD CHOSEN BY FATE'S DICE.
RATTLE
I HAD INTENDED TO PASS MY POWER ON TO HIM.
BUT IT WOULD SEEM THAT HE IS INCOMPATIBLE WITH IT.
THEN I JUST HAPPENED TO COME ALONG WITH MY GRAVITY POWERS.
HMM... YOUR DICE... ROLL SOME INTERESTING NUMBERS.

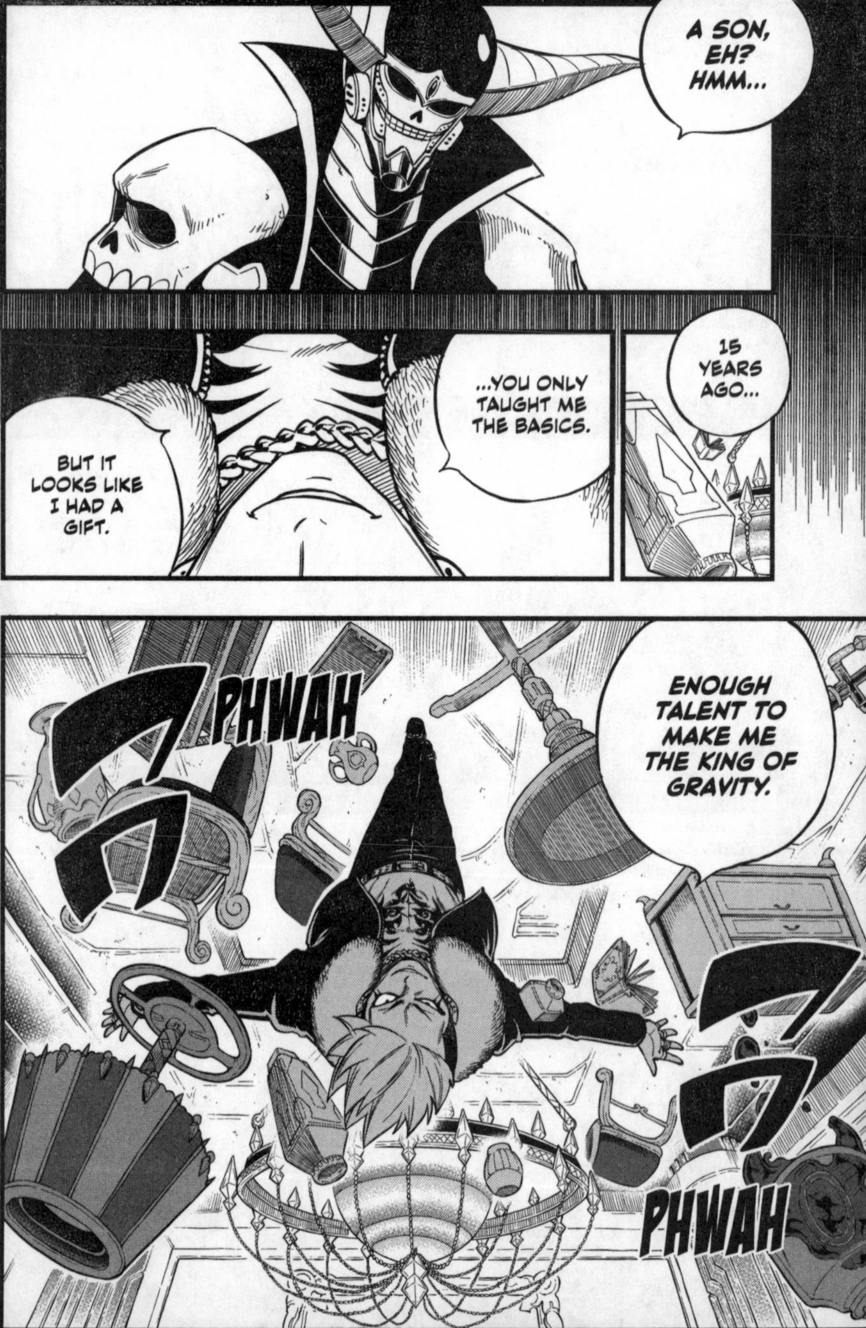
A SON, EH? HMM...
15 YEARS AGO...
...YOU ONLY TAUGHT ME THE BASICS.
BUT IT LOOKS LIKE I HAD A GIFT.
ENOUGH TALENT TO MAKE ME THE KING OF GRAVITY.
PHWAH
PHWAH

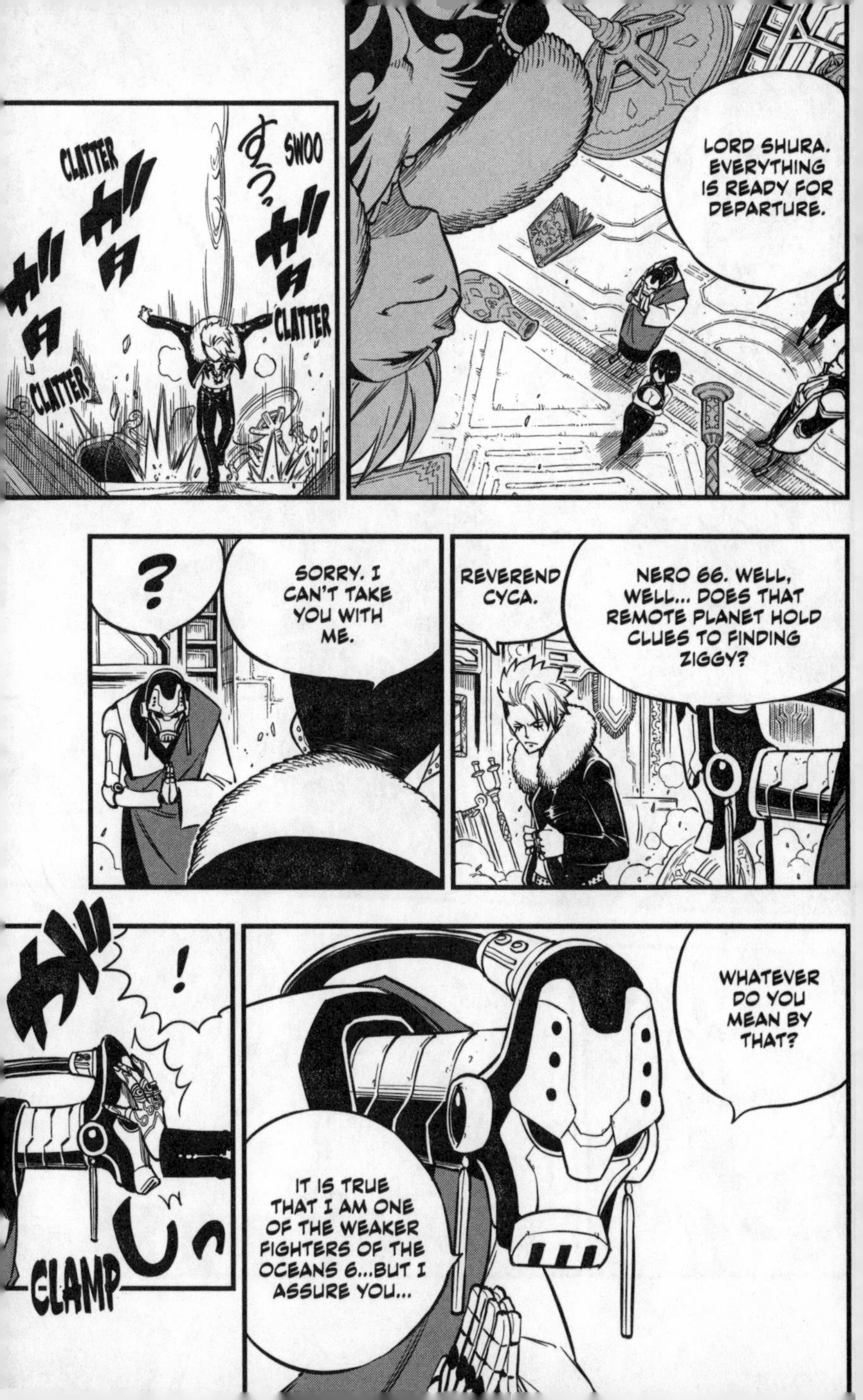
LORD SHURA. EVERYTHING IS READY FOR DEPARTURE.
SWOO
CLATTER
CLATTER
CLATTER
NERO 66. WELL, WELL... DOES THAT REMOTE PLANET HOLD CLUES TO FINDING ZIGGY?
REVEREND CYCA.
SORRY. I CAN'T TAKE YOU WITH ME.
?
WHATEVER DO YOU MEAN BY THAT?
IT IS TRUE THAT I AM ONE OF THE WEAKER FIGHTERS OF THE OCEANS 6...BUT I ASSURE YOU...
!
CLAMP

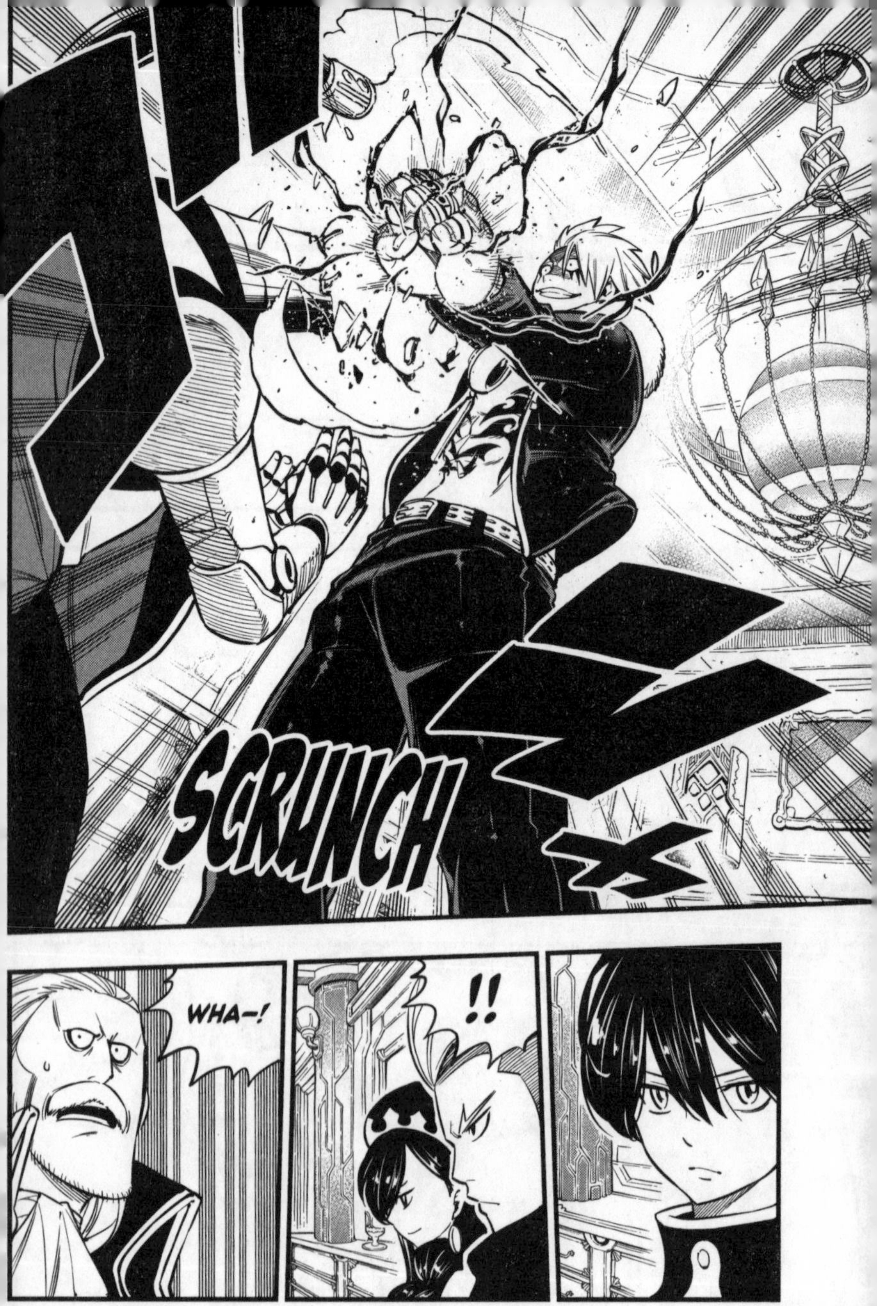
SCRUNCH
!!
WHA-!

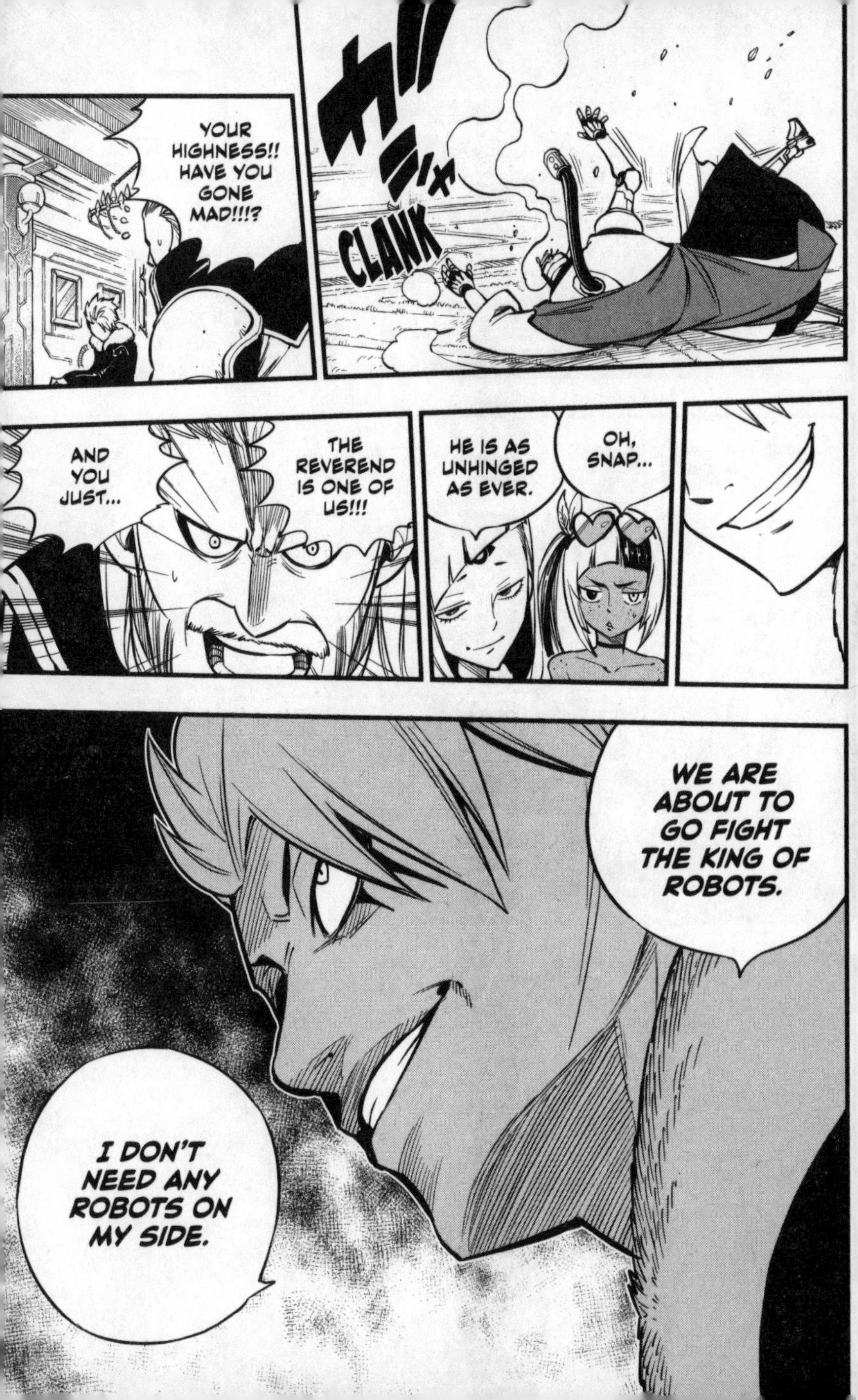
CLANK
YOUR HIGHNESS!! HAVE YOU GONE MAD!!!?
OH, SNAP...
HE IS AS UNHINGED AS EVER.
THE REVEREND IS ONE OF US!!!
AND YOU JUST...
WE ARE ABOUT TO GO FIGHT THE KING OF ROBOTS.
I DON'T NEED ANY ROBOTS ON MY SIDE.

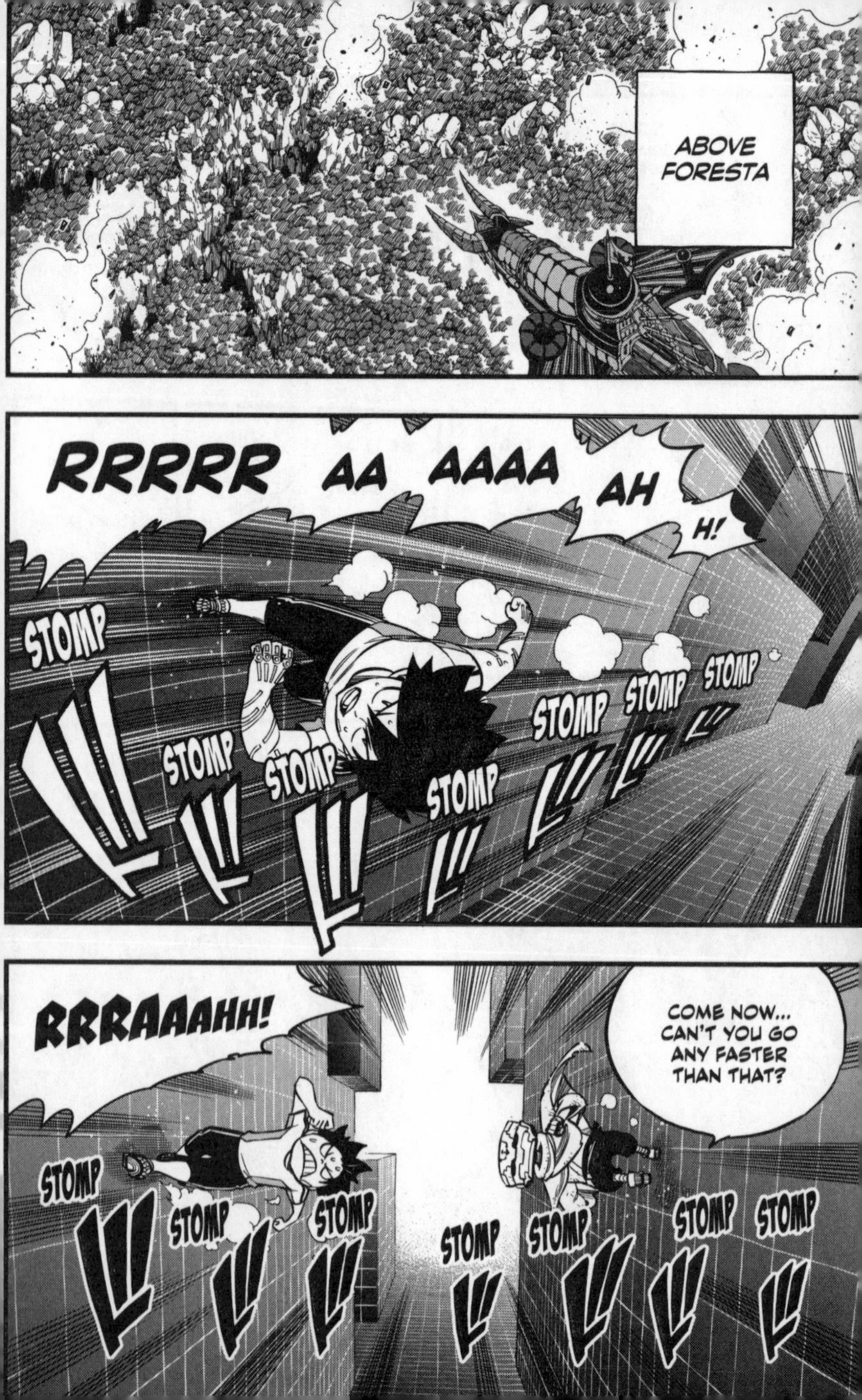
ABOVE FORESTA
RRRRR AA AAAA AH H!
STOMP STOMP STOMP STOMP STOMP STOMP STOMP
COME NOW... CAN'T YOU GO ANY FASTER THAN THAT?
RRRAAAHH!
STOMP STOMP STOMP STOMP STOMP STOMP STOMP

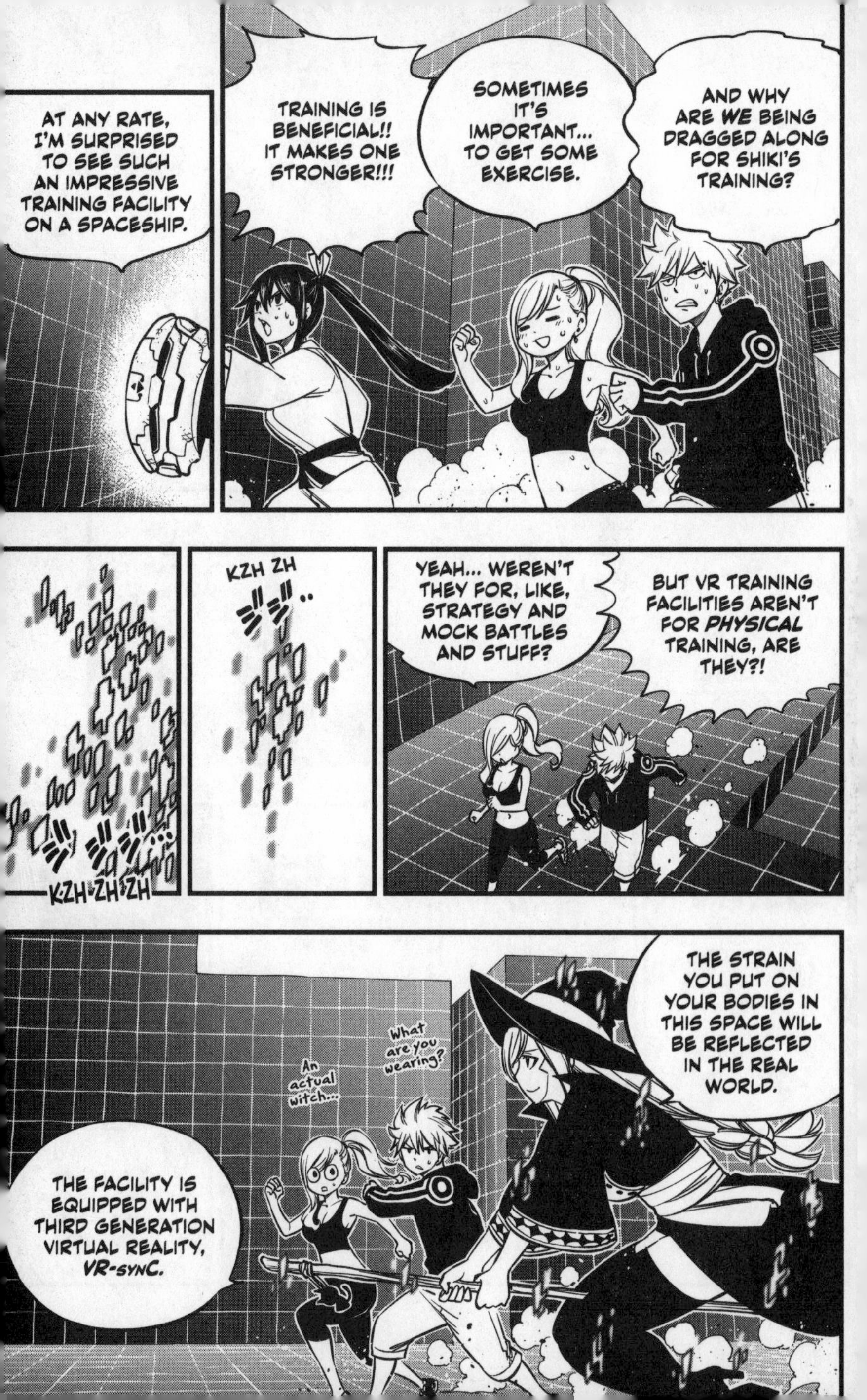
AND WHY ARE WE BEING DRAGGED ALONG FOR SHIKI'S TRAINING?
SOMETIMES IT'S IMPORTANT... TO GET SOME EXERCISE.
TRAINING IS BENEFICIAL!! IT MAKES ONE STRONGER!!!
AT ANY RATE, I'M SURPRISED TO SEE SUCH AN IMPRESSIVE TRAINING FACILITY ON A SPACESHIP.
BUT VR TRAINING FACILITIES AREN'T FOR PHYSICAL TRAINING, ARE THEY?!
YEAH... WEREN'T THEY FOR, LIKE, STRATEGY AND MOCK BATTLES AND STUFF?
KZH ZH
KZH ZH ZH
THE STRAIN YOU PUT ON YOUR BODIES IN THIS SPACE WILL BE REFLECTED IN THE REAL WORLD.
What are you wearing?
An actual witch...
THE FACILITY IS EQUIPPED WITH THIRD GENERATION VIRTUAL REALITY, VR-SYNC.

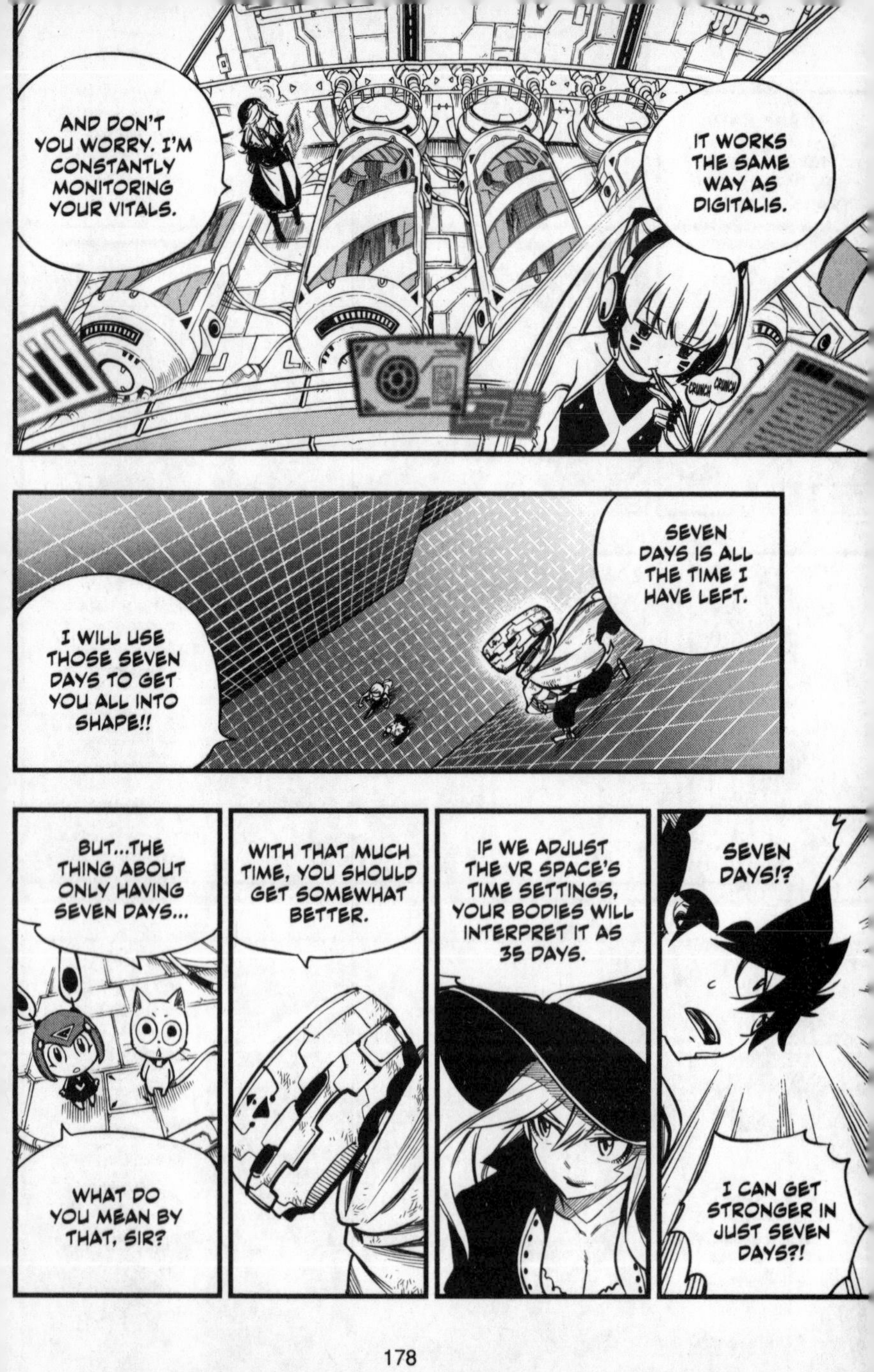
IT WORKS THE SAME WAY AS DIGITALIS.
CRUNCH CRUNCH
AND DON'T YOU WORRY. I'M CONSTANTLY MONITORING YOUR VITALS.
SEVEN DAYS IS ALL THE TIME I HAVE LEFT.
I WILL USE THOSE SEVEN DAYS TO GET YOU ALL INTO SHAPE!!
SEVEN DAYS!?
I CAN GET STRONGER IN JUST SEVEN DAYS?!
IF WE ADJUST THE VR SPACE'S TIME SETTINGS, YOUR BODIES WILL INTERPRET IT AS 35 DAYS.
WITH THAT MUCH TIME, YOU SHOULD GET SOMEWHAT BETTER.
BUT...THE THING ABOUT ONLY HAVING SEVEN DAYS...
WHAT DO YOU MEAN BY THAT, SIR?

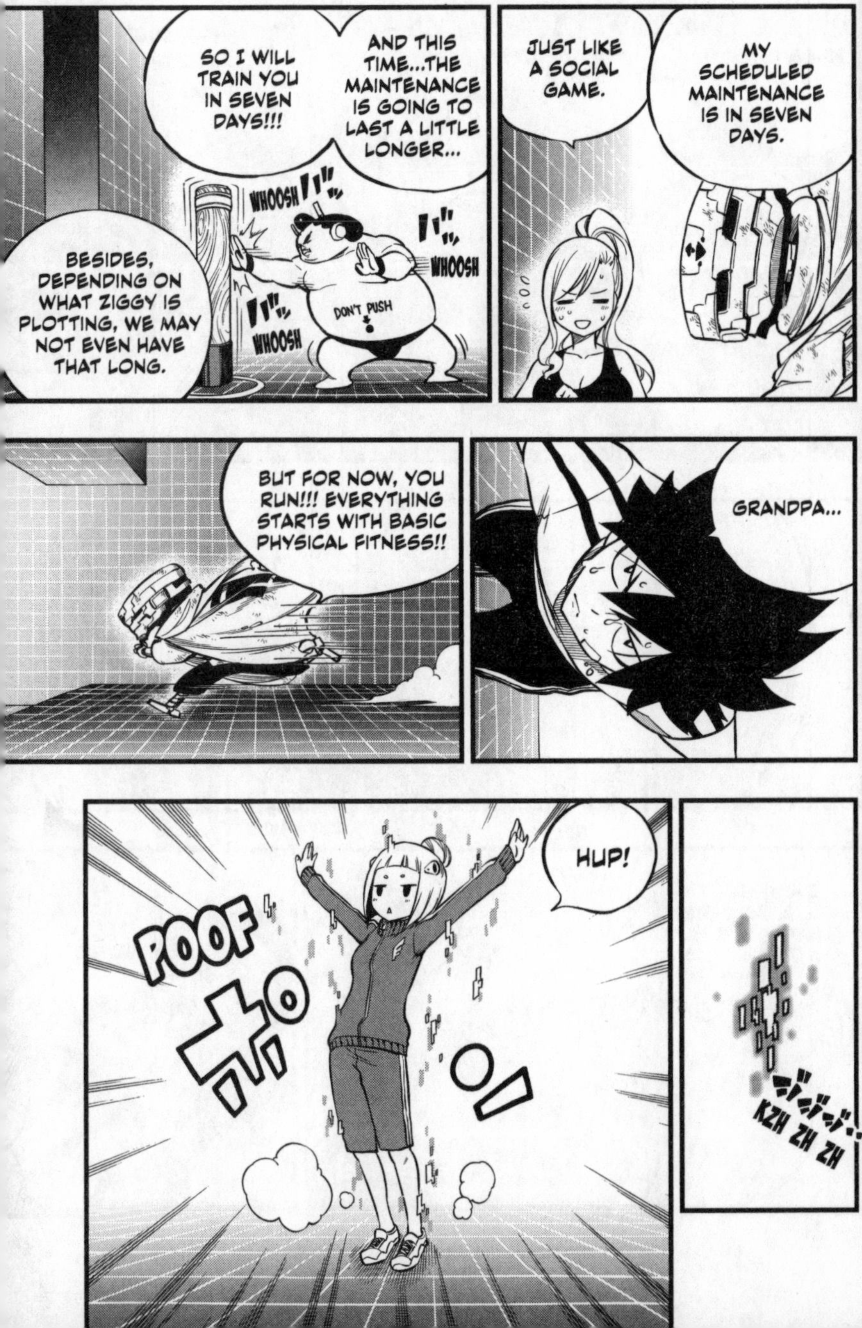
MY SCHEDULED MAINTENANCE IS IN SEVEN DAYS.
JUST LIKE A SOCIAL GAME.
AND THIS TIME...THE MAINTENANCE IS GOING TO LAST A LITTLE LONGER...
SO I WILL TRAIN YOU IN SEVEN DAYS!!!
WHOOSH
WHOOSH
WHOOSH
DON'T PUSH
BESIDES, DEPENDING ON WHAT ZIGGY IS PLOTTING, WE MAY NOT EVEN HAVE THAT LONG.
GRANDPA...
BUT FOR NOW, YOU RUN!!! EVERYTHING STARTS WITH BASIC PHYSICAL FITNESS!!
KZH ZH ZH
HUP!
POOF

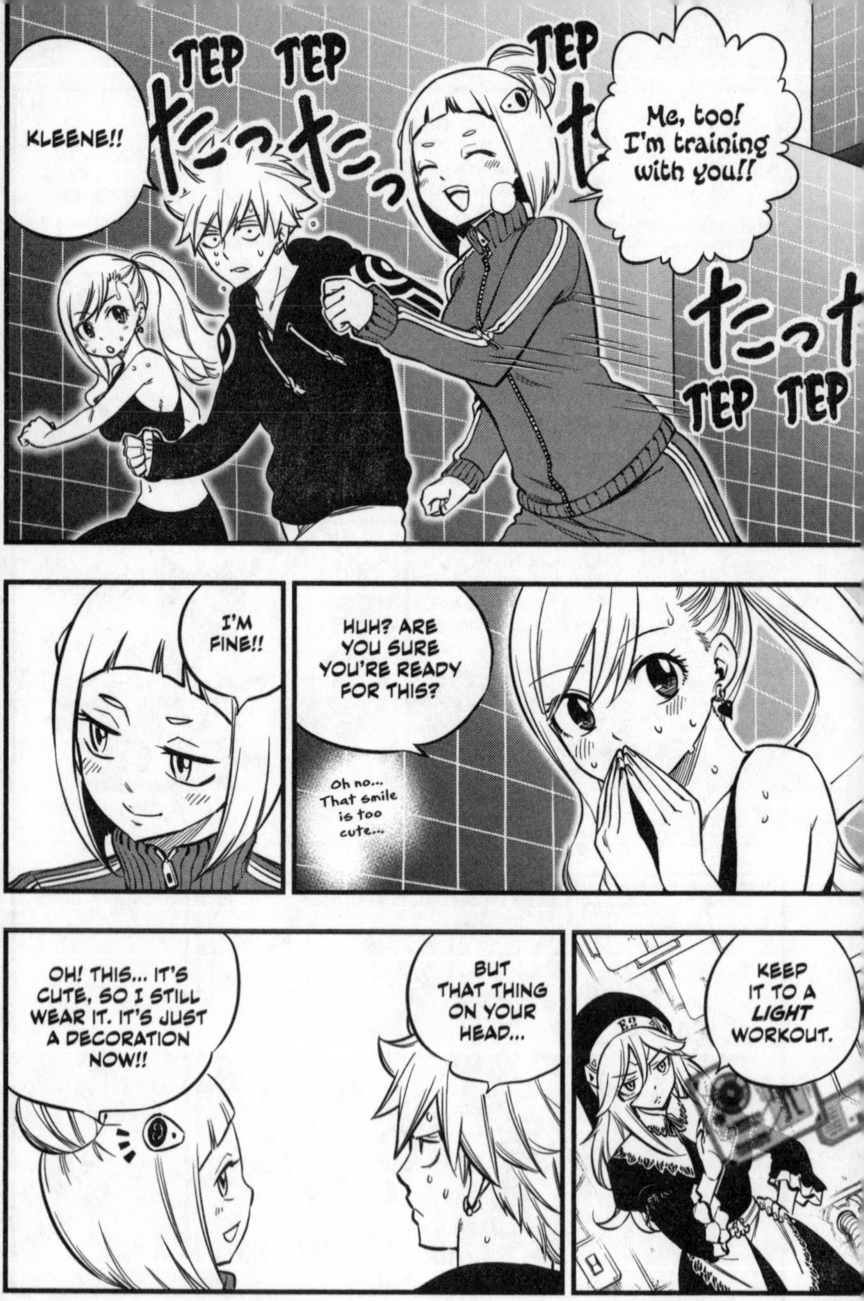
TEP
Me, too! I'm training with you!!
たっ
TEP TEP
TEP TEP
たったっ
KLEENE!!
HUH? ARE YOU SURE YOU'RE READY FOR THIS?
Oh no... That smile is too cute...
I'M FINE!!
KEEP IT TO A *LIGHT* WORKOUT.
BUT THAT THING ON YOUR HEAD...
OH! THIS... IT'S CUTE, SO I STILL WEAR IT. IT'S JUST A DECORATION NOW!!

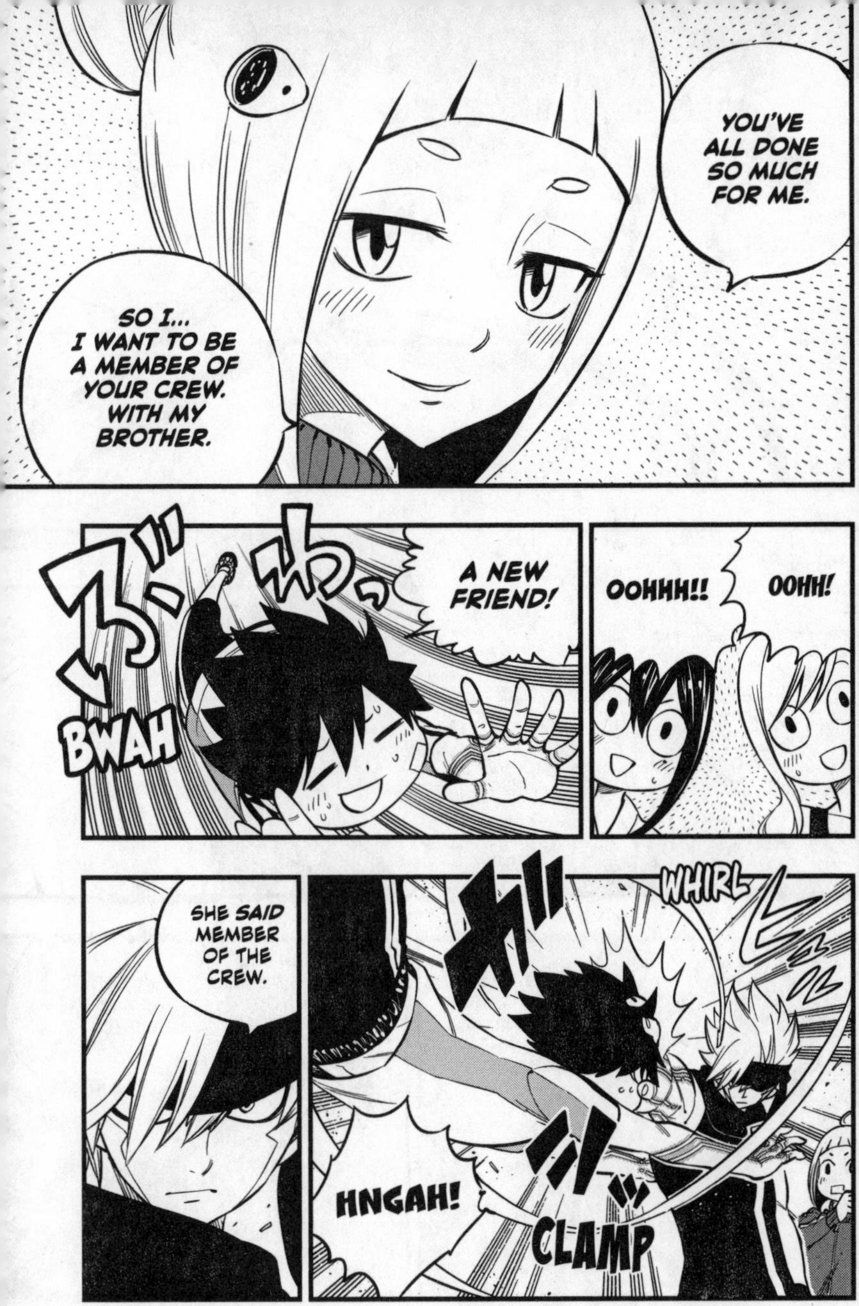
YOU'VE ALL DONE SO MUCH FOR ME.
SO I... I WANT TO BE A MEMBER OF YOUR CREW. WITH MY BROTHER.
OOHH!
OOHHH!!
A NEW FRIEND!
BWAH
WHIRL
HNGAH!
CLAMP
SHE SAID MEMBER OF THE CREW.

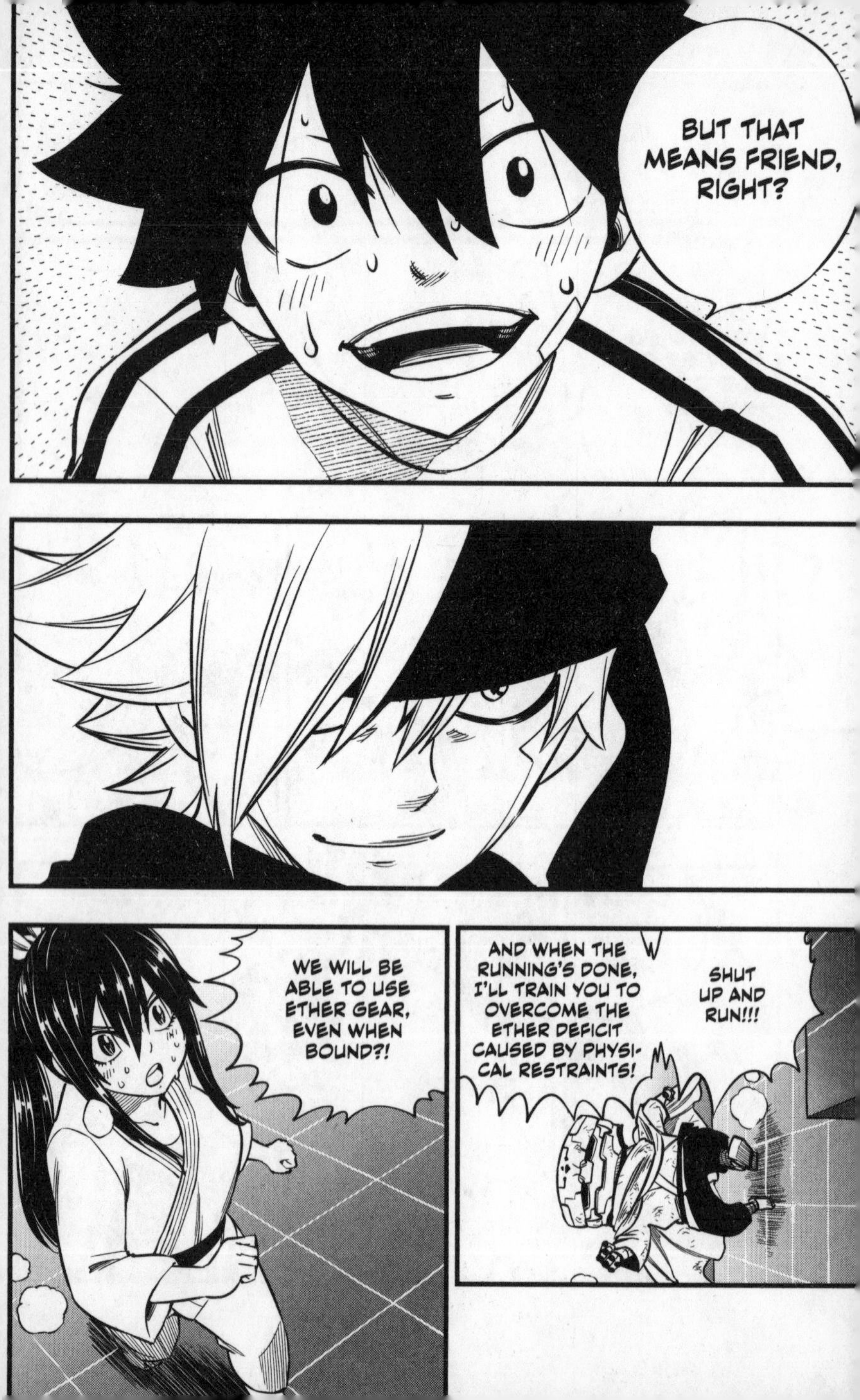
BUT THAT MEANS FRIEND, RIGHT?
SHUT UP AND RUN!!!
AND WHEN THE RUNNING'S DONE, I'LL TRAIN YOU TO OVERCOME THE ETHER DEFICIT CAUSED BY PHYSICAL RESTRAINTS!
WE WILL BE ABLE TO USE ETHER GEAR, EVEN WHEN BOUND?!

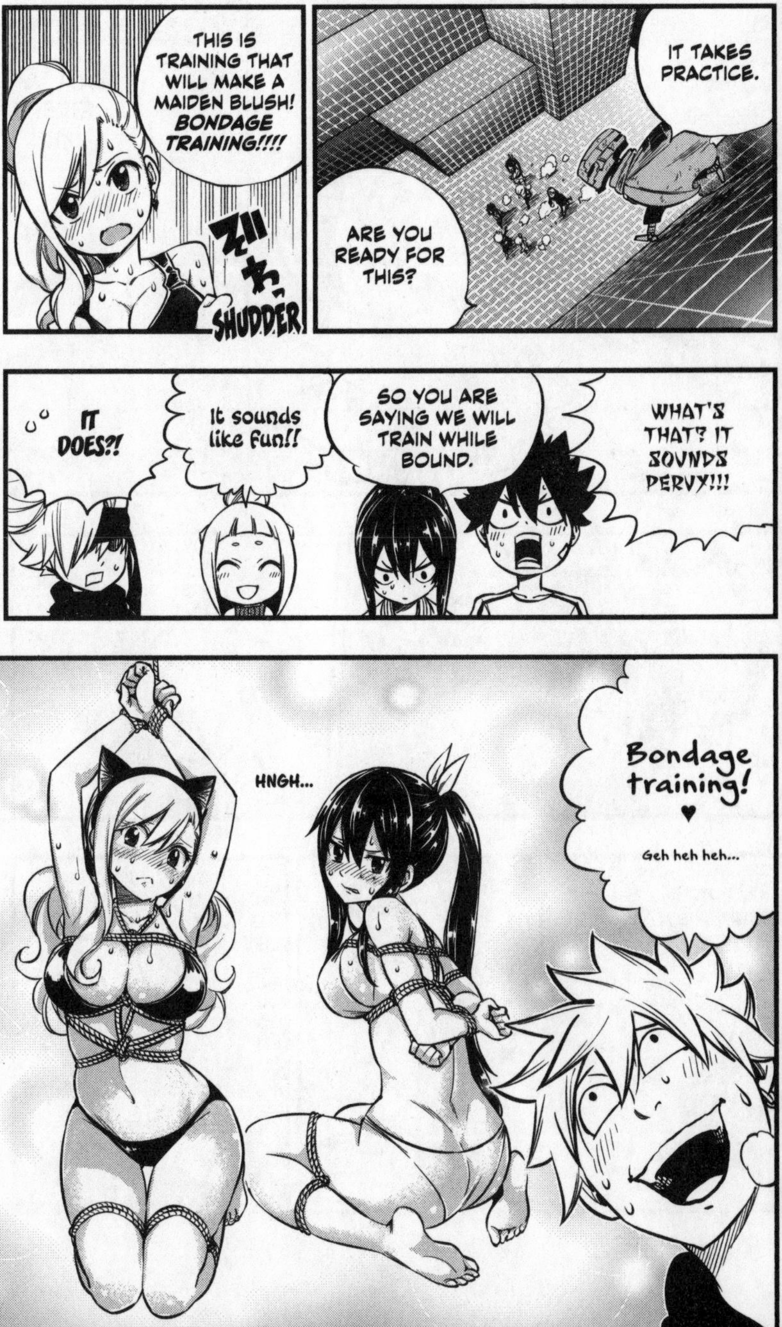
IT TAKES PRACTICE.
ARE YOU READY FOR THIS?
THIS IS TRAINING THAT WILL MAKE A MAIDEN BLUSH! BONDAGE TRAINING!!!!
SHUDDER
WHAT'S THAT? IT SOUNDS PERVY!!!
SO YOU ARE SAYING WE WILL TRAIN WHILE BOUND.
It sounds like fun!!
IT DOES?!
Bondage training! ♥
Geh heh heh...
HNGH...

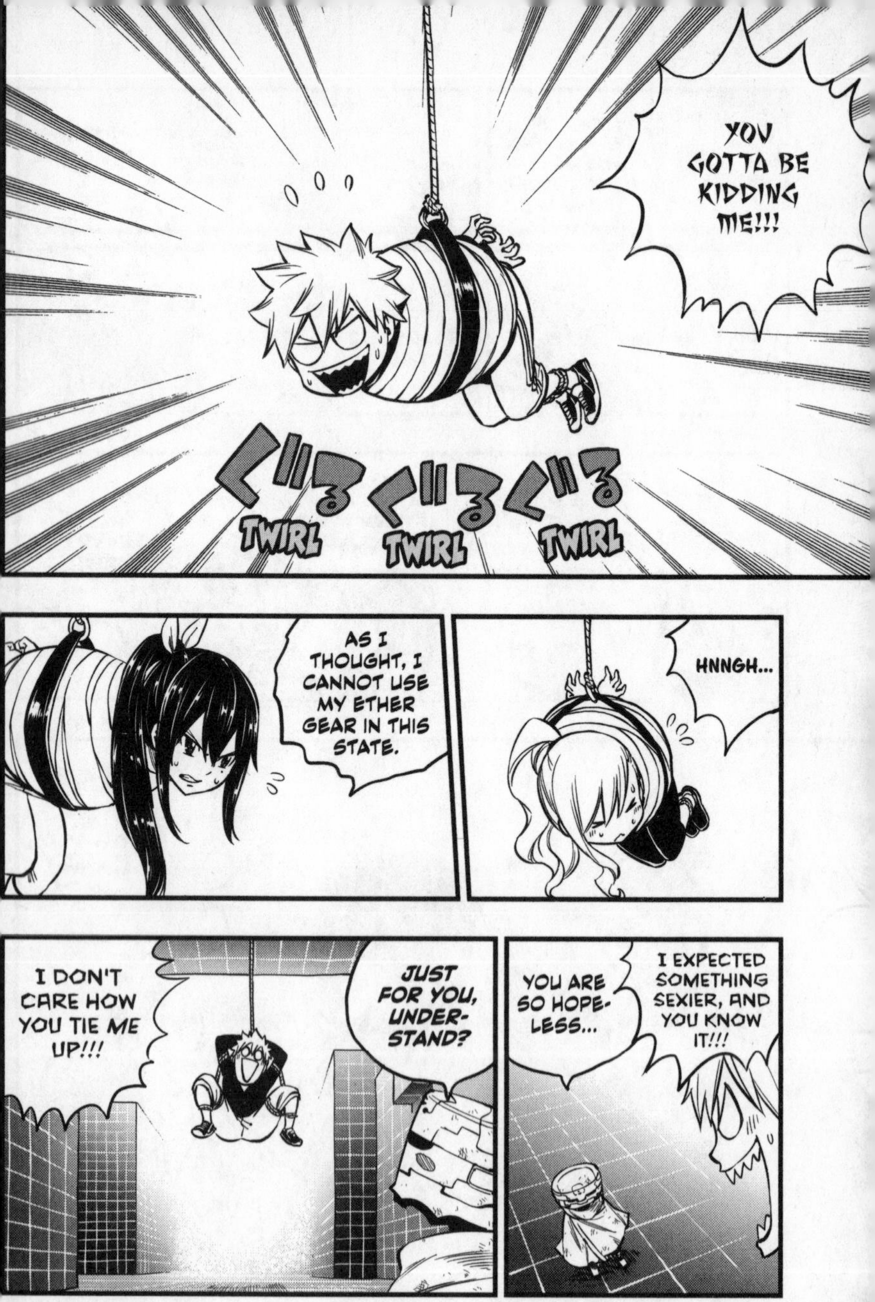
YOU GOTTA BE KIDDING ME!!!
ぐるぐるぐる
TWIRL TWIRL TWIRL
HNNGH...
AS I THOUGHT, I CANNOT USE MY ETHER GEAR IN THIS STATE.
I EXPECTED SOMETHING SEXIER, AND YOU KNOW IT!!!
YOU ARE SO HOPE-LESS...
JUST FOR YOU, UNDER-STAND?
I DON'T CARE HOW YOU TIE ME UP!!!

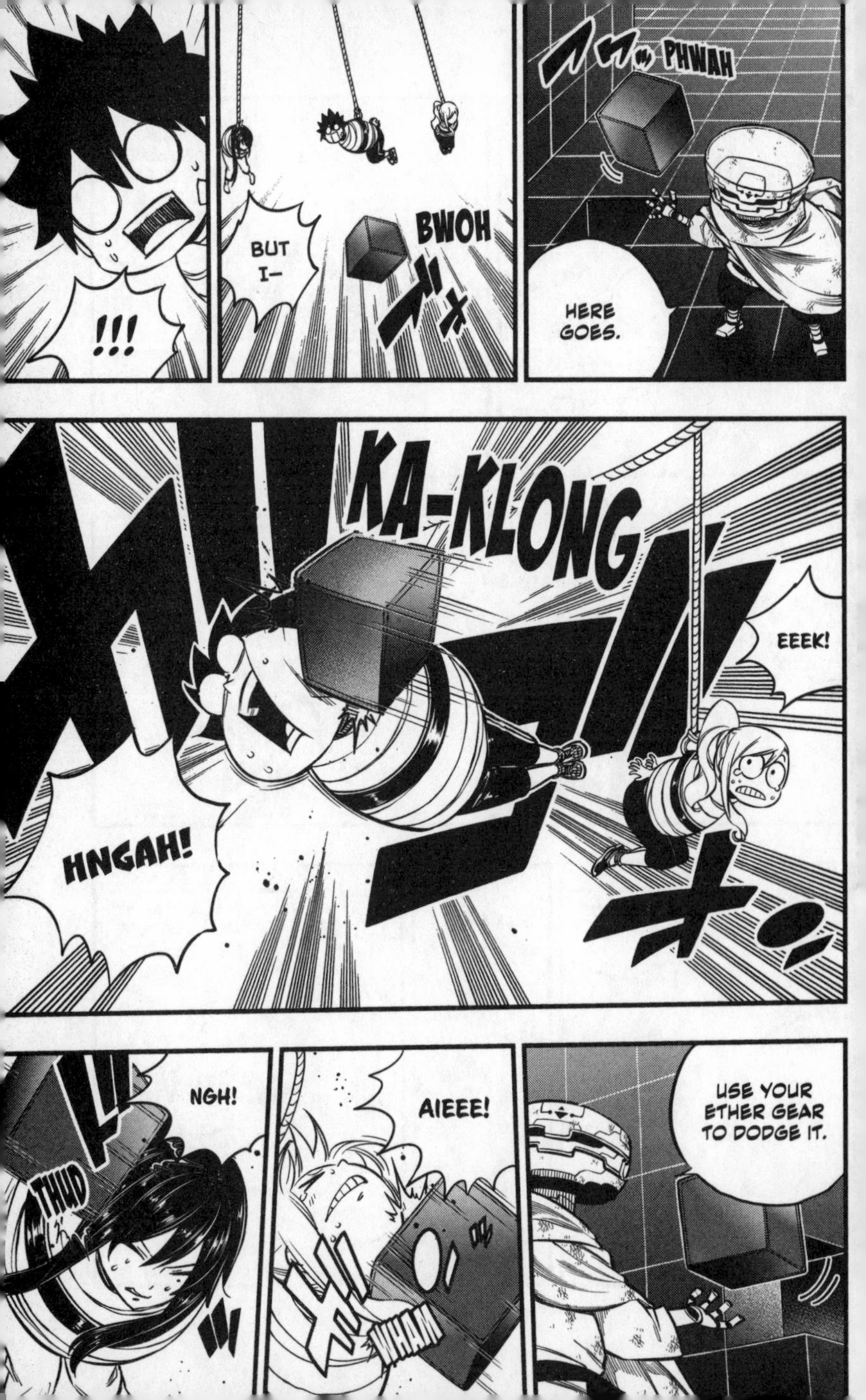
PHWAH
HERE GOES.
BWOH
BUT I—
!!!
KA-KLONG
EEEK!
HNGAH!
USE YOUR ETHER GEAR TO DODGE IT.
AIEEE!
WHAM
NGH!
THUD

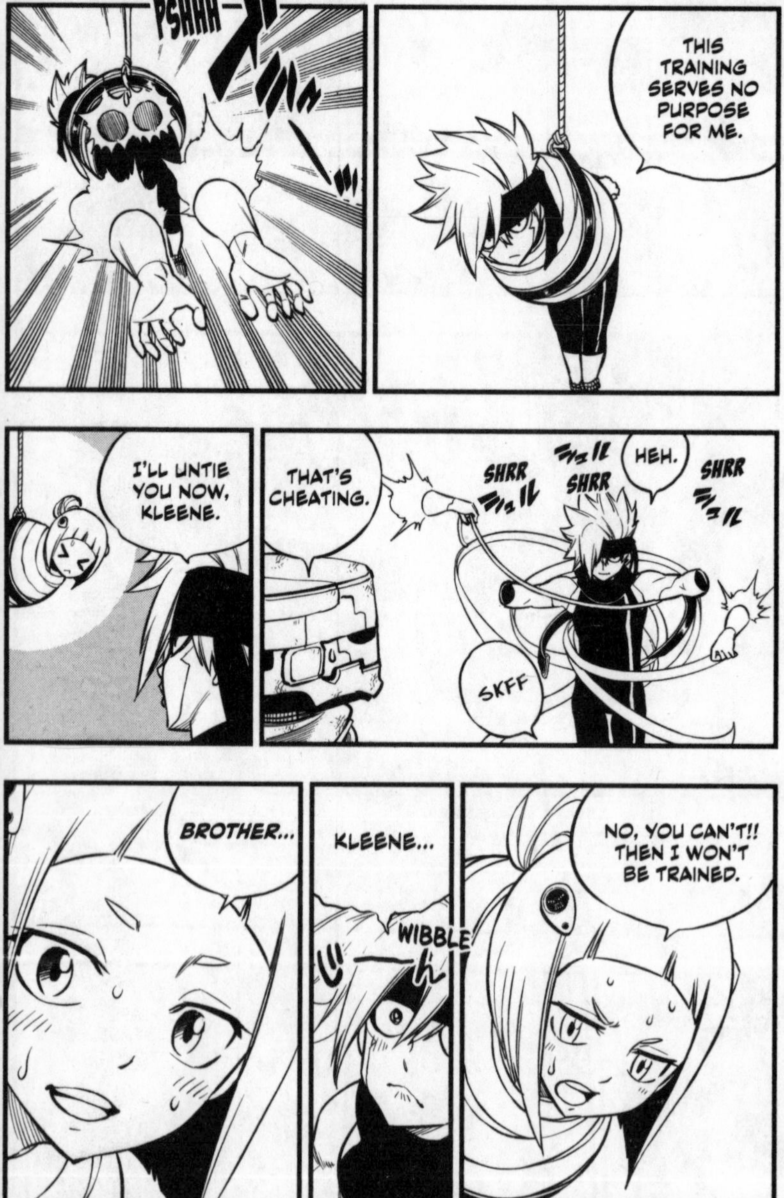
THIS TRAINING SERVES NO PURPOSE FOR ME.
PSHHH
SHRR
HEH.
SHRR
SHRR
THAT'S CHEATING.
SKFF
I'LL UNTIE YOU NOW, KLEENE.
NO, YOU CAN'T!! THEN I WON'T BE TRAINED.
KLEENE...
WIBBLE
BROTHER...

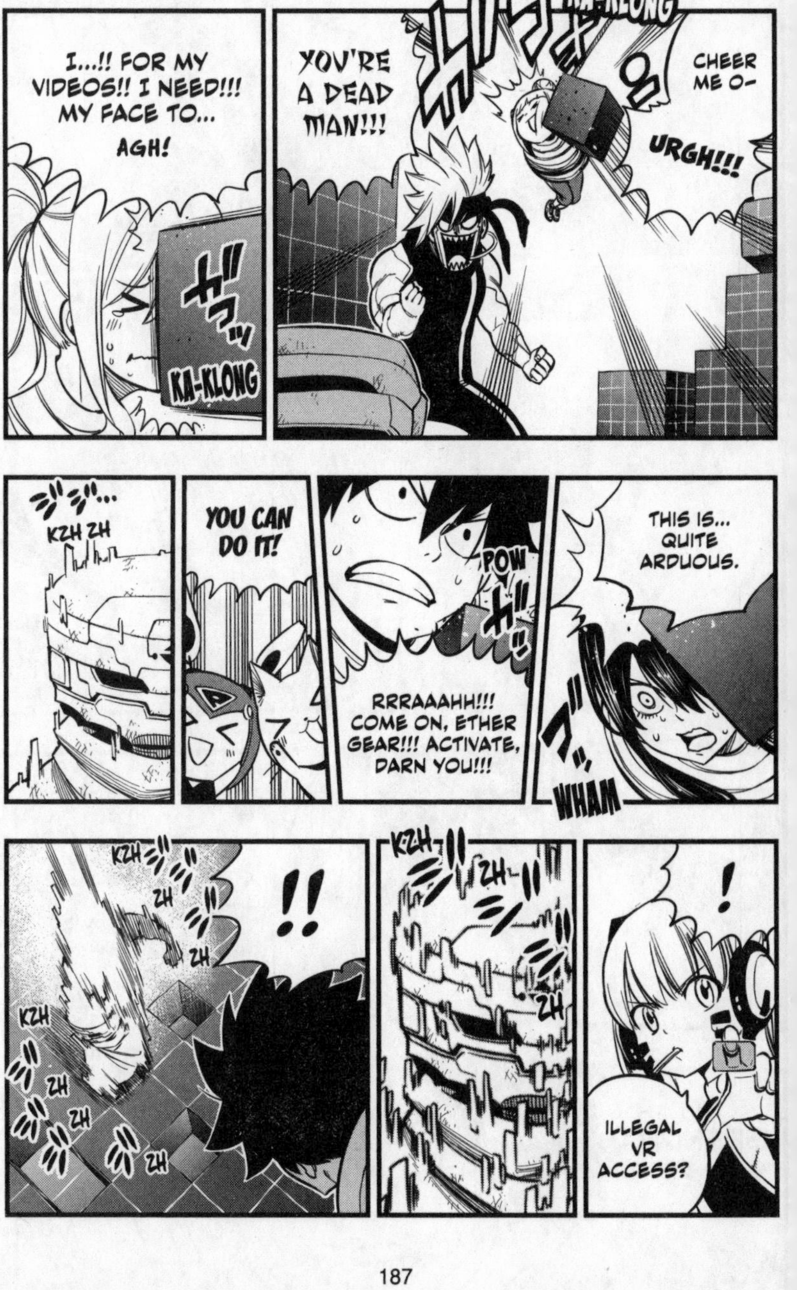
KA-KLONG
CHEER ME O-
URGH!!!
YOU'RE A DEAD MAN!!!
I...!! FOR MY VIDEOS!! I NEED!!! MY FACE TO...
AGH!
KA-KLONG
THIS IS... QUITE ARDUOUS.
WHAM
POW
RRRAAAHH!!! COME ON, ETHER GEAR!!! ACTIVATE, DARN YOU!!!
YOU CAN DO IT!
KZH ZH
!
ILLEGAL VR ACCESS?
KZH
ZH
ZH
KZH
ZH
!!
ZH
KZH
ZH
ZH
ZH

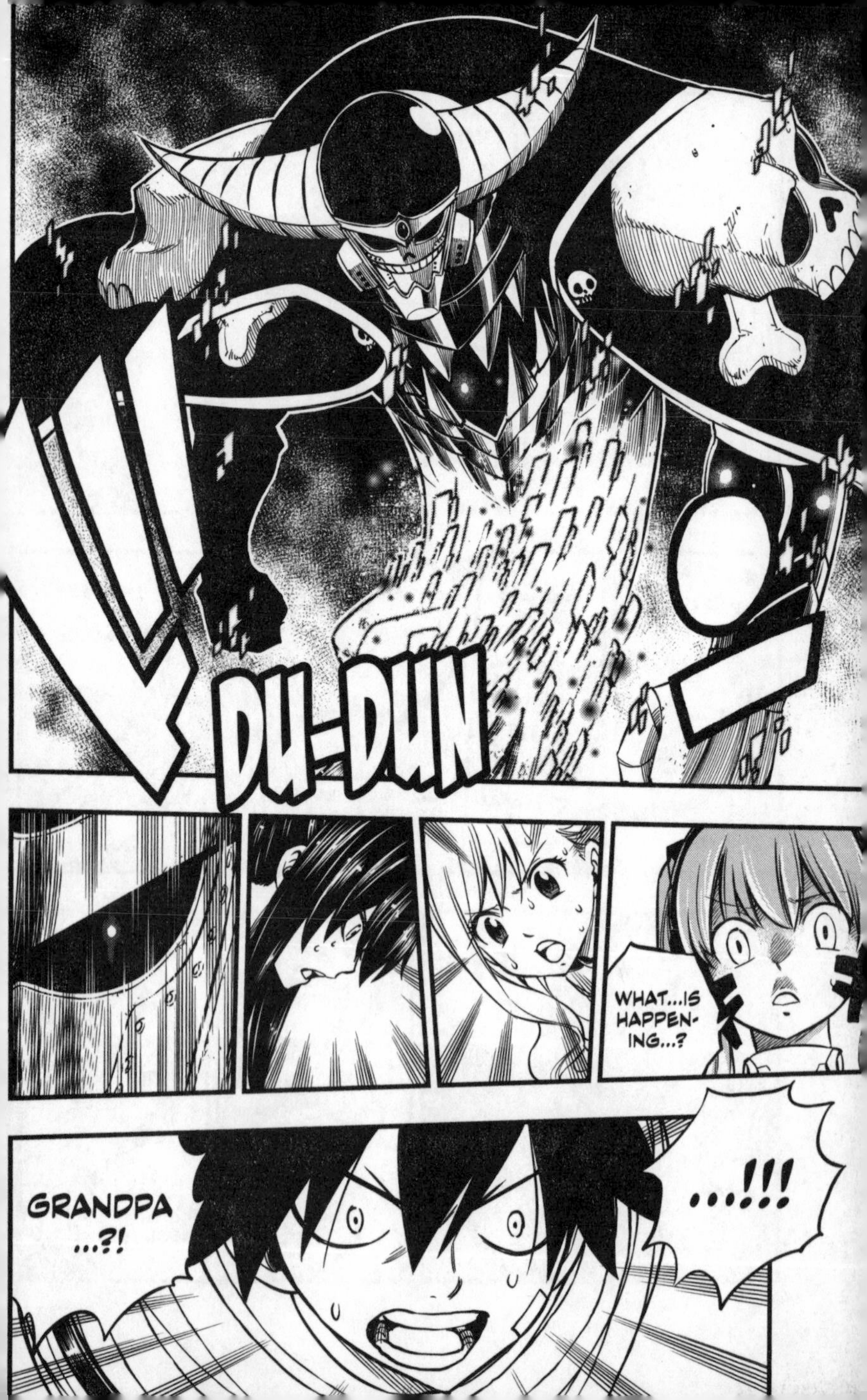
DU-DUN
WHAT...IS HAPPEN-ING...?
...!!!
GRANDPA ...?!

AFTERWORD

In this volume we see Oceans 6 and Ijuna (Shura's secretary). Actually, we had a contest on Twitter where we asked all you readers to design original Ether Gear, and these are the characters that were chosen. To be more precise, Callum, Lyra, Nasseh, and Mirrani are the characters we used. And Ijuna. It was a really fun project, so I'd love to do it again, but all of the characters selected ended up as enemy characters, so there's a possibility that they will die miserable deaths. So I hope all the happy winners will please forgive me.

That reminds me, there was a bit of an issue with this project, which did occur to me before we started it, and it was, "What if someone sends in an Ether Gear power that I was already planning to use in the series in the future?" Currently, there are a few characters who have appeared in the series but haven't used their abilities. I figured it would be bad if the powers were the same, and in fact, someone did submit a power that overlapped a lot with one that I was planning to put in the story very soon. But the character's look was great, and I couldn't bring myself to reject them just because the powers were the same, so I changed the powers just a little bit (because the powers I was already planning were a very important element in the story that could not be changed), and used the character anyway. I'll just tell you—it was Lyra. The submission had her using dice powers, but I had settled on Nero having dice powers a long time before that, so I changed the dice into cards. Thank you very much for kindly agreeing to that change. For Callum, Mirrani, and Nasseh, I chose them because I was immediately able to come up with battle ideas for them. As for Ijuna, I thought of an interesting development to go with her Ether Gear powers, so she's not a member of Oceans, but I think she'll have her time in the spotlight.

Xenolith appeared in this volume, too. He's another one of the rare characters in my manga whose story was decided on a pretty long time ago, so I hope you'll all look forward to seeing what part he has to play.

Finally, the relationship between Justice and Elsie… These two have a very star-crossed destiny awaiting them.

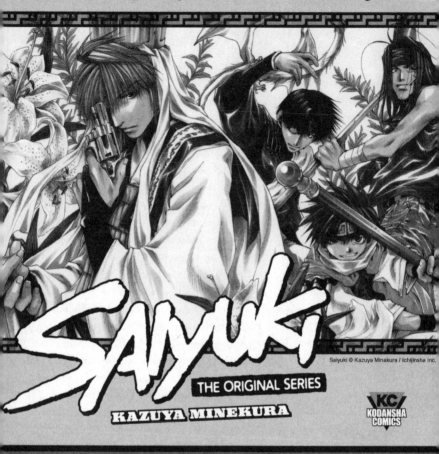

Young characters and steampunk setting, like *Howl's Moving Castle* and *Battle Angel Alita*

Beyond the Clouds © 2018 Nicke / Ki-oon

A boy with a talent for machines and a mysterious girl whose wings he's fixed will take you beyond the clouds! In the tradition of the high-flying, resonant adventure stories of Studio Ghibli comes a gorgeous tale about the longing of young hearts for adventure and friendship!

A Kodansha Comics Trade Paperback Original
EDENS ZERO 15 copyright © 2021 Hiro Mashima
English translation copyright © 2021 Hiro Mashima

Published in the United States by Kodansha Comics, an imprint of Kodansha USA Publishing, LLC, New York.

Publication rights for this English edition arranged through Kodansha Ltd., Tokyo.

First published in Japan in 2021 by Kodansha Ltd., Tokyo.

ISBN 978-1-64651-286-7

Original cover design by Narumi Miura (G x complex).

Printed in the United States of America.

www.kodansha.us

1st Printing
Translation: Alethea Nibley & Athena Nibley
Lettering: AndWorld Design
Editing: David Yoo
Kodansha Comics edition cover design by Phil Balsman

Publisher: Kiichiro Sugawara

Director of publishing services: Ben Applegate
Associate director, publishing operations: Stephen Pakula
Publishing services managing editors: Madison Salters, Alanna Ruse
Production managers: Emi Lotto, Angela Zurlo